CHINA IN THE CYBER DOMAIN

By

Maj Gen PK Mallick, VSM (Retd)

Prints Publications Pvt Ltd

In collaboration with

The Vivekananda International Foundation

Published by

Prints Publications Pvt Ltd
Viraj Tower-2, 4259/3, Ansari Road,
Darya Ganj, New Delhi-110002
Tel. : +91-11-45355555
Fax: +91-11-23275542
E-mail : contact@printspublications.com
Website :www.printspublications.com

First Edition : 2022 (Hardbound)

ISBN: 978-93-936740-4-3

Price: Rs. 1495/-

Published and Printed by Mr. Pranav Gupta (Director) on behalf of Prints Publications Pvt Ltd, New Delhi.

This book is dedicated to my late parents who would have been very happy to see this book in print

Foreword

Over the last four decades, China has built up its comprehensive national power with a clear strategic objective of the Chinese people's 'great rejuvenation'. It is challenging the US-led international system and hopes to become the most powerful country someday. Building cyber capabilities is an important component of China's emergence as a major military and technological power.

China's record in the development of its cyber capabilities is impressive. It has developed indigenous capability in artificial intelligence, big data, robotics, 5G, quantum computing and a host of other areas. The "Made in China" programme is aimed at the indigenisation of high technology. The Military-Civil Fusion approach, the focus on human resource development and R&D show China's seriousness in creating an impressive innovation ecosystem in which the government, the academia and the Chinese companies work closely under the tight supervision of the Chinese Communist Party. The efforts to become self-reliant by building a 'dual-circulation' economy is a major departure from the earlier export-led growth model. China has constructed a large digital-industrial base to support its technological rise.

The Peoples' Liberation Army (PLA) is rapidly assimilating new technologies for warfighting purposes having made impressive advances in hypersonic weapons, counter space technologies, deep-sea exploration, space exploration and advanced manufacturing. Massive investments have been made in artificial intelligence and quantum computing. In the social sphere, modern technologies have been harnessed to strengthen surveillance and control. China has built cyber armies, which rope in even civilians. Many cyber-attacks around the world are suspected to be carried out by Chinese hackers. Leading Chinese information technologies companies are suspected of being closely linked with the PLA and doing its bidding. The PLA is adopting new doctrines suitable for information warfare. Its psyop operations across the world have become increasingly frequent and sophisticated.

China's growing cyber capabilities raise apprehensions. Several Chinese tech companies have been banned in different countries due to national security apprehension. Cybersecurity has become a major area of contention between China and the U.S.

China has realized that mastery of emerging technologies, particularly in the cyber domain, is key to its emergence as a global power. Thanks to its economic and technological strength, China is today in a position to exert influence in major international professional bodies and platforms on technology governance issues.

The military confrontation between India and China in eastern Ladakh in 2020 makes it imperative for India to be extremely watchful of the national security implications of a rising China.

In the present book, *China in the Cyber Domain,* Major General PK Mallick (Retd) explores China's rise as a cyber power in some detail. He has been associated with the VIF as a Consultant and has a deep interest in the issues of technology. I am confident that this timely book will enrich the ongoing strategic discourse on China.

New Delhi
January 2022

Dr. Arvind Gupta
Director VIF

Acknowledgements

I have been observing China and its activities in cyber domain for a long time. This book is the culmination of all those studies.

Number of people from academia, industry, practitioners and subject matter experts have helped me immensely to do my research and complete the book. I owe a debt of gratitude to all of them.

At the outset I want to thank the Vivekananda International Foundation (VIF) for giving me the opportunity to write the book. Without the support provided by VIF I could not have dreamt of writing this book.

I would like to place on record my gratitude to Dr. Arvind Gupta, Director VIF and all the experts of VIF for their kind encouragement, motivation, advice which helped me a lot.

My special thanks to Mrs Anuttama Ganguly, Secretary VIF, for providing all the administrative and moral support for my project. The contributions of Mrs Manisha Bhadula of the Library, Library & Web Coordinator Abhijit Biswas, the IT & Web Manager Krishan Redhu and Office Assistant Naresh Singh can never be forgotten.

No amount of gratitude would be enough for the guidance, support and painstaking efforts taken by Lt Gen Gautam Banerjee, PVSM, AVSM, YSM (Retd). He has been a mentor to me and has been extremely patient with me for pointing out the mistakes, giving valuable suggestions and goading me in every step to complete this book. I have no doubt, without his constant encouragement this book would not have seen light of the day.

I am thankful to my brother in arms from the Corps of Signals of Indian Army who have been standing behind me like a rock in all my endeavours. My grateful thanks to Subedar S Nayak, Havildar (Now Naib Subedar) Shantanu Nandi, Havildar Kamal Mahata, Havildar Sunder Singh and Havildar Dhirender Kumar.

I would like to convey my gratitude to Mr. Pranav Gupta (Managing Director) of Prints Publications Pvt Ltd, the Editorial Team of Miss Princee Singh and Miss Shyaloo for their help and Mohit Gupta and the Technical Team for their untiring work in finalising the book.

As always my grateful thanks to my ever supporting wife Ratna for suffering all my idiosyncrasies and giving me moral and material support. Not to forget my daughters Piyali and Pritha for keeping me in good humour.

At the end all errors and omissions are mine.

Maj Gen PK Mallick, VSM (Retd)

Dated: 19 January, 2022

Contents

Illustrations

Photos

Tables

Figures

Abbreviations

3GPP	–	3rd Generation Partnership Project
A2/AD	–	Anti-Access/ Area Denial
AI	–	Artificial Intelligence
AMS	–	Academy of Military Science
APT	–	Advanced Persistent Threats
ARB	–	Aerospace Reconnaissance Bureau
ASEAN	–	Association of Southeast Asian Nations
ATC	–	Air Traffic Control
BaBe	–	Baca Berita
BBC	–	British Broadcasting Corporation
BNCC	–	Beijing North Computing Center
C2	–	Command and Control
C3I	–	Command, Control, Communications and Intelligence
C4ISR	–	Command, Control, Communications, Computers, Intelligence, Surveillance and Reconnaissance
CAC	–	Cyberspace Administration of China
CAIFC	–	China Association for International Friendly Contact
CASC	–	China Aerospace Science and Technology Corporation
CASIC	–	China Aerospace Science and Industry Corporation
CASS	–	Chinese Academy of Social Sciences

CCC	– Comprehensive Command Centre
CCCWS	– China Center for Contemporary World Studies
CCIC	– China Crime Information Centre
CCMCFD	– Central Commission for Military Civilian Fusion Development
CCP	– Chinese Communist Party
CCSA	– China Communications Standards Association
CCTV	– China Central Television
CDAA	– Circularly Disposed Antenna Array
CERT	– Computer Emergency Response Team
CESI	– China Electronic Standards Institute
CETC	– China Electronic Technology Group Corporation
CETC	– China Electronics Technology Group
CGTN	– China Global Television Network
CI	– Confucius Institutes
CICIR	– China Institutes of Contemporary International Relations
CII	– Critical Information Infrastructure
CIIS	– China Institute of International Studies
CIISS	– China International Institute for Strategic Studies
CILG	– Cybersecurity and Informatization Leading Group
CINGAIDS	– Chinese Institute of New Generation AI Development Strategies
CIO	– Cyber-Influence Operations
CIP	– Center for International Policy

CISAW	– Certified Information Security Assurance Worker
CLSGISI	– Central Leading Small Group for Internet Security and Informatisation
CMC	– Central Military Commission
CMI	– Civil-Military Integration
CNA	– Computer Network Attack
CNCERT/CC	– National Computer Network Emergency Response Technical Team/Coordination Centre of China
CND	– Computer Network Defence
CNE	– Computer Network Exploitation
CNIS	– China National Institute of Standardization
CNITSEC	– China Information Technology Security Evaluation Center
CNN	– Cable News Network
CNNIC	– China Internet Network Information Center
CNO	– Computer Network Operations
CO	– Cyberspace Operations
COMINT	– Communications Intelligence
COSTIND	– Commission for Science, Technology and Industry for National Defense
CPC	– Communist Party of China
CPD	– Central Propaganda Department
CRR	– Cybersecurity Review Regime
CSET	– Center for Security and Emerging Technology
CSSA	– Chinese Students and Scholars Association

CYBERCOM	– Cyber Command
DARPA	– Defense Advanced Research Projects Agency
DDoS	– Distributed Denial-of-Service
DIA	– Defense Intelligence Agency
DISA	– Defense Information Systems Agency
DNI	– Directorate of National Intelligence
DoD	– U.S. Department of Defense
DPP	– Democratic Progressive Party
ECCM	– Electronic Counter-Countermeasures
ECM	– Electronic Counter Measures
ELINT	– Electronic Intelligence
ELINT	– Integrates Electronic Intelligence
EMS	– Electro-Magnetic Spectrum
EMSO	– Electro Magnetic Support Operations
EU	– European Union
EW	– Electronic Warfare
FYP	– Five-Year Plan
GAD	– General Armament Department
GDPR	– General Data Protection Regulation
GGE	– Group of Government Experts
GII	– Global Innovation Index
GLD	– General Logistics Department
GONGO	– Government Organized Non-Government Organisations
GPD	– General Political Department
GSD	– General Staff Department
HF	– High Frequency

HRD	–	Human Resource Development
HUST	–	Huazhong University of Science and Technology
IADS	–	Interactive Analysis and Display Software
IANA	–	Internet Assigned Numbers Authority
ICANN	–	Internet Corporation for Assigned Names and Numbers
ICB	–	Information and Communications Bureau
ICS	–	Industrial Control Systems
ICT	–	Information and Communication Technologies
IDS	–	Intrusion Detection System
IEC	–	International Electrotechnical Commission
IEU	–	Information Engineering University
IGOs	–	Intergovernmental Organisations
IISS	–	The International Institute for Strategic Studies
IIWAM	–	Information/Influence Warfare and Manipulation
IM	–	Instant Messaging
INEW	–	Integrated Network Electronic Warfare
IO	–	Information Operations
IOG	–	Independent Operational Group
IoT	–	Internet of Things
ISCCC	–	Information Security Certification Center
ISO	–	International Organisation of Standardization
ISPs	–	Internet service providers
IT	–	Information Technology

ITI	– Information Technology Industry
ITU	– International Telecommunications Union
IW	– Information Warfare
JOCC	– Joint Operational Control Centre
JSD	– Joint Staff Department
JSD-NEB	– Joint Staff Department's Network-Electronic Bureau
MCF	– Military-Civil Fusion
MIIT	– Ministry of Industry and Information Technology
MiTM	– Man-in-the-middle
MLPS	– Multi-level Protection Scheme
MLPS 2.0	– Multi-level Protection Scheme 2.0
MOOTW	– Military Operations Other Than War
MPS	– Ministry of Public Security
MR	– Military Regions
MRHQ	– Military Region Headquarters
MSS	– Ministry of State Security
MUCD	– Military Unit Cover Designator
NCC	– National Cybersecurity Center
NCL	– National Cybersecurity Law
NCSE	– National Center of Standards Evaluation
NCW	– Network Centric Warfare
NDU	– National Defense University
NDWP	– National Defense White Paper
NGOs	– Nongovernmental organisations
NISEC	– National Information Security Engineering Technology Center

NISSTC	–	National Information Security Standardisation Technical Committee
NSA	–	National Security Agency
NSACE	–	Network Security Authentication Certification Engineer
NSD	–	Network Systems Department
NTIA	–	National Telecommunications & Information Administration
NUDT	–	National University of Defense Technology
OBOR	–	One Belt One Road
OEWG	–	Open-Ended Working Group
OODA	–	Observe, Orient, Decide, Act
OPM	–	Office of Personnel Management
PAP	–	People's Armed Police
PB	–	Petabytes
PLA	–	Peoples' Liberation Army
PLAAF	–	Peoples' Liberation Army Air Force
PLAJLSF	–	Peoples' Liberation Army Joint Logistic Support Force
PLAN	–	Peoples' Liberation Army Navy
PLARF	–	Peoples' Liberation Army Rocket Force
PLASSF	–	Peoples' Liberation Army Strategic Support Force
PMS	–	Preparations for Military Struggle
PPP	–	Public Private Partnership
PRC	–	People's Republic of China
PSI	–	Public Security Intelligence
PWD	–	Political Work Department
R&D	–	Research and Development

RATs	– Remote Access Tools
REC	– Radio Electronic Combat
RMA	– Revolution in Military Affairs
RMAs	– Revolutions in Military Affairs
RT	– Russian Television
S&T	– Science and Technology
SAARC	– South Asian Association for Regional Cooperation
SAC	– Standardization Administration of China
SAF	– Second Artillery Force
SAMR	– State Administration of Market Regulation
SAR	– Synthetic Aperture Radar
SARFT	– State Administration of Radio, Film, and Television
SASAC	– State-Owned Assets Supervision and Administration Commission of the State Council
SASTIND	– State Administration for Science, Technology and Industry for National Defense
SCIO	– State Council Information Office
SCO	– Shanghai Cooperation Organisation
SIGINT	– Signals Intelligence
SIIO	– State Internet Information Office
SILG	– State Informatization Leading Group
SIS	– Super Intelligence System
SMS	– Science of Military Strategy
SNISCG	– State Network Infosec Coordination Group
SOEs	– State-Owned Enterprises

SSD – Space Systems Department
SSF – Strategic Support Force
SVM – Support Vector Machine
TAO – Tailored Access Operations
TC – Theatre Command
TRADOC – Training and Doctrine Command
TRB – Technical Reconnaissance Bureaus
TT&C – Tracking, Telemetry and Control
TTP – Thousand Talents Program
UAVs – Unmanned aerial vehicles
UFWD – United Front Work Department
UN – United Nations
USA, U.S. – United States of America
USSTRATCOM – U.S. Strategic Command
VOIP – Voice over Internet Protocol
VPN – Virtual Private Network
WTC – Western Theater Command

China in the Cyber Domain

ABSTRACT

China is one of the most active cyberspace players in the world. It is developing cyber capacities in pursuit of its economic, political and strategic objectives. President Xi Jinping has made it clear that his objective for China is to emerge as a cyber superpower. Harvard Kennedy School of Government in a recent study of cyber power of various countries has ranked China as the second most powerful nation after U.S.

The People's Liberation Army (PLA) of China has been keenly following all the advancements that have taken place recently in warfare. It has studied the foreign military experiences, especially from the U.S., and learned what works, what should be ignored and what should be adopted to serve PLA's goals. The PLA differs considerably from its Western counterparts in its approach to cyber and network operations. The PLA is not interested in only acquiring new equipment. It is trying to figure out how to best exploit all the equipments, whether new or old, by developing an appropriate set of doctrine and attendant tactics, techniques and procedures to implement that doctrine. PLA has been innovative enough to develop solutions to its operational challenges, creating entirely new capabilities or operating in new and creative ways to challenge its adversaries operating in proximity to its borders.

The PLA of China believes that with the rise of the Information Age, future wars will be contests to exploit information. Controlling the information through the cyber domain is a prerequisite for achieving victory in a modern war. Wars will be decided by the side who is more capable of generating, gathering, transmitting, analyse and exploit information. Informationised warfare blurs the lines between peacetime and wartime. The PLA's concept of the information domain and information operations includes the network, electromagnetic, psychological and intelligence in cyber domains.

China has undertaken a major transformation of the PLA in 2015. The PLA Strategic Support Force (PLASSF) is the first step in the development of a cyber force by combining cyber reconnaissance, cyber attack and cyber defence capabilities into one organisation to reduce bureaucratic hurdles and centralise command and control of PLA cyber units. The PLA continues to augment capabilities to conduct cyberspace, space and electronic warfare operations. Along with the technical aspects of cyber operations, the PLA combines psychological warfare in manipulating public opinion, media warfare and the legal warfare that influences legal arguments to strengthen China's diplomatic and security position. China calls this as the 'Three Warfares'. China effectively integrates this Three Warfare in a comprehensive cyber-information operations doctrine.

The National Defense White Paper (NDWP, 2019) on China's National Defense in the New Era published in July 2019, stated: "Driven by the new round of technological and industrial revolution, the application of cutting-edge technologies such as artificial intelligence (AI), quantum information, big data, cloud computing and the Internet of Things (IoT) is gathering pace in the military field." It said, "War is evolving in form towards informationized warfare, and intelligent warfare is on the horizon." President Xi

Jinping has enunciated the latest concept of intelligentized warfare.

China has been progressively expanding its ability to operate in cyberspace, including electromagnetic spectrum, information and outer space. It is forcefully pursuing indigenous innovation of emerging technologies especially AI, big data, robotics, 5G technology, cloud computing and quantum information systems which will give it new capabilities in cyberspace. While China has not fought a war since its 1979 conflict with Vietnam, the PLA is going ahead in the domains of intense integrated electronic and computer network warfare or counter space operations as compared to other nations.

Notes:

1. *English translations have over time led to the usage of three terms: informationization, informatization and now intelligentization. More or less synonyms, the changing nomenclatures emphasise the degree to which information, and its processed version intelligence, are to be imbibed into the military system for the conduct of modern era warfare.*

2. *The People's Liberation Army (PLA) blurs the fine distinction between cyber operations and informationized warfare. For the PLA, the two are but part of one whole – Information Warfare (IW).*

* * *

INTRODUCTION

"Cyberspace is the common space of activities for mankind. The future of cyberspace should be in the hands of all countries. Countries should step up communications, broaden consensus and deepen cooperation to jointly build a community of shared future in cyberspace." – **Xi Jinping, President of the People's Republic of China, 16 December 2015.[1]**

The globe today is characterised by cyberspace. Internet access is available to more than half the global population today. In near future, the implementation of smart cities and Internet of Things (IoT), where entire cities and personal appliances are driven by information and communication technologies (ICT), will digitise and enhance the daily human existence. With the increased access to the internet and rapidly developing technologies comes increased vulnerability in the cyber domain. China sees cyber as an extension of their foreign policy and will try to use the *information* to influence, not only neighbouring countries but international and inter-governmental organisations (IGOs) also in cyberspace.

In 1995 the internet made its entry to the public in China. Today China has the biggest population of netizens in the world. It is the world's biggest producer of desktop computers. Two of its telecommunications equipment manufacturers are among the world's largest. China is already a dominant force in cyberspace. Since military operations, espionage and political warfare depend on information and data, China invests hugely to gain the advantage in cyberspace, including physical architecture, operating systems and hardware.[2] China is thus one of the most active cyberspace players in the world. It is developing cyber capacities in pursuit of its economic, political and strategic objectives. The middle kingdom is also forcefully pursuing the indigenous innovation of emerging technologies especially 5G technology, big data, robotics, AI, cloud computing and quantum information systems which will give it new capabilities in cyberspace. President Xi Jinping has elucidated clearly that his objective for China is to emerge as a cyber super power. China aims to become the world's largest and most powerful nation in cyberspace. The information technology revolution has produced both historic opportunities and potential vulnerabilities for China. It remains a major victim of cyber crime.

China's Military Strategy, May 2015 states: "Cyberspace has become a new pillar of economic and social development and a new domain of national security. As international strategic competition in cyberspace has been turning increasingly fiercer, quite a few countries are developing their cyber military forces. Being one of the major victims of hacker attacks, China is confronted with grave security threats to its cyber infrastructure. As cyberspace weighs more in military security, China will expedite the development of a cyber force, and enhance its capabilities of cyberspace situation awareness, cyber defense, support for the country's endeavours in cyberspace and participation in international cyber cooperation, so as to stem major cyber crises, ensure national network and information security, and maintain national security and social stability."

The People's Liberation Army (PLA) of China believes that with the rise of the Information Age, future wars will be contests to exploit information. Wars will be determined by the side who is more capable of generating, gathering, transmitting, analyse and exploit information. PLA believes controlling the information domain is a prerequisite for achieving victory in a modern war. The PLA's concept of the information domain and information operations includes the network, electromagnetic, psychological and intelligence domains. The 'network domain' and corresponding 'network warfare' are more or less similar to the U.S. concept of the cyber domain and cyber warfare.

The Communist Party of China's (CPC) propaganda apparatus continues to adapt and modernise as the cyber domain grows in importance, seeking to promote 'positive energy' online and to 'tell China's story well'. The Directorate of National Intelligence (DNI) of the United States of America (USA, U.S.) assessed that "China presents a persistent cyber espionage threat and a growing attack threat to our core military and critical infrastructure systems. China remains the most active strategic competitor responsible for cyber espionage against the U.S. Government, corporations and allies. It is improving its cyber attack capabilities and altering information online, shaping Chinese views and potentially the views of U.S. citizens".[3]

The new currency of 'comprehensive national power', the measurement of a state and society's power, including economic, political, diplomatic, military, science and technology and cultural components, is measured in terms of information. China has risen as a cyber super power. It has enormous economic and military capabilities that augment its overall national power. This would empower China to flourish in the Fourth Industrial Revolution that is currently unfolding. China's cyber power is a critical part of its comprehensive national power. The Harvard Kennedy School of Government in a recent study of cyber power of the countries has ranked China as the second most powerful nation after U.S.

2020 NCPI Rankings

Belfer Center National Cyber Power Index 2020 "Top 10"			Specific Rankings	
#	Country	Overall score	Capability	Intent
1	United States	50.24	1	2
2	China	41.47	2	1
3	United Kingdom	35.57	3	3
4	Russia	28.38	10	4
5	Netherlands	24.18	9	5
6	France	23.43	5	11
7	Germany	22.42	4	12
8	Canada	21.50	11	9
9	Japan	21.03	8	14
10	Australia	20.04	16	8

Source: Julia Voo et al., National Cyber Power Index 2020, Harvard Kennedy School of Government, September 2020 available at: https://www.belfercenter.org/publication/national-cyber-power-index-2020

As per the study by the Center for Strategic & International Studies, China along with Russia, North Korea and Iran are today's most prolific users of offensive cyberspace operations. But they fail to mention the capabilities of USA, Israel, France and the United Kingdom. In 2018, the People's Republic of China (PRC) was blamed for election hacking in Cambodia and Malaysia, theft of intellectual property from countries like the United States, Singapore and Taiwan. China has implemented a policy that enables them to spy on their own people.

Cyber power has become a cornerstone of PRC policy within the last decade. Cyber power facilitates four Chinese national priorities:

- The insurance of a harmonious Internet.

- Reduction of foreign dependence on digital and communications equipment.
- Development of their cyber-forces and cybersecurity.
- Promotion of 'cyber sovereignty' as a principle of Internet governance.

These priorities are integral in China's use of cyberspace to influence international governmental organisations like the United Nations. China wants to achieve global "electronic dominance" by 2050. This includes targeting its adversary's critical infrastructure, financial markets, military and civilian communications capabilities before traditional military operations begin. A 2016 NATO Cooperative Cyber Defence Centre of Excellence study concluded that the "Chinese government, together with the Chinese military, private corporations, and unaffiliated citizens, conduct intrusions against major Western powers as well as in the neighbouring region every day, targeting academia, industry and government facilities for the purpose of amassing technological secrets."

The National Defense White Paper China's National Defense in the New Era (NDWP, 2019), published in July 2019 states: "Driven by the new round of technological and industrial revolution, the application of cutting-edge technologies such as AI, quantum information, big data, cloud computing and the IoT is gathering pace in the military field." The PLA recognises that military use of such state-of-the-art technologies holds the key to the outcome of future warfare. Adopting the new trend for military revolution may enable the PLA to "overtake (the U.S. forces) at the bend."[4] The PLA continues to augment capabilities to conduct cyberspace, space and electronic warfare operations. PLA's modernisation includes command and force structure reforms to improve operational flexibility and readiness for future deployment. The PLA many a time uses the term 'informatization' to describe the transformation to become a modern military that can function in the digital age.

The Chinese do not use the word cyber as regularly as in the West. Cyber warfare takes place in the electromagnetic spectrum. China's military thinkers view cyber and network operations occur in an information domain which includes network, psychological, media operations and electronic warfare. In the next chapter various aspects of Information Warfare, Cyber Warfare and Local War will be discussed.

Endnotes

1. Full Text: International Strategy of Cooperation on Cyberspace available at: http://www.xinhuanet.com/english/china/2017-03/01/c_136094371.htm
2. "China's Cyber Power in a New Era," in Tim Huxley and William Choong, eds. Asia-Pacific Regional Security Assessment 2019, (London, UK: Routledge, International Institute for Strategic Studies, 2019), available at: https://www.iiss.org/publications/ strategic-dossiers/asiapacific-regional-security-assessment-2019 /rsa19-07-chapter-5
3. Louisa Lim and Julia Bergin, 'Inside China's audacious global propaganda campaign', Guardian, 7 December 2018, available at: https://www.theguardian.com/news / 2018 / dec / 07 / china-plan-for-global-media-dominance-propaganda-xi-jinping
4. PRC State Council, China's National Defense in the New Era.... available at: https://china.usc.edu/prc-state-council-china%E2%80%99s – national - defense-new-era-%E6%96%B0%E6%97%B6%E4%BB%A3%E7%9A%84%E4%B8%AD%E5%9B%BD%E5%9B%BD%E9%98%B2-july-24-2019

* * *

CHAPTER 1

Information, Cyber and Local Warfare

Introduction

Information has become critically important in the conduct of current and future wars. As per the Chinese thinking, in the Information Age future wars will be contests in the ability to exploit information as mechanised warfare was for the Industrial Age. Informationized warfare will be the feature of the Information Age. The side better able to generate, gather, transmit, analyse and exploit information will win the war. This will require the PLA to sustain its efforts to focus more on quality than quantity and to improve its ability to conduct joint operations. The PLA is reorienting itself to better conduct informationized warfare.

China's academic discussions of information warfare (IW) and cyber warfare started in the early 1990s. The PLA saw the effect of modern information operations (IO) on the battlefield and in the international arena from the application of high technologies in the Balkans, the first Gulf War and subsequent operations in Kosovo, Afghanistan and Iraq. China realised that there is no way it can defend itself without following the changes in the forms of war in which high tech, mainly information technologies, play vital roles. The PLA has been keenly studying U.S. military publications on the evolution of American doctrine on IW and network-centric warfare. The

PLA started implementing its own form of IW. The Chinese military has adopted IW concepts suited to its own organisation and doctrine. It blended its own traditional tactics, U.S. doctrine and expanded on Cold War Soviet doctrine of radio-electronic combat to bring the PLA into the information age.

The Chinese do not use the word 'cyber' as regularly as in the West. For the Chinese, cyberspace is only a subset of information space. The PLA's broader concept of the information domain and of IO encompasses the network, electromagnetic, psychological and intelligence domains, with the "network domain" and corresponding "network warfare" roughly analogous to the current U.S. concept of the cyber domain and cyber warfare. The PLA military strategists include cyber warfare as a part of IW. Cyber warfare takes place in the electromagnetic spectrum. The PLA differs appreciably from its Western counterparts in its approach to cyber and network operations. China does not see cyber power as a distinct capability as the air, land, sea and space. China's military thinkers view cyber and network operations as occurring in an information domain which includes network, psychological, media operations and electronic warfare (EW).

The PLA's command, control, communications, computers, intelligence, surveillance, and reconnaissance programs support the ground forces, navy, air force, missile forces, nuclear warfare and space warfare. China's military doctrine depends on incorporating information technology and networked IO. The PLA's operational concepts for employing traditional signals intelligence and EW have expanded to include cyber warfare, kinetic and cyber attacks on satellites and information confrontation operations across the electromagnetic spectrum.

Information Warfare

Information operations comprise of reconnaissance operations, offensive and defensive operations and deterrence operations in the electromagnetic, network and psychological realms. It consists of the employment of physically destructive means against key information infrastructure targets. Information warfare has a broader definition than IO and refers to a struggle for initiative between two hostile parties involving the use of information technology in the political, economic, science and technology, diplomatic, cultural, military and other domains.

China feels that controlling the cyber-information spectrum in the modern battlefield is a critical enabler and a fundamental prerequisite in a conflict. The PLA assesses 'information blockade' or 'information dominance' is necessary to seize the initiative and set the conditions necessary to gain land, sea and air superiority. China's investment in developing capabilities in cyber operations, EW systems and counter-space capabilities reflects the priority the PLA places on information advantage. The PLA emphasises that the seizure of electromagnetic dominance in the early phases of a campaign is one of its foremost tasks to ensure battlefield success. The PLA writers have coined the term 'Integrated Network Electronic Warfare (INEW)' to describe the use of computer network operations, EW and kinetic strikes to disrupt battlefield information systems that support an adversary's war-waging capabilities. The PLA has developed the Integrated Network and Electronic Warfare doctrine to organise and structure its forces for seizing information superiority.

In an assessment of China's capabilities, the International Institute for Strategic Studies (IISS) noted: "The PLA has devoted much attention to IW over the past decade, both in terms of battlefield EW and wider, cyber-warfare capabilities. The main doctrine is the 'Integrated Network Electronic Warfare' document, which guides the PLA computer-network operations. The PLA thinking appears to have moved beyond INEW towards a new concept of 'information confrontation' which aims to integrate both electronic and non-electronic aspects of IW within a single command authority. The PLA thinking sees warfare under informationized conditions as characterised by opposing sides using complete systems of ground, naval, air, space and electromagnetic".

Cyber Warfare

Cyber warfare is considered to be part of IO. In the PLA's glossary of military terms, IO is defined as: "integrating modes such as EW, cyber warfare, and psychological warfare to strike or counter an enemy to interfere with and damage the enemy's information and information systems in cyberspace and electromagnetic space; to influence and weaken the enemy's information acquisition, transmission, processing, utilization, and decision-making capabilities; and to ensure the stable operation of one's own information systems, information security, and correct decision making."

China's Military Strategy, May 2015 states: "Cyberspace has become a new pillar of economic and social development, and a new domain of national security. As international strategic competition in cyberspace is becoming fierce, many countries are developing their cyber capabilities. China is one of the major victims of hacker attacks and has to deal with grave security threats to its cyber infrastructure. As cyberspace weighs more in military security, China will expedite the development of a cyber force, and enhance its capabilities of cyberspace situation awareness, cyber defense, support for the country's endeavours in cyberspace and participation in international cyber cooperation, to stem major cyber crises, ensure national network and information security and maintain national security and social stability".

The PLA could use its cyber warfare capabilities to support military operations in the following key areas:

- Cyber reconnaissance allows the PLA to collect technical and operational data for intelligence and potential operational planning for cyber attacks because the accesses and tactics, techniques, and procedures for cyber reconnaissance translate into those also necessary to conduct cyber attacks.
- The PLA could employ its cyber attack capabilities to establish information dominance in the early stages of a conflict to restrict an adversary's actions or slow mobilisation and deployment by targeting network-based C2, C4ISR, logistics and commercial activities. Cyber warfare capabilities can serve as a force multiplier when coupled with conventional capabilities during a conflict.

The PLA writings note the effectiveness of IO and cyber warfare in recent conflicts. They credit cyber attacks on an enemy's C2 system with the potential to "completely disrupt" these systems, paralysing the victim and thus gaining battlefield superiority for the attacker. The PLA researchers believe that building strong cyber capabilities are necessary to protect Chinese networks and advocate seizing 'cyberspace superiority' by using offensive cyber operations to deter or degrade an adversary's ability to conduct military operations against China. Chinese writings suggest cyber operations allow China to manage the escalation of a conflict because cyber attacks are a low-cost deterrent. The writings also suggest that cyber attacks demonstrate capabilities and resolve to an adversary.

It is important to differentiate between cybersecurity and information security. The West sees cybersecurity as the security of computer and information systems as physical and logical entities, and information assurance or information security as referring to security of the content. On the contrary, the Chinese view both the information systems and the content of the information as integral and connected parts of information security. The Chinese have adopted IW as a distinct, yet integrated and discrete discipline, which is incompatible with the Western view. The west now divides the concept into smaller and separate disciplines, such as psychological operations and strategic communications. The Chinese use cyber warfare only when describing Western countries and their cyber operations.

The 2016 U.S. Department of Defense (DoD) report states: "The PLA conducts military exercises simulating operations in complex electromagnetic environments and likely views conventional and cyber operations as a means of achieving information dominance. The PLA would likely use EW, cyberspace operations (CO), and deception to augment counter space and other kinetic operations during a wartime scenario to deny an adversary's attainment and use of information. Chinese military writings describe informationized warfare as an asymmetric way to weaken an adversary's ability to acquire, transmit, process, and use information during war and force an adversary to capitulate before the conflict. "Simultaneous and parallel" operations would involve strikes against U.S. warships, aircraft, and associated supply craft and the use of information attacks to affect tactical and operational communications and computer networks. These operations could have a significant effect on an adversary's navigational and targeting radars".

International Strategy for Cooperation in Cyberspace, released by China in March 2017, stated that the PLA would play an important role in cyberspace. The strategy also stated that the country would expedite the development of a cyber force and enhance capabilities in situational awareness, cyber defence, supporting state activities and participate in international cooperation, to prevent major cyber crises.

Like many other states, China is seriously involved in computer network operations. These are conducted primarily for the following reasons:

- To strengthen political and economic control in China.
- To complement other forms of intelligence collection and gather economic, military, or technology intelligence and information.
- To reconnoiter, map and gather targeting information in a foreign military, government, civil infrastructure or corporate networks for later exploitation or attack.
- To conduct the exploitation or attacks using the collected information.
- To develop defences or conduct defensive operations in the PLA and China's own cyber systems.

Chinese military analysts feel that cyber warfare is strategic warfare in the information age, as nuclear warfare was in the 20th century. This definition clarifies that cyber warfare has much broader significance to national security. It involves competition in areas beyond the military, such as the economy, diplomacy and social development. The PLA considers cyber capabilities as a critical component in its overall integrated strategic deterrence posture, alongside space and nuclear deterrence.

Local War

The Science of Military Strategy states: "It has two distinctive features: one is the high-tech feature, and the other is the local feature. The former refers to the high-tech as the material and technological foundation of war, for a large amount of high-tech weapons and equipment are used and a lot of traditional military systems are improved by the employment of high technologies. The latter means that the war is controlled within the local range. Moreover, the aim, range, tools of war and time and space of engagements are all limited. These two features determine the fundamental orientation of the future development of the local war."

The PLA theorists feel that in contrast to the previous PLA belief in Total War, Local Wars are characterized by the pursuit of limited political goals through a relatively constrained use of force. Under this concept, military force supports diplomatic efforts aimed at securing attainable, limited political goals rather than the complete destruction of the enemy. A RAND report states, "Military action is intended to create conditions for the achievement of the desired political outcome." However, they estimate that the high technology levels and lethality present in Local Wars will ensure that wars will be brief but highly destructive contests between vastly lethal and networked military forces. Armed forces in Local Wars at the operational level will be agile, capable of high-tempo deep operations, resource-intensive, critically dependent on information and present in all domains of warfare.

Local War under Conditions of Informatization (or Informationization)

Active Defence provides the basic strategic posture for the PLA. This concept has been improved upon as the doctrine of Local War under Conditions of Informatization. In the

Chinese view, informationized warfare extends beyond cyber activities and is instead about establishing information dominance. One cannot wait until the outbreak of war to gather intelligence, carry out influence and psychological operations, develop satellite and antisatellite systems or design computer software weapons. Informationized warfare includes the conduct of political warfare, which shapes and influences friendly, adversary and third-party views and assessments.

The Local War under Conditions of Informationization concept has been the official military doctrine of the PLA since 1993. This doctrine states that now warfare will be local geographically, primarily along China's periphery, limited in scope, duration, means and conducted under 'conditions of informatization'. As per Chinese military experts, informationized warfare is an asymmetric way to weaken an adversary's ability to acquire, transmit, process, and use information during war and to force an adversary to capitulate before the onset of conflict. The U.S. DoD describes these as "conditions in which modern military forces use advanced computer systems, information technology and communication networks to gain the operational advantage over an opponent." The DoD interprets this doctrine as "high-intensity, information-centric regional military operations of short duration."

The PLA frequently uses the term 'informatization' also to describe the transformation process of becoming a modern military that can operate in the digital age. China views informatization as a comprehensive system of systems. In the next chapter how informatization has evolved over the tears under different regimes will be reviewed.

* * *

CHAPTER 2

Cyber-Informatization and Evolution of Chinese Concepts of War

"We should be fully aware of the importance and urgency of internet security and informatization. Without cybersecurity there is no national security; without informatization, there is no military modernization."

–President Xi Jinping

Introduction

From the early 1970s, the proliferation of micro-electronics, computers and telecommunications technology tremendously improved the ability to gather, store, manage and transmit information. Information technology, including computers and telecommunications systems affects all segments of society and national economies. IT is now an integral part of the nation's infrastructure. Informatization is the consequence of the Information Age and the widespread introduction of information technology.

Threats to security and national interests have also become informationized as the economic, political and social issues are under informatization. The two warring sides today have unprecedented access to each others' national economies, the broader population and the top decision makers. The proliferation of IT into all aspects of economics and society makes them more susceptible to a range of new pressures and threats. These threats extend beyond the information networks and the component computers. The information itself can become a threat. Information can erode the morale of key decision makers, popular support for a conflict, or the will of the military to fight. In step with the increasing impact of information, China's understanding of its national interests has expanded.[1]

The Chinese do not use the word *cyber* as is done in the West. They distinguish everything related to cyber as part of a broader conversion from an industrial society to an information society. The process is referring to as informationisation or informatisation (the latter is normally used in translations and has wider use). As per the People's Liberation Army's (PLA), cyberspace is only a subset of information space. China views Informationisation as a comprehensive system of systems.[2]

China feels that warfare has also become informationized. Information itself is a new domain and what connects other domains such as the land, sea, and air with each other. Warfare "under informatized conditions" refers to the application of IT to all aspects of military operations, including sensors and electronics on weapons systems and platforms, automated command and control (C2) systems and information operations (IO) including cyber, electronic, public opinion, psychological and legal warfare. IT has made various weapons systems more precise and lethal. The networking of sensors and shooters allows for higher operational tempos. It facilitates the command, control, communications, computers, intelligence, surveillance and reconnaissance (C4ISR) systems gather and process large amounts of information to command "informatized" weapons, platforms and units to increase efficiency and flexibility, responsiveness and effectiveness of military forces. Night and weather conditions are not constraints for military forces as it used to be in the past.

However, informationized warfare goes beyond the incorporation of information technology into weapons systems. It is the making of systems-of-systems, including the integration of IT into every aspect of military activities like intelligence collection and exploitation, logistics and transportation etc. One of the characteristics of "informationized warfare" is that conflicts are not platform-versus-platform or even system-versus-system, but battles between rival arrays of systems-of-systems.[3]

As per China 'Informatization' means that IT is of paramount importance to expanding military effectiveness. This involves dominating the electromagnetic spectrum through integrated network electronic warfare (EW) as well as exploiting technological advances in microelectronics, sensors, propulsion, stealth and especially cyber to equip the PLA with new capacities for long-range strike and disruption. Informatization is an awkward translation of the Chinese term '*xinxihua*'. In China, informatization is a national-level concept used in civil as well as military affairs to describe the transition from the Industrial Age to the Information Age generated by the development, spread, and application of information technology. As Joe McReynolds and James Mulvenon explain, informatization "describes the process of moving toward greater collection, systematization, distribution, and utilization of information."

According to the 2019 U.S. Department of Defense (DoD) report on China's Military Power, the term 'informatization' is 'approximately analogous to the U.S. military's concept of network centric operations: a force's capability to use advanced IT and communications systems to gain operational advantage over an adversary'. The PLA's view of informatized local wars was, 'defined by real-time, data-networked C2 and precision strike'. According to PLA, informatization provides the PLA with military capabilities that allow it to 'leapfrog' the capabilities of currently technologically superior adversaries.

Space, cyber and electromagnetic warfare capacities have the potential to adversely affect a high-tech enemy's 'operational system of systems' and thwart their command-level 'system of systems'. By introducing added information and communications technologies, including cyber capacities, across its theatre commands and forces The PLA aims to make 'basic progress' by 2020, to improve information-enabled command, control and communications capabilities. Informatization is also central to the PLA's efforts to improve its military education and training.

President Xi Jinping has called for the PLA to create a highly informatized force capable of dominating all networks and expanding the country's security and development interests. Under Xi Jinping, the PLA is now ready to undertake "informationized local wars," reflecting the new circumstances or new conditions now challenging it. These new circumstances have come up because of a series of transformations in the broader socio-techno-economic background. These include:[4]

- Technological transformation, mainly in big data, cloud computing and other changes in IT.
- Industrial transformation, because of networking and the development in artificial intelligence (AI) and other elements that have raised traditional industries to new heights.
- Military transformation, as a consequence of weapons combining more and more intelligence and units becoming more digitised.

Evolution: Informatization to Intelligentized Warfare

China's national military strategy gives the military strategic guidelines. It is the direction from the Central Military

Commission (CMC) of the Chinese Communist Party (CCP) on all aspects of the PLA combat-related activities. Marshall Peng Dehuai stated in 1957, "the strategic guidelines affect army building, troop training and war preparations." The guidelines give out how China plans to wage its next war. When CMC changes a strategic guideline, it can be a major departure from China's past strategy, or minor change indicating an alteration to an existing strategy. China had eight unique military strategies or strategic guidelines since 1949. Those approved in 1956, 1980 and 1993 represent major changes in China's military strategy, while the others have constituted minor changes.[5]

China's Preparations for Informatized Warfare can be categorised under the following phases:[6]

- The Era of Mao Zedong (1927–1976): Active Defense and the Curse of the Final War.
- The Era of Deng Xiaoping (1976–1989): A Break from the Final War and Shift to Local War.
- The Era of Jiang Zemin (1989–2004): An agenda setter. Set the stage for strategy, deterrence, psychological warfare and the use of stratagems. Local Wars under High-Tech Conditions. Release of the 2001 Science of Military Strategy.
- The Era of Hu Jintao (2004–2012): Innovation starts rolling. Introduced several technological concepts and achievements like interest in system of systems and advanced the development of information technologies. Published the 2013 book *Science of Military Strategy*. Informatized Local Wars.
- The Era of Xi Jinping (2012–Present): Most dynamic, exciting and progressive shift to Informatized Warfare and Intelligentized Warfare.

Past and Present Leaders, the Science and Technologies Emphasized by the PLA, and Military Strategy are shown below:

Leader	Science, technologies, and weapons emphasized by the PLA	Military strategy that was adopted (besides active defense which has been adopted throughout)
Mao Zedong	Atomic bomb, hydrogen bomb	People's war (while its content has changed, the term itself has survived in succeeding eras)
Deng Xiaoping	Advanced conventional weapons	Local wars under modern conditions
Jiang Zemin	High tech, high-tech weapons	Local wars under high-tech conditions
Hu Jintao	Information and weapons operated based on information	Local wars under the conditions of informatization
Xi Jinping	Information, intelligence, and weapons operated on their basis	Informatized warfare (shift to intelligentized warfare)

Source: NIDS China Security Report 2021 China's Military Strategy in the New Era Published by The National Institute for Defense Studies 5-1 Honmura-cho, Ichigaya, Shinjuku-ku, Tokyo 162-8808 Japan Website: http://www.nids.mod.go.jp, Page 15

China has been keenly observing the use of technology by the U.S. and the western powers since the 1990-1991 Gulf War, the 1995-1996 Taiwan Straits Crisis and the 1999 Belgrade embassy bombing. It has followed the concepts of Revolution in Military Affairs (RMA), the Network Centric Warfare (NCW), System of Systems, the Transformation concept etc.[7] Chinese analysts critically have reviewed U.S. network warfare prowess during Operation Desert Storm. As an Academy of Military Science (AMS) textbook describes, "Several recent local wars, especially the 1999 Kosovo War and the 2003 Iraq War, gave us a glimpse of the vivid realities of local wars under informatized conditions, providing us with many lessons."

The Chinese were alarmed by the PLA's outdated and inadequate military capabilities and supporting systems. Most aspects of the campaign reminded the PLA high command of its deficiencies in EW, precision guided munitions, stealth technology, precision bombing, campaign coordination through airborne C2 systems, space-based early warning and surveillance in targeting and intelligence gathering etc. Immediately after the first Gulf War, the Chinese decided that they must prepare for what they termed "local wars under modern, high-technology conditions." Features of such wars specified that:[8]

- Quality and the quantity of weapons matters. Technologically sophisticated weapons would give advantage to the side which would be able to determine the limits of the conflict and effectively control its scale and extent.
- Battlefields are three-dimensional. Conflicts expand deeper into the strategic rear areas.
- Conflict is conducted around the clock marked by high operational tempos, under all-weather environments.
- The basic approach is different. Greater emphasis is placed on joint operations, aerial combat, long-distance strike and mobile operations.
- Role of command, control, communications and intelligence (C3I) is vital. C3I functions are essential to successful implementation of such wars. Accordingly, the ability to interfere with an opponent's C3I functions also became much more important.

Two years after the Gulf War, in 1993, the PLA modified its military strategic guideline as the basic aim of Preparations for Military Struggle (PMS) which set at "winning local wars in conditions of modern technology, particularly high technology". The PLA analysed informatized conditions and informatized warfare used in the 1999 Kosovo War intensely. Jiang Zemin in a speech to the CMC in December 2000, said that "high-technology local wars since the Gulf War demonstrate that information technology plays an extremely important role in modern warfare. The main characteristic of high technology war is informatization. The new military transformation is essentially a revolution in military informatization. Informatization is becoming a multiplier of the combat effectiveness of the armed forces. The new transformation in military affairs is entering into a new stage of qualitative changes and will likely develop into a profound military revolution that spreads around the globe and involves all military fields." Jiang identified four core trends:

- Informatized weapons and equipment would determine the core of a military's combat capability.
- Role of stand-off strikes, described as noncontact and nonlinear operations, would become more important. Such strikes would be used to target an opponent's C4ISR, air defence, and other systems.
- Confrontations among systems will become the basic feature of battlefield confrontations.
- Space had become "the new strategic high ground."

After witnessing Western military operations in Afghanistan and the Balkans, by the early 2000s, the PLA began preparing for 'local wars under informationized conditions'.

One year after the Iraq War, in 2004, the military's PMS was changed to "winning local wars under conditions of informationization." As explained in white paper entitled China's National Defense in 2004, the basic understanding is that "informationization has become the key factor in enhancing the war-fighting capability of the armed forces." Hu Jintao summarised in June 2006, "Local wars under informatized conditions are a confrontation of systems of systems and the basic form of operations is integrated joint operations." The 2004 guideline remained focused on local wars but highlighted the role of 'informatization' in warfare and marked a shift in the main form of operations from joint operations to integrated joint operations. The 2004 strategic guideline did not constitute a major change in China's military strategy. The 2004 guideline enriched and improved the 1993 guideline, indicating a limited adjustment in military strategy and not a major change.

The 2004 guideline was adopted at a June 2004 meeting of the CMC. At the meeting, Jiang Zemin stated that "we must clearly place the basis of PMS on winning local wars under informatized conditions." This change reflected the CMC's judgment that "the basic characteristic of high-technology warfare is informatized warfare. Informatized warfare will become the basic form of 21st century warfare." Jiang instructed that the PLA "must adapt to the transformation in the basis of PMS, promote deeper development of a military transformation with Chinese characteristics, and realize the strategic goals of building an informatized force and winning informatized wars."

Under the leadership of Hu Jintao the National Defense White Paper published in 2006 states that the PLA would:[9]

- Follow the military strategic guideline for active defense.
- Lead informatization and promote the composite development of informatization and mechanization.
- Expedite upgrades of the PLA's main equipments to conform to informatization.

- Augment maritime information systems, set up an informatized air fighting force and improve the informatization level of the Second Artillery Force's weapon and equipment systems.

China's 2008 National Defense White Paper had placed the following goals within a specific developmental time frame to:

- Establish a 'foundation' for military 'informatization' by 2010.
- Achieve major progress towards this goal by 2020.
- Fully realize this transformation by 2050.

Hu Jintao, as General Secretary and Chairman of the CMC at the 17th CCP National Congress in 2012, vowed to increase the capability to complete varied military tasks, at the root of which was the capability for 'local wars under the conditions of informationization'. Hu's report advocates that the PLA placed greater priority on informatization than on mechanization.

The 2013 White Paper

On April 16, 2013 China released another defense white paper. It was entitled 'The Diversified Employment of China's Armed Forces'. It highlighted China's adherence to the following principles and policies:[10]

- Safeguarding national sovereignty, security and territorial integrity and aiding the country's peaceful development.
- Planning to win local wars under the conditions of informationization and expanding and intensifying military preparedness.
- Formulating the concept of overall security and effectively conducting military operations other than war (MOOTW).

- Deepening security cooperation and fulfilling international obligations.
- Acting according to laws, policies and disciplines.

Winning Informatized Local Wars

In July 2014, the PLA formalised on winning informatized local wars. The 2014 strategy did not constitute a major change in China's military strategy. It stressed the role of informatization in warfare and justifying far-reaching organisational reforms that the PLA needed to undertake in order to effectively execute joint operations. The change from the 2004 strategy was altering from "winning local wars under the conditions of informatization" to "winning informatized local wars". It also addressed cybersecurity for the first time in an official military document. This encouraged important changes in the PLA's force structure, operational doctrines and training priorities to support a high-tech networked military force.

China's 2015 National Defence White Paper, subtitled 'China's Military Strategy' provided a broad view of China's strategic goals. It states, "The world RMA is proceeding to a new stage.[11] Long-range, precise, smart, stealthy, and unmanned weapons and equipment are becoming increasingly sophisticated. Outer space and cyberspace have become new commanding heights in strategic competition among all parties. The form of war is accelerating its evolution to informatization. World major powers are actively adjusting their national security strategies and defence policies and speeding up their military transformation and force restructuring. The aforementioned revolutionary changes in military technologies and the form of war have had not only a significant impact on the international political and military landscapes but also posed new and severe challenges to China's military security." It also called upon the PLA to expedite the development of a cyber force and to enhance its capabilities in cyberspace situation awareness as well as cyber defence in order to stem major cyber crises, ensure national network and information security and maintain national security and social stability.

The U.S. DoD's 2015 report on Chinese military power assessed that cyber operations are a key component of informationization. It could serve Chinese military operations in three key areas as cyber operations:[12]

- Allow data collection for intelligence and probable offensive cyber operation purposes.
- Can be employed to restrain an adversary's actions or slow response time by targeting network-based logistics, communications and commercial activities.
- Coupled with kinetic attacks during conflict can serve as a force multiplier.

China's informationized battlefield is a battlefield between networks. Attacking the enemy's military information systems and defending against an enemy's attacks through cyberspace are essential means of its informatized warfare. China's use of cyberspace in warfare will therefore continue to increase in importance and the cyberspace will become a major battlefield in informatized warfare.

Scope of 'Intelligentized Warfare'

President Xi's strategic vision calls for the PLA to build a highly informatized force capable of dominating all networks and expanding the country's security and development interests. The PLA considers IO as a means of achieving information dominance early in a conflict. He wants the PLA to create a highly informatized force capable of dominating all networks and expanding the country's security and development interests. It should set up an operational system-of-systems, which would facilitate the PLA to acquire, transmit, process and use information during a conflict to conduct joint military operations across the ground, maritime, air, space, cyberspace and electromagnetic spectrum domains.

Published four years after National Defense White Paper (NDWP, 2015), the 2019 edition of the NDWP, 'China's National Defense in the New Era', presents the new concept of *intelligentized* warfare. It said, "War is evolving in form towards informationized warfare, and intelligent warfare is on the horizon." The paper turned out to be a disappointment for many reasons, not the least of which was the absence of the phrase 'winning informatized local wars'. The discourse in the white paper changed to: "Driven by the new round of technological and industrial revolution, the application of cutting-edge technologies such as AI, quantum information, big data, cloud computing and the IoT is gathering pace in the military field. International military competition is undergoing historic changes. New and high-tech military technologies based on IT are developing rapidly. There is a prevailing trend to develop long-range precision, intelligent, stealthy or unmanned weaponry and equipment. War is evolving in form towards informationized warfare, and intelligent warfare is on the horizon."[13]

An associate professor at the National Defense University, Li Minghai, explains intelligentized warfare as "integrated warfare based on IoT systems that uses intelligent weaponry and equipment and their corresponding operational methods in the land, sea, air, space, electromagnetic, cyber and cognitive domains." Further, ideally for fighting an informatized warfare, armed forces builds on informatization and combines land, sea, air, space, cyber and electromagnetics into an integrated system. To make command and strategic guideline decisions, equipment with high computing skills are to be introduced. Emerging technologies like AI, machine learning and game theory will be utilised to accurately analyse and determine the opponent's intentions to be fed to commanders. Command systems will be created to integrate humans and machinery. Non-tangible targets in cyber and cognitive spaces would be included in the target list. Thus the operational spaces of intelligentized warfare will exceed those of informatized warfare.

Major General Wang Peng, Vice Chief of Staff of the Eastern Theater Command, summarises the characteristics of intelligentized warfare compared with informatized warfare as follows:[14]

- The objective of information dominance is to seize the initiative in land, sea, air, space, cyber and electromagnetic battlefields. In intelligentized warfare, 'intelligence dominance' is the new domain for grasping the initiative resulting in struggle for superiority in human cognitive speed and cognitive quality.
- Development of autonomous weapon and equipment is a primary part of intelligentized warfare. Capacities similar to human thinking are passed on to weapon and equipment to conduct autonomously reconnaissance, movement, attack, defence and other activities.
- Intelligentized warfare includes the operational spaces of land, sea, air, space, cyber and electromagnetic so that the operational domains can complement each other.

- The battles are not entirely devoid of human involvement though AI-equipped weaponry are given some autonomy and the battles themselves may be unmanned. Human beings control the battles.
- AI is presumed to help commanders make decisions by processing large quantities of data quickly and accurately. AI will support decision-making by commanders.

In a 2019 Jamestown Foundation write-up of a Chinese book titled 'Winning Mechanisms of Electronic Countermeasures', the Chinese authors indicated that the PLA was one of the world's leading militaries and it plans to conduct electro-magnetic spectrum (EMS) conflicts in the future. The text notes that the winning mechanism of EMS conflicts is "the inherent basis and path to realising electromagnetic dominance through electronic offence and defence by way of electro-magnetic energy, directed energy, sound energy, and other technical means."[15]

The following are some key takeaways from the PLA's understanding of how AI and smart weaponry are affecting operational planning:[16]

- Technical domain will combine with various conventional physical domains to form a cross-domain battlefield. Advances in the brain and cognitive technologies will give rise to the cognition domain of war which, together with other domains, will forge a mega-domain operational system.
- Drone swarm operations will attempt to overload an opponent's defensive systems and responses. Swarms will be used in the air, sea and land domains. One huge drone swarm could involve reconnaissance, jamming,

attack and other capabilities that fulfil multiple missions.

- A group of 'smart warfare systems' is being built where AI is the brain, operational networks the nerves and operational big data the blood. Counters to an adversary's use of smart wars must also be considered and topics such as algorithmic and anti-algorithmic warfare must be researched in depth.
- The focus of military engagements will change from system confrontations to algorithm competition, due to the use of AI. It was noted that algorithms are stratagem mechanisms for resolving various issues.
- Intelligent power will become the most crucial factor in determining war's outcome. It will utilise innovation in areas such as intelligent perception, intelligent decision-making, intelligent control and unmanned platforms.
- Cross-domain unconventional and asymmetrical fighting will be the new normal and intelligence control will replace territorial control as the centre of gravity in war. Perhaps this will cause the definition of war to be redefined.
- Attrition warfare launched with intelligent swarms, cross-domain mobile warfare and cognition control warfare will become basic types of combat operations.
- Civil-military integration, which involves the collaborative industry-university-research innovation system, will open society's innovative power and promote the development of military intelligence. The development of the Chinese Institute of New Generation AI Development Strategies (CINGAIDS) is but one civilian development that will be integrated with the military response.

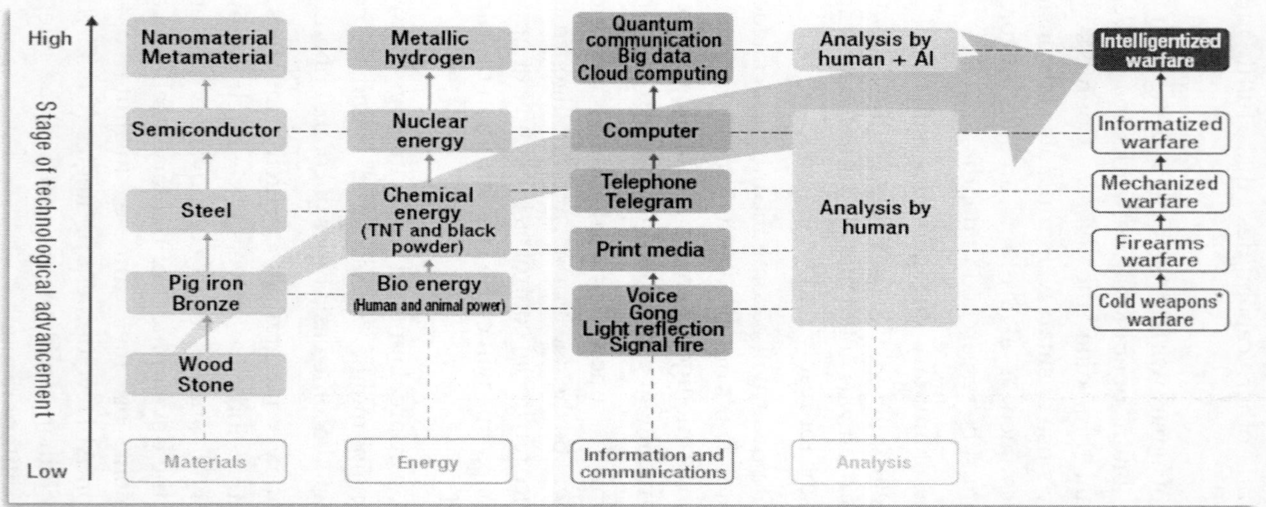

Relationship between the Technological Advancement and Evolution of War

Source: NIDS China Security Report 2021 China's Military Strategy in the New Era Published by The National Institute for Defense Studies 5-1 Honmura-cho, Ichigaya, Shinjuku-ku, Tokyo 162-8808 Japan Website: http://www.nids.mod.go.jp, Page 17

Evolution of China's Military Strategy

	Mao Zedong era	Deng Xiaoping era	Jiang Zemin era	Hu Jintao era	Xi Jinping era
Worldview and national strategy	• Readiness for war based on theory of unavoidable final war	• Break from the theory of unavoidable final war • Nation building and military buildup in a peaceful environment	• Break from Cold War structure • Nation building and military buildup in peacetime	• Nation building and military buildup in the process of turning China into an economic power	• Nation building and military buildup as an economic power
Military strategy	Nature of warfare: people's war (content changed with the times)				
	Active defense strategy (content changed with the times) From "striking only after the enemy has struck" to "striking before the enemy strikes" From "lure the enemy troops in deep" operations to "deny enemy penetration" operations				
	People's war	Local wars under modern conditions	Local wars under high-tech conditions	Local wars under the conditions of informatization	Informatized warfare (Intelligentized warfare in the future)
Defense domain	Ground, sea, air	Ground, sea, air + space		Ground, sea, air + space, cyber, electromagnetic	Ground, sea, air + space, cyber, electromagnetic (+ cognitive)
Service	Army, Navy, Air Force	Army, Navy, Air Force, Second Artillery Force			Army, Navy, Air Force Rocket Force Strategic Support Force
Main enemy	United States and Soviet Union	United States			

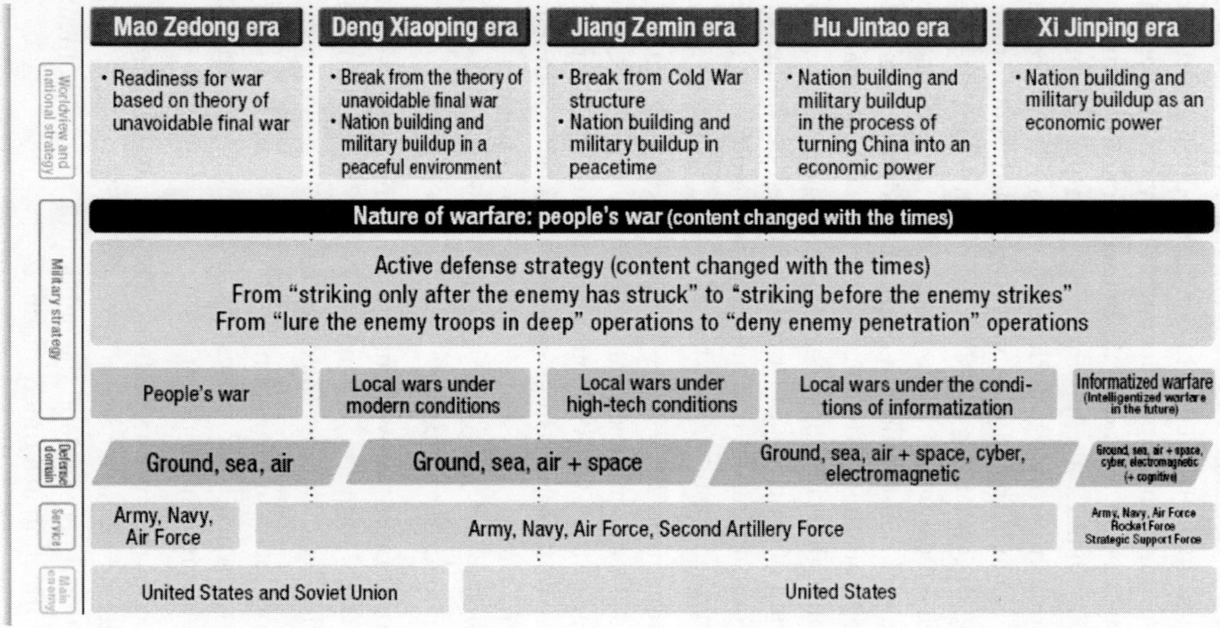

Source: NIDS China Security Report 2021 China's Military Strategy in the New Era Published by The National Institute for Defense Studies 5-1 Honmura-cho, Ichigaya, Shinjuku-ku, Tokyo 162-8808 Japan Website: http://www.nids.mod.go.jp, Page 18

Action Taken by the PLA for Informatization

Lot of introspection was undertaken when the PLA found that "The main contradiction in our army building is that the level of our modernisation is incompatible with the demands of winning a local war under informatized conditions, and our military capabilities are incompatible with the demands of carrying out the army's historic missions in the new century and new stage." The PLA is very concerned about matters regarding organisation, logistics, force structure, training, personnel education and C2. Jiang Zemin emphasised the importance of non-technical aspects of modernisation in the context of personnel education: "Though we're unable to develop all high-technology weapons and equipment within a short period of time, we must train qualified personnel first, for we would rather let our qualified personnel wait for the equipment than the other way round."

By November 2013, a set of sixty reform measures or principles were endorsed at a plenum of the Central Committee of the CCP. Without using the term 'informatization' many of these measures called for the establishment of relevant information systems and their exploitation as an underpinning of national advance. For example, the leadership made demands for:

- More rapid movement to an innovative society, national uniform economic accounting systems and 'other basic data for the entire society.'
- More open information on budgets and finance for state-owned enterprises (SOEs), more interdepartmental information sharing.
- Acceleration of the perfection of leading structures for internet management, guarantees for the security of the national network and the publication of environmental information in a timely manner.

- Full utilisation of informatised means to stimulate a balanced distribution of high-quality healthcare resources.
- Perfection of leadership systems and the unified management of Information assets and technologies in the armed forces.

Three PLA departments, Informatization, Strategic Planning and Training, were made to help enable this transformation. Since 2008, all major PLA military exercises have cyber and IO components that have been both offensive and defensive in nature. The PLA found ten dialectical aspects of relations when planning operational guidance under informatized conditions. From a Chinese perspective, it was important, since the dialectical grasp of opposite concepts helps in directing future operations and enabling victories in war and neither of the elements of the pairs that follow can be totally eliminated. The important point to remember is that both of the opposites can apply, depending on the circumstances and their creative application. These opposing aspects were as follows:[17]

- Relations between contact and non-contact operations.
- Relations between linear and non-linear operations.
- Relations between regular and non-regular operations.
- Relations between hard strikes and soft kills.
- Relations between decisive operations and protracted operations.
- Relations between battlefield transparency and the fog of war.
- Relations between full-spectrum superiority and partial superiority.
- Relations between technological gap and cost gap operations.

- Relations between dynamic energy concentration and force concentration.
- Relations between armament and natural environment.

Establishing Information Dominance

For fighting and winning 'informationized local wars' means establishment of information dominance. Information dominance is the ability to gather, transmit, analyse and exploit information more rapidly and more accurately than the adversary. The best way to deter is to demonstrate that one can fight and win. That requires fielding capable forces, demonstrating the willingness to use them and communicating both capability and will to the adversary. Only with information dominance can land, sea, air or outer space capabilities operate to their full potential. Increase of various sources of information, as well as the growing capability to move huge amounts of data, provide opportunities to create a common situational picture among all the participating forces. The PLA analysts assume that both sides will be constantly trying to achieve information dominance and will be trying to weaken and damage the adversary's information networks.

Common situational awareness would allow commanders to better track not only adversary forces but also friendly units. This common situational picture is built upon the following key pillars:

- Real-time information.
- Accurate data.
- Collection of many diverse kinds of information for many different users.
- Intelligent information processing.
- Reliable communications.

For conducting information warfare and pursuing information dominance the priority targets will be the adversary's high technology weapons platforms, intelligence and surveillance systems; their bases where they are located and their command, control, and communications networks. The winner is the side that maintains better connectivity among the various essential systems. Achieving information dominance in the face of the hard-kill and soft-kill weapons and tactics is not solely a matter of computer network attack or defence. In its place, the Chinese consider information warfare as comprising several key lines of operations, including EW, network warfare and space warfare.[18]

The concept of information plays a central role in Chinese military thinking. The PLA has put considerable attention to IW over the past decade, both in terms of battlefield EW and cyber warfare capabilities. In the next chapter, the concepts and doctrines of cyber warfare will be analysed.

Endnotes

1. State Council Information Office, Tenth Five Year Plan for National Economic and Social Development, Informationization Key Point Special Plans, October 18, 2002 available at: http://www.cia.org.cn/information/information_01_xxhgh_3.htm
2. Tan Wenfang, "The Impact of Information Technology on Modern Psychological Warfare," National Defense Science and Technology, No. 5 (2009), p. 72.
3. Bai Bangxi and Jiang Lijun, "Systems of Systems Conflict Is Not the Same as Systems Conflict," National Defense Newspaper, January 10, 2008.
4. Dean Cheng, Getting to Where the PLA Needs to Be, Testimony before U.S.–China Economic and Security Review Commission, June 20, 2019 available at: https://www.uscc.gov/sites/default/files/Cheng_USCC%20Testimony_FINAL.pdf
5. M. Taylor Fravel, China's New Military Strategy: "Winning Informationized Local Wars",China Brief Volume: 15 Issue: 13,

July 2, 2015 available at: https://jamestown.org/program/chinas-new-military-strategy-winning-informationized-local-wars/

6. Honmura-cho, Ichigaya, Shinjuku-ku, NIDS China Security Report 2021 China's Military Strategy in the New Era Published by The National Institute for Defense Studies 5-1, Tokyo 162-8808 Japan, available at: http://www.nids.mod.go.jp
7. Maj Gen P K Mallick, VSM (Retd), Defining China's Intelligentized Warfare and Role of Artificial Intelligence. Vivekananda International Foundation, March 2021 available at: https://www.vifindia.org/sites/default/files/defining-china-s-intelligentized-warfare-and-role-of-artificial-intelligence.pdf
8. Dean Cheng, Getting to Where the PLA Needs to Be, Testimony before U.S.–China Economic and Security Review Commission, June 20, 2019 available at: https://www.uscc.gov/sites/default/files/Cheng_USCC%20Testimony_FINAL.pdf
9. NIDS China Security Report 2021 China's Military Strategy in the New Era Published by The National Institute for Defense Studies 5-1 Honmura-cho, Ichigaya, Shinjuku-ku, Tokyo 162-8808 Japan, available at: http://www.nids.mod.go.jp/publication/chinareport/pdf/china_report_EN_web_2021_A01.pdf
10. White Paper 2012 - Ministry of National Defense. available at: http://eng.mod.gov.cn/publications/2016-07/13/content_4768293.htm
11. China Military Power Report 2019 - The Frontier Post. available at: https://thefrontierpost.com/china-military-power-report-2019/
12. DOD report cites China's focus on cyber as a weapon of...., available at: https://defensesystems.com/articles/2015/05/14/dod-report-china-cyber-ew-space-uavs.aspx
13. "NIDS China Security Report 2021 China's Military Strategy in the New Era.", National Institute for Defense Studies, Japan available at: http://www.nids.mod.go.jp/publication/chinareport/pdf/china_report_EN_web_2021_A01.pdf
14. *ibid*
15. Zi Yang, "PLA Stratagems for Establishing Wartime Electromagnetic Dominance: An Analysis of 'The Winning

Mechanisms of Electronic Countermeasures,'" OE Watch, March 2019, pp. 18-19, republished in collaboration with the Jamestown Foundation, China Brief, Vol. 19, Issue 3, dated 1 February 2019.

16. Maj Gen P K Mallick, VSM (Retd), Defining China's Intelligentized Warfare and Role of Artificial Intelligence. Vivekananda International Foundation, March 2021 available at: https://www.vifindia.org/sites/default/files/defining-china-s-intelligentized-warfare-and-role-of-artificial-intelligence.pdf

17. Yang Baoming, Zhao Changjun, and Xu Jianhua, "Dialectical Considerations on Operational Guidance under Informatized Conditions," China Military Science, No. 4, 2010, pp. 73-83

18. Dean Cheng, Getting to Where the PLA Needs to Be, Testimony before U.S.–China Economic and Security Review Commission, June 20, 2019 available at: https://www.uscc.gov/sites/default/files/Cheng_USCC%20Testimony_FINAL.pdf

* * *

CHAPTER 3

Concepts and Doctrines of Cyber Warfare

Introduction

The PLA keenly observed the stunning victories by U.S. led coalitions in the 1991 Gulf War and the 1999 Kosovo War, which heralded a new era of warfare. The PLA was quick to recognise the advantages of U.S. network-centric warfare capabilities, so vividly demonstrated in the Gulf War. It was also well aware of the resultant vulnerabilities that resulted from American reliance on those battle networks. These assessments encouraged the development of Chinese asymmetric capabilities, including cyber warfare, electronic counter-measures and counter-space capabilities to target those potential vulnerabilities. Simultaneously, the PLA launched a strategy of 'informatization' through which it has developed military command and information systems along with a new and rapidly expanding architecture of space systems. Today, the PLA is undertaking mechanisation, informatization, and 'intelligentization' simultaneously. It wants to advance modernisation on multiple fronts, leveraging emerging technologies including AI to enhance its system of systems.

The PLA has not copied the U.S. concept blindly. It has tried to adapt the concept with the Chinese requirements and peculiarities. The PLA differs considerably from its Western counterparts in its approach to cyber and network operations. The PLA does not use the word 'cyber' as extensively as the West. They perceive everything related to cyber developments as processes of informationisation or informatization. Rather than seeing cyber power as a distinct capability like air, land, sea and space, PLA's planners view cyber and network operations as occurring in an information domain. This domain encompasses network, psychological and media operations as well as electronic warfare.[1]

The concept of information plays a central role in Chinese military thinking. As cyberspace is strongly related to information, one can find relevant contents within general military documents which explain the PLA's ambitions in cyberspace. The Chinese emphasise information warfare in general and cyber warfare in particular more ardently than the U.S. does.

The PLA has devoted much attention to information warfare over the past decade, both in terms of battlefield EW and cyber warfare capabilities. The main doctrine is the 'Integrated Network Electronic Warfare' (INEW), which guides PLA computer network operations. The PLA thinking appears to have moved beyond INEW towards a new concept of 'information confrontation' that aims to integrate electronic and non-electronic aspects of information warfare within a single command authority. The PLA thinking sees warfare under informationized conditions, as characterised by opposing sides, using complete systems of ground, naval, air, space and electromagnetic forces.

The PLA strategists consider that 'network-electronic operations' will be critical to combat effectiveness as modern means of warfare. Cyber and network operations may become an 'indispensable method for deterring powerful enemies' with the probability of even winning without fighting under certain conditions.

Doctrine

Doctrine is an important component of a nation's cyber power. It not only indicates the relative importance of cyber operations, but it may also provide clues about their effectiveness. After the Communists came to power in 1949, the PLA generally followed the then Soviet Union's concepts and doctrines, organisation, weapon profile etc. As China opened up, it started following the western, especially the U.S, concepts and use of technology in modern warfare. The PLA has examined U.S. military publications on network centric warfare and the evolution of American doctrine on IW for more than a decade. It studied the effect of modern information operations on the battlefield and started implementing its own version of IW.

The PLA has adopted IW concepts suited to its own organisation and doctrine, blending its traditional tactics, U.S. concepts and concepts from the Soviet military to bring itself into the information age. It has modernised and improved upon its own psychological warfare operations, and expanded the role for its legal experts in justifying its military action and territorial claims.[2]

Its military doctrines rely on incorporating information technology and networked information operations. Its concepts for employing traditional signals intelligence and EW have expanded to include cyber warfare, kinetic and cyber attacks on satellites and information confrontation operations across the electro-magnetic spectrum. Along with these technical aspects of information operations, the PLA's combination of psychological warfare, manipulation of public opinion or media warfare and the manipulation of legal arguments to strengthen China's diplomatic and security position - what China calls 'legal warfare' - join together in a comprehensive information operations doctrine.

At least in the initial stages, the PLA could not get out of the Soviet Union mindset. The Soviets followed the concept of Radio Electronic Combat (REC) by developing their EW capabilities into an integrated system. REC combines signals intelligence, direction finding, intensive jamming, deception and destructive fires to attack enemy organisations and systems through the means of their control. The purpose of REC was to limit, delay or nullify the enemy's use of his command and control systems while protecting Soviet systems by electronic counter-counter-measures. The system's estimated goal was to destroy or disrupt a majority of the enemy's command, control, and weapon system communications, either by jamming or by destructive fires.

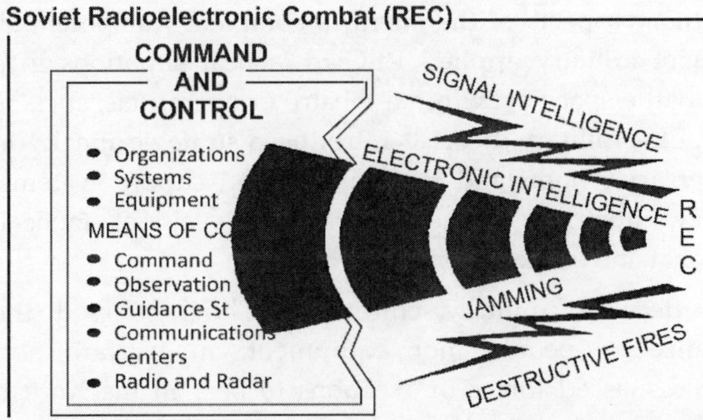

Source: FM 100-2-1, THE SOVIET ARMY: Operations and Tactics, Headquarters Department of the Army, 16 July 1984, https://fas.org/irp/doddir/army/fm100-2-1.pdf

During the Cold War, the Soviets expected their forces would inflict 60 percent casualties or combat damage on enemy forces in the opening moves of any conflict through a combination of traditional EW and combat strikes by aircraft, helicopters, missiles, rockets and artillery. The U.S. Army described REC as "the total integration of EW and physical destruction resources to deny us the use of our electronic systems." The goals of Soviet REC were to:

- Sow confusion and disrupt and paralyse enemy C2 and logistical structure.
- Support expanded special operations forces against enemy rear areas.
- Employ a reconnaissance-strike concept task organised across a front.
- Destroy or neutralise enemy nuclear delivery systems.

The PLA has added additional dimensions to the older Soviet concept in terms of cyber attacks and space warfare to its offensive operations. It expects to weaken and paralyse an enemy's decision-making abilities and the political, economic and military aspects of the enemy's complete war potential. The Soviet military applied REC to tactical situations in a limited battle space or within a theatre of operations, such as Europe. PLA military theorists introduced strategic attacks on an adversary's homeland sustainment and supply systems. This new doctrine extends across all levels of tactical, operational and strategic levels of war.

For decades, military culture in China stressed the importance of people, not equipment, in warfare and employed massed forces or weapons to bear in the Korean War, the Sino-Indian War and the Sino-Vietnam War. Although the PLA had electronic systems, it did not modernise with the intent to use and even depend on these systems. Now the PLA is updating 20th century mechanised and joint operations and combining them with EW and precision strike to integrate mobility and precision fires to secure operational success on the modern battlefield. Ultimately, the PLA must execute integrated operations combining computer network warfare, networked firepower warfare, EW and sensor systems.[3]

Information Warfare. As explained in the previous chapter, one of the main principles of the Local War concept is that IW will play a central role in future warfare. Within the realm of IW, the PLA must be capable of quickly seizing and retaining information superiority, or the ability to access and process information within effective Command, Control, Communications, Computer, Intelligence, Surveillance and Reconnaissance (C4ISR) networks while denying the enemy the same ability. The PLA believes that collecting, transmitting and processing information will lead to significant advantages at the operational and even strategic level.

Cyber Warfare. Cyber warfare takes place in the electromagnetic spectrum. There is enough conceptual and operational overlap with the traditional EW. China has publicly identified cyberspace as a critical domain for national security and declared its intent to expedite its cyber forces' development. Cyber operations are designed to penetrate, exploit and damage or sabotage, through electronic means, an adversary's "information systems and networks, computers and communications systems, and supporting infrastructures".[4]

Science of Military Strategy

The PLA's The 'Science of Military Strategy' states that, in contrast to conventional forces, "computer network operations require only small numbers of personnel and relatively low investment of funds to achieve operational goals; computer network operations thus have the characteristics of low cost, high benefit, and low risk." It describes three types of network operations: network reconnaissance, network attack and defence operations and network deterrence. It describes network reconnaissance as the 'most common' form of military cyber operation today, suggesting a substantial identity between what the U.S. military would regard as computer exploitation activities on the one hand and reconnaissance on the other. Reconnaissance includes, for example, "exploiting loopholes in the adversary's computers to sneak into the adversary's network systems, and via spyware collect and steal information stored and processed in those computers."

The Science of Military Strategy defines network deterrence as "actions which display network attack and defence operational capability, and the firm resolve for retaliation, to prevent the adversary from daring to carry out large-scale network attacks." Deterrence operations are designed primarily to prevent large-scale network attacks, which are defined as attacks with a strategic quality, or those that could have an impact on security and development interests of the state. Notably, the means of deterrence are not limited to network attack and defence capabilities but also include the traditional military strike forces and means. The most frequently employed Chinese term for 'deterrence' can also mean 'coercion'. The 2000 version of the Science of Military Campaigns, a book published by the Chinese National Defense University Press, suggests, "We must send a message to the enemy through computer network attack, forcing the enemy to give up without fighting."

There is a basic difference with the U.S. concepts of computer network operations. In U.S doctrine of Computer Network Operations include computer network offence, computer network defence and computer network exploitation. It does not talk about deterrence.

Chinese military leaders contemplate to defeat the U.S. by attacking its centre of gravity, particularly its dependence on networks. China is looking for niche capabilities that can thwart plans for the U.S. to operate in East Asia. While the PLA emphasises the importance of defence, it also sees cyber warfare as inherently offence-dominant. One function of network attack is to retard the movement of U.S. logistics across the Pacific by targeting "harbors, airports, means of transportation, battlefield installations, and the communications, command and control and information systems." A second function is to frustrate enemy C4ISR more broadly, including communications, radar, space-based systems and military command and control.

China's strategy calls for developing capabilities and capacity of governance in four major areas:

- Managing internet content and creating positive energy online.
- Ensuring general cybersecurity including protecting critical information infrastructure.
- Developing an independent, domestic technological base for the hardware and software that provide security of the Internet in China.
- Increasing China's role in building, governing and operating the Internet globally.

In March 2017, China released an 'International Strategy for Cooperation in Cyberspace', to state that the PLA will play an 'important role' in cyberspace.[5] The strategy also stated that the country would 'expedite the development of a cyber force and enhance capabilities in terms of situational awareness, cyber defense, support of state activities, participation in international cooperation, prevention of major cyber crisis, safeguarding cybersecurity and maintaining national security and social stability'. In 2017, China also announced the establishment of a 'Central Commission for Integrated Military and Civilian Development', which seeks to integrate civilian technologies, including in the fields of information and communications technologies and AI, into the PLA.

Ultimately, the PLA has rolled all these concepts into what it terms as the Integrated Network Electronic Warfare. INEW is a systems-versus-systems form of military confrontation on the 21st-century battlefield, dependent on space, cyber and various information technologies. Cyber operations are a component of INEW.

Integrated Network Electronic Warfare

The PLA has traditionally been an artillery dominant force with good EW capabilities. The PLA's concept of INEW, which dates back to the early 2000s, combines precision strike, cyber attack and EW. Taking a cue from U.S. military operations in Iraq and the Balkans, China has elevated INEW to a strategic level of war, moving beyond the tactical and theatre realms of operations. The PLA has also added cyber attacks and attacks on satellites, or space warfare, to its offensive operations toolkit. According to the U.S. DoD, INEW was designed "to deny an adversary access to information essential to conduct combat operations" to accomplish China's strategic objective of information dominance. Chinese military theorists see INEW as a fundamental characteristic of IW and the informationized battlefield. The PLA defines the INEW concept as "network-electronic integration warfare as a form of information warfare where one implements information attacks against the enemy's networked information systems through highly melded EW and network warfare."

As network warfare expands and EW systems are networked, the Chinese see these as inextricably linked. In future local wars under informationized conditions, there will be steady merger of network and EW. EW highlights attacking the signal layer, using strong electro-magnetic energy to drown out target signals whereas network warfare stresses attacking the information layer, using disruptive information flow transported into the enemy's network systems as the means of attack. From a technical angle, EW and network warfare can be broadly complementary. However, network warfare will be affected by efforts aimed at dominating the electro-magnetic spectrum but neither EW nor network warfare alone can comprehensively disrupt a system-of-systems. Nevertheless, given the complementary nature of the two types of warfare in terms of attack concepts, attack methods and operating environments, they do constitute a highly effective integrated attack methodology.[6]

The PLA believes that in future conflicts, the electro-magnetic spectrum will be the key influence upon operation in network space, with network and EW organically linked and operating under a single unified direction. It thinks that as individual facilities and their attendant information systems are networked together, the physical infrastructure upon which information passes and the information itself becomes an integrated whole. Treating networked information systems as the common domain of operations, INEW envisages using electro-magnetic attack and defence as well as information attack as the main techniques for degrading the adversary's ability to gather and exploit information. INEW therefore joins the physical aspects and virtual aspects of IW, merging them into a single concept of operations.[7] By undertaking attacks on both of these elements, the PLA is more likely to establish information dominance. Successful conduct of integrated network and EW should lead to the dominance of the entire battlefield information space.

The INEW incorporates targeting and defence of the physical element of the information networks as part of network warfare. This is what makes INEW more than merely adding EW techniques to network warfare. It enlarges IW beyond the predominantly virtual world of data to include the physical, tangible world. INEW is envisaged as a vital example of the new kind of unified jointness necessary to successfully fight local wars under informationized conditions.

Presently, the PLA's thinking appears to have moved beyond INEW, towards a new concept of 'information confrontation' that aims to integrate electronic and non-electronic aspects of IW within a single command authority. Since 2008, major PLA military exercises have had components of cyber and information operations both offensive and defensive in nature.

Network Warfare or Netwar

Network warfare is the facet of IW involving the range of activities that occur within networked information space when two sides seek to reduce the adversary's networks' effectiveness while retaining one's own. The purpose of network warfare is to create 'network dominance'. When one has network dominance, the full range of one's networks, includeing computer networks, can operate efficiently. The information on these networks is secured while being moved and applied rapidly. At the same time an adversary's networks are prevented from doing the same. Certain networks that are integral to network warfare include the command and control network, intelligence information network and air defence network. Network space is sometimes characterised as the sixth domain alongside land, sea, air, space and the electro-magnetic spectrum. In some cases, it is seen as the fifth domain encompassing the electro-magnetic spectrum.

The 2013 Science of Military Strategy, an important PLA document published approximately once a decade, stipulates that "The side holding network warfare superiority can adopt network warfare to cause dysfunction in the adversary's command system, loss of control over his operational forces and activities, and incapacitation or failure of weapons and equipment and thus seize the initiative within military confrontation, and create the conditions for gaining ultimate victory in war." Network warfare is the partner of EW. Like EW, it includes not only offensive and defensive components, but also reconnaissance of adversary and others' networks.

Network warfare occurs in the realm of 'network space', a term that approximately matches that of cyberspace. While computer network operations remain integral to network warfare, the latter is seen as moving beyond just the computer networks.

Informatization followed by Networking

The PLA's informatization process is both long and dynamic. The PLA embraces information age operations in support of all forms of military operations. It expands the traditional concepts of air, land and sea battle space to include the electromagnetic spectrum, cyberspace and space. This virtual battle space is defined as the space created by technology, computers and the web (Internet) that is subject to human control and reflects human will, its components being cyberspace, information space and digital space. As per the PLA doctrine, information power and various types of firepower are merged. Eventually, the PLA must execute integrated operations combining computer network warfare, networked firepower warfare, EW and sensor systems.

The PLA's problem is to develop new cyber warfare doctrine appropriate for the PLA's level of modernisation. It has to take advantage of the Chinese armed forces' existing strengths in EW, electronic information gathering, precision attack and massed firepower. The PLA is apprehensive about bandwidth, which is the basis for supporting a high volume of transmissions and system survivability and to confront enemy information systems.

As per Chinese writings, EW and network warfare, which includes but goes beyond cyber, are actually flip sides of the same coin. This is different from western thinking, where EW and Cyber Warfare are two different sets of operations.

System Destruction Warfare[8]

The PLA now understands modern warfare as a confrontation between opposing operational systems and not merely opposing armies. The Chinese theory of victory in modern warfare recognises system destruction warfare as the current method of modern warfighting. No longer war is a contest between particular units, arms, services or specific weapons platforms of competing adversaries. *War is won by the side that can disrupt, paralyse or destroy the operational capability of the enemy's operational system.* This is referred to as 'systems confrontation'. Systems confrontation is fought not only in the conventional physical domains of land, sea and air. It is also waged in outer space, nonphysical cyberspace, electro-magnetic and even psychological domains.

China's current victory theory is based on successfully waging system destruction warfare that seeks to paralyse and even demolish the critical functions of an adversary's operational system. As per this theory, the enemy "loses the will and ability to resist" once its operational system cannot function effectively. The PLA recognises systems confrontation as the basic mode of warfare in the 21st century. System destruction warfare, not annihilation warfare, is the PLA's current theory of victory. This requires joint operations capability and the seamless linking of all systems and units through an extremely robust information network. This can be achieved through kinetic and non-kinetic strikes against critical points and nodes while at the same time employing a more robust, capable and adaptable operational system of its own. Systems thinking significantly impacts how the PLA is currently organising, equipping and training itself for future warfighting contingencies.

Systems Confrontation in System Destruction Warfare[9]

Military experts of PLA think that the operational system comprises five main component systems: command system, firepower strike system, information confrontation system, reconnaissance intelligence system and the support system. These five component systems is likely to exist within an operational system to some degree. Recent PLA publications advocate that there are four target types that PLA planners seek when attempting to paralyse the enemy's operational systems. These are:

- Strikes that disrupt or degrade the flow of information within the adversary's operational system.
- Disrupting or degrading that operational system's essential factors, which include but are not limited to, its Command and Control (C2), reconnaissance, intelligence and firepower capabilities.
- Disrupting or degrading the operational architecture of the adversary's operational system. These include the entire C2 network, reconnaissance intelligence network or firepower network.
- Disrupting the time sequence and/or tempo of the enemy's operational architecture. This is to degrade and ultimately undermine the operational system's own "reconnaissance-control-attack-evaluation" process.

With AI technology rapidly getting into the military domain, it will inevitably lead to a sweeping change in the way combat power establishes itself. The PLA aims to use AI algorithms, autonomous systems, machine learning, human-machine teaming collaboratively to paralyse its enemies. The Chinese military's ultimate objective appears to be gaining a cognitive advantage, the ability to adapt one's system-of-systems faster than one's adversary. The Chinese want to use AI to deliver precise effects to immobilise their adversary while defending their own system-of-systems. Any adversary of China would be wise to understand the implications of how future AI capabilities may be employed to realise Chinese goals in system-of-systems confrontation.[10]

Intelligentized Warfare

President Xi Jinping gave the latest theory of Intelligentization. In his report to the 19th Party Congress in October 2017, he pushed the PLA to "accelerate the development of military intelligentization and improve joint operations capabilities and all-domain combat capabilities based on network information systems."[11] This would be the guiding principle for the future of Chinese military modernization. China does not seek to merely integrate AI into existing warfighting functions. China wants to use it to shape a new cognitive domain and thus revolutionise their entire approach to warfighting. Xi Jinping and China's leadership believes that China should pursue global leadership in AI technology and reduce its dependence on imports of international technology.

Chinese strategists profess that integration of military and non-military domains takes place in Intelligentized Warfare and cross-domain asymmetrical and unconventional fighting in battle will become the new normal. The rules of engagement and the support process will have to be rewritten for unmanned operations. Intelligent control will become the centre of gravity. There will be integration of human and machine intelligence in intelligentized warfare in terms of 'Machine-on-machine warfare'. Combining wearable devices and gadgets implanted into human bodies, humans and machines into brain-machine interfaces, external skeletal systems will "comprehensively enhance the inherent cognitive and physiological capacity of human fighters and will forge out superman combatants."[12]

PLA experts have discussed data processing, using data from geographic information systems and 'human social and cultural data and social media data' and from reconnaissance, surveillance or intelligence. As military forces try to integrate big data into their structures, operations would increasingly be characterised by human–machine interaction, combinations of human–machine intelligence, data-centric analytical processing and, ultimately, independent decision-making and autonomous-attack capabilities. In short, 'the key to winning quickly is how to shorten the OODA (observe, orient, decide, act) loop and revolutionising C2'. China recognises that big data-driven research and development and AI-enabled technologies will result in the PLA's acquisition of 'smarter' and more autonomous platforms and systems. However, PLA leaders are sure that 'big data and AI technology cannot completely replace people and cannot change their decisive position in war'.[13]

Psychological Warfare

Aim of Psychological Warfare is to force an enemy to submit without a fight based on preemptive attacks that indicate strength and influence designed to overpower an opponent mentally. Political, economic, military, diplomatic, technical and cultural channels can be used to demonstrate China's comprehensive national strength. The combination of destruction and soft influence may be used together. Destruction involves attacks on centers of gravity and vital points of an enemy's strength, while soft influence relies on collecting, processing, and controlling capabilities to attack or disturb the attitudes and behaviour of opponents.[14]

Based on using information systems or media influence to affect the psyche of citizens and leaders, there are following types of Psychological Warfare:

- **Information Deterrence.** It uses political, military and economic superiority to deliver accurately, effectively and sufficiently information about one's dominance over the enemy side, making an opponent scared and unsure of war's outcome. War games, weapon exhibitions and public weapon development plans are used as a psychological deterrence strategy.
- **Information Blockades.** It uses information superiority to cut off an adversary's information sources and place an adversary in the dark and at a loss to take any effective countermeasures, making them feel helpless, nervous and panic-stricken.
- **Information Deception.** It spreads false information and disrupts an adversary's awareness, causing confusion, hesitation and misgivings.
- **Information Disruption.** It causes congestion and confusion through interruption of information circulation channels via jamming and the disturbance of information systems. Computer viruses, logic bombs and hacking techniques can disrupt, destroy or attack information networks and cause harm to people's psychology due to a hacker's ability to cause financial or other crises.

Technologies for the use of Psychological Warfare have improved. Unmanned aerial vehicles can distribute leaflets, audio leaflets, etc., as a part of soft warfare today. Computer viruses, stealth technologies, satellite television and operational platforms with high mobility can neutralise the other sides' use of information through jamming, deception and other means. Laser, microwave, particle beam and dynamic energy weapons can indirectly affect the war process due to their killing power's cognitive impact.

Psychological Warfare requires integrated participation of both military and civilian expertise. Informationized warfare has blurred the line between war and peace and encouraged the so-called 'civilianisation' of war, resulting in the recruitment of society's information experts to reinforce Psychological Warfare.

The PLA sees psychological warfare as an integral part of the 'three warfares' and modern information operations. Chinese legal scholars and members of the CMC's Political & Legal Affairs Commission are also active in what the PLA has named 'legal warfare'. The second of the three forms of warfare, Psychological Warfare, has been a major responsebility of the Political & Legal Affairs Commission since it was established. The PLA targeted Nationalist forces and the Japanese with psychological operations and used them in the Korean War. It believes that Psychological Warfare targets the adversary's will to fight and is designed to lower enemy forces' efficiency by creating dissent, disaffection and dissatisfaction in their ranks.

Historically in China, psychological operations involved the use of stratagem and deception. In its psychological warfare operations, the PLA may target an enemy's values, its motivation for fighting, both in peacetime or wartime, the logic of an adversary's foreign policy, security policy or national decisions. Psychological operations may target an adversary's civil populace and its leaders, as well as military personnel. The PLA's objectives were to cause an adversary's allies to take a neutral position or become disaffected from the ally. This is still the focus of psychological operations today.

Quoting a former U.S. military attaché to China, one study sums up the means and methods of PLA psychological operations. It states that political signals may be sent through:

- Public or private diplomacy at international organisations, such as the United Nations, and/or directly to other governments or persons.
- The use of the Chinese and foreign media in official announcements or articles written by influential persons.
- Nonmilitary actions, such as restrictions on travel or trade.
- Using military announcement, demonstrations, deployments or tests, which do not involve the use of deadly force.

Mark Stokes, a former U.S. Air Force attaché in China, in an analysis of the PLA's psychological warfare operations, quotes PLA strategist Yu Guohua, in China Military Science that the PLA: Should sap the enemy's morale, disintegrate their will to fight, ignite the anti-war sentiment among citizens at home, heighten international and domestic conflict, weaken and sway the will to fight among its high level decision-makers and in turn lessen their superiority in military strength.

In perception management, a nation or organisation undertakes conscious actions to convey specific information or indicators of intent to foreign audiences to influence their emotions and reasoning. Perception management may deny specific items of information to foreign audiences for the same reasons. The goal is to influence foreign public opinion, leaders and intelligence systems and to influence official assessment. The purpose of perception management operations is often to mould foreign behaviour in ways that favour the original actor's objectives.[15]

When the PLA Navy or the maritime or coastal patrol organisations in China stage incidents with foreign navies or fishing fleets, it is part of psychological operations. Whether in the South China Sea or the East China Sea, such actions intimidate neighbours and other claimants to disputed territories. By creating the impression that acting counter to China's interests or desires may cause China to use force, the PLA can dissuade or deter an adversary without resorting to combat.

China's 'Three Warfares Doctrine' has inspired information operations initiatives since approval by the country's CMC in 2003. Further understanding of this sophistication is apparent in China's division of Strategic Psychological Warfare into five discrete but highly complementary parts:

- Information deterrence that accurately communicates examples of Chinese economic, political and other forms of superiority. These superiorities can be limited, but the examples have some basis. Chinese ability to control parts of the South China Sea can intimidate neighbours and more distant adversaries even though this control is contested and replicating the qualified geographic superiority elsewhere would be difficult, if not impossible.
- Information deception is somewhat of a yang to information deterrence's yin, using false information to disrupt awareness and promote confusion and hesitation in decision-making.

- Information blockades employ one or more forms of information superiority to deny foes access to information, effectively blinding them.
- Information disruption interrupts the circulation or exchange of information by jamming or otherwise disrupting those systems.
- Use of computer viruses, logic bombs and hacking to undermine confidence and cause confusion via the disruption of financial, management, or other networks.[16]

Each member of this quintet has the potential to enhance the effects of the others. Falsehoods cultivate belief in light of previous information based on accurate depictions of Chinese superiority. Employing multiple elements of the five in the service of a single objective complicates the effective response. As a notional example, seeking to influence voting in a targeted country by disrupting voting machines would undermine the electoral process's legitimacy in the eyes of voters while drawing attention away from parallel hacking assaults to alter tallies. In a military-specific example, the use of falsehoods combined with accurate reports of, say, Chinese long-range surface-to-surface missile capabilities could instill doubts in the minds of an enemy preparing to deploy forces. Elsewhere, state social media would target the adversary's military family members, seeking to undermine perceptions regarding the legitimacy of pending operations. Disinformation programs could simultaneously target broader community support while cyber attacks interfere with the computer, traffic control, scheduling and other systems essential to deploying forces. The outcomes of all are similar: the accomplishment of Chinese ends without triggering unacceptable responses by the targeted party.

China has launched the most far-reaching restructuring of China's national defence establishment in 2015. Before the reforms, experts in PLA felt that its structure and organisation are the main roadblocks facing PLA modernisation efforts. PLA took the opportunity of the major reforms to readjust its extensive cyber, space and EW capabilities into a unified force. In the next chapter China's cyber organisations are analysed in details.

Endnotes

1. Maj Gen P K Mallick, VSM (Retd),The PLA's Developing Cyber Warfare Capabilities and India's Options, Strategic Study India, Occasional Paper No – 02/2021, available at: https://indianstrategicknowledgeonline.com/web/PLA%20CYBER%20CAPABILITIES%20AND%20ITS%20ADAPTION%20IN%20WARFARE.pdf
2. Larry M. Wortzel, The Chinese People's Liberation Army and Information Warfare, Strategic Studies Institute and U.S. Army War College Press, March 2014 available at: https://apps.dtic.mil/sti/pdfs/ADA596797.pdf
3. Ye Zheng, Xinxihua Zuozhan Gailun (An Introduction to Informationalized Operations), Beijing, China: Military Science Press, 2007, pp. 17–18
4. Magnus Hjortdal, "China's Use of Cyber Warfare: Espionage Meets Strategic Deterrence," Journal of Strategic Security, Vol. 4, No. 2, 2011, p. 1
5. Full Text: International Strategy of Cooperation on Cyberspace http://www.xinhuanet.com › 2017-03 › c_136094371_3, 01-Mar-2017
6. Maj Gen P K Mallick, VSM (Retd),The PLA's Developing Cyber Warfare Capabilities and India's Options, Strategic Study India, Occasional Paper No – 02/2021, available at: https://indianstrategicknowledgeonline.com/web/PLA%20CYBER%20CAPABILITIES%20AND%20ITS%20ADAPTION%20IN%20WARFARE.pdf
7. Ye Zheng, Concepts of Informationized Operations (Beijing, PRC: Military Science Publishing House, 2007), p. 157, and YE Zheng, Science of Information Operations Teaching Materials (Beijing, PRC: Military Science Publishing House, 2013), p. 27.

8. Engstrom, Jeffrey, Systems Confrontation and System Destruction Warfare: How the Chinese People's Liberation Army Seeks to Wage Modern Warfare. Santa Monica, CA: RAND Corporation, 2018, available at: https://www.rand.org/pubs/research_reports/RR1708.html

9. *ibid*

10. Yang Wenzhe, "How to Win Intelligentized Warfare by Analyzing what are Changed and What are Unchanged," Jiefangjun Bao, 22 October 2019. http://www.81.cn/jfjbmap/content/2019-10/22/content_245810.htm

11. Xi Jinping's Report at the Chinese Communist Party 19th National Congress], Xinhua, October 27, 2017, available at: http://www.china.com.cn / 19da / 2017-10 / 27 / content_41805113_3.htm.

12. 199. "Intelligentization" and a Chinese Vision of Future War, Dec 19, 2019 available at: https://madsciblog.tradoc.army.mil/199-intelligentization-and-a-chinese-vision-of-future-war/

13. Military Balance 2020.

14. Chang Yan'e and Ou Lishou, "Important Issues Covering Strategic Psychological Warfare under Informationized Conditions," China Military Science, No. 3 2005, pp. 77-83.

15. Stephen Collins, "Mind Games," NATO Review, Summer 2003, available at www.nato.int/docu/review/2003/issue2/english/art4.html.

16. Timothy Thomas, "The Chinese Way of War: How Has It Changed?" MITRE paper, April 2020, 13.

* * *

CHAPTER 4

Organisations Dealing with Cyber Domain

Introduction

Under the leadership of Xi Jinping, President of the People's Republic of China (PRC) and Chairman of the Central Military Commission (CMC), the Chinese Communist Party (CCP) launched the most far-reaching restructuring of China's national defence establishment since the reforms of the 1980s under Deng Xiaoping. The aim was to transform the PLA into a capable joint force and further strengthen control of the PLA in the hands of Xi Jinping and the CCP.

On New Year's Day 2016, the CMC issued a blueprint to develop PLA into a "modern military with Chinese characteristics that can win information-age wars" by 2020. Xi Jinping announced that the four general departments, i.e. the General Staff Department (GSD), General Political Department, General Logistics Department (GLD), and General Armament Department (GAD), had been disbanded. The general departments were replaced by 15 smaller functional CMC departments, commissions and offices that would report directly to the CMC. Xi Jinping declared that China's military modernization process would be complete by 2035 and China will have a "world class military" by 2049, in time to mark the 100th anniversary of the PRC in 2049.

The PLA has taken several steps to achieve its first objective of optimising its structure for joint operations. The PLA has been downsized and streamlined at all levels to shift from a quantity-and-scale to a quality-and-efficiency model. PLA's command and control structures have been streamlined. More control has been given to the CMC and its chairman. The missile force, earlier known as the Second Artillery, was elevated to a full service and renamed as the PLA Rocket Force. It has created the sub-service Strategic Support Force and Joint Logistics Support Force to facilitate other services to operate seamlessly together. The CMC has distributed resources more equitably among the services, reduced troop numbers, and the PLA Army's overall prevalence, which used to be the dominant service of the PLA.

The PLA had been making considerable progress in enhancing its technical capabilities to conduct space, counter space, Electronic warfare (EW) and cyber space operations. However, before the reforms, experts in PLA felt that its structure and organisation were the main roadblocks facing its modernisation efforts. The PLA sees cyber, electronic, and psychological warfare as inter-connected sub-components of Information Warfare (IW). The specialists advocated greater integration of these forces as an operational necessity as the crucial organisations responsible for cyber, space and EW missions remained stove-piped in a silo. PLA took the opportunity of the significant reforms to readjust its extensive cyber, space and EW capabilities into a unified force.

After the reorganisation the PLA command structure in simplified form is given below:

China's Military Leadership

CENTRAL MILITARY COMMISSION

Chairman Xi Jinping

Vice Chairman Gen Xu Qiliang, Gen Zhang Youxia

Members Gen Wei Fenghe, Gen Li Zuocheng, Adm Miao Hua, Gen Zhang Shengmin

DEPARTMENTS	COMMISSIONS	OFFICES
CMC General Office	Discipline Inspection Commission	Agency for Offices Administration
Joint Staff Department	Politics and Law Commission	Audit Office
Political Work Department	Science and Technology Commission	Office for International Military Cooperation
Logistic Support Department		Reform and Organization Office
Equipment Development Department		Strategic Planning Office
Training and Administration Department		
National Defense Mobilization Department		

THEATER COMMANDS	SERVICES AND SUPPORT FORCES	SCHOOLS	PARAMILITARY FORCES
Eastern Theater	PLA Army	Academy of Military Science	People's Armed Police
Southern Theater	PLA Navy	National Defense University	China Coast Guard
Western Theater	PLA Air Force	National University of Defense Technology	Militia
Northern Theater	PLA Rocket Force		People's Armed Forces Maritime Militia*
Central Theater	PLA Strategic Support Force		
	PLA Joint Logistic Support Force		

**These forces can fall under both civilian and PLA command*

This Chart does not depict the Ministry of National Defense (which is not in the chain of command), general offices, military districts, garrisons, sub-districts, and People's Armed Forces Departments (which command the militia)

Source: Military and Security Developments Involving the People's Republic of China 2020, Annual Report to Congress

The raising of the Strategic Support Force (SSF) in December 2015 was a critical milestone in the history of the PLA. The SSF consolidated cyber, space, electronic and psychological warfare and intelligence capabilities and responsibilities. The creation of the SSF shows China's understanding of information as a strategic resource in today's warfare. SSF's structure is planned to create synergies between disparate IW capabilities to execute specific strategic missions that will be decisive in future wars.

The PLA reforms can be correlated to U.S. reforms after the Goldwater-Nichols Department of Defense Reorganization Act of 1986. This act was aimed at transforming a peacetime military structure to more optimised for joint warfare. The SSF is partly designed on U.S. Strategic Command (USSTRATCOM), with modifications reflecting China's unique approach and challenges.

In this chapter, only those organisational issues relevant to the information domain, including the cyber domain, are discussed. The space domain is not included.

Overall PLA Organisational Structure Prior to Reform

The PLA's organisation was based on a Soviet Union model imported in the early 1950s. Its three main pillars were:

- Three services of the army, navy air force and the Second Artillery Force (SAF) responsible for China's conventional and nuclear missiles.
- Four general departments: The General Staff Department (GSD), General Political Department (GPD), General Logistics Department (GLD) and the General Armaments Department (GAD).
- Seven geographic Military Regions (MR): Shenyang, Beijing, Jinan, Nanjing, Guangzhou, Chengdu and Lanzhou, with subsidiary units drawn from the services.

The CMC was head of these organisations and exercised the highest command authority in the PLA. Since 1978, China is trying to transform the PLA from an infantry-heavy, low-technology, ground forces-centric force into a leaner, meaner, highly networked and high-technology force with stress on joint operations and power projection.

For a better understanding of the organisational reforms, it is essential to comprehend the older organisation and its roles. The organisation of CMC and the various departments under it before the PLA reorganisation of 2015 is given in Appendix.

Broad structure of the PLA before the reform of 2015-16 is given below:

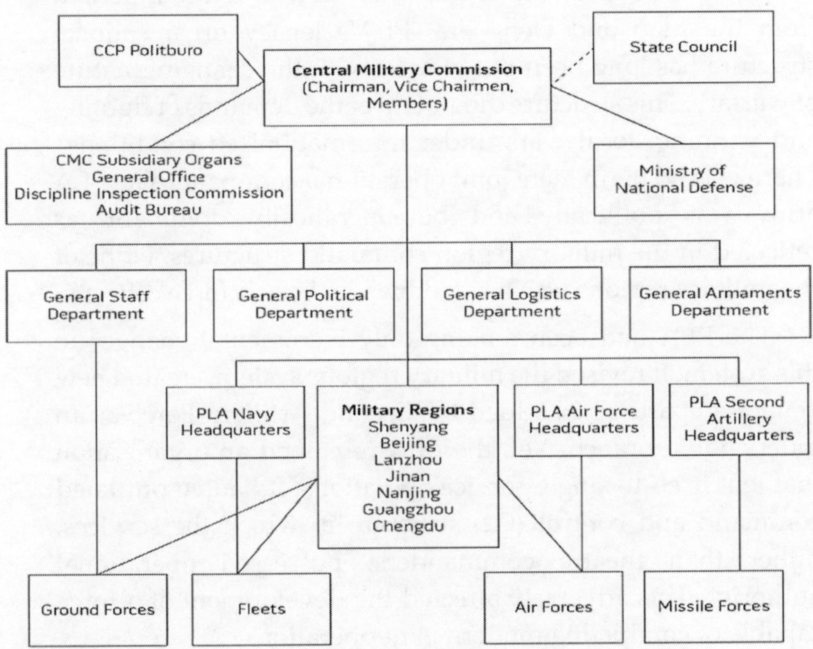

PLA Structure Prior to Reform

Source: https://ndupress.ndu.edu/Media/News/Article/793267/chinas-goldwater-nichols-assessing-pla-organizational-reforms/

Before the PLA's reorganisation, space, cyber and Electronic Warfare (EW) units were organised according to their missions like reconnaissance, attack or defence rather than their warfighting domains. Earlier espionage and technical reconnaissance in the cyber domain were handled by the GSD Third Department, while the GSD Fourth Department dealt with the targeting and attack missions. The GSD Informatisation Department handled the defence of essential information systems.

Post Reforms PLA Organisation

Though the PLA has undertaken several modernisation efforts since the 1980s, it largely retained a structure inherited from the Mao and Deng era. PLA's legacy organisational structure has long been out of sync with the changing nature of warfare. This structure did not meet the demands of fighting and winning 'local wars under informationised conditions'. There was no permanent joint operational command. The PLA army was politically and bureaucratically dominant, as reflected in the military region command structures. None of the military regions was headed by naval or air force officers.

The PLA had been making only incremental changes to this system. It revised the military regions system, created new general departments, added the Second Artillery Force as an independent branch. Yet, the PLA remained an organisation that lent itself to single-service operations. It had an outdated command and control (C2) structure in which the services, rather than theatre commanders, possessed operational authority. This adversely affected the development of a force capable of conducting modern joint operations.

In late 2015 and early 2016, CMC Chairman and CCP General Secretary Xi Jinping announced the most ambitious reform and reorganisation of the PLA since the 1950s.

The reforms have two primary aims: reshaping and improving the PLA's command and control structure to enable joint operations among the services and ensuring the PLA is loyal and responsive to the Party and Xi. Before the reforms, the rapid development of the technical proficiencies of Chinese cyber, space and EW forces stood in glaring contrast with the PLA's stagnant operational structure, despite significant shifts in operational realities. There was a growing realisation in PLA scholarly circles that the PLA's structure and organisation, not its technological capabilities, had become the primary roadblock facing PLA modernisation efforts. The vital organisations responsible for space, cyber and EW missions were silo-based where operational necessity demanded greater integration of these forces. PLA took this opportunity to realign its growing space, cyber and EW capabilities into a unified force.

To restructure the PLA for modern warfare, the following major organisational changes were made:

- To enhance the operational effectiveness of the PLA in the information age, the four general departments within the CMC responsible for managing the ground forces were reshuffled into 15 organs into a new PLA Army (PLAA) leading organ under the CMC leadership to streamline the chains of command.
- The Second Artillery Force, responsible for China's missile forces, was redesignated as the PLA Rocket Force (PLARF). It was elevated to equal footing with the PLAA, PLA Navy (PLAN), PLA Air Force (PLAAF) and the new PLA Strategic Support Force (PLASSF).
- To enhance integrated joint operations capacity, the PLA Joint Logistic Support Force (PLAJLSF) was established.

- The PLA's four former general departments were converted into 15 joint force "functional organs" within an expanded CMC. The GSD became the new CMC Joint Staff Department, the GPD converted to the CMC Political Work Department, the GAD changed to the CMC Equipment Development Department and the GLD became the CMC Logistics Support Department.
- The seven military area commands, headquartered in Shenyang, Beijing, Lanzhou, Jinan, Nanjing, Guangzhou and Chengdu, were disbanded and have been organised into five theatre commands, called by their strategic locations in north, south, east, west and central China headquartered in Nanjing, Guangzhou, Chengdu, Shenyang and Beijing respectively.
- The headquarters of Western Theater Command is in Chengdu. Its responsibility is virtually the entire western half of China, including borders with India and Russia and the regions of Tibet and Xinjiang.
- 300,000 personnel have been cut to trim down the forces and keep the total active force at two million.

The Western Theater Command (WTC) is geographically the largest theatre command within China. The WTC is responsible for responding to conflict with India and terrorist and insurgent threats to and within western China. PLA units located within the WTC include two group armies, other Army units under the region's two military districts of Xinjiang and Tibet, three Air Force bases and one Rocket Force base. People's Armed Police (PAP) units responsible for Xinjiang operations are likely to be under the control of the Western Theater Command.

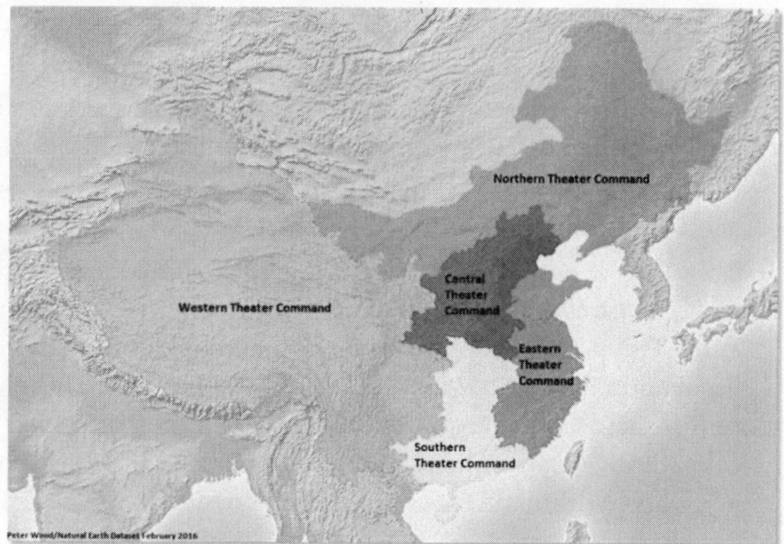

Source: Peter Wood, Natural Earth Dataset, February 2016

PLA has pursued a "bricks, not clay" approach to reorganisation. Instead of building whole organisations from scratch, the PLA made structural changes by renaming, resubordinating or moving entire existing organisations and their component parts and then redefining their command relationships within the PLA. Some of the old organisations remained with the earlier set-up and were not shifted.

Major Changes

The CMC Reforms. New expanded CMC comprising 15 departments, offices and commissions replaced the four former general departments:

- The General Staff Department became the new CMC Joint Staff Department,
- The General Political Department became the CMC Political Work Department,

- The General Armament Department converted to the CMC Equipment Development Department,
- The General Logistics Department changed to the CMC Logistics Support Department.

The GPD's law enforcement functions were shifted to a new CMC Political and Legal Affairs Commission. The oversight of party discipline in the PLA was relocated to the CMC Discipline Inspection Commission. The GAD's Science and Technology Commission, accountable for defence innovation, was placed under direct CMC oversight. These are not exact equivalents to their predecessors; specific capabilities, tasking and modules have been transferred elsewhere within the PLA, particularly in the case of the SSF.

Blanket transfer of the former GPD into the current Political Work Department (PWD) of the CMC has dramatically altered the new organisation's nature, focus and responsibilities. The new PWD has been considerably reduced in size in comparison to its earlier version. However, a significant proportion of the personnel taken away from the GPD/PWD was transferred to form the political work organs of the newly established PLA Army service headquarters. Therefore, it does not represent a net loss to the PLA's political work system as a whole. Various components of the former GPD have been combined in the propaganda domain, the bureaucratic overhead has been reduced and propaganda work has been modernised. The PWD's Cultural Arts Center has been formed by amalgamating the former GPD's various artistic and creative components.

The reforms have significantly changed the command and control arrangements for joint operations and redefined time-honoured organisational relationships and created new responsibilities across the PLA command structure. It has created an expanded CMC, including a new Joint Staff Department (JSD) which succeeds the former Army General Staff Department. JSD is responsible for supervising joint operations and holds direct command over the traditional Services, the Theatre Commands and the Strategic Support Force and Rocket Forces, the two services which retain dual responsibilities for 'force construction' and strategic operations.

CMC now supervises a dual command structure where the services are responsible for force construction while the five theatre commands are responsible for traditional joint operations in their respective regions. The SSF and Rocket Force are outside this bifurcated arrangement, maintaining responsibility for their own force construction and strategic operations. Through its various bureaus, the JSD oversees overall military command including operations, intelligence, cyber and electronic warfare, communications and battlefield environment support.

The Strategic Support Force

The Strategic Support Force's creation comes at an inflection point for the PLA.[1] China has increased the speed of the current shift of its military posture from land-based territorial defence to extended power projection. The creation of the SSF unmistakably signals the importance of information dominance for China's military planners. China's leaders want to protect their country's interests in the strategic frontiers of space, cyberspace and the far seas. It is also a direct recognition that the strategic frontiers of space and cyberspace are vital to China's expanding hard power and its broader strategic interests, including economic growth and technological development.

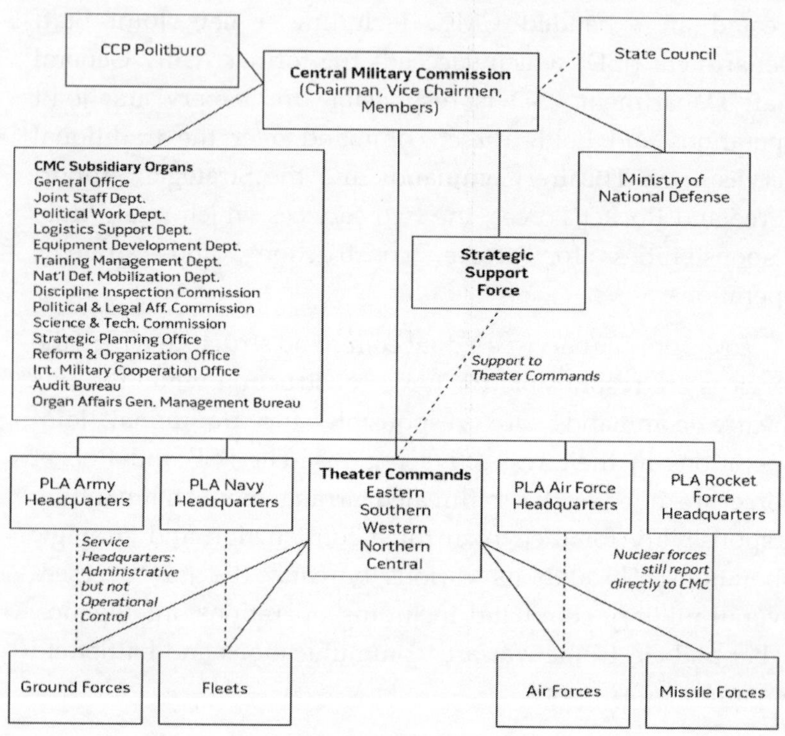

PLA Structure after Reform

Source: Phillip C. Saunders and Joel Wuthnow, *China's Goldwater-Nichols? Assessing PLA Organizational Reforms,* National Defense University, April 2016, http://inss.ndu.edu/Portals/68/Documents/ stratforum/SF-294.pdf

The SSF shows the evolution of Chinese thought on information as a strategic resource in warfare. It emphasises the need to exploit cyber, space and the electro-magnetic spectrum for military superiority while denying their use to adversaries. The PLASSF symbolises the evolution of some basic Chinese warfighting principles into a unified command structure. It combines various capabilities to employ them in a more structured and coherent way than the earlier mostly piecemeal approach used by the PLA. The PLASSF was developed to reduce the PLA's known shortcomings in joint operations. The joint command is a primary objective of the reforms. The Strategic Support Force's ability to provide the information umbrella of space-based C4ISR, intelligence support and battlefield environment assessments facilitates stitching up a common intelligence picture among joint forces within Theatre Commands. The SSF ensures the centralised management, centralised employment and centralised development of support resources and acts as an essential support for the PLA's joint operation system of systems. The objective of the reform is to improve the PLA's ability to fight informationised conflicts and improve joint operations and power projection capabilities in support of China's strategic aims.

China's intelligence apparatus is complex, huge and almost completely opaque to outsiders. It has various and occasionally competing intelligence organisations that deal with domestic and external intelligence gathering. The PLASSF integrates electronic intelligence (ELINT), signals intelligence (SIGINT), long-range surveillance and information operations capabilities under a single command. National-level assets have been retained at the top level of command. Lower-level assets are distributed to Theatre Commands on as required basis. PLASSF intelligence operations are split into strategic intelligence and tactical intelligence. Strategic intelligence consists of collection efforts focused on long-term issues of national importance. Tactical intelligence is composed of collection efforts that directly support PLA operations, such as ground intelligence, air- and space-based surveillance, deep ELINT, and tactical-level information operations.

According to China's Defence White Paper published in July 2019: "The PLASSF is a new type of combat force for safeguarding national security and an important driver for the growth of new combat capabilities. It comprises supporting forces for battlefield environment, information, communications, information security, and new technology testing. In line with the strategic requirements of integrating existing systems and aligning civil and military endeavours, the PLASSF is seeking to achieve big development strides in key areas and accelerate the integrated development of new-type combat forces to build a strong and modernized strategic support force."[2]

The primary mission of the SSF is to win informatised warfare by:

- Providing strategic information support for joint operations, including in the new operational domains of space, cyber and electromagnetic spectrum.
- Achieving information dominance.
- Endeavouring to convert advanced technologies into military capabilities.

Joe McReynolds, a research fellow at the Jamestown Foundation, and John Costello at the U.S. Department of Homeland Security identified the following concrete missions of strategic information support:[3]

- Centralising technical intelligence collection and management.
- Providing strategic intelligence support to theatre commands.
- Enabling PLA power projection.
- Supporting strategic defence in the space and nuclear domains.
- Enabling joint operations.

The PLASSF has a critical role in information security, communications and new technology testing via increasingly advanced C4ISR means. The PLASSF is the driving force behind the intelligentisation of the entire PLA. The SSF's mission is focused on IW and strategic-level information support for space, cyber, electronic and psychological warfare. One of the main tasks of SSF is the strategic denial of the electro-magnetic spectrum. The SSF has also assumed responsibility for the use of quantum computing and artificial intelligence (AI). One of the missions of SSF is destroying U.S. satellite and communications systems globally to force a "no satellite, no fight" environment on the U.S. SSF is likely to have a role in promoting or fielding other capabilities such as directed and kinetic energy weapons. The SSF is also strengthening its electronic warfare capability to jam U.S. ship and aircraft radars.

The SSF will address the rapid changes in emerging disruptive technologies, usually driven by research and development in the private sector. SSF would pursue civil-military integration or "military-civil fusion" as an integral facet of its task. It would take advantage of advances in dual-use technologies and leverage civilian talent. SSF has formed partnerships with over nine units and enterprises, such as the University of Science and Technology of China and the China Electronics Technology Group (CETC), to focus on cultivating high-end talent through education, training, cooperation and exchanges.

Electronic Warfare (EW). The PLA has initiated an aggressive modernisation program and its organisational reforms, including its EW and Electro Magnetic Support Operations (EMSO) capabilities. EW comprises a range of capabilities involving interfering with or disrupting electronic and communications equipment, emphasising jamming and anti-jamming. The PLA has fielded a comprehensive set of jammers and other electronic counter-measures targeting U.S. sensors and communications. PLA EW systems are designed to suppress, degrade, disrupt, or deceive enemy electronic systems operating in radio, microwave, radar, infrared and optical frequency ranges and rival computer and information systems. China has also fielded several types of unmanned aerial vehicles (UAVs) with EW payloads. China displayed several of these during the PLA 90th anniversary parade in July 2017. The information operations group included an information support formation, electronic reconnaissance formation, electronic countermeasures formation, and UAV formation in the parade. The SSF electronic reconnaissance formation provides highly mobile, integrated, flexible and multi-domain IW capabilities. The unit's mission is seizing and maintaining battlefield information control.

PLA EW units regularly train to conduct jamming and anti-jamming operations against multiple communication and radar systems or GPS satellite systems in force-on-force exercises. These exercises test operational units' understanding of EW weapons, equipment and performance. They also allow operators to improve confidence to operate effectively in a complex electromagnetic environment. In addition, the PLA tests and validates advances in EW weapons research and development during these exercises.[4]

The SSF, in 2018, increased joint communications and reconnaissance training with the PLAA and the PLAAF to improve operational support capabilities and joint operations in advanced electromagnetic environments. In the LUOYANG-2018 series of force-on-force exercises, a SSF base challenged a PLA group army brigade's communications with hostile jamming and interruptions to their operational electromagnetic environment. The SSF operates in the fuzzy zone between peacetime and wartime to achieve "escalation dominance, a condition wherein China maintains the initiative in shaping adversary behaviour in a crisis scenario that has not yet become a full-on conflict."[5]

Cyber Operations. Chinese scholars describe computer network operations as an important new form of that has the potential to change traditional operational concepts, thinking and methods. Computer network operations have both coercive and warfighting applications and can have a large effect on an opponent's political, economic and military capabilities. It is considered as an important means for a military equipped with inferior weapons to effectively counter a high-technology opponent.[6]

Cyber operations require a relentless cycle of cyber reconnaissance, capabilities development and deployment of cyber weapons to leverage cyber effects in a conflict. There is a close relation between computer network exploitation and computer network attack. Once inside the adversary network, only the change of intention converts reconnaissance into the attack. The computer network exploitation continues in peacetime. It involves mapping computer networks and their communication nodes and retrieving, collecting, and analysing information found from these sources. Reconnaissance includes cyber espionage against military, civilian or commercial targets, theft of military technological know-how, intellectual property, etc. Given the functional integration of these peacetime and wartime activities in cyber operations, the integration of PLA's cyber offence and espionage capabilities became a practical necessity.

Computer network operations, called network warfare is defined by the Chinese People's Liberation Army as "within the information network space, destroying an enemy's network systems and information and degrading its operational effectiveness; and protecting one's network systems and network information and the conduct of operational activities."[7] The PLA divides computer network warfare into three components: computer network reconnaissance, computer network strike and computer network defense.[8] The PLA's cyber capabilities, defence, offence and reconnaissance have been centralised under the SSF. The PLA wants to use offensive cyber operations to disrupt, degrade or damage adversary systems, including critical infrastructure, before and during multiple stages of a conflict in different conflict scenarios. It would use defensive cyber operations to defend against the same capability from an adversary.

By consolidating cyber and other Information Operations related elements, the SSF generates synergies by combining national-level cyber reconnaissance, cyber attack and cyber defence capabilities into one organisation to centralise command and control and reduce bureaucratic hurdles.

The SSF Organisational Structure and Composition

The SSF is characterised as a "force" and not a "service." In late 2015, the earlier Second Artillery Force was promoted to Rocket Force as a full military service as part of a reorganisation. It seems that the SSF corresponds to an independent military branch, similar to the Second Artillery Force before the military reforms. As a strategic organisation, the SSF reports directly to the CMC and not to the Theatre Commands. On 12 December 2019, the Commander of the PLA Strategic Support Force Li Fengbiao was promoted to the rank of full General (4 stars) as part of modernising and streamlining of the PLA High Command.[9]

The Grade Structure. The PLASSF and its commander are assessed to hold a Theatre Command (TC) leader grade. Its headquarters elements and operational departments have a grade of TC deputy leader. In the PLA, only an organisation of a higher grade can exercise command over another. There may be complications of how command and control will work within the PLASSF. Many of the component elements under these organisations, such as the headquarters departments of the Space and Network Systems Departments, along with their underlying bases and bureaus, are of corps leader grade. This grade structure seems to be excessively compressed compared to PLA organisations' typical structuring, causing bureaucratic challenges. It is likely that the grade of elements of the PLASSF will be readjusted as the reforms continue.

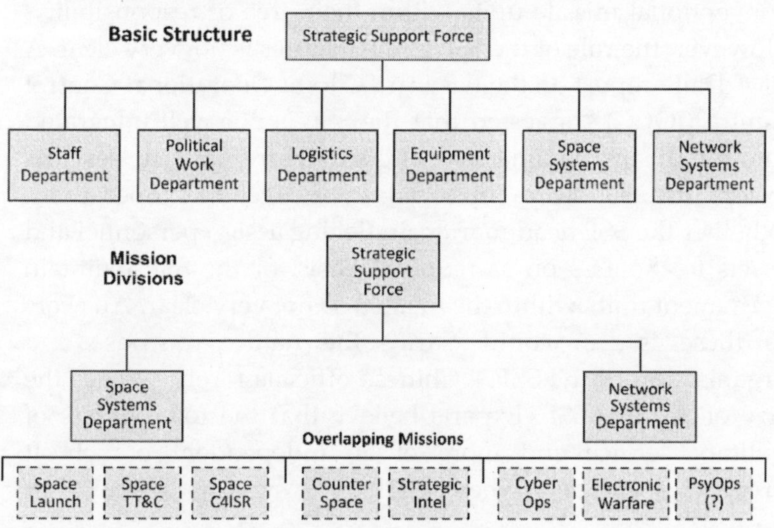

Organisational Structure and Composition of SSF

Source: Elsa B. Kania and John k. Costello, the Strategic Support Force and the Future of Chinese Information Operations, the Cyber Defense Review, Spring 2018.

Key Departments	Roles
Staff Department	Works with the Central Military Commission's Joint Staff Department on supports for joint operations, including logistics support planning and training
Political Work Department	Three Warfares (public opinion, psychological, legal), compliance with party guidance, and organizational management
Discipline Inspection Commission	Combatting corruption inside the organization
Network Systems Department	Reconnaissance, defense, and offense in the cyber and electromagnetic domains; technical reconnaissance
Space Systems Department	Administration of satellite launch centers; satellite launches, tracking, and control; space information support

Key Departments and Roles of the SSF

Source: NIDS China Security Report 2021, National Institute for Defense Studies, Japan http://www.nids.mod.go.jp/publication/chinareport/pdf/china_report_EN_web_2021_A01.pdf

Theatre Command commanders have been given operational authority over army, navy, air force and potentially conventional missile units within their area of responsibility. However, the role of the SSF in the theatres is not very clear. A PLA Daily report on the Eastern TC Joint Operational Control Centre (JOCC) suggested that the SSF is not well integrated into the theatre commands as personnel from all the services except the SSF were involved in the centre's operations. Whether the SSF headquarters in Beijing assign personnel and assets to the TCs on as required basis, or the SSF maintain permanent units within the theatres is not very clear. Answers to these issues would clarify the nature, purpose and organisation of the SSF.[10] Chinese officials rarely discuss the size of the PLASSF. Experts believe that the force is less of military service and more of an independent branch. It provides space and cyber information support to the other services.

The SSF consist of the Staff Department, Political Work Department, Discipline Inspection Commission, Network Systems Department (NSD), the Space Systems Department (SSD), Equipment Department and the Logistics Department.

The SSF was formed from organisations formerly subordinate to the PLA services and the CMC's GSD. The aim was to create operational synergies between previously disparate IW capabilities to enable information dominance to be decisive in future wars. Instead of building the organisation from scratch, the PLA has renamed, re-subordinated or moved existing organisations and their parts and then redefined their command relationships. These changes are part of a far-reaching transformation of PLA institutions, force structure and policy. China's leaders want to tighten central political control over a force that was seen as increasingly corrupt and build the PLA into a credible joint warfighting entity.

Operationally, the SSF consists of two main branches. The Space Systems Department supervises almost all PLA space operations, including satellite launch, tracking, telemetry and space warfare. The Network Systems Department combines former PLA organisations responsible for IW, cyber warfare, electronic warfare and psychological warfare.[11] The SSF oversees these two co-equal, semi-independent branches - the Space Systems Department is responsible for military space operations; and the Network Systems Department is responsible for information operations (IO), including EW, cyber warfare and psychological operations. Through its Space Systems Department and Network Systems Department, the SSF provides information support derived from space-based and cyber-based means to all PLA services and the five theatre commands.

The SSF has been designed for dominance in cyber space, space and the electromagnetic domain, considered critical "strategic commanding heights" for the PLA. Under its Space Systems Department, the SSF has consolidated control over a critical mass of the PLA's space-based and space-related assets.

Through these capabilities, the SSF has taken responsibility for strategic-level information support for the PLA in its entirety, enhancing its capacity to engage in integrated joint operations and remote operations.

The PLA is also building up network-electronic operations capabilities within its national Joint Staff Department headquarters and new regional theatre commands. The Joint Staff Department's Network-Electronic Bureau (JSD-NEB) makes a new force structure for managing the cyber and EW missions in the SSF, theatre commands and other services. It reflects the emergence of a multi-level force structure specialising in information operations. The PLA's individual services may retain their own technical reconnaissance bureaus and at least limited information operations capabilities, such as electronic countermeasures units. This means that the SSF force is responsible for strategic national-level operations that previously rested with former GSD units. At the same time, the services and theatre commands will remain responsible for cyber and EW operations at the operational and tactical levels.

Administrative Departments. The SSF is split into several administrative and managerial Departments such as political work, staff, logistics etc. The SSF has a four-department administrative structure at the headquarters level that includes the Staff, Equipment, Political Work and Logistics Departments. The Staff Department is responsible for operations and planning, training, project management and oversight and personnel management. It has four subordinate bureaus: the Operational Planning Bureau, the Training Bureau, the Direct Subordinate Works Bureau and the Navigation Bureau. Interestingly, the SSF has its own security and counter-intelligence elements, reflecting its exclusive importance and the assessment of the external threats arrayed against it.

Redefining the Reforms. PLA reforms have thus considerably altered the command context for many missions now under the SSF, redefining longstanding organisational relationships and creating new responsibilities across the PLA command hierarchy. The SSF has been given technical reconnaissance capabilities supporting operations but not with intelligence capabilities supporting strategic decision making. This reform gives the PLA more leeway to move away from its army-dominated past and focus intelligence resources toward critical operational needs.

The SSF Space Systems Department is responsible for almost all PLA space operations, including space launch and support, space information support, space telemetry, tracking and space warfare. In its 2015 Defence White Paper, China officially designated space as a new domain of warfare. China thinks that space will play an essential role in enabling long-range precision strikes and denying other militaries the overhead C4ISR systems. The Space Systems Department seeks to resolve the bureaucratic power struggles that existed over the PLA space mission. The elements of the mission had been dispersed across several national and service-subordinate organisations.[12]

This combination of the Space Systems Department and Network Systems Department may reflect the PLA's recognition of the inherent synergies among these domains and capabilities, from integrating network and EW to potential cyber operations against satellites.

The SSF Network Systems Department

The Network Systems Department (NSD) is responsible for IW. Its missions include signals intelligence, technical reconnaissance, cyber espionage, computer attack, electro-magnetic warfare and psychological operations. China wants to solve the operational coordination challenges of information sharing during the pre-reform organisational structure by putting these missions under the same organisational umbrella. Integrating cyber and EW elements under one organisation is a critical step to operationalise the concept of integrated network and electronic warfare (INEW) that the PLA has envisioned since the early 2000s.[13] The Network Systems Department also provides intelligence support to the theatre.

The NSD is built around the former General Staff Department's 3rd Department. It combines all strategic Information Operations (IO) units in the PLA. This helps in operational coordination between the PLA's cyber espionage

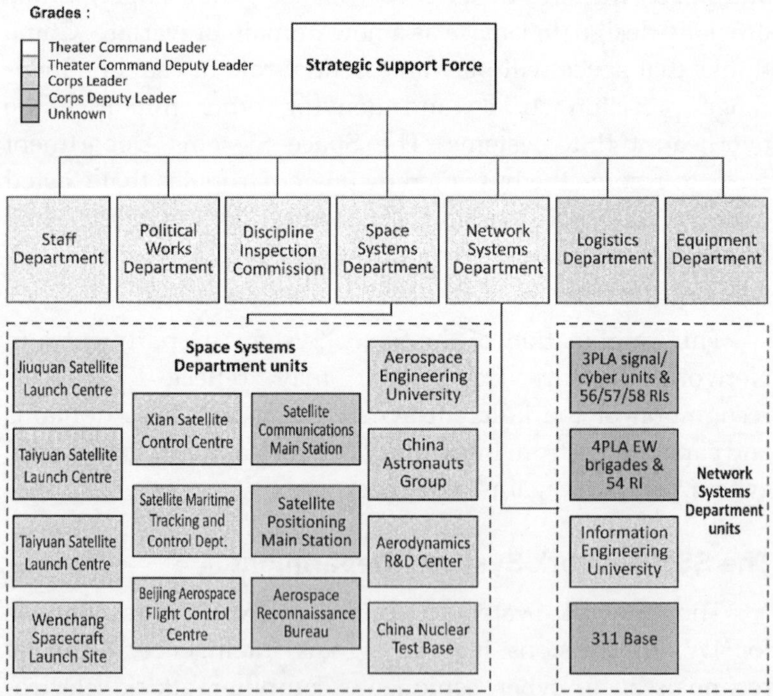

Source: China Brief, Volume 19, Issue 10, May 29, 2019

and cyber attack forces. Below the strategic level, the NSD shares operational and tactical level tasks with units under the services and regional Theater Commands.

Organisational Structure and Composition of NSD. A commander and political commissar head the NSD. Both carry Theatre Command deputy leader grades. Deputy commanders and deputy political commissar of the Network Systems Department have corps leader grades. Senior PLASSF Network Systems Department officers exercise some administrative authority over corps leader, corps deputy leader, division leader and division deputy leader-grade units. They were earlier subordinate to the former GSD Third and Fourth Departments. Selected divisions under former Military Region, PLAN and PLAAF Technical Reconnaissance Bureaus (TRB) may have been assimilated into at least six corps leader or corps deputy leader-grade base commands. Corps leader-grade base leaders would report to officers at the next higher grade, in this case directly to the PLASSF Chief of Staff or PLAASF Deputy Commander overseeing the Network Systems Department. While administratively subordinate to the PLASSF, five of these base commands could provide national level ISR support to Theater Commands during peacetime. They could be formally assigned to Theater Command operational control during a contingency.

NSD Units. The NSD is built around the former GSD Technical Reconnaissance Department which was responsible for signal intelligence and cyber espionage. The former 3/PLA is the organisational core around which the Network Systems Department is built.

Units from Former GSD Third Department (3/PLA). The NSD maintains the former Third Department's headquarters, location and internal bureau-centric structure. In one official statement, the NSD has been referred to as the 'SSF Third Department'. The 3/PLA consisted of administrative third level departments, 12 operational bureaus, a computing centre and three research institutes. The NSD has absorbed most of the 12 operational bureaus previously under the 3/PLA, including the 2nd (Unit 61398), 4th (Unit 61419), 8th (Unit 61786) and 12th Bureaus (61486). One of the main hacking arm of the PLA was the Shanghai based Second Bureau of Unit 61398. Shanghai-based Twelfth Bureau (Unit 61486) specialises in hacking targeted economic organisations to enable China gain technological advantages. The 3/PLA's Second and Twelfth Bureaus were fully integrated into the NSD. They have been significantly expanded and improved and given greater hacking and spying authority over computers, the Internet and telecommunications. The NSD operates five theatre designated technical reconnaissance bases and most of the former GSD Third Department's (3/PLA's) numbered bureaus.

Units from GSD Fourth Department or 4/PLA. Before the 2015/2016 reform, electronic warfare (EW) and computer network attack was the responsibility of the GSD Electronic Countermeasures and Radar Department (4/PLA). The 4/PLA consisted of administrative departments, division leader-grade bureaus, probably two air defence Electronic Counter Measures (ECM) brigades, a satellite ECM command, an ECM Center and the GSD Fourth Department research institute. The GSD Informatization Department handled computer network defence. The 4/PLA was responsible for all forms of electronic warfare - both defensive and offensive. Some of these capabilities have been integrated into the NSD, including the two electronic warfare brigades that were previously under the 4/PLA.[14]

Research Institutes. The NSD has taken over essential research agendas that could support capability development.

The 3/PLA had its own research institutes, mainly the 56th, 57th and 58th Research Institutes. These research institutes earlier reported directly to 3/PLA headquarters and were tasked with military research, development, testing and acquisition supporting 3/PLA's missions. The NSD has taken control of these Research Institutes.[15] The 4/PLA has its own research institutes, the 54th Research Institute and the Information Engineering University. It focused on electronic and network countermeasures. These were transferred to the NSD.[16] The Information Engineering University trains the future officers, scientists and experts and supervises all basic research relevant for the SSF. This university controls and runs more than a dozen highly specialized academies and research centres all over China that come under the Network Systems Department. The Information Engineering University oversees the following second level departments:

- Political Department.
- S&T Research Department.
- Training Department.
- Command Information Systems Academy.
- Electronic Technology Academy.
- Encryption Engineering Academy.
- Luoyang Foreign Language Academy.
- Geospatial Information Academy.
- Cyberspace Security Academy.
- Navigation and Aerospace Target Engineering Academy.
- Command Officer Basic Education Academy.
- Blockchain Academy.
- National Digital Switching Engineering Research.
- National Key Laboratory of Mathematical Engineering and Advanced Computing.

- Information Technology Research Institute.
- Fuzhou Sub-Academy.
- Changshu Sub-Academy.
- Songshan Training Base.

311 the 'Three Warfares' Base. The elements of the GPD responsible for psychological operations were amalgamated into the NSD. This is in line with the PLA's concept of cyber, electronic and psychological warfare as inter-connected sub-components of IW. The psychological domain is a core element of the PLA's "Three Warfares" concept that calls for the integrated use of psychological operations, public opinion warfare and legal warfare to gain an advantage over an adversary. The SSF's psychological warfare mission is performed by the 311 Base. This base is the only organisation in the PLA that is publicly known to perform psychological warfare operations. The 311 Base is the PRC's crucial instrument for political warfare that is closely affiliated with the Liaison Bureau within the Political Work Department. Notably, the 311 Base is a content creating unit. Its integration into the NSD reveals the political reliability of the SSF and China's understanding of the remarkable pace of information activities and the importance of quick utilisation of opportunities and swift reaction to moves by others.[17]

Other units. Miscellaneous units under the NSD include the SSF Network Security Base and the Luoyang Electronic Equipment Testing Center, a key military and national base for testing electronic information systems under electromagnetic environments.

SSF Cyber Operations

The hacking and cyber espionage activities are under strict military control. Units receive their specific tasks and priorities directly from the very top, *i.e.* Xi Jinping's CMC. These can be snooping on foreign governments and institutions and acquiring sensitive technologies and know-how. Because of the sensitivities, PLA does not involve outside entities such as academic institutions and commercial companies or State-Owned Enterprises (SOEs). Interaction with the Chinese industries happens only if there is a need to plant specialised components inside pieces of equipment produced in China. For this, the SSF has special channels through the CPC and the Ministry of State Security (MSS) to make available the PLA SSF experts safe access to the government-controlled production lines and personnel. The party and state security cadres tightly control this.[18]

PLA scholar Major General Ye Zheng in his 2013 Lectures on the Science of Information Operations gives a detailed examination of the unique properties, advantages, and limitations of information operations and their use in warfare. Ye names four fundamental principles of Chinese thinking on IW that inform the SSF's approach to information operations:[19]

- Information operations are offence-oriented. Information dominance is the core of the "three dominances" of information, air and space that would ensure victory.
- Information operations are offence-dominant. Cyber and intelligence operations are sensitive to changing circumstances. They rely on techniques and access methods that lose their power once they have been used and the element of surprise is lost. Cyber accesses are generally more effective in the starting stages of a conflict.
- "Pre-positioning" and "massing on the border" manifest differently in IW. In the information domain place, priority is on timing and blurring the distinction

between peacetime and wartime. This blurs the distinction between intelligence and military preparations.

- Information advantage can be substituted for space and time on the battlefield. Prepositioned effects and capabilities, achieved through cyber implants in an adversary's systems or an intelligence advantage enabled by strategic information support, can be utilised at strategic times to anticipate, delay and disable an opponent's ability to defend himself or project power.

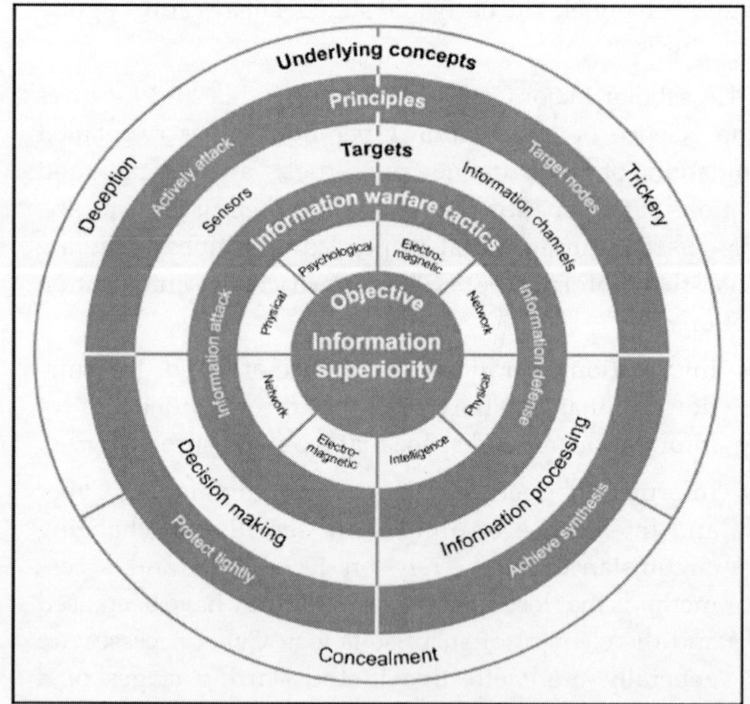

Chinese Information Operations.

Source: Chinese Tactics, ATP 7-100.3, August 2021 available at: https://armypubs.army.mil / epubs / DR_pubs / DR_a / ARN33195-ATP_7-100.3-000-WEB-1.pdf

Integrated IW

The Strategic Support Force is the core of China's IW force, central to China's pre-emptive and asymmetric warfare strategy. China's recent military reforms want to combine military preparations into a "combined wartime and peacetime military footing." At the outset of the war, PLA wants to get into an advantageous position and launch a preemptive attack or quickly respond to aggression.

The Science of Military Strategy (SMS), a PLA Textbook, states space, cyber and EW means working together as strategic weapons to "paralyse enemy operational system of systems" and "sabotage enemy's war command system of systems." This includes launching space and cyber-attacks against political, economic and civilian targets as a deterrent. The Strategic Support Force will play a central role as the IW component of China's warfare strategy. It will be the "tip of the spear" in its war plans and strategic disposition.

The SSF wants to unify China's large number and dispersed forces across three key dimensions:

- It merges espionage and offence disciplines across electronic, cyber and space warfare.
- It merges all the types of strategic warfighting operations primarily in information domains under a single cohesive force.
- Peacetime-wartime integration. The PLA is better prepared to conduct the battle space's intelligence preparation, cohesively plan, cross-domain and cross-discipline information operations campaigns and develop capabilities suited to conflict's evolving realities.[20]

Integrating Cyber Espionage and Offence. China has correctly understood that Cyber Espionage and Cyber Offence are heavily intertwined. When left uncoordinated in a conflict, they draw on shared resources and can even risk interfering with each other. The integration of China's military cyber offence and espionage capabilities has become a functional necessity. SSF reduces the degree of separation between its espionage and offensive activities. Before the reorganisation, espionage was handled by the Third Department of the former GSD (3/PLA), the Fourth Department (4/PLA) dealt with the offensive elements. The former Informatization Department undertook certain aspects of defence. Under the SSF, the idea of "integrated reconnaissance, offence and defence" could involve integrating disciplines to enhance full-spectrum war-fighting capabilities. This new organisational structure could also enable unified research and development, planning, force construction and operations that would not have been possible under the previous system.

The SSF brings crucial advantages in this context. Integrating espionage and offence for strategic information operations allows both missions to benefit from shared reconnaissance which is critical for identifying vulnerabilities and weaknesses around which their capabilities can be built, and offensive effects can be planned. The conditions do not remain static and are sensitive to changes in an adversary's defence posture, readiness, the shift from peacetime to wartime scenario and prevailing attitudes. Armed forces have to be in a state of "perpetual mobilisation." If two disciplines are kept separated, both suffer.

This grouping enables commanders to balance conflicting objectives and inherent trade-offs that can occur between the two disciplines. Espionage operations prioritise maintaining access to adversary systems and communications for the intelligence gains they may provide. In contrast, offensive operations may involve sacrificing those access methods to undermine the rival's systems and limit his operations, even if the cost is losing a key source of information. Commanders must continually evaluate both options against each other and overall campaign objectives and evolving military needs. If espionage and offence authorities are separated, it will become difficult for the commanders.

Unified IW Command and Control. The Strategic Support Force is taking responsibility for achieving "escalation dominance." It means that China should maintain the initiative in shaping adversary behaviour in a crisis scenario that has not yet become a full-blown conflict. This requires considerable intelligence capabilities and a varied set of measures for countering, influencing or deterring an adversary before and after the crisis. This capability to engage in "calibrated escalation" is a highly complex mission that necessitates coordinating across multiple domains, including the military bureaucracy, to produce a set of options that can be clearly communicated up the chain of command. It has to be evaluated against other political, economic and military costs. A singular service would not be able to do these tasks.

Independent Operational Group (IOG)

For strategic-level information operations, transitioning from peacetime posture to a war scenario just before or immediately after starting a war would have demanded unprecedented coordination across entrenched divisions between national-level departments, services and military region to form an information operations group conflict. The IOG would bring together the disparate elements responsible for cyber, electronic and psychological warfare into an operational command at the strategic, campaign and tactical levels. The SSF attempts to knock down the last silos of different departments and create a cohesive force in peacetime to smooth over the transition to wartime and construct a more effective war fighting force. IOG's tasks would include kinetic, cyber warfare, space, EW, psychological warfare, air defence electronic countermeasures and information support through all phases of conflict. Operations groups are further separated at the strategic, theatre and tactical levels of warfighting.

PLA information operations forces can be separated among strategic information operations forces, which include:

- Satellite information attack and defence forces, 'new concept' electronic assault forces and Internet assault forces.
- Campaign information operations forces include conventional EW forces, anti-radiation assault forces and battlefield cyber warfare forces.
- Tactical information operation forces, which include satellite information attack and defense forces and battlefield cyber warfare forces.

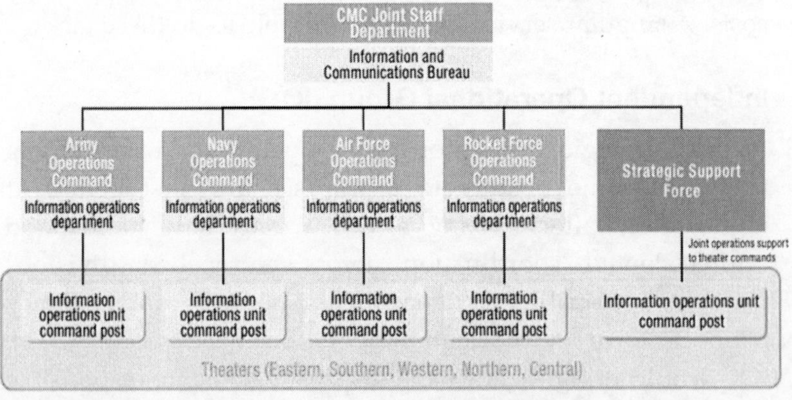

Command Organisation during Information Operations.

Source: http://www.nids.mod.go.jp / publication / chinareport / pdf / china_report_EN_web_2021_A01.pdf

The SSF keeps dedicated regional branches at the five joint force Theater Commands and national-level elements of the Rocket Forces, the Air Force and the Navy, with distinct cyberspace command elements down to the IOG level to support combat operations particularly during major wars against sophisticated militaries. The key wartime information support missions include the following:

- Centralising collection and management of intelligence collected by technical means.
- Providing strategic intelligence support to theatre and IOG commands.
- Enabling long distance and power projection operations.
- Supporting strategic defence in the space and nuclear domains.
- Enabling three-dimensional joint operations through the intelligence, communications and informatisation domains.

Outside the SSF, the PLA is creating network-electronic operations capabilities within its national Joint Staff Department headquarters and within new regional theatre commands. This shows the emergence of a multi-level force structure specialising in information operations. The PLA's 90th anniversary parade in July 2017 included SSF IOG's participation, combining an information support formation, electronic reconnaissance formation, electronic countermeasures formation and UAV formation.

The parade formally identified the SSF's role as the primary fighting force for information operations and information support. The SSF serves as the central component of the IOG. Though the SSF is the primary fighting force for information operations, it is not the only one. Outside the SSF, units from former military regions and within services will fall under the new joint theatre commands and focus on campaign-level operations. For example, the electronic countermeasures (ECM) formation came from the PLA in the parade, specifically from an air defence brigade and an Army Division ECM detachment. In a conflict scenario, each service's and branch's information counter-measures forces would combine with the information combat group. This focus on the SSF and one of its premier units suggest that the PLA is increasing the priority and prominence of the SSF and its assigned missions to tackle the military's deficiencies in controlling complex electromagnetic environments.[21]

Centralised Technical Intelligence Collection and Management. The SSF has a vast array of national-level technical collection assets from the former organisations that now constitute the majority of its force. This includes synthetic aperture radar, space-based electro-optical imagery intelligence, electronic intelligence platforms from across the GSD and GAD, electronic support capabilities from the former Fourth Department, and strategic long-range ground-based collection systems from the former Third Department. Before the reorganisation, management of these systems was stove-piped and answerable only to their parent general department. Strategic Support Force can now get a comprehensive perspective, identify gaps in intelligence collection, assess emerging needs and fit operations and acquisitions to address deficits and new challenges.

One of the primary tasks of the SSF is to provide strategic intelligence collected from various technical means starting from satellites to hacking. Intelligence Bureau within the PLA's Joint Staff Department does the analysis and delivery of the collected intelligence. It controls the country's most leading think tanks and research institutions.

Information and Communications. Reorganised from the former GSD Informatization Department, the new Joint Staff Department's Information and Communications Bureau (ICB), has inherited responsibilities for force-wide management of information systems, communications and support for high-level warfighting command and control. The ICB is at the apex level of CMC. It includes the PLA's Information Assurance Base. The Strategic Support Force's control of critical ground-based satellite communication infrastructure and primacy in operating space-based data relays show it is a primary organisation responsible for routing and supporting information flows through outer space.[22]

Conflict Situations. The PLASSF's role would shift from coercion and deterrence to enable joint warfighting in a conflict scenario. Critical PLA assets of technical intelligence under the PLASSF would become an integral element of PLA military intelligence in support of decision-making at the CMC JSD level. Concurrently it would be supporting the various theatre commands. Simultaneously, the PLASSF would try to achieve dominance in space, cyber space and the electromagnetic spectrum. The PLASSF would be responsible for providing vital information support to PLA services, particularly the PLARF, to enable targeting and joint operations to augment China's power projection. It would integrate PLA operations across domains and allow the system of systems confrontation.

The most crucial role of SSF will be cyber operations. Cyber operations allow China to manage the escalation of a conflict because cyber attacks are a low cost deterrent. The cyberattacks demonstrate capabilities and resolve to an adversary. To support Area Denial Weapon or Anti-Access/ Area Denial (A2/AD), Chinese cyber attack operations aim to target critical military and civilian infrastructure to deter or disrupt adversary intervention. SSF retains the option to scale these attacks to achieve desired conditions with a minimal strategic cost.

Psychological Warfare

According to Chinese thinking, psychological warfare is an integral part of IW. The task of PLA's psychological warfare is to weaken the enemy's will, shape international public narratives, shape diplomatic and political stories and advance the PRC's interests through all phases of conflict. PLA intellectuals have emphasised the importance of psychological and political operations in shaping the strategic situation ahead of conflict. About psychological warfare, the 2001 edition of the Science of Military Strategy explains that "the target of modern psychological warfare is not limited to the enemy forces as it also includes all people of the hostile country. Meanwhile, it assumes the mission of educating our own military and civilians... Its key target, however, is the enemy's decision making level, meaning it uses all kinds of means to attack that level's thinking, conviction, will, feeling and identifying systems in order to cause wrong understandings, assessments, and decisions and shake its thinking and conviction and will of resistance to achieve the objective of defeating the enemy without fighting. It is implemented not only in wartime but also in massive and continued scale in peacetime."

Psychological warfare conducted in the cyber domain has the following advantages:

- There is no limits in terms of geography or time. As an expert states, "wherever a network exists network psychological warfare can be conducted."
- It can be used to distribute information, including fictitious or misleading information that can be detrimental to an enemy's warfighting effort.

- It can be conducted in many forums, including websites and mass e-mails directed at groups of people or individuals.
- It is flexible and can be changed or updated rapidly.

Chinese psychological warfare includes those information operations (IO) activities in which a combatant employs information and media to target human thought, emotion and spirit. At tactical levels, the objective of psychological warfare is to create a psychological condition favourable to friendly forces and unfavorable to the enemy and reduce enemy morale and its will to resist. An effective psychological warfare campaign is considered the best possible trade-off, paying a small price in lives and material for big a victory. Psychological warfare wants to attain the soft kill, the only thing that can achieve Sun Tzu's definition of supreme excellence—subduing one's opponent without fighting.

Applications of hard-kill and soft-kill techniques simultaneously. The PLA considers that modern weapons and a well integrated approach to psychological warfare can achieve a hard-kill effect through soft-kill capabilities. The use of overpowering firepower together with an effective psychological warfare campaign, can create hard-kill results through psychological damage. Also new weapons are coming up that are technically nonlethal but have powerful psychological effects like sonic weapons, microwave weapons etc. Traditional soft-kill capabilities like propaganda and media manipulation should be fully integrated into the campaign.

For the PLA, psychological warfare used to be the responsibility of the GPD, working in close coordination with the balance of the PLA. The authority of the GPD was second only to the GSD. Given the authority and span of the GPD, Chinese psychological operations are likely to be integrated into broader military operations and incorporated into the earliest stages of military planning. The SSF's psychological warfare mission is performed by the 311 Base. The 311 Base is a content creating unit. It performs missions and tasks associated with the PLA's 'Three Warfares' concept, which comprises psychological warfare, public opinion warfare, and legal warfare. The 311 Base is still closely associated with the Liaison Bureau within the Political Work Department. This change removes organisational hindrances to coordinate across the information operations disciplines. It helps to integrate these operations in peacetime to transit into a wartime structure.

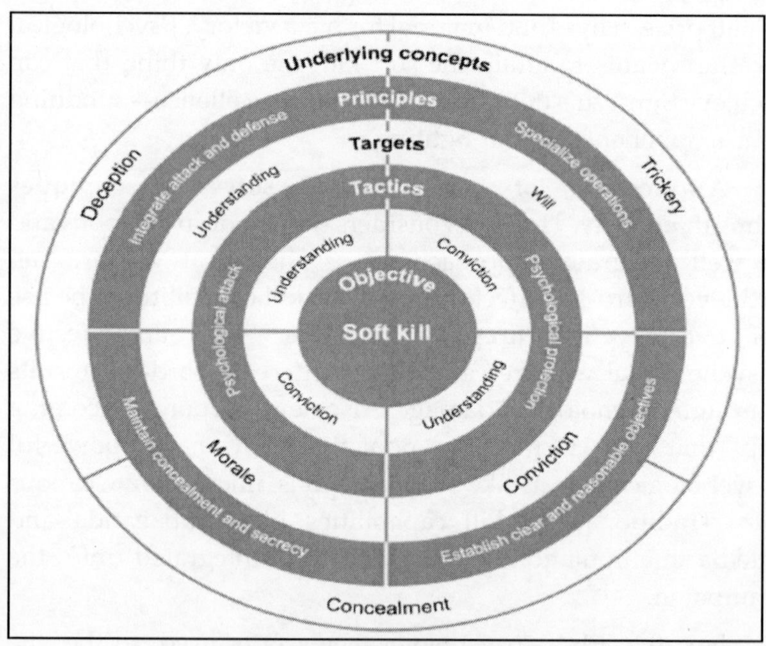

Psychological Warfare

Source: Chinese Tactics, ATP 7-100.3, August 2021 available at: https://armypubs.army.mil/epubs/DR_pubs/DR_a/ARN33195-ATP_7-100.3-000-WEB-1.pdf

As a Party-army imposes on its psychological operations, the PLA's status forces an additional necessity to ensure ideological loyalty and push Party ideals as part of its operational strategy. It seems that the 311 Base's move signals a 'decoupling' between political and psychological warfare. The revised 2010 Political Work Guidelines and 2013 edition of the Science of Military Strategy point to the need for psychological operations to be more closely aligned with traditional, nonpolitical military IW forces. The SSF's responsibility for psychological warfare could enable the PLA to exploit its cyber and psychological warfare capabilities together.

The present state of the former GPD Liaison Department is not very clear. An Epoch Times article from December 2016, citing unnamed military sources in Beijing, states that, except for some personnel specifically engaged in intelligence work who was transferred to the Strategic Support Force, the whole staff of the former GPD Liaison Department was being converted into civilian, non-active duty personnel. It merged with the CPC's own International Liaison Department.[23]

SSF and the 'Three Warfares' Concept. The 311 Base, now part of the NSD, performs missions and tasks associated with the PLA's 'Three Warfares' concept, which comprises psychological warfare, public opinion warfare, and legal warfare.[24] This base is the only publicly known organization in the PLA that performs psychological warfare operations. The PLA's psychological warfare mission is to shape international public narratives, weaken the enemy's will, shape diplomatic and political narratives and advance the PRC's interests through all phases of conflict. The SSF is responsible for the Three Warfares that utilize cyberspace. Jeffrey Engstrom, a political scientist at the RAND Corporation, notes that the SSF's

Political Work Department manages the Three Warfares and that information operations units are responsible for psychological warfare during wartime. Organisations responsible for IW through cyberspace in peacetime are entities including the party's media organizations under the Publicity Department of the Central Committee of the CCP, the Ministry of Public Security (MPS) of the State Council and the Ministry of State Security of the State Council. It remains to be seen whether the Three Warfares conducted by the SSF are different from the operations of these organizations or whether they engage in the operations with some overlaps.

SSF and Educational Institutions. The SSF oversees educational institutions, including the Information Engineering University, Space Engineering University and Research Institutes and has the role of training specialists in the cyber and space domains. For training personnel for cyber warfare, the SSF not only has jurisdiction over Information Engineering University but also has signed framework agreements for strategic cooperation with six universities: University of Science and Technology of China, Shanghai Jiao Tong University, Xi'an Jiao Tong University, Beijing Institute of Technology, Nanjing University and Harbin Institute of Technology—and three military enterprises: China Aerospace Science and Technology Corporation (CASC), China Aerospace Science and Industry Corporation (CASIC) and China Electronic Technology Group Corporation (CETC). The SSF is working with several organisations to develop talent responsible for cyber warfare, including academic exchanges with these educational and research institutions, interactions among experts, implementation of specialised educational programs, supplying outstanding talent and cooperating on educational technology research.

Gray Areas

It is not clear from where the people for 'national cyber protection' are coming from. It is unclear how any SSF cyber defence and protection mission would engage or coordinate with China's Ministry of Public Security and Cyberspace Administration, responsible for maintaining the security and defence of China's critical information infrastructure. There will be challenges in overlapping roles and responsibilities and establishing necessary legal, procedural and technical means of operational coordination and incident response to ensure the security of the critical infrastructure.

Balancing between cyberattacks and espionage is a difficult task. PLA units responsible for operations planning have less experience in this. At least in the open domain, it is not seen that PLA has a doctrine for using force in cyber space. While the PLA has developed its own theories on the strategic use of cyber operations in a conflict, these ideas have not yet been tested against the complex reality of operational and organisational implementation. The restructuring of the SSF will put those ideas to the test, pushing Chinese cyber operations into unfamiliar territory. SSF is yet to be tested in this field.

Unlike U.S. Cyber Command that solely focuses on cyber, the SSF includes cyber, space and Electronic Warfare (EW) capabilities. SSF is also responsible for organising, training and equipping strategic cyber and EW forces. However, surprisingly, military services continue to be responsible for training and providing operational and tactical level cyber and EW units. When deployed, these units are under the operational control of theatre commanders. This seam between the SSF, military services, and theatre commanders may be a problem area that its adversaries can exploit. Consolidation of information operations under the SSF could become a limiting factor for the development of services cyber and electronic warfare capabilities necessary for tactical warfighting.

It is not very clear how the SSF will manage conflicting or overlapping responsibilities between its space and cyber forces. Force integration at lower organisational and administrative layers is challenging. Any deficiencies in integration may hinder the SSF's ability to integrate its in-house space and cyber missions and its coordination with theatre commands and other entities.

Major Changes in the Organisation

The Chinese follow a different path than the Russian military. To achieve information dominance, the PLA has taken a far-reaching radical step. It focuses on its most influential IW forces. This will affect future PLASSF doctrinal development, training and unit structures and numbers. The structure of the PLASSF realises the concept of 'Integrated Network and EW' that has strengthened PLA thinking on IW since the 1990s. The former 4/PLA headquarters have been elevated to a joint capability to support strategic level 'network-electronic countermeasures'. The former 4/PLA's subordinate EW brigades have been incorporated into the PLASSF. Still, its headquarters has been shifted to the CMC Joint Staff Department with the new Network Electronic Bureau or Network Electronic Countermeasures. Details are as follows:

Details of the Former Fourth Department Units Now under SSF

Name of Unit	Notes
Operational and Administrative Units	
4/PLA Headquarters	Transferred to Joint Staff Department as a new Network-Electronic Bureau
Electronic Countermeasure Brigade (ECM) (Langfang)	Assessed to be transferred to Network Systems Department (NSD)

Name of Unit	**Notes**
Langfang ECM Brigade Detachment (Yingtan)	Assessed to be transferred to NSD
Electronic Countermeasure Brigade (Beidaihe)	Transferred to NSD
Beidaihe ECM Brigade Detachment (Nicheng)	Transferred to NSD
Electronic Countermeasure Center	Potentially merged with Joint Network Electronic Countermeasure dadui
Satellite Main Station (Beijing)	Assessed to be transferred to NSD or Space Systems Department (SSD)
Regional Satellite Station (Hainan)	Assessed to be transferred to NSD or SSD
Research Institutes	
54th Research Institute	Transferred to NSD
Academic Institutions	
Electrical Engineering Institute	Now National University of Defense Technology Electronic Countermeasures Institute

Source: John Costello and Joe McReynolds, China's Strategic Support Force: A Force for a New Era, National Defense University, October 2018 available at: https://ndupress.ndu.edu / Portals / 68 / Documents / stratperspective/china/china-perspectives_13.pdf

Network-electronic counter-measures bureaus and teams are now available with the new theatre commands. Their tasks and the institutional mechanisms for coordination with the JSD-NEB and PLASSF are not clear. It remains to be seen, at the macro level, how the PLA will organise information operations across these units and the various network and EW capabilities with the existing organisations and those which are being raised under multiple services and the new theatre commands.

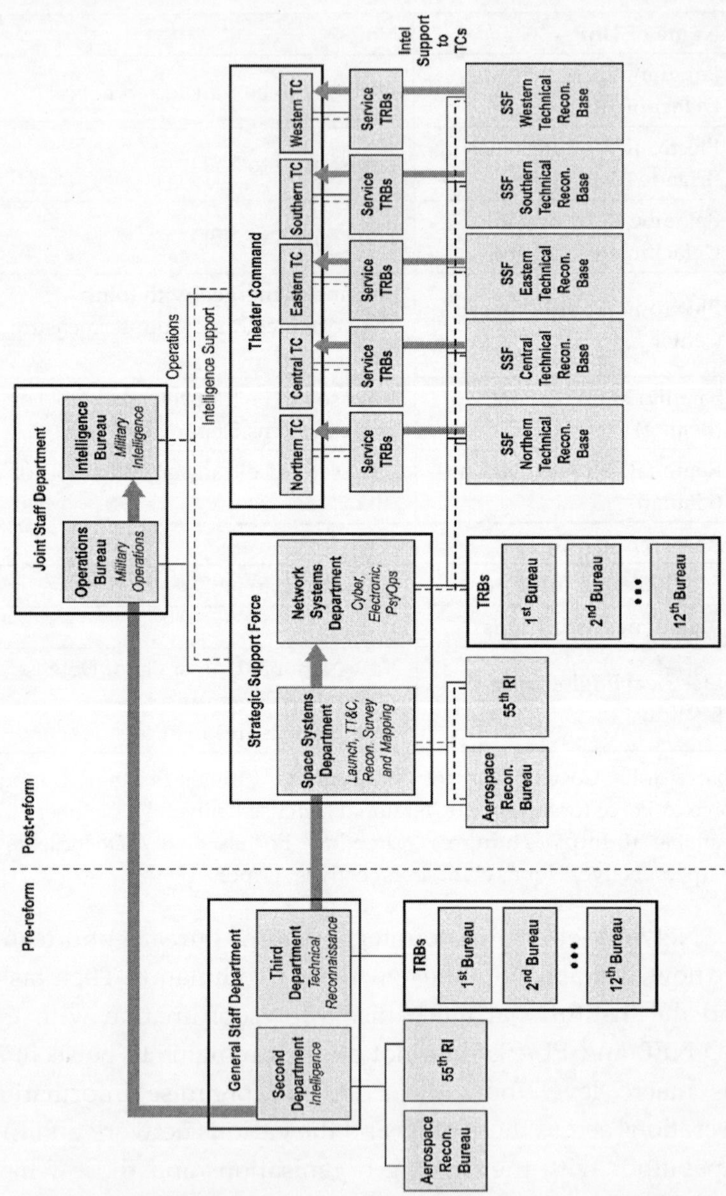

Organisation of the SSF and its Predecessor Organizations

Source: Costello and McReynolds, China's Strategic Support Force

The JSD under the CMC includes the 1PLA's command and control, recruitment, planning and administrative bureaus. Information support branches like the survey and mapping bureau, meteorology and hydrology bureau and targeting bureau moves to the SSF.

The 2/PLA, GSD's intelligence department, moved to the SSF. There are some question marks whether it will keep its clandestine intelligence operation or this will be sent to a separate unit. The Aerospace Reconnaissance Bureau (ARB), responsible for the GSD's overhead intelligence, surveillance, and reconnaissance mission will be the centre of the SSF's space corps. The 2/PLA's second bureau, responsible for tactical reconnaissance, will shift to the SSF. This includes one of its primary tasks: operating China's long-range UAVs.

The complete Informatization Department moves to the SSF. This includes communications, information management, network administration, computer network defence (CND) and satellite downlinks. This reform reduces the power and influence of the Army by removing its most strategic capabilities. Earlier, the PLA Army was split into two echelons, its GSD-level headquarters departments and units and Military Region level operational units. Most of the personnel in the joint force GSD units were Army personnel, and generally, these units were considered Army units. The SSF now has its own administrative branches and personnel. It allows the PLA Army to concentrate on ground combat, land defence and its intended roles in the context of China's national defence strategy.

Network-Electronic Units in Transition

Implications of Change. While the SSF has consolidated many capabilities, the PLA's information operations forces have a complex and multi-level structure. The SSF has not included and strengthened the complete PLA's cyber espionage and technical reconnaissance capabilities. Earlier each service and military region (MR) maintained its own Technical Reconnaissance Bureau (TRB) for signals intelligence and cyber espionage activities. It is not clear to what extent the SSF will integrate these other services or military region TRBs. The cyber defence mission is associated with the former GSD Informatization Department's Information Assurance Base and its subordinate Network Security and Defense Center remains with the new Joint Staff Department's Information and Communications Bureau. While the SSF can have a defensive task to complement its reconnaissance and offensive capabilities, the Ministry of Public Security and Cyberspace Administration of China is primarily responsible for national-level cyber defence, including critical infrastructure protection and law enforcement and regulatory responsibility. The 4/PLA headquarters has been integrated into the JSD as the Network-Electronic Bureau. It would be driving the INEW concept supervising force development and warfighting efforts of the SSF, other services and theatre commands. The 'network-electronic' grouping has been observed in other post-reform PLA organisations like the national joint force Network-Electronic Countermeasures and a Theater Command Network-Electronic Countermeasure. It is unclear whether it will create new bureaus to lead the new operational EW units under its command.

SIGINT. Even though cyber was one of its primary tasks, the 3/PLA was also responsible for traditional signals and communications intelligence. This is a significant part of the 3/PLA's personnel, facilities and organisational mass. If the Network Systems Department is exclusively meant for cyber warfare, then TRB's nation-wide network's traditional signals intelligence operation would require a new organisation. It is not clear if the CMC will split this task away from the 3/PLA.

Educational Institutions. It is not clear about the bureaucratic standing of specific key organisations equivalent to military regions. Commanders and political officers of the Academy of Military Sciences (AMS), the PLA's National Defense University (NDU) and the National University of Defense Technology (NUDT) have each been historically treated as the equivalent of a military region commander, reflecting their institutional importance. The AMS is a top-level think tank and brain trust for the senior military leadership. It is similar to the U.S. Army's Training and Doctrine Command (TRADOC). It develops the latest doctrines for the entire PLA and consequent training plans. It has some roles similar to the inspector general for assessing training activities. It is not known whether it will relinquish these roles to the new CMC Training Management Department. The status of these institutions, whether they will be treated as the equivalent of a war zone or will be reorganised into an entirely new format, is not clear.

Comparison : Cyber Organisations of U.S. and China

China surprised the world by the reorganisation of PLA and the creation of the PLASSF in December 2015. It appears that the structure of PLASSF has been influenced by U.S. Cyber Command (CYBERCOM). However, there are significant differences. A better appropriate comparison will be USCYBERCOM's parent organisation, U.S. Strategic Command (USSTRATCOM). Like the PLASSF, USSTRATCOM is responsible for space, cyber operations and strategic C4ISR support to "combatant commands". The U.S. combatant commands are akin to PLA's new theatre commands.

There is a feeling that China has followed the U.S DoD example of restructuring of the Goldwater-Nichols Department of Defense Reorganization Act of 1986. By this act, authority flowed from the U.S President and Secretary of Defense to the regional unified combatant commands commanders, who lead joint forces within their respective theatres. The Service chiefs were given an advisory role, with responsibilities to organise, train and equip troops. There is some similarity with the evolving PLA operational and administrative chains of command. However, the PLA command and control system has some key differences from the U.S. system. The Chinese theatres cover territory only within China, unlike the U.S. combatant commands, which span the globe. The JSD will centrally direct operations far beyond China's borders from Beijing. The PLA keeps the CMC as its highest decision making body, unlike a U.S. style commander-in-chief. Chinese scholars inform that this organisation was arrived at after careful analysis of western militaries. The distribution of strategic support across the various services caused redundancies in force development and a counter-productive rivalry for funding and resources.

The PLA's concept of the information domain and information operations includes the network, electromagnetic, psychological and intelligence domains. The 'network domain' and corresponding 'network warfare' are similar to the current U.S. cyber domain and cyberwarfare concept. But the PLASSF is a unique force structure that is different from both USSTRATCOM and USCYBERCOM in several key areas. The PLASSF is a military service and not a joint force command. It lacks a nuclear mission which is originally USSTRATCOM's primary task. The differences are more significant and more qualitative for cyber operations. It integrates all aspects of information operations.

The PLASSF differs from the U.S. Strategic Command in the following areas:[25]

- STRATCOM is responsible for strategic C4ISR support to the U.S. Combatant Commands as a joint force construct. PLASSF does it as a singular service.
- STRATCOM is a joint functional combatant command. It manages subordinate elements from the Army, Navy, Air Force and Marine Corps to carry out its primary tasks of nuclear, space and IW, strategic C4ISR support and ballistic missile defence. In contrast, PLASSF does not have responsibility for nuclear forces. The PLA Rocket Force is tasked to do this.
- The head of USCYBERCOM and the National Security Agency (NSA) of the United States are the same. After over 12 years, efforts are on to separate USCYBERCOM from the NSA for independent action and planning without losing the reconnaissance capabilities required to inform military targeting. In China's case, the Ministry of State Security (MSS) and PLA are primarily responsible for cyber operations, including espionage and offensive action. Now MSS focuses on foreign intelligence, economic espionage and political dissent and the PLA concentrates on military intelligence and warfighting.

A major difference between the SSF Cyber Force and USCYBERCOM is the inclusion of psychological operations within the ambit of PLASSF. The Chinese Communist Party and PLA scholars think cyber operations is a primary means for psychological operations. Chinese leaders feel manipulating information by an adversary would have undesirable societal effects and undermine Chinese domestic information control. China's civilian cyber security establishment's task extends beyond computer networks to physical devices, online content, broadcast airwaves, and propaganda. Chinese leaders feel that failure to control information threatens the CCP's political power and stability.

Question Marks

The PLA has its weaknesses and limitations like limited combat experience, the inadequate capability to conduct joint operations, limited expeditionary capabilities, a new and primarily untested organisational structure and dependence on foreign suppliers for specific critical equipment and materials. The PLA is aware of its shortcomings and is working to address these challenges. On the whole, 'Chinese cyber threat' is often overstated and not placed into proper context, especially by the Americans. A well known China expert, Greg Austin, draws attention to factors such as:

- Commercial lobbying and attention-seeking by American cybersecurity firms.
- Media environment is too receptive to cyber space intrigues and anti-China rhetoric.
- General lack of knowledge even among the highest decision-makers on the details and conduct of the US's own cyber espionage and operations against China.

The PLA defines cyberspace to include all capabilities within the information domain—both at peacetime and wartime. However, this has come at the cost of implementing a more complex, multi-layered structure within the SSF to manage all of these capabilities. In implementing this multi-layered structure, it isn't clear whether some elements of the technical reconnaissance made it over to become part of the SSF, or if they did, how they were fit in. At the worst, this leaves a critical capability isolated outside of the SSF. At best, the interactions will be complex within the SSF's layered organisation.

The exact separation of responsibilities between the JSD and SSF remains unclear, including how the PLA will integrate SSF espionage and offence-oriented cyber operations with CMC management of the PLA's cyber defence mission.

Organisational Issues

It is still unclear how the PLA will integrate the SSF's cyber operations, mainly focused on espionage and offence, with the PLA's cyber defence mission. The responsibility for PLA network protection remains with the Information Support Base under the Joint Staff Department's Information and Communications Bureau. This arrangement is similar to USCYBERCOM and the Defense Information Systems Agency (DISA).

Does the SSF have the responsibility for the cyber defence of private, civilian and critical infrastructure networks? It is unclear where the SSF would get the resource in terms of the personnel or capabilities to fulfil this role. The SSF would have to create this capability from scratch. They will require something like USCYBERCOM's Cyber Protection Teams under its Cyber National Mission Force.

The coordination between SSF cyber defence and protection mission and the Ministry of Public Security and Cyberspace Administration of China, charged with maintaining China's security and defence of China's critical information infrastructure, is unclear. China would face challenges in explaining roles and responsibilities and establishing necessary legal, procedural and technical means of operational coordination and incident response to protect critical infrastructure security. This would require maturity and foresight as civilian and military authorities' requirements are sometimes contradictory or overlapping.

PLA units responsible for operations planning have less experience in anticipating and balancing between the two missions of computer network attack (CNA) and computer network exploitation (CNE). The PLA has not developed a doctrine for using force in cyberspace under which consistent judgments can be made in a crisis. The PLA will have to decide critical issues about peacetime and wartime targeting, escalation in situations where peacetime and wartime divide is blurred, battlespace prepositioning and the viability and wisdom of utilising cyber operations to attain specific strategic military objectives. PLA information operations forces may be different from strategic information operations forces, which include:

- Satellite information attack and defence forces.
- 'New concept' electronic assault forces.
- Internet assault forces.
- Campaign information operations forces include conventional EW forces, anti-radiation assault forces and battlefield cyber warfare forces.
- Tactical information operation forces, which include satellite information attack and defence forces and battlefield cyber warfare forces.

Interoperability between strategic and operational level information operation forces has to be clarified. The SSF has not included and consolidated the entirety of PLA's cyber espionage and technical reconnaissance capabilities. Under the PLA's previous structure, each service and MR maintained its own Technical Reconnaissance Bureau (TRB), responsible for signals intelligence and cyber espionage. At this point, it is unclear to what extent the SSF will incorporate these other services or military region TRBs, though there are preliminary indications that a number of them have been transferred into the SSF. The cyber defence mission associated with the former GSD Informatization Department's Information Assurance Base and its subordinate Network Security and Defense Center remains under the new JSD's Information and Communications Bureau. The SSF is likely to develop a defensive mission to complement its reconnaissance and offensive capabilities.

Cyberspace Administration of China (CAC) is the central Internet regulator, censor, oversight and control agency for the PRC. It appears that the CAC, along with the MPS, would take primary responsibility for supporting cyber defence at the national level, including the protection of critical infrastructure and regulatory and law enforcement responsibility, respectively. Cyberspace Administration of China has authority over military and local cyberspace coordination centres, supporting defensive operations.

Given this complex force structure, there are some unresolved questions regarding command. It appears that the SSF, not unlike the former Second Artillery Force, and now Rocket Force, falls under the direct authority of the CMC rather than being commanded by theatre commands. However, the new theatre commands and subordinate service elements may possess or construct their own cyber or network-electronic operations capabilities. According to one notional schematic by an SSF scholar, theatre command joint operations command departments, through their joint operations cyberspace operations command centres, will exercise command over cyberspace operations forces under each of the services; the CMC Joint Operations Command, through a CMC Joint Command. Cyberspace Operations Command Center commands over the SSF, which commands cyberspace strategic reconnaissance, assault, defence, and support forces and capabilities.

Although this is not necessarily entirely consistent with the official command structure, the critical elements reflect a three-tiered approach to China's cyber capabilities. At present, the construction of more robust cyber or network-electronic combat forces within theatre commands likely remains a work in progress. In addition, there are no functional mechanisms for coordination among cyber operations forces at different levels.

Challenges of Talent Management

While China produces 15,000 cyber specialists every year, it does not meet the demand for 700,000–1.4 million professionals, creating severe workforce shortages. The PLA faces problems including an education-demand gap, unbalanced assignment of personnel and outflow of talent to the private sector. These problems are prominent in the nascent SSF. The Office of the CCP Central Cyberspace Affairs Commission has announced that for 10 years starting from 2017; it will designate seven institutions including the SSF's Information Engineering University, as cybersecurity model institutions and put efforts into talent training. In response to the government's intention, the private-sector information security firm 360 Enterprise Security Group has established educational and research institutes about cybersecurity in rapid succession in recent years. Nevertheless, it will not be easy to resolve problems such as talent outflow from the military.

Joint Force Structure

There are many reasons to question the positive impact of the reforms on PLA operational effectiveness in promoting joint war-fighting. Potential obstacles are:

- **Ground force dominance.** At least initially, joint billets and the CMC will be filled up predominantly from ground force officers. The army perspectives, interests and biases will continue to disturb efforts to build a real joint force. Much will be contingent on the PLA's ability to use joint PME, joint billets and rotational assignments between the services.

- **Interservice rivalry.** Competition for resources and influence may limit practical cooperation between the various services. As China's economic growth continues to slow, there will be a premium on access to scarce budgetary resources.
- **Lack of combat experience.** China has taken several actions to develop a credible joint warfighting capability, including developing joint doctrine, conducting joint exercises and establishing a joint C2 structure. Lack of experience in real-world joint combat operations could hinder the PLA's ability to field a strong joint force.
- **Leninist features.** The PLA maintains party control over the military, such as the CMC which is an organ of the CCP Central Committee, political commissars and Party committees. The reforms have stressed the need to strengthen the "absolute leadership" of the party. This could reduce the flexibility and autonomy of commanders, especially at the operational level.

Command and Control

The new theatre commands and subordinate service elements are likely to have cyber or network-electronic operations capabilities. This raises the following questions:

- The effectiveness of China's SSF in overcoming the PLA's organisational and technical weaknesses and integrating China's war-fighting capabilities successfully to fulfil joint operations requirements on the modern battlefield especially beyond China's near-seas remains to be seen.

- It is unclear what the SSF's specific responsibilities are for kinetic counter-space capabilities like ASATs, directed energy weapons, lasers and how it will coordinate with the PLA Rocket Force to win future informatised warfare.
- The progress of China's next-generation dual-use innovations like quantum computing, cyber-warfare, space-based ISR, directed energy devices, AI etc.

Education

It is not clear about the status of the Academy of Military Science, National Defense University and National University of Defense Technology. The following questions emerge:[26]

- Will they continue to be directly under the CMC?
- Will new academies be formed or former academies transformed into new entities based on personnel and force structure changes?
- Will more NCO schools or more command academies be established?
- What changes will occur in the PLA system of educational academies and schools?
- Will the number of new students be reduced because of the 300,000-person reduction?
- Will PLA-wide guidance be issued establishing education and experience requirements for officers to be considered qualified as joint officers?

Since its establishment in late-2015, the SSF has consolidated most of China's military space and information warfare capabilities. It is still a force in transition. There would be further changes to its organisational structure, composition and operational thinking.

Conclusion

Raising of the PLASSF reveals Chinese thinking on future warfare when an evolving fourth industrial revolution is transforming the character of warfare from informatised to intelligentized warfare. The PLASSF will be at the vanguard of these new strategic frontiers of conflict and competition, devising and designing capabilities for the future battlefield milieu. In any conflict scenario, the PLASSF would be the tip of the spear of the PLA's power.

The reorganisation has to be seen in two contexts. The reforms aim to usher PLA into the present era and convert them into a force capable of winning "informatized local wars." Simultaneously, the reforms are driven politically to reassert party leadership to transform the PLA into a more dependable, effective political instrument.

The PLASSF is to help the PLA's effective implementation of joint operations and IW. Creating an exclusive military service for IW confirms two things: China's emphasis on information in its strategic concepts and the CMC's wish to proclaim more control over these forces as political instruments. With the CMC at the helm of affairs, IW will be visible in all facets of PLA operations, both in war and peace.[27] In due course, the reforms would lead to a leaner and meaner warfighting organisation. Changes like a dedicated SSF responsible for cyber, space and EW, advances in long range precision strike and other capabilities, realistic, combat oriented training, better Professional Military Education, tighter control of PLA finances, a force structure that places more emphasis on naval and aerospace forces would facilitate the PLA to execute joint operations in multiple domains with greater confidence and capacity.

China has been carrying out cyber espionage activities against western countries to collect sensitive public and private information. China is particularly interested in space, infrastructure, energy, nuclear power, technology firms, clean energy, biotechnology and healthcare. These cyber-espionage operations are part of a sophisticated, long term campaign to get inside targeted networks so that once intruders are inside the network, they can exfiltrate information, manipulate data and implant stay-behind devices or software for future action.

Remaining Challenges

In the course of PLA reforms, the CMC has focused on making broad strokes and affecting change in larger, leading organizations first, in what has been characterised as 'above the neck' reforms. Such an approach minimises the disruptiveness of these reforms. These initial steps seek to create a foundation upon which future reforms can be built. For the SSF, this has meant that the old siloed nature of space, cyber, and electronic warfare have been broken and reorganized into new verticals through the Space Systems Department and the Network Systems Department. Such high-level changes alone, however, will not be enough to enable more profound reform. However, the SSF's force structure reflects significant progress towards synergy.

In the next chapter, various organizational facets of China's cyber operations including cyber espionage and signal intelligence will be looked into.

*

Appendix

Pre-reform Status of Key PLA Organisations

(Note: This part is described in present tense as the entire gamut and final status of the re-organisation remains hazy, and much of the old system is likely to remain replicated.)

The Central Military Commission (CMC). The Chinese armed forces, including the PLA, the People's Armed Police (PAP) and the militia, are headed by the CMC. The head of the CMC is its chairman, who is usually also the head of the CCP (the General Secretary of the party) and the Chinese government's head (the Premier). Till 2016, the CMC leadership exercised command of the armed forces through four general departments and the PLAN, PLAAF, and Second Artillery headquarters and the People's Armed Police. The role of the four general departments is given below.

The General Political Department (GPD). The GPD ensures that the PLA remains firmly under the CCP's control. The GPD controls the political officer system, with a political officer at every level of command, party committees at battalion level and above and party branches at company level and below. The GPD is responsible for the management and organisation of Communist Party work within the PLA; full-spectrum personnel management; development and dissemination of Party propaganda, culture, liaison, security, legal and judicial issues and investigations. The GPD leads the all-PLA military discipline and inspection system and the conduct of political warfare.

The General Logistics Department (GLD). The GLD is responsible for the management of logistics and logistics support work for the entire PLA. It is responsible for military finance, supply, subsistence, transportation, fuel, infrastructure construction, facilities management, health services and auditing. The GLD maintains a transportation department, to ensure that items can be moved where needed. As the PLA increasingly operates far away from Chinese shores, the GLD's responsibilities have become more complex.

The General Armaments Department (GAD). The GAD was raised in April 1998 to establish more military control over weapons and equipment development and procurement. The GAD is responsible for the PLA's weapons and equipment research, development, acquisition and maintenance. It determines, formulates, supervises and implements the policies, laws and regulations regarding weapons and equipment for the entire military. The GAD is also responsible for weapons and equipment budgeting, including oversight and auditing. In conducting these tasks, the GAD operates China's test, evaluation and training bases and a network of military representative bureaus and offices. The GAD guides the direction of PLA modernisation through its Science and Technology Committee. The GAD assumed responsibility for the nuclear test site at Lop Nor, Xinjiang; China's various space launch, tracking, telemetry and control (TT&C) and mission control facilities; as well as other test ranges and facilities.

The General Staff Department (GSD). The General Staff Department is the heart of the PLA and driver of its future. GSD develops policies, plans and programs, establishes requirements and allocates resources to support the PLA mission to protect the interests of the CCP. The GSD is responsible for day to day joint operations, intelligence, strategic planning and operational requirements, training and mobilisation. In addition to its role in military diplomacy and security of senior party and state leadership, GSD concurrently functioned as Army headquarters. GSD had increased its role in computer network operations (CNO) and space operations.

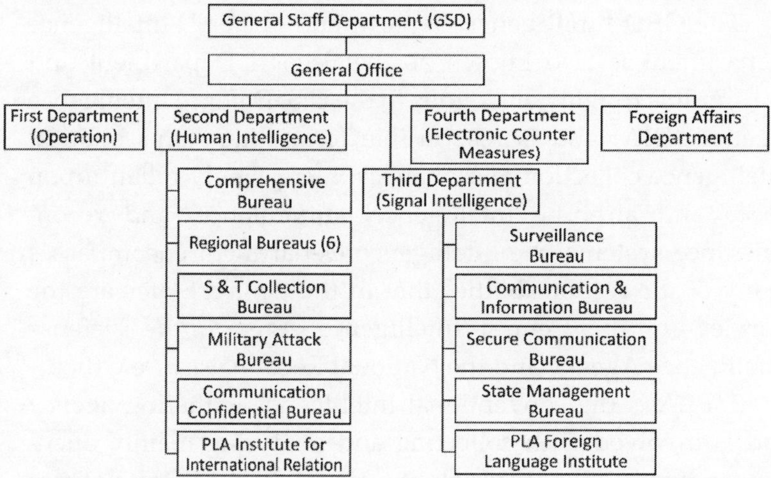

Source: James Mulvenon, "PLA Computer Network Operations: Scenarios, Doctrine, Organizations, and Capability," in Roy Kamphausen, David Lai, and Andrew Scobell, eds., Beyond the Strait: PLA Missions Other than Taiwan (Washington, DC: National Bureau of Research, 2009).

The GSD Operations Department. The GSD Operations Department, also known as the First Department, is responsible for current military operations, including managing the PLA Joint Operations Command Center, airspace surveillance and air traffic control (ATC), border defence and survey and mapping hydrological and meteorological support to current operations. The Operations Department's Political Department is responsible for internal political work. The Comprehensive Bureau is responsible for overall integrated force planning. The GSD Operations Department also develops requirements for and manages joint military use of navigation, geodetic, meteorological and oceanographic space systems. It operates the Beidou satellite navigation ground segment, with the Satellite Navigation Control Center and oversees many survey and mapping units around the country.

The GSD Intelligence Department. The GSD Intelligence Department is also known as the Second Department and 2/PLA. It is roughly analogous to the U.S. Defense Intelligence Agency (DIA) and is responsible for military and political intelligence collection and analysis. Increasingly reliant upon space and airborne intelligence, surveillance, and reconnaissance systems, the Intelligence Department encompasses many of the responsibilities that in the United States are the purview of the Central Intelligence Agency, the Defense Intelligence Agency and the National Reconnaissance Office.

2/PLA is the conventional intelligence gathering agency and is involved with collecting and analysing mainly open-source information through its global network of defence attachés. Defence attachés are all cadre 2/PLA officers. They are selected mainly on the basis of their analytical capabilities and language skills. This global network has focused primarily on collecting and analysing open source information and does not appear to engage in covert collection operations out of legal residencies. It may not be engaged with covert operations. Its non-official cover officers are believed to have had significant success in collecting valuable data about high-grade U.S. and Western weapons systems including the B-1 bomber, the B-2 stealth bomber, the Quiet Electric Drive submarine propulsion system and the W-88 miniaturised nuclear warhead.

The Intelligence Department conducts both overt and covert intelligence collection and intelligence analysis. The GSD Intelligence Department has a role in developing space-based reconnaissance operational requirements and ground receiving stations' operation. The Intelligence Bureau or GSD Intelligence Department First Bureau is responsible for defence-related HUMINT collection, with a particular focus on Taiwan. The Tactical Reconnaissance Bureau is responsible for joint airborne reconnaissance operations and dissemination. The 55th Research Institute, subordinate to the Second Bureau, supports the Intelligence Department to develop operational and technical requirements for intelligence collection systems, particularly unmanned aerial vehicle (UAV) sensors. The Technology Bureau also known as the Space Reconnaissance Bureau and the Seventh Bureau, are responsible for space based intelligence collection and analysis.

The Intelligence Department manages the PLA Institute of International Relations and China International Institute for Strategic Studies (CIISS). It oversees the Peacekeeping Bureau. The GSD Second Department manages China's military attaches.

Each of the military region headquarters (MRHQ) has a subordinate GSD Second Department cell. This military intelligence section provides focused intelligence support to the MRHQ staff supporting potential military operations within their area of responsibility.

Third Department (3/PLA) of the General Staff Department

The 3 PLA or Technical Reconnaissance Department oversees a huge setup for monitoring communications traffic from various sites within China, from embassies and other facilities abroad and space-based assets. The Technical Department also has responsibility for assuring PLA computer systems' security to prevent foreign adversaries from gaining access to sensitive information. 3/PLA's headquarters is in Beijing, where it runs political and logistics departments together with the Science and Technology Intelligence Bureau and the Science and Technology Equipment Bureau. The GSD Third Department is often compared to the National Security Agency (NSA) in the United States.

The 3/PLA is responsible for signals intelligence (SIGINT). Before introduction of the Internet 3/PLA operated as a conventional military signals intelligence agency with various collection platforms within China. Since the early 1990s, a gradually increasing overseas presence consisting of a chain of SIGINT stations were observed:

- Along the coast of Myanmar, including a substantial facility at Great Coco Island in the Andaman Sea targeting Indian naval capabilities.
- In Laos.
- In Cuba, where since 1998 China has operated SIGINT stations in Bejucal and Santiago de Cuba to collect US telecommunications and US military satellite communications.
- Embassy-based SIGINT facilities in Ankara and Baghdad during the First Gulf War and Belgrade during the Kosovo conflict.[28]

The 3/PLA has a variety of air and ship-borne SIGINT collection capabilities. Recently there are reports that 3/PLA has extended its reach through joint operations with selected states. It has been reported that Indonesia has been using Chinese-supplied equipment to monitor Australian telecommunications and sharing the informations with China. It includes undertaking computer network operations, encompassing computer network espionage, computer network attack and computer network defence. It has both a research and an operational side. The former includes a Science and Technology Intelligence Bureau and a Science and Technology Equipment Bureau. The latter controls three research institutes, dedicated to computer science, sensor technology and cryptography.

The 3/PLA has its core competency in signals intelligence (SIGINT), high performance computing and technical encryption capabilities and China's largest employer of well-trained linguists. It appears to be diversifying from its traditional SIGINT mission to CNE. The GSD Third Department directly commands 12 operational bureaus. These 12 operational bureaus play the most crucial role in 3/PLA's structure. Each of the bureaus usually carries out a specific task like intercepting radio or satellite communications, conducting cryptology, translation, or intelligence analysis on diplomatic communications, foreign militaries, economic entities, educational institutions, and individuals considered worthy of surveillance.

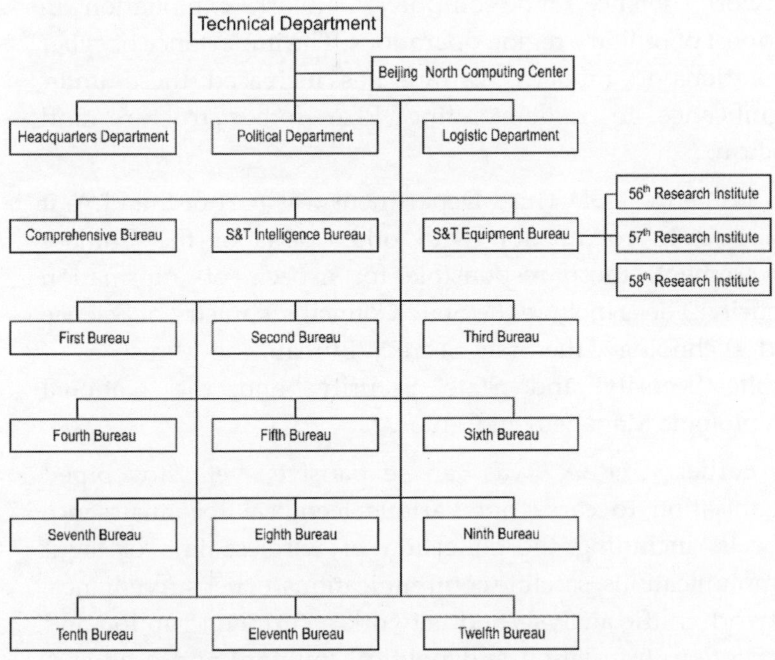

Organisation Tree of the Technical Department

In addition to its traditional SIGINT mission, the Third Department is the national authority for CND and CNE. It seems that there is no Third Department bureau dedicated to the CNE mission. Eight of these bureau headquarters are in Beijing. Shanghai has two other bases. Balance two are in Qingdao and Wuhan. The operational bureaus are distinctly separate from technical reconnaissance bureaus (TRBs) under the PLA's seven Military Regions (MR), PLAN, PLAAF and PLARF. TRB directors report to MR, PLAN, PLAAF, and PLARF Chiefs of Staff. However, the Technical Department provides TRBs with policy guidance and tasking for collection and analysis.

The TRBs conduct communications intelligence, direction finding, traffic analysis, translation, cryptology, computer network defence and computer network exploitation in support of military region operations. The importance of cyber operations in modern warfare has increased these units' significance in understanding PLA force structure and doctrine.

While the GSD Third Department was part of the PLA, it operated in conjunction with other parts of the Chinese government, those responsible for aspects of information security. These include the State Council's Ministry of Science and Technology, the State Secrecy Bureau, the Ministries of Public Security and State Security, and the National Cryptologic Management Center.

Earlier 3/PLA was an expansive yet stovepiped organisation to carry out various technical reconnaissance aspects, including the collection of wireless line of sight communications, satellite communications, cyber surveillance, network traffic analysis and network security encryption and decryption, translation and political, military and economic analysis. It targets military activity, foreign diplomatic communications, financial entities, public education institutions and individuals of interest. This amalgamation of civilian and military efforts in computer network operations leads to the three broad categories of Chinese computer network warfare forces. These are:

- Specialised network warfare forces that implement network offensive and defensive operations. These are primarily PLA Units. These units are assigned a military unit cover designator (MUCD) Number.
- Specialist nonmilitary units as authorised forces comprising non-uniformed operators drawn from local capabilities from within a military region or war zone including the Ministry of State Security (MSS), the Ministry of Public Security (MPS) and other relevant government departments.
- Civilian forces, including cyber militia/auxiliary forces who conduct network operations. They are embedded within civilian institutions like universities and telecommunications companies.

Military Unit Cover Designators

Often media reports, for example, say, Unit 61398 targets the US and Canada to obtain political, economic and military intelligence. These five-digit numbers are known as "military unit cover designators" (MUCDs). These are used in place of unit names like the Fifth battalion of 11 Gorkha Rifles. The MUCD is used for referring to specific units in public discussions while obscuring the identity. It is not clear whether the major reorganisation of the PLA will change the MUCD system.

Endnotes

1. People's Liberation Army Strategic Support Force – A Comprehensive Look, Air Power Asia available at: https://airpowerasia.com / 2021 / 03 / 08 / peoples-liberation-army-strategic-support-force-a-comprehensive-look/

2. China's National Defense in the New Era, The State Council Information Office of the People's Republic of China, July 2019 available at: https://www.andrewerickson.com/2019/07/full-text - of - defense – white – paper - chinas-national-defense-in-the-new-era-english-chinese-versions/
3. People's Liberation Army Strategic Support Force – A Comprehensive Look, Air Power Asia available at: https://airpowerasia.com / 2021 / 03 / 08 / peoples-liberation-army-strategic-support-force-a-comprehensive-look/
4. Office of the Secretary of Defense, Annual Report to Congress: Military and Security Developments Involving the People's Republic of China, China Military Power, 2019, May 2019, pp. 63-64
5. John Costello and Joe McReynolds, China's Strategic Support Force: A Force for a New Era, National Defense University Press, 2018
6. Academy of Military Science Operational Theory and Regulations Research Department Information Operations Theory Laboratory, *Information Operations Theory Study Guide: 400 Questions on Information Operations,* Beijing: Military Science Press, 2005, 97
7. Academy of Military Science, Chinese People's Liberation Army Military Terminology, Beijing: Military Science Press, 2011, 286.
8. Academy of Military Science Information Operations Theory Laboratory, Information Operations Theory Study Guide, 97.
9. Yossef Bodansky, The Real Culprit – The PLA's Strategic Support Force, Institute for Strategic, Political, Security and Economic Consultancy, February 2020 available at: https://css.ethz.ch/content / dam / ethz / special-interest / gess / cis / center – for - securities-studies/resources/docs/ ISPSW_669_Bodansky.pdf
10. Rachael Burton and Mark Stokes, The People's Liberation Army Strategic Support Force: Leadership and Structure, Project 2049 Institute, September 25, 2018 available at: https://project2049.net / wp-content / uploads / 2018 / 09 / 180925_PLA_SSF_Leadership-and-Structure_Stokes_Burton.pdf
11. John Costello and Joe McReynolds, China's Strategic Support Force: A Force for a New Era, National Defense University Press, 2018
12. Office of the Secretary Of Defense, Annual Report to Congress: Military and Security Developments Involving the People's

Republic of China, China Military Power, 2019, May 2019, pp. 48-49

13. John Costello and Joe McReynolds, China's Strategic Support Force: A Force for a New Era, National Defense University Press, 2018
14. China Net, December 19, 2014; China Military Online, May 16, 2017
15. Ministry of Education, May 12, 2018; Sichuan Education News, April 1, 2017, Student Examination Network, December 30, 2016
16. Beijing Guotai Jianzhong Management and Consulting ; October 31, 2016; PLA Daily, June 13, 2016
17. The People's Liberation Army Strategic Support Force: Update 2019, By Adam Ni and Bates Gill, ChinaBrief, Volume 19, Issue 10, May 29, 2019 available at: https://jamestown.org/wp-content/uploads/2019/05/Read-the-05-29-2019-CB-Issue-in-PDF2.pdf?x55109
18. Yossef Bodansky, The Real Culprit – The PLA's Strategic Support Force, Institute for Strategic, Political, Security and Economic Consultancy, February 2020 available at: https://www.ispsw.com/wp-content/uploads/2020/02/669_Bodansky-1.pdf
19. People's Liberation Army Strategic Support Force – A Comprehensive Look, Air Power Asia available at: https://airpowerasia.com / 2021 / 03 / 08 / peoples-liberation-army-strategic-support-force-a-comprehensive-look/
20. John Costello and Joe McReynolds, China's Strategic Support Force: A Force for a New Era, National Defense University Press, available at: https://inss.ndu.edu / Portals / 68 / Documents / stratperspective/china/china-perspectives_13.pdf
21. Elsa B. Kania, John K. Costello, The Strategic Support Force and the Future of Chinese Information Operations, The Cyber Defense Review, Spring 2018
22. John Costello and Joe McReynolds, China's Strategic Support Force: A Force for a New Era, Center for the Study of Chinese Military Affairs Institute for National Strategic Studies National Defense University, October 2018 available at: https://ndupress.ndu.edu/Portals/68/Documents/stratperspective/china/china-perspectives_13.pdf

23. The GPD Liaison Department merges with the Central Liaison Department, Epoch Times, December 26, 2016.

24. Office of the Secretary of Defense, Annual Report to Congress: Military and Security Developments Involving the People's Republic of China, China Military Power, 2019, May 2019, pp. 48-49.

25. Components, U.S. Strategic Command, 2017 available at: http://www.stratcom.mil/components/

26. The PLA's New Organizational Structure: What is Known, Unknown and Speculation (Part 1), China Brief Volume: 16 Issue: 3, Jamestown Foundation, 4 February 2016 available at: https://www.refworld.org/docid/56baf0bb4.html

27. Military and Security Developments Involving the People's Republic of China 2020, Annual Report to Congress, Office of the Secretary of Defense available at: https://media.defense.gov/2020/sep/01/2002488689/-1/-1/1/2020-dod-china-military-power-report-final.pdf

28. Bradley Martin, China for Real: Embassy Bombing 'Part of Espionage War,' Asia Times Online, July 23, 1999

* * *

CHAPTER 5

Signals Intelligence, Computer Network Defence and Electronic Counter-Measures Organisations

PLA's SIGINT Mission

Traditionally the Third Department (3 PLA) of the General Staff Department (GSD) has the core competency in signals intelligence (SIGINT), advanced high-performance computing and encryption/decryption technical capabilities. It is China's largest employer of well-trained linguists. Like its American equivalent, the National Security Agency (NSA), 3 PLA manages one of the world's largest intelligence collection and information security infrastructures. 3 PLA was also responsible for the security of PLA computer systems to prevent foreign opponents from gaining access to sensitive national security related information.

The SIGINT consists of communications intelligence (COMINT) and electronic intelligence (ELINT). ELINT involves the collection, analysis and storing of radar emissions. The Third Department is responsible for COMINT, while the GSD Fourth Department has the ELINT portfolio.[1]

The 3 PLA is expanding its traditional SIGINT mission. Computer Network Exploitation (CNE) represents the cutting edge of SIGINT. It seems that 3 PLA is the national executive agent for CNE. Operational 3 PLA entities play a prominent role within a broader Computer Network Operations (CNO) network, with the Technical Reconnaissance Bureaus (TRB) under Military Regions (MR). While unclear, entities engaged in CNO likely are fragmented and stove-piped. The most important entities that are dedicated to the technical aspects of CNO include 3 PLA's First Bureau, the Ninth Bureau, the Beijing North Computing Center and the GSD 58th Research Institute. It is unclear which organisation within the PLA has responsibility for Computer Network Attack (CNA). It is believed that the GSD Electronic Counter-measures (ECM) and Radar Department (also known as the GSD Fourth Department), which traditionally has been responsible for radar-related planning and ECM operations are responsible for this task.

This chapter examines 3 PLA's command structure and its subordinate research institutes. An overview of 3 PLA's 12 operational bureaus has been taken. The technical reconnaissance resources under each of the PLA's seven MR, Navy, Air Force, and PLA Rocket Force are discussed.

The 3 PLA

The Network Systems Department of the Strategic Support Force (SSF) has been handed over the Third Department or 3 PLA's mission set, headquarters location and much of its organisational structure. The previous 3 PLA SIGINT bureaus are organised primarily according to geographical location, with the lion's share of departments focused on targets in the United States, East Asia and Europe. The GSD 3 PLA has command over 12 operational bureaus. Eight of the 12 bureau headquarters are located in and around Beijing. Two bureau headquarters are based in Shanghai, one in Qingdao and one in Wuhan. The 12 operational bureaus report to the

Headquarters Department. Political commissars and Bureau-level directors have grades equivalent to that of an army Division commander and oversee 6 to 14 subordinate sites or offices.[2]

The 3 PLA, headquartered in the northwestern hills of Beijing's Haidian District, manages a large SIGINT and cyber reconnaissance system targeting foreign diplomatic communications, military activity, economic entities, public education institutions and individuals of interest. The 3 PLA bureaus have definite tasks like radio or satellite communications intercept, translation, cryptology, information assurance and intelligence analysis. Intercept stations located around China's fringes can monitor radio traffic and pinpoint emitters' location through radio direction finding. Leadership, staff, technical personnel and linguists in 3 PLA are distributed in general headquarters staff positions, 12 operational bureaus, a computing centre and three research institutes. The 3 PLA bureau, office, and section facilities and sites, located throughout China, report directly to Beijing and are not under the administrative jurisdiction of military region commanders or political commissars.

Collecting foreign intelligence through cyber espionage has been thoroughly institutionalised and prioritised for 3 PLA. However, 3 PLA's operations are often in parallel with those of the Military Region TRB, which operate under seven MR and are independent of 3 PLA. Like 3 PLA, the TRBs' responsibilities include CNE and cryptology and COMINT. Located next to the military region HQs, the TRBs intercept communications in areas related to their interests, such as the Air Force or the Navy. TRBs are now integrated with the SSF. Regional bureaus are responsible for translation, analysis and reporting of unprocessed communications intercepts collected by the Third and 12th Bureaus and information gathered through CNE assets. Whether the regional bureaus have authority to task collection is unknown.

The militia is the third component of China's armed forces along with the PLA and People's Armed Police. It is not clear about the degree of control that operational bureaus and TRBs exercise over militia and reserve assets in military districts.

Beijing North Computing Centre

The 3 PLA Beijing North Computing Center (BNCC) is responsible for cyber reconnaissance architecture design, technology development, systems engineering and acquisition. Minimum ten subordinate divisions are responsible for designing and developing CNA, defence, and exploitation systems. BNCC is one of China's path-breaking organisations working on high-performance computing. BNCC, is also referred to as the GSD 418th Research Institute. It has a military cover designation of the 61539 Unit. BNCC is also known as the Beijing North Commercial College.

China's leading cybersecurity experts have felt the need for active defence involving intrusions of and attacks against enemy systems. BNCC plays a leading role in command-and-control network management, advanced malware development, code breaking, data storage and vulnerability assessment. BNCC personnel have practical experience in network intrusion monitoring and control, CNA and defence and information collection. BNCC software source code has been given to enterprises for commercialisation. BNCC developed one of China's first stealthy remote access tools (RATs). BNCC introduced China's most advanced network Intrusion Detection System (IDS) for analysing threats and assessing vulnerabilities, including those of operating systems such as Android. Super-computing power is needed to crack advanced encryption systems. Its advanced computing networks servers appear sufficient to handle vast databases containing electronic communications and files, radio chatter including recorded phone calls, private e-mails, passwords, Internet search records, password-protected computer files and a vast amount of personal data.

BNCC maintains a close relationship with China's broader CNO community. BNCC engineers have served as advisors in the Information Security Working Group. BNCC divisions depend on at least a dozen cybersecurity companies for day-to-day work. BNCC-affiliated companies also support information security engineering bases in Beijing, Shanghai, and Tianjin.

Training and Education

Training and education for 3 PLA personnel are normally conducted at the two institutions. Most linguists assigned to 3 PLA bureaus and TRBs receive language education at the PLA University of Foreign Languages in Luoyang. After graduation, they are assigned to a bureau for mission-specific technical training.

Technical training for computer scientists, electrical engineers, communications specialists and network security personnel is carried out at the PLA Information Engineering University in Zhengzhou, Henan Province. Here, personnel security requirements are more strict than in other parts of the PLA.

The SIGINT Operational Bureaus

The Third Department has direct authority over 12 operational bureaus. Eight of the 12 bureau headquarters are bunched up in Beijing. The other two are based in Shanghai, one in Qingdao and one in Wuhan. The department's 12 operational bureaus report to the Headquarters Department. These operational bureaus are separate and distinct from TRBs under the PLA's seven MR and the three services: Air Force, Navy, and PLARF. TRB directors report to the military region and armed services chiefs of staff. However, 3 PLA is likely to provide TRBs with policy guidance and tasking for intelligence collection and analysis.

A major part of the 3 PLA collection and analytical resources are devoted to the former Soviet Union. Three bureaus out of 12 have Russia-related tasks. These are the Fifth 10th and 11th Bureaus based in different parts of Beijing. The Fifth Bureau has a translation, analysis, and reporting mission while the 10th and 11th Bureaus have operational missions. The 10th Bureau monitors Russian and Ukrainian missile tests and space launches. The task of the 3 PLA 11th Bureau, the 2020 Unit, remains a mystery.

Bureau-level directors and political commissars have grades comparable to that of a division leader. They supervise between 6 and 14 subordinate sites or offices. The Office directors have a grade equivalent to a deputy division and regiment leader. Sites/offices under bureaus are divided into sections, though some sections report directly to bureau headquarters. 3 PLA manages a Hong Kong and Macao Liaison Bureau in Shenzhen, in addition to a liaison office in Shanghai. Each of the bureaus carries out a specific task like intercepting radio or satellite communications, conducting cryptology, translation or intelligence analysis on diplomatic communications, foreign militaries, economic entities, educational institutions and individuals considered worthy of surveillance.[3]

Roles and organisational structures of operational bureaus are explained below.

The First Bureau (Unit 61786)

The bureau is responsible for maintaining information security within the former 3/PLA and handling cryptography. The headquarters is co-located with the Third Department command complex in northwestern Beijing. It manages at least 12 offices operating in various parts of China. The bureau's mission includes decryption, encryption and other information security tasks. The First Bureau is the only military representative on the National 863 Program Information Assurance Expert Working Group. The First Bureau keeps a close, mutually supportive relationship with related organisations like the Information Security and Network Attack and Defense Laboratory of Sichuan University. The First Bureau is responsible for encrypting communications intercepts to be transmitted via dedicated and secure security of internal 3 PLA networks. It may be responsible for decoding intercepted communications.

The Second Bureau (Unit 61389)[4]

Known as APT-1, the Second Bureau collects data on military targets and carries out industrial espionage activity. This unit targets the U.S. and Canada to obtain political, economic and military intelligence. It is responsible for translating information obtained from communications intercepts and cyber-surveillance and creating intelligence reports based on translated materials. It is based in Shanghai.

The bureau came into the limelight in 2013 when the cybersecurity firm Mandiant published its activities against the United States. APT-1 had obtained hundreds of terabytes of data from at least 141 organisations over 20 industries by the

PROBABLE THIRD DEPARTMENT SECOND BUREAU SATELLITE GROUND STATION
SHANGHAI BAOSHAN DISTRICT

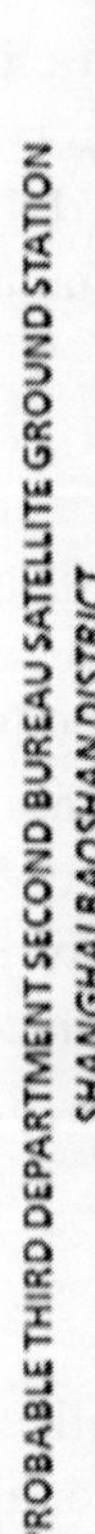

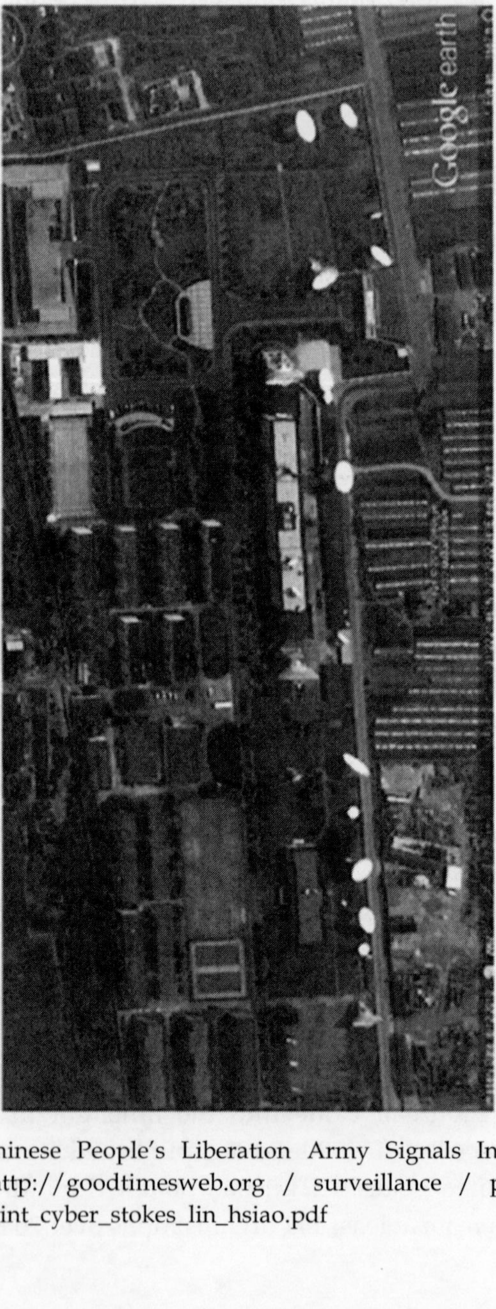

Source: The Chinese People's Liberation Army Signals Intelligence available at: http://goodtimesweb.org / surveillance / pla_third_department_sigint_cyber_stokes_lin_hsiao.pdf

time of the report's publication. According to the size of its physical infrastructure, APT-1 is staffed by thousands of people, all required to be competent in CNO and English. Mandiant reports that 87 percent of APT-1's victims are in English-speaking countries and belong to industries that, China feels, have strategic importance to its national growth.

GSD 3 PLA Second Bureau Organizational Breakdown is given below:

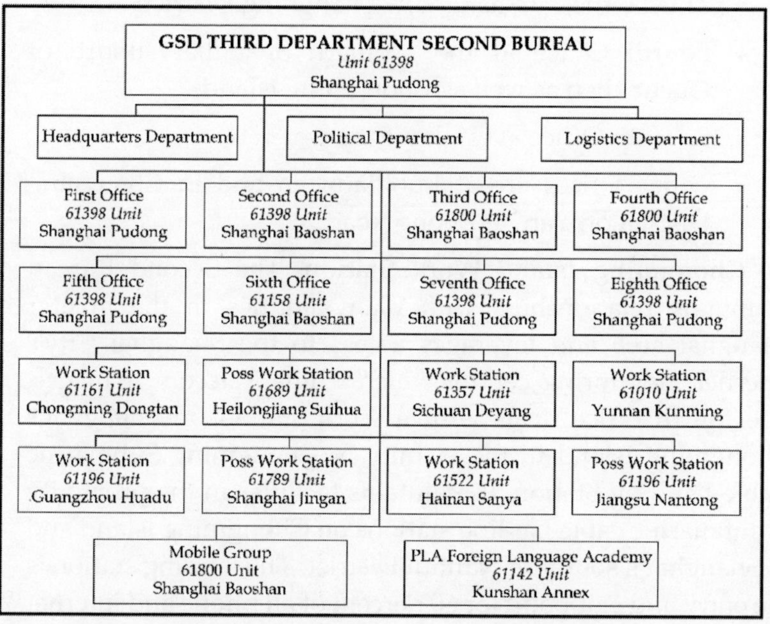

Source: Mark A. Stokes, *The PLA General Staff Department Third Department Second Bureau: An Organizational Overview of Unit 61398,* Project 2049 Institute, July 27, 2015.

The Second Bureau managed the establishment of 3 PLA's information security engineering base in Shanghai. Based on the number of technical studies produced jointly by members from both organisations, it seems that the Second Bureau enjoys a cooperative working relationship with Shanghai

Jiao Tong University's School of Information Security Engineering. The Second Bureau command is located in Shanghai's northeastern Gaoqiao district. The First Division is co-located with Second Bureau headquarters and appears responsible for analysis. Lower offices are concentrated in Shanghai, although one may be in Kunming. The bureau's offices are located as under:

- Second Office at Dachangzhen.
- Third Office at Shanghai's Changning District.
- Fourth Office at the northern Shanghai suburb of Gucunzhen as well as Chongming Island.
- Seventh Office at Gaohangzhen.
- Other offices are at Luodianzhen and in Changning District on Yan'an Zhong Road.

Chongming Island Work Station. The Second Bureau maintains relationships with many entities in the greater Shanghai area and leverages access to the Shanghai City's Internet monitoring centre, which China Telecom manages. The fourth office deals with a work station on Shanghai's Chongming Island in the vicinity of Chongming Submarine Cable Landing Station. It maintains facilities in the proximity of submarine cable landing stations on Chongming Island and in Shanghai's southern Nanhui District. The landing station is the entry and exit point for 60 percent of all phone and internet traffic entering and leaving China. It has fibre optic connectivity with China Telecom's internet monitoring centre known as the Shanghai 005 Center. The centre is located in the China Telecom Information Park in Pudong. The centre functions as a gateway for submarine cable landing stations.

The Chongming facility is subordinate to the 61161 Unit (possibly the Second Bureau's Third Office). As an additional informations, a GSD Fourth Department brigade (61251 Unit) supervises an element in the Nichangzhen area and possibly on Chongming Island. In 2007, the Second Bureau funded a 150-kilometre fibre-optic network linking Chongming Island with other locations in Shanghai.

The Second Bureau's technical reconnaissance network expands much beyond Shanghai. The distributed network includes at least three circularly disposed antenna array (CDAA) systems positioned in north, south and southwest China. They provide a network controller in Shanghai with real-time geolocation and intercept of regional high frequency (HF) transmissions.

National (Shanghai) Information Security Engineering Technology Centre. The Second Bureau has a role in establishing the National Information Security Engineering Technology Center (NISEC). The Third Department manages the centre in support of the National Crypto Management Center, State Council's Ministry of Science and Technology, State Secrecy Bureau, Ministry of Public Security and Ministry of State Security.

The Third Bureau (61785 Unit)

The Third Bureau is responsible for intercepting radio communications from areas in China's periphery, including North and South Korea, Taiwan and Central Asia. The headquarters is in the southern Beijing suburb of Daxing. Third Bureau's tasks are front end collection of the line of sight radio communications, including border control networks, direction finding, emission control and security. The bureau has at least 13 subordinate offices located in Beijing, Harbin, Dalian, Hangzhou, Ningdu County (Jiangxi), Xiamen, Kunming, Shenzhen, Xian and Ürümqi. Dalian (61120 Unit) is the Third Bureau's First Office. Formerly designated the 57346 Unit, the Sixth Office (61542 Unit; 121 Institute) is located in Xian and functions as a networking centre.

The Kunming office of the Third Bureau has been involved in counter-drug operations. The Fifth Office of the Third Bureau in Beijing's southern Daxing District is responsible for PLA emission security like electromagnetic shielding (TEMPEST). The Shenzhen office is responsible for coverage of Hong Kong/Macao wireless networks. Members of the Third Bureau's Third Division have conducted studies on cyber warfare, including analysis of weaknesses in Android operating systems and NTLM (Windows NT Local Area Network Manager) authentication protocols. Members also have carried out joint studies with Shanghai Jiao Tong University's Department of Computer Science and Engineering.

The Fourth Bureau (61419 Unit)

It is responsible for collecting signals intelligence on Korean and Japanese targets. Its headquarters is in Qingdao.

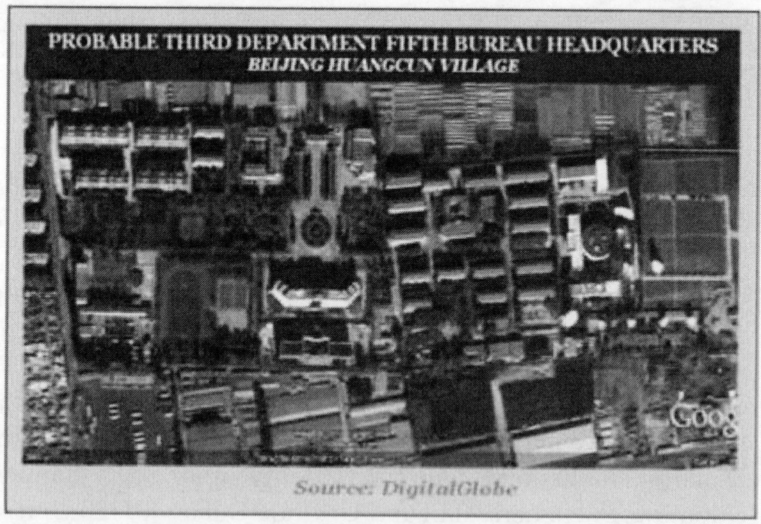

Source: The Chinese People's Liberation Army Signals Intelligence available at: http://goodtimesweb.org / surveillance / pla_third_department_sigint_cyber_stokes_lin_hsiao.pdf

The bureau was formerly based in the Shanxi provincial city of Xinzhou, specifically Huanglong Wanggou village. While its headquarters moved to Qingdao, the Fourth Bureau may still maintain its training base in Xinzhou. Fourth Bureau offices are located at Qingdao, Hangzhou, Jimo City, Wenlongzhen, Xinzhou, Dalian, Beijing, and Shanghai. The Second Office incorporates Korean linguists.

The Fifth Bureau (61565 Unit)

It is responsible for collecting signals intelligence on Russian targets. Its headquarters is in Beijing's Daxing District Huangcun Village. A large number of parabolic dish antennas can be seen at the eastern end of the compound. Fifth Bureau offices are located in Xinjiang, Heilongjiang's Suihua City and Jiuquan.

The Sixth Bureau (61726 Unit)

This Bureau is responsible for surveillance targets in South and Southeast Asia and Taiwan. Its headquarters is in Wuhan's Wuchang District. Sixth Bureau offices stretch across central China from the eastern coastal city of Xiamen to the Yunnan city of Kunming, indicating a Taiwan and South Asia mission. Its offices are located in Xiamen, Kunming's Panlong District (Fourth Office), Xiangfan, Ningdu County's Xiaobu Village, Wuhan, Jingmen and Nanchang (Seventh Office). The Nanchang office has a training mission.

Jingmen Zone B has been associated with Sixth Bureau Second Office and is possibly located in Luoji Village, southeast of Jingmen. Reference to a 3 PLA affiliated Jingmen Zone A has also been noted. The Sixth Bureau also had a presence in the village of Ziling, possibly the Sixth Office.

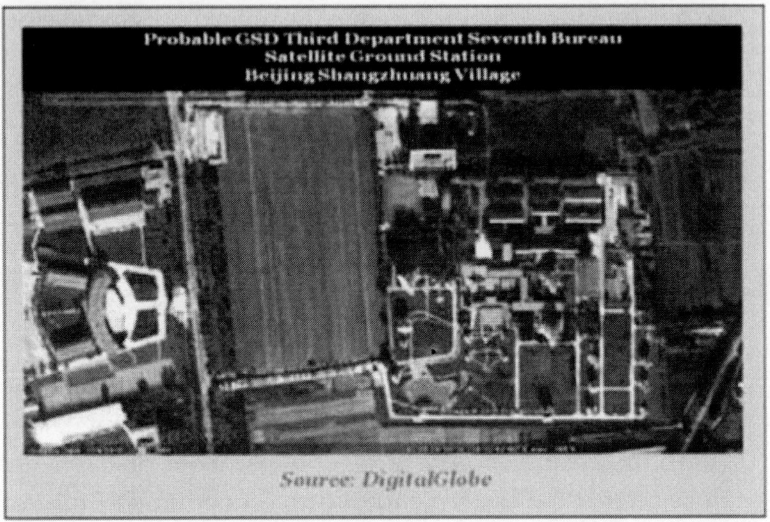

Source: The Chinese People's Liberation Army Signals Intelligence available at: http://goodtimesweb.org/surveillance/pla_third_department_sigint_cyber_stokes_lin_hsiao.pdf

The Seventh Bureau (61580 Unit)

The exact mission of the Seventh Bureau's mission is unclear. Selected bureau engineers specialise in computer network defence and attack and have conducted joint studies with the PLA Information Engineering Academy Computer Network Attack and Defense section. It provides a supporting role to the rest of the former 3/PLA. Its Headquarter is in Shucun area of Beijing's northwest Haidian District. It has wide network attack and defence capabilities and other means for network-centric warfare. Seventh Bureau has been linked with technical aspects of cyber operations. The Seventh Bureau employs English translators. It has at least ten offices. The bureau oversees a satellite ground station in the northwest Beijing suburb of Shangzhuang and manages one element at least in Ürümqi area.

One Seventh Bureau study examined support vector machine (SVM) applications for detecting intrusion patterns. Two senior engineers outlined network-centric warfare, while another published an assessment of the future of the Internet and dense wavelength division multiplexing. Another study focused on psychological and technical aspects of reading and interpreting written foreign language. Another addressed legal aspects of the global economy. These studies indicate the focus of the Seventh Bureau.

The Eighth Bureau (61046 Unit)

The Eighth Bureau focuses on Western and Eastern Europe and perhaps the rest of the world like the Middle East, Africa and Latin America. Its headquarters is at Beijing‘s northwest suburbs in Hanjiachuan, adjacent to 3 PLA headquarters. It has ten offices, with one central office located in the Hainan Island city of Haikou. The Seventh Office is located in Hubei Province's Xiangfan City. Satellite receiving station of the Eighth Bureau is in the northwestern Beijing suburb of Xibeiwang. It seems to have a presence in Wenquanzhen in far northwest Beijing.

The Ninth Bureau (61221 Unit)

It is the Third Department‘s primary strategic intelligence analysis and database management and audiovisual technology entity. It focuses on the absorption and analysis of strategic intelligence. The Ninth is the most opaque among all the bureaus. Headquartered near the Summer Palace in Beijing, the Ninth Bureau has at least one office responsible for computing equipment.

The Tenth Bureau (61886 Unit)

The Tenth Bureau (61886 Unit), sometimes referred to as the ‘7911 Unit’, focuses on surveillance of Russian based missile sites. Its headquarter is in Beijing's northwest suburb of Shangdi on Xinxi Road. It has a Central Asia or Russia-related mission, focused specifically on telemetry and missile tracking and nuclear testing. The 10th Bureau First Office is collocated with the 10th Bureau headquarters. The Second Office is located in Xinjiang's Yining City, near the Kazakhstan border. The Third Office is based in Kashgar's Baren Village and 10th Bureau Office is in Ürümqi.

The Eleventh Bureau (61672 Unit)

It is also known as the 2020 Unit. The exact nature of this bureau's mission is not clear. Its headquarters is in Beijing, east of the 3 PLA headquarters compound. The offices are distributed throughout northern China. Assignment of Russian linguists suggests that it focuses on Russian targets. Since Russian linguists are assigned to both the 11th and Fifth Bureau entities, differences between the two missions are unknown.

Source: The Chinese People's Liberation Army Signals Intelligence available at: http://goodtimesweb.org / surveillance / pla_third_department_sigint_cyber_stokes_lin_hsiao.pdf)

The Twelfth Bureau (61486 Unit)

It is responsible for intercepting satellite communications and collecting space-based SIGINT and support China's space surveillance network. Its assets are dedicated to intercepting foreign satellite communications from sites around China's periphery. The 12th Bureau also operates specialised equipment onboard satellites capable of intercepting communications worldwide from Chinese space-based systems.

According to the CrowdStrike report, the Bureau, also called 'Putter Panda', has been active since 2007, targeting the aerospace industries in U.S. and Europe through attacks on the government, defence, research and technology sectors. The group's methodology relies on deploying malware through targeted e-mails in the form of spear phishing. This shows that China can use cyber espionage at two strategic levels - illegally obtained intellectual property allows it to speed up its space-related developments and it also enables exploitation of an opponent's satellite weaknesses during an actual conflict.[5] The report concluded the Second Bureau shared cyber-related resources with the 12th Bureau.

The headquarters of 12th Bureau is located in Shanghai's Zhabei District. Subordinate offices and sites are in the Shanghai area and in southeast, northeast, southwest and northwestern China. The Third Office is located in Shanghai's Baoshan District and has sponsored research into extracting synthetic aperture radar (SAR) satellite images. The bureau's southeast station is located in Fuzhou's Gangtouzhen. Other 12th Bureau offices are located in Taicang, just outside Shanghai, and Hangzhou's Daxiaogu Village. Its southwest site is located outside Kunming in Songming County's Yuejia Village. The 12th Bureau's northeast station is located in Changchun's Xinglongshan Village. A southern site is positioned within Guangzhou Huadu District. Sites in Northwestern direction are located in Gansu and Xinjiang.

Science and Technology (S&T) Equipment Bureau

The 3 PLA S&T Equipment Bureau has administrative oversight of three research institutes responsible for computing, sensor technology and cryptography located in Shanghai, Beijing and Tianjin.

The National Information Security Engineering Technology Center (NISEC) within 3 PLA was established in Shanghai in 2001. Experts from here sit on the 863 Program Information Security Expert Working Group (863-917 Program), which financed establishment of the Great Firewall of China security system and the two information security standardization committees (WG-3 and WG-7).

The National Research Center for Information Security Technology, established in 2005, serves as the national authority on risk assessment for China's network security. This has been referred to as the PLA Information Security Center.[6] Also referred to as the Information Security Research Institute or National Information Center, the organisation maintains a close affiliation with 3 PLA S&T Equipment Bureau.

Central authorities approved the creation of a third information technology security base in Tianjin in 2009. It specialises in cryptographic keying material, systems integration and CNA technology. Collocated with these engineering centres are National Information Security Industrial Bases, with additional industrial bases located in Wuhan and Chengdu.

The Third Department supports the State Council's Ministry of Science and Technology, State Secrecy Bureau, National Crypto Management Center, Ministry of Public Security and Ministry of State Security. It coordinates with

Shanghai-based equipment and technology suppliers and may work as a material supply depot for the East China region. The headquarters is in Shanghai. The S&T Equipment Bureau supervises three research institutes responsible for computing, sensor technology and cryptography. These are:

- **56th Research Institute.** The institute is based in the Chengdu area and is also known as the Southwest Institute of Electronics and Telecommunications Technology. The PLA possesses some of the fastest supercomputers in the world. It is the PLA's oldest and largest computing R&D organisation. Situated in Wuxi in Jiangsu Province, the institute has invested heavily in high-performance computing. It supports the 3 PLA and other national-level computer centres. Super-computing allows the making and breaking of sophisticated codes and passwords. The director of the 56th Institute is a member of the 863 Program Expert Working Group on Computing and Software.
- **57th Research Institute.** The 57th Research Institute is responsible for developing communications intercept and signal processing systems. The institute is located in Chengdu. Its institute's primary focus is satellite communications technology. It has been found working with the China Academy of Space Technology on satellite R&D. It has subordinate offices in Guangdong and Chengdu. The 57th Research Institute may also host a Signal Processing Key Defense Laboratory.
- **58th Research Institute.** The 58th Research Institute's focus is on cryptology and information security technology. It is located in Mianyang (Sichuan Province). It has a close relationship with 3 PLA First Bureau and Nanjing University of Science and Technology.

Technical Reconnaissance Bureaus of MR and Services/Branches

The Third Department's 12 operational bureaus are separate and distinct from TRBs under the seven military region headquarters in Beijing, Chengdu, Guangzhou, Jinan, Lanzhou, Nanjing, and Shenyang. Each of China's military regions and the PLAAF, PLAN and SSF has assigned to its headquarters department at least one technical reconnaissance bureau that monitors foreign communications and cyber activity.

Each MR Headquarters Chief of Staff exercises authority over at least one TRB. However, senior 3 PLA authorities in Beijing issue policy guidance and general tasking for TRB collection, analysis and reporting. TRB missions may be comparable to those of 3 PLA and include computer network defence, CNE, COMINT, cryptology direction finding, translation and traffic analysis. Nevertheless, their primary job is to support the MR command; they also support border security forces.

The amount of control that the GSD 3 PLA and subordinate bureaus exercise over the TRB of the seven MRs, Air Force, Navy, SSF and Military Districts is not clear. If monitoring of the cyber space and intrusion of foreign computer networks is an extension of SIGINT, then it is highly likely that the 3 PLA would prefer to operate surreptitiously. Doing the same thing by two different agencies may alert adversary defenders of communications and computer networks vulnerabilities.

Beijing MR (66407 Unit). The headquarter of Beijing MR TRB is located in Beijing's Xiangshan Mountain area. It has Russian linguists assigned. Subordinate offices are based along the border in Inner Mongolia. One office is at the Hohhot township of Qiaobaozhen, with another in the Hailar area. The Eighth Office is located in Neimeng Linhe.

Chengdu MR (78006 Unit). The Chengdu MR has two TRBs. The headquarters of Chengdu MR First TRB is in Chengdu. Chengdu MR First TRB is involved in CNE operations. The Chengdu MR Second TRB (78020 Unit) is based in the northern suburbs of Kunming with lower offices in Baoshan, Malipo and other border cities.

Guangzhou MR (75770 Unit). The headquarters of Guangzhou MR TRB is in the Guangzhou suburbs and oversees at least eight offices operating in southern China. Its offices are located in Guangzhou's Huadu District, Guangzhou's Baiyun District, Shantou's Nan'Ao County, Shenzhen and west of Sanya on Hainan Island. It is suspected to carry out network-related work, including possible surveillance of voice over internet protocol (VOIP) and internet viruses.

Jinan MR (72959 Unit). The headquarter of Jinan MR TRB is located in Jinan City. It supervises 670 technical specialists, including an element dedicated toward microwave relay intercept. It controls eight offices staffed by Korean, Japanese, English, and other language specialists.

Lanzhou MR (68002 Unit). The Lanzhou MR oversees two TRBs. The headquarters of Lanzhou MR First TRB is located in the southern Lanzhou City's Qilihe District. No subordinate offices of the Lanzhou MR First TRB could be recognised unlike other MRs. The Lanzhou MR's Second TRB (69010 Unit) has an important role in China's SIGINT community. The headquarters of Lanzhou MR Second TRB is in Ürümqi's Shuimogou. Its subordinate offices are located in Kashi's Shule County, Altay and Yining. It monitors military activities along China's borders with India, Pakistani, Afghanistan, Tajikistan, Kyrgyzstan, Kazakhstan, Russia, and Mongolia.

Nanjing MR (73610 Unit). The Nanjing MR Headquarters Department supervises two TRBs that concentrate on military and other communications and computer networks of Taiwan and U.S. activity in the Western Pacific area of operations. The headquarters of Nanjing MR First TRB is located in Nanjing City. Its offices are located at Nanjing's Zhuzhuang suburbs, Shanghai's Songjiang District's Dongshi Village, Zhoushan Island, Shanghai's Minhang District and Hangzhou's Jianggan District. Nanjing MR's Second TRB headquarters is in an underground bunker complex in Fuzhou City's Zhenbancun. It concentrates exclusively on Taiwan. The First, Second, Fourth and Sixth Office are found in Fuzhou's Hongshan village, in a bunker complex in an area on Dafu Mountain. The Third Office is located near the bureau headquarters on Feifeng Mountain in the Fuzhou community of Jianxin Village. The Fifth Office conducts political, military and economic translation work, including from English to Chinese. The Seventh Office, situated on Gushan in Fuzhou's eastern Jin'an District, is responsible for the collection of front-end signals. With the same task, the Eighth Office is located along the Chinese mainland coast opposite Taipei on Dongjing Mountain in Donghanzhen.

Shenyang Military Region (65016 Unit). The headquarters of Shenyang MR TRB is located in Shenyang's Dongling District. It focuses on Russian, Korean and Japanese targets. Its subordinate offices are located in Harbin, Dalian, Jiamusi, Heilongjiang's Dongning County, Qiqihar's Fuyu County, Inner Mongolia's Hulunber and Hunchun City.

Service Specific Technical Reconnaissance Bureaus

Service specific TRBs focus on monitoring communications networks related to their specific areas of interest. Since the last several years, technical reconnaissance assets have been merged under Air Force and Navy Headquarters Departments in Beijing to better leverage resources under centralised control.

Air Force. The PLAAF Headquarters Department runs three TRBs responsible for monitoring neighbouring air forces and air activity around China's periphery. PLAAF TRBs carries out airborne SIGINT missions using military or civilian aircraft as platforms. The headquarters of PLAAF First TRB (95830 Unit) is located in Beijing's Huangsi District. It manages an underground network control centre in the Western Hills. It maintains a network of direction finding sites in north-eastern and eastern China that support the national air defence mission. Another subordinate PLAAF First TRB office is collocated with the bureau headquarters and supervises Xiaogan and Shenyang elements. The PLAAF First TRB may support special airborne SIGINT collection missions launched from Nanyuan Airbase in Beijing's southern suburbs. The headquarters of PLAAF Second TRB (95851 Unit) is located in Nanjing and manages a network of collection and direction-finding sites along the coast in Fujian and Guangdong. Its primary task is to monitor Taiwan Air Force's communications networks in Taiwan, air to air communications including air tower and ground control intercept. Its offices are located in Fuqing City's Donghanzhen, Shanghai, Fuzhou, Xiamen and Guangzhou's Xintang District. The headquarter of PLAAF Third TRB (95879 Unit) is located in Chengdu's Fenghuang Mountain. It monitors air activity and air defence communication networks along China's southwestern, western and northwestern borders. The Third TRB has 13 subordinate regimental-level sites, including one in the Hetian area, Ürümqi and Ningxia.

Navy. The Navy supervises two TRBs bureaus that are organised geographically. The headquarters of Navy's First

TRB (91746 Unit), is located in at Beijing. It oversees ten subordinate offices in northern China, including sites in Qingdao, Hunchun and Yantai. The headquarters of the Second TRB (92762 Unit) of Navy is located in Xiamen's Si'men District. Lower offices are located in Ningbo, Wenzhou, Xiamen, Shantou and Haikou. The PLAN's First and Second TRBs supervise ship-based SIGINT collection assets.

The SSF. The headquarters of TRB of the SSF (96669 Unit) is located in Beijing's Huilongguan suburb. Locations of subordinate elements have not been identified yet.

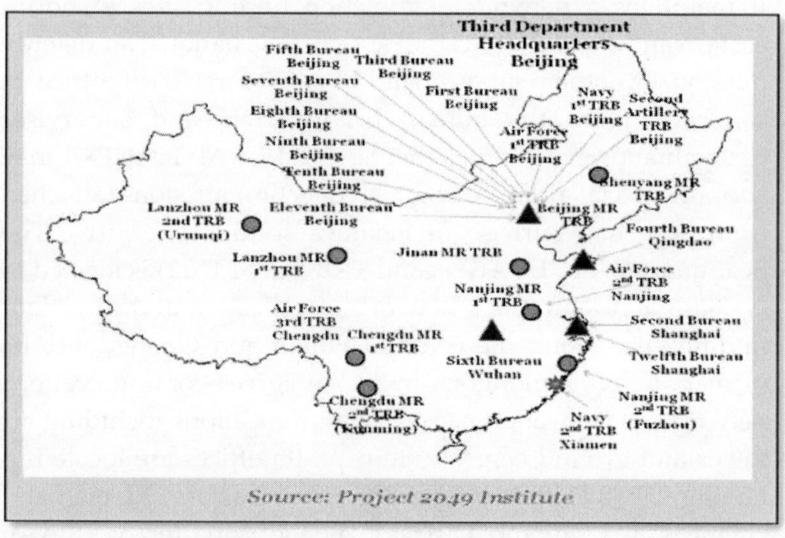

Source: Project 2049 Institute

Computer Network Management

Computer Network Defence (CND). The GSD Third Department is also responsible for PLA CND. It has a central role in China's national-level information security community. CND-related organisations supervised by the 3 PLA are:

- **The PLA Communications Security Bureau.** China North Computation Center and the 3 PLA Computing

Center are in Beijing. Inaugurated in 2005, the National Research Center for Information Security Technology serves as the national authority on risk assessment for China's network security.

- **The PLA Information Security Evaluation and Certification Centre.** Information Security Research Institute and National Information Center maintains a close affiliation with the 3 PLA S&T Equipment Bureau.
- **The National Information Security Engineering Technology Center.** Based in Shanghai, it is supervised along with the State Secrecy Bureau, State Council's Ministry of Science and Technology, National Crypto Management Center and Ministry of State Security.
- **The National Research Center for Information Technology Security** is located near GSD 3 PLA Seventh Bureau command headquarters on Nongda Road in northern Beijing suburb of Shangdi.

Computer Network Operations and Psychological Warfare. The PLA experts have recommended greater integration of psychological operations and CNO. The PLA psychological warfare training includes cyber network attack/defence. The concerned units should be able to identify and counter perception management and ideological campaigns launched against China through computer networks. China wants to counter the ideas and concepts deemed harmful to the CCP's monopoly on state power rather than a narrow technical concern over hostile CNA. Important General Political Department (GPD) psychological warfare units with probable CNO missions include the 61023 Unit in Beijing and the 61716 Unit in Fujian.

Computer Network Exploitation. The 3 PLA does not enjoy a monopoly over cyber espionage. Technical reconnaissance bureaus subordinate to MR, the PLAAF, PLAN, and

SSF also may collect against foreign targets of interest. Public security bureaus at the city and provincial levels also have computer-monitoring groups, as does the Ministry of State Security.

GSD Electronic Counter-Measures and Radar Department (Fourth Department or 4 PLA)

Known as the GSD Fourth Department or 4 PLA, it is responsible for radar related joint operational requirements development and ECM. Its priorities are satellite jamming and counter-stealth radar systems. The 4 PLA is capable of disrupting adversary use of communications, navigation, SAR and other satellites. Unlike 3 PLA, this department's task is offensive rather than defensive EW or pure intelligence collection and analysis. The 4 PLA was traditionally responsible for electronic warfare. However, now it has assumed the task of carrying out CNA also. The 4 PLA can also engage in collecting ELINT and providing tactical electronic support measures. In addition, it manages ECM units.[7] It also collects ELINT, primarily at the operational and tactical levels of war. The interaction between 3 PLA and 4 PLA is done in R&D, intelligence collection and managing a joint network warfare training system overlap.

The Fourth Department consists of the following bureaus:

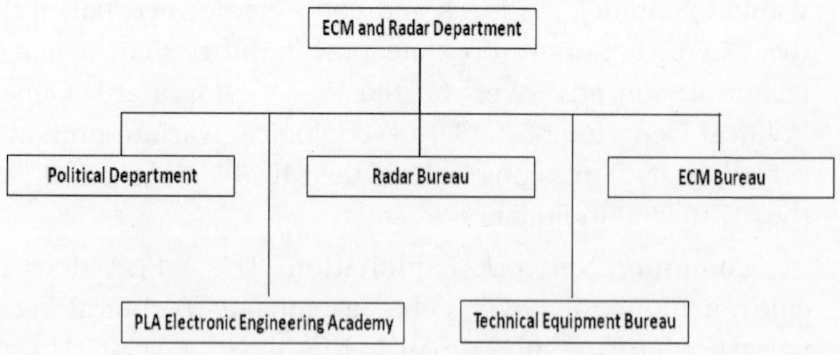

- The Radar Bureau specialises in counter-stealth force modernisation. It improves radars and detection programs and develops systems to counter stealth and low-observable technologies. It does research on space surveillance systems to support space situational awareness.
- The ECM Bureau is responsible for planning, programming and budgeting for ECM systems. It develops counters to adversary electronic systems and electronic counter-countermeasures (ECCM), allowing Chinese systems to operate in the face of adversary ECM. The Fourth Department is likely to operate its own ELINT satellite ground stations, as well as satellite jamming regiments.
- The Technical Equipment Bureau is responsible for acquisitions.
- The PLA Electronic Engineering Academy in Hefei, Anhui Province, is the department's institution for cadet education and technical training and officer Professional Military Education.

The 4 PLA has Operational units in terms of one ECM brigade (61906 Unit) with its headquarters in Langfang, Hebei Province and subordinate battalion level units located in Anhui, Jiangxi, Shandong and other locations in China. Another unit, possibly an ECM brigade (61251 Unit), is headquartered in the Qinhuangdao area of Hebei Province. The Fourth Department operates electronic reconnaissance satellite ground receiving stations to support joint targeting and one or possibly two satellite jamming regiments, including the 61764 Unit on Hainan Island. A regimental level unit located on Hainan Island has operational or experimental satellite jamming responsibilities, with one dedicated to jamming U.S. satellite assets. Military Regions, Air Force and

Navy have at least one ECM regiment. The GSD Third Department and Fourth Department jointly manage a network attack/defence training system.

The 4 PLA is responsible for running many research institutions related to developing new ECM. The most important of these is the 54th Research Institute, which provides engineering support and facilitates the department's connection with other entities under the China Electronic Technology Corporation, including the 29th Research Institute in Chengdu, the 36th Research Institute in Jiaxing and the 38th Research Institute in Hefei. The 4 PLA also oversees the PLA Electronic Engineering Academy located in Hefei as the primary academic EW centre in China and trains junior officers. A number of the research institutes under 4 PLA have concentrated on how to counter critical American command, control, communications, computers, and intelligence (C4ISR) systems. Methods used are GPS jamming, Joint Tactical Information Distribution System countermeasures and synthetic radar jamming. Such EW capabilities would be coordinated with CNA tools to conduct an all-out attack against the enemy's key command and networks.

GSD Informatisation Department

Often referred to as the Communications Department, it is responsible for developing, operating, constructing and maintaining the PLA's C4ISR system. It works with civilian ministries and companies at the national and provincial levels to enhance PRC's telecommunications infrastructure. The Informatization Department supports the development of PLA operational and technical requirements for telecommunications. The GSD Informatization Department leverages long-range unmanned aerial vehicles (UAVs), such as those used for strategic reconnaissance.

Securing Information Dominance. To conduct "local wars under informationized conditions," the PLA will rely on organisations like the GSD, GPD and GAD who are responsible for key IW and information operations portfolios.

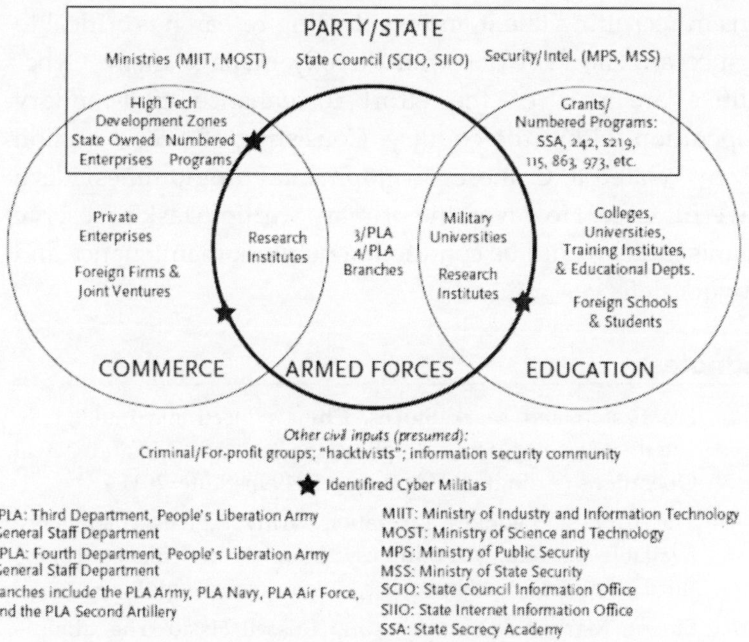

China's CNO and Civil-Military Integration

Source: Jon R. Lindsay, Tai Ming Cheung and Derek S. Reveron (edited), China and Cybersecurity: Espionage, Strategy, and Politics in the Digital Domain, Oxford University, 2015

Hacktivist Units and Cyber Militia

Other than the PLA cyber units, various other groups operate from the Chinese cyberspace. Most of the confirmed attacks originate from such independent hacktivist units. The groups are uncontrolled and more nationalistic than the state. The PLA has recruited civilians into its 'cyber militias units' since 2002 for hacking activities. These units are staffed by academics and civilians consisting of hackers, IT companies, scientists, network engineers, foreign language speakers and others with valuable skills with information technology backgrounds. The PLA's collaboration with civilian organisations in recruiting talent and conducting research is critical to its success. The PLA does not directly manage them. Cyber militias are part of the effort to enhance civil-military cooperation within the country. Consisting of over 8 million citizens related to Chinese developmental programmes, it is a powerful force. However, the primary wartime task of reserve organisations would be conducting network maintenance and network defence.

Endnotes

1. Ian Easton and Mark Stokes, China's Electronic Intelligence Satellite Developments: Implications for U.S. Air and Naval Operations (Arlington, VA: Project 2049 Institute, 2011.)
2. The Chinese People's Liberation Army Signals Intelligence available at: http://goodtimesweb.org / surveillance / pla_third_department_sigint_cyber_stokes_lin_hsiao.pdf
3. Stokes, Mark A., Jenny Lin, and Russell Hsiao. The Chinese People's Liberation Army Signals Intelligence and Cyber Reconnaissance Infrastructure. Report by Project 2049 Institute, 2011, p. 3. Available at: https://project2049.net / documents / pla_third_department_sigint_cyber_stokes_lin_hsiao.pdf.
4. Mark A. Stokes July 27, 2015, The PLA General Staff Department Third Department Second Bureau: An Organizational Overview of Unit 61398, Project 2049 Institute, July 27, 2015.
5. CrowdStrike Intelligence Report: Putter Panda. Report by CrowdStrike, 2014. Available at: https://cdn0.vox-cdn.com/ assets / 4589853 / crowdstrike-intelligence-report-putter-panda.original.pdf.
6. National Information Technology and Security Research Center, ISRA website, undated, available at: http://www.isra.org.cn/

about/index.htm; and China Futures Association Information Director Liu Tiebin: Ideas for IT System Security Design, China Information Network, September 4, 2009, available at: http://www.cio360.net/Page/1802/InfoID/307354/SourceId/11300/PubDate/2009-09-04/Default.aspx.

7. Easton, Ian, and Mark A. Stokes. China's Electronic Intelligence Satellite Developments. Report by Project 2049 Institute, 2011, p.5.

* * *

CHAPTER 6

China's Management of Cyber Security

"Cybersecurity and informatization are mutually constitutive. Security is the precondition of development, development is the guarantee for security, security and development must progress simultaneously."

"Without cyber security, there will be no national security."

–Xi Jinping, April 19, 2016, Speech at the Work Conference for Cybersecurity and Informatization

Introduction

The information revolution has been a mixed blessing for the world and China. The Internet has improved economic productivity, national security and social interaction. China has leveraged information technology (IT) to integrate its firms into the global economy and modernise its infrastructure. An increase in internet penetration has helped to boost export-led growth. China has one of the fastest growing Internet populations in the world. If civil society exists in China, it exists on the Internet, even as the government censors content online.

However, the cutting edge of technology is a double-edged weapon. Critical information infrastructure (CII) and the data stored on it are lucrative targets for adversaries. Losses to financial theft and online fraud range are estimated as trillion droller to tens of billions of dollars per year. As cyber technology creates prosperity, it facilitates cybercrime, espionage and cyber warfare. Like many other advanced industrial states, China is the source and target of extensive cyber exploitation.

Internet Users in China. In January 2021, China had a population of 1.44 billion. China started to adopt the Internet in 1994, and connectivity grew exponentially over the last 25 years. In January 2021, there were 939.8 million internet users in China. In China, the number of internet users increased by 85 million between 2020 and 2021. In January 2021, internet penetration in China stood at 65.2 percent.

China's Social Media Statistics. In January 2021, there were 930.8 million social media users in China. China's number of social media users increased by 110 million between 2020 and 2021. The people using social media in China was equivalent to 64.6 percent of the total population in January 2021.

Mobile Connections in China. In January 2021, there were 1.61 billion mobile connections in China. The number of mobile connections in China increased by 8.0 million between January 2020 and 2021. In January 2021, the number of mobile connections in China was equivalent to 111.8 percent of the total population. Number of mobile connections may exceed 100 percent of the total population as many people have more than one mobile connection.

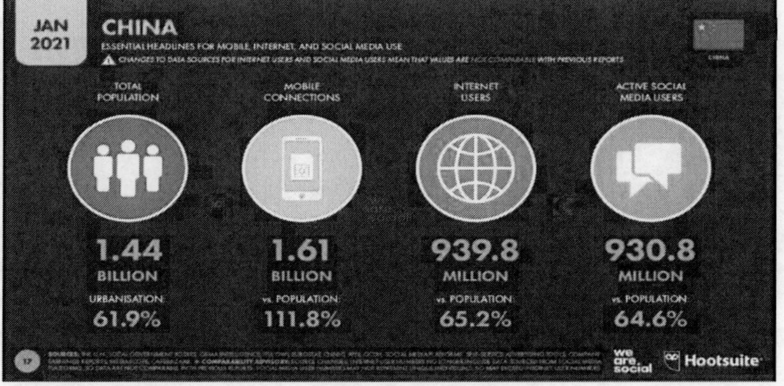

China has a relatively independent ecosystem composed of many world-class Internet firms like Huawei, ZTE, Alibaba, Tencent, Baidu and TikTok. China's digital behemoths Alibaba, Baidu and Tencent, with combined annual revenues estimated at US$87.3 billion, have established a dominant position within China's internet ecosystem. They also invest heavily in start-ups and for research and development. Successful Chinese companies are seeking new markets and opportunities worldwide in a manner that dovetails with China's geopolitical objectives.

Promotion of a digital economy is an integral component of China's strategy to secure its future development, especially at a time when its overall growth is slowing. Chinese Premier Li Keqiang has highlighted in his 2019 work reports the importance of integrating the digital with the real economy as a source of growth.

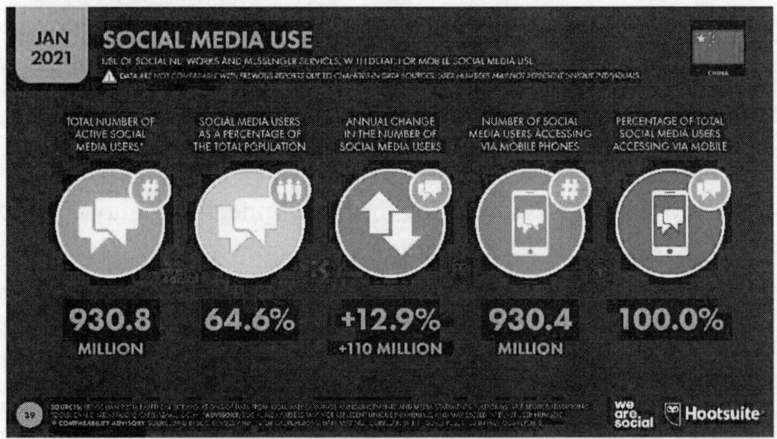

After the Snowden revelations, China's cyber security approach has evolved from a 'whole-of-government' and 'whole-of-nation' approach to that of 'whole-of-systems' approach that advocates a systematic formula characterising cyber security as holistic rather than fragmented, dynamic rather than static, open rather than closed, relative rather than absolute and common rather than isolated.

China's cybersecurity strategy has three main drivers: economic, political and military. Important symptoms of those drivers are:[1]

- Maintaining economic growth and stability. It involves cyber espionage of U.S. and other western targets.
- Using cyber operations to signal discontent with foreign powers over developments outside of China like territorial disputes, allegations of Chinese hacking activity that adversely affect China's reputation.
- Protecting the power of the Chinese Communist Party (CPP) through propaganda, information control and targeting of domestic sources of potential unrest.
- Preparing for armed conflicts and ensuring cyber superiority over an opponent through modernisation, research and cultivation of human resources.
- Studying and realising potential adversaries' military infrastructures, capabilities, motivations, objectives and limitations in the cyber domain.
- Advancing alternative narratives of government handling of cyber security internationally and domestically.

Cyber Policy Initiatives

China's cyber security concept is much broader than the usual emphasis on cyberwar, cybercrime and protection of critical infrastructures. Cyber security and information security are intertwined, critical for maintaining the viability of the Chinese nation, society and the CCP. The most important part of cyber security for China is internal security, with a heavy emphasis on content security. This had led to actions ranging from the Great Firewall of China to the use of human censors to monitor and delete online content the CCP thinks harmful.

China has made many important legislative, institutional and developmental adjustments for its cyber security initiatives. Some of these are:

- Earlier, cyber policy decision-making was distributed amongst various ministries. The Chinese government has now consolidated it to a centralised body, Cyberspace Administration of China (CAC), with President Xi himself as the head of the CAC joined by heads of various relevant ministries and governmental units.
- A number of cyber laws and policies have been passed at various levels in the last few years to address internal needs and respond to external geopolitical and policy trends.
- The government issued several large-scale industrial policies to boost the country's technological capacities like the "Made in China 2025" plan to produce higher value products and services, the "Internet Plus" plan to upgrade the nation's traditional industries from agriculture to manufacturing and the "Digital Silk Road" to seek new technological markets around the world.

China's National Cyberspace Security Strategy

On December 27, 2016 the Cyberspace Administration of China published its National Cyberspace Security Strategy.[2] China has principally economic, political and military objectives in the cyber security strategy. China tries to take the lead on international cyber governance and proliferate President Xi's call to establish a community of shared future in cyberspace. This document outlines the principles of peace, sovereignty, shared governance and shared benefits and unequivocally states: "Countries should reject the Cold War mentality, zero-sum game and double standards, uphold peace through cooperation..." and "The tendency of militarization and deterrence buildup in cyberspace is not conducive to international security and strategic mutual trust." While China tries to take the moral high ground, it wishes to establish a global Internet governance framework based on state sovereignty. There is an inherent dichotomy here.

China has identified the following grave challenges for cyber security:

- China faces grave risks and challenges in national politics, national defence, the economy, security, culture, society and citizens' lawful rights in cyber-space.
- Cyber penetrations harm political security. The use of networks to introude in the internal affairs of other countries and cyber surveillance, cyber espionage and other such activities harm national security and users' information security.
- Cyber attacks threaten economic security. It will lead to paralysis of critical infrastructure harm national economic security and the public interest.
- Harmful online information corrodes cultural security. Excellent traditional culture and standard value views are facing attacks. Online rumours and harmful information violate the Socialist core value.
- Online terrorism, crime and law-breaking are destroying social security. Terrorism, separatism, extremism and other such forces use the network to incite, plan, organise and carry out violent terrorist activities.
- International competition in cyberspace is rapidly unfolding. There is strife for controlling strategic resources in cyberspace to occupy norm-setting power and strategic commanding heights. A small number of countries is aggravating an arms race in cyberspace.

- Opportunities and challenges coexist in cyberspace. The opportunities are greater than the challenges. China must persist in positive use for the development potential of cyberspace to extend it to China's 1.3 billion people.

China's Cyber Objectives:

- Implementation of innovative, coordinated, green, open and shared development concept.
- Strengthening risk consciousness and crisis consciousness.
- To comprehensively handle both domestic and foreign large pictures.
- To comprehensively plan the development of the two great matters of internal and external security.
- To defend vigorously, respond effectively, promote peace, security, openness, cooperation and order in cyberspace.
- To safeguard the interests of national sovereignty, security and development.
- To realise the strategic objective of building a strong cyber power.
- **Peace.** Information technology abuse is to be effectively curbed, arms races in cyberspace and other such threats to international peace are to be effectively controlled, conflicts in cyberspace are to be effectively prevented.
- **Security.** Cyber security risks are to be effectively controlled, national cybersecurity protection systems are to be completed and perfected, core technologies and equipment are secure and controllable and network and information systems operate stably and

reliably. Cyber security talents are to satisfy demands. The cyber security consciousness of the entire society, basic protection capabilities and their confidence in using the network will increase considerably.

- **Openness.** Information technology policies, standards and markets are to be open and transparent. The digital divide should be closed with every passing day. All countries worldwide are to develop closer cooperation in technology exchange, attack on cyber terrorism and cybercrime, a multilateral, democratic and transparent international Internet governance system.
- **Order.** The public's right to know, participate, express opinions, supervise and other such lawful rights and interests in cyberspace are to be fully protected. Domestic and international legal structures, standards and norms for cyberspace are to be established progressively.

Established Principles

- Respecting and protecting sovereignty in cyberspace.
- Peaceful use of cyberspace.
- Governing cyberspace according to the law.
- Comprehensively manage cybersecurity and development.

Identified Strategic Tasks

- Resolutely defending sovereignty in cyberspace.
- Resolutely safeguard national security.
- Protect critical information infrastructure.
- Strengthening the construction of online culture.
- Attacking cyber terrorism, law-breaking and crime.

- Perfect network governance systems.
- Enhancing cyberspace protection capabilities.
- Strengthening international cooperation in cyberspace.

China's National Defence in the New Era (2019)

The White Paper on China's 'National Defense in the New Era' provides more details of China's cyber military strategies. This document evaluates the current national and international security situations and outlines China's defence missions, reforms, and spending. It paints the U.S. as the ultimate cyberspace hegemon. The paper recommends that the PLA adapt to the new era of strategic competition by strengthening its preparedness and improving its combat capabilities while preserving world peace. This document clarifies that China should apply cutting-edge technologies to the military domain, including artificial intelligence, cloud computing, big data, quantum computing and the Internet of Things (IoT).

International Strategy of Cooperation on Cyberspace

China's Ministry of Foreign Affairs and Cyberspace Administration published, on 1st March 2017, a document on 'International Strategy of Cooperation on Cyberspace'. This document elucidates the following:

- Militarisation of cyberspace and use of it as an area for deterrence.
- Attempts that damage international security and stability.
- Cyberspace shall be audited and controlled by multi-sided governance, in which states, international organisations, international companies, non-governmental organisations and even individuals shall be the sides.

- United Nations (UN) is an appropriate agency for determining the auditing committees in question.
- Foreign investments in international informatics and technology companies will be encouraged.
- Any kind of support will be given to the foreign companies for them to make investments in the country, providing that public benefit and national security will be watched.
- Governance of the internet will not be monopolised, the PRC prefers a multi-sided governance system.

Regulations for the Control of the National Cyber Space Area

Several national laws have been issued to strengthen China's cyber defence capabilities. The Cyber Security Law of 1st June 2017 provides the broad framework for national security and cyber security to the PRC. The Cyber Security Law:

- Pays more attention to the protection of personal information and individual privacy. It standardises the collection and usage of personal information. Enterprises should give greater importance to data security and individual privacy protection.
- Presents clear definitions of network operators and security requirement concerning these network operators.
- Places higher demands on the protection of critical information infrastructure.
- Stipulates that sensitive data must be stored domestically.
- Lays down penalties for violating cyber security.

Stakeholders in China's Cyber Security

Chinese concept of information security has the unique characteristic of giving more importance to Internet content than to technical cyber security. This is in contrast to the Western idea of emphasising the technical threats to computer networks. This emphasis has led to a focused national effort to increase censorship and surveillance infrastructure rather than coordinate technical standards and enforcement mechanisms. China puts more effort into defence against the real or imagined threats of terrorism, separatism and extremism than defending against and technical exploitation by foreign intelligence services and economic cybercrime.

Actors in the PRC Cyber Security Strategy Management

The agencies involved in China's Cyber Security Strategy Management can be divided mainly into civil and military sides. The military side consists of units within PLA. This has been shown on the left side of the diagram given.

The civil side includes CPC, working groups and institutions affiliated to the Chinese government, technology, telecommunication, globally active informatics companies, hacker groups, and cyber civil militia. The top decision-making bodies of the civil side are Politburo Standing Committee, State Council and Central Military Commission as it exists in all decision-making processes of China.

The diagram next page depicts the mesh of official institutions that play a role in managing Chinese cybersecurity policy. At the centre of the chart are CCP entities, including the new Cybersecurity and Informatization Leading Group (CILG) chaired by Xi Jinping, which subsumed State Informatization Leading Group (SILG) and State Network Infosec Coordination Group (SNISCG). The CCP State Secrets

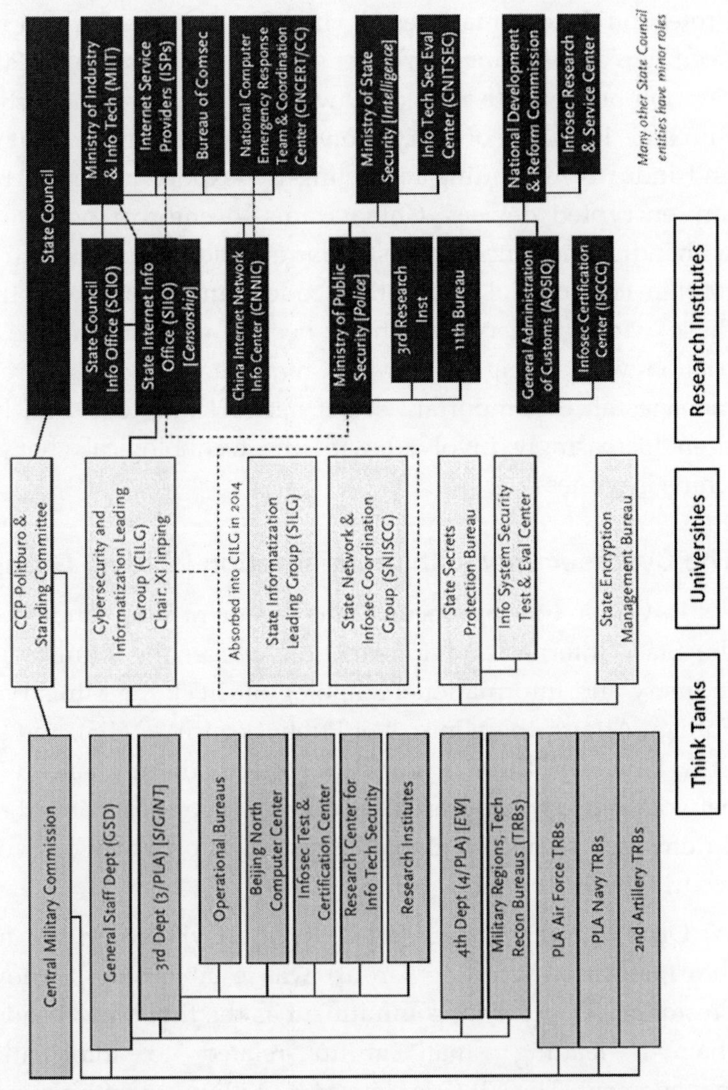

China's National Cyber Security Systems

Source: Jon R. Lindsay, Tai Ming Cheung and Derek S. Reveron (ed), China and Cybersecurity: Espionage, Strategy, and Politics in the Digital Domain, Oxford University Press, 2015

Protection Bureau manages all classified information and has been active increasingly in cyber security policy since the 2009 revision of the State Secrecy Law. The CCP State Encryption Bureau is in charge of encryption for the government, military and industry, including restricting the export and import of any encrypted devices. China wants to enforce compliance with indigenous encryption standards. It demands access to all foreign commercial encryption codes, and later exempting those without encryption have been a constant source of friction with foreign firms in China. State Secrets Bureau manages all the important secret networks systems and has been increasingly involved with the technological changes China is witnessing.

The Cybersecurity and Informatization Leading Group

In China, Internet security management was handled by the State Internet and Information Office, the Ministry of Industry and Information Technology (MIIT), the Ministry of Foreign Affairs, the Ministry of Public Security (MPS), and the PLA. However, there is no clear coordination mechanism for network security between these different agencies, nor is there an effective means of global communication when network security events occur.

On February 27, 2014, new Cybersecurity and Informatization Leading Group was established. It shows President Xi's personal commitment as the first party head to chair a leading small group related to information management. The CILG is chaired by Xi Jinping with Premier Li Keqiang and Standing Committee member Liu Yunshan as vice chairs, with nineteen other Politburo or ministerial-level officials as members. Significantly ten of the eleven Politburo members are also on Xi Jinping's new Leading Group for the

Comprehensive Deepening of Reform. The leading group prioritises internet security and information management as a single concept, trying to resolve the lack of an integrated approach that has been the root cause. The new group, with Xi as its head, is expected to make firm demands and solve internal discrepancies where necessary. President Xi has attributed to internet security and information management as 'two wings of one bird, two wheels on one car.'

Leading small groups and central leading groups have become a common facet to deal with issues that the bureaucratic machine cannot solve. Possibly a better mechanism to adopt successful reforms, they comply directly with the orders of the CCP's highest leaders. The State Informatisation Leading Group (SILG) and the State Network and Information Security Coordination Small Group (SNISCSG) were guided by the State Council. However, the recently established Central Leading Small Group for Internet Security and Informatisation (CLSGISI) acts directly under President Xi Jinping and has extraordinary authority.

The State Council Elements

State Internet Information Office (SIIO). SIIO was founded in 2011 to coordinate the 'rectification' of the internet, working in close cooperation with the MIIT and MPS to observed social media, where user-created content become a serious concern to the government. State Council Information Office (SCIO) established SIIO for managing the general domestic information flow.

Ministry of Industry and Information Technology. MIIT was established in 2008 to centralise IT development. Its duties and responsibilities are similar to the Department of Homeland Security of the U.S. It sets standards, inspects network security, holds exercises and coordinates information and telecoms security through a special department.[3] MIIT controls China's six Internet service providers (ISPs), which monitor and filter content on their networks as per the censorship guidelines given by the SCIO and the SIIO. MIIT controls the following:

- **National Computer Network Emergency Response Technical Team/Coordination Centre of China (CNCERT/CC).** Founded in 2002, CNCERT is a non-governmental organization acting under MIIT. CNCERT/CC which is responsible for emergency response to serious public computer infections. It publishes a yearly report of cyberattacks against China, a source of statistics frequently quoted by officials to highlight Chinese vulnerability. CNCERT/CC works closely with the China Internet Network Information Center (CNNIC), managing Chinese Internet domain names. It is responsible for detecting malicious software in the networks of the country, developing necessary measures against them, and informing MIIT about the processes. MIIT supports its work by helping to build virus and vulnerability databases, getting malicious IP and domain name providers and supervising CNCERT to engage in international cooperation.
- **State Administration for Science, Technology and Industry for National Defense (SASTIND).** SASTIND works under MIIT. It drafts guidelines, policies, laws, and regulations regarding science, technology, and industry for national defence. Before establishing MIIT, a separate body called the Commission for Science, Technology and Industry for National Defense (COSTIND) used to carry out similar tasks.

The Ministry of Public Security. MPS investigates cybercrime primarily through its Eleventh Bureau. It takes measures to protect CII together with development work through a wide network of research labs. MPS also has a key rule in counter-espionage by auditing the Chinese commercial information security companies and products to be exported. Significantly, MPS operates the Great Firewall of China and conducts domestic intelligence activities. The MPS Third Research Institute conducts information security research through several institutes, such as the National Research Center for Anti-Computer Invasion and Virus Prevention.

Ministry of State Security (MSS). MSS is China's foreign intelligence service. MSS has an important role in the intelligence structure of the PRC. MSS has substantial technical cyber expertise. MSS's cyber capabilities have grown considerably to collect political and economic data on foreign governments, NGOs and domestic dissidents. Through the China Information Technology Security Evaluation Center (CNITSEC), MSS conducts vulnerability assessment and software reliability tests. Remarkably, Microsoft handed over the source code of its Windows operating system to CNITSEC for review in 2003. It is not known whether MSS access to Windows code has helped Chinese cyber exploitation activities.

Cyberspace Administration of China

The Cyberspace Administration of China was raised in May 2011 as a subordinate office under SCIO. The CAC is the central Internet regulator, censor, oversight and control agency for China. The CAC signifies an attempt to combine propaganda with technological innovation and development. The CAC has been working under the direct supervision of the Office of the Central Leading Group for Cyberspace Affairs since April 2014. The CAC is responsible for cyberspace security and internet content regulation. Its major functions are directing, coordinating and supervising online content management and handling administrative approval of businesses related to online news reporting. The CAC is known as the State Internet Information Office also.

Cyberspace Administration of China has shown its prowess by blocking foreign VPNs, closing and monitoring the most popular messaging application in China, WeChat and coordinating cyber-attacks against anti-censorship groups like GreatFire.org, an organisation seeking to bring transparency to the Great Firewall. It has the following departments/ responsibilities:

- **Bureau of Policies and Regulations.** Focuses on internet issues; drafts internet policies, regulations and other key documents; offers policy suggestions for internet and IT and reviews documents for standardisation.
- **Bureau of Network Security Coordination.** Supervises the general management of network security and cooperation.
- **Bureau of Network Data and Technology.** Looks after issues on network data and resolves technical problems.
- **Bureau of International Cooperation.** Coordinates and handles international communication and coordination on internet issues.
- **Bureau of Mobile Network Management.** Coordinates and manages mobile networks.
- **Bureau of Informatization Development.** Promotes the advancement of IT and the development of digitization in other sectors.

- **Bureau of Network News Information Communication.** Overseas the distribution of public information, news in online media.
- **Bureau of Comprehensive Coordination Management and Law Enforcement Supervision.** Supervises coordination between bureaus and law enforcement inspection on internet issues.
- **Bureau of Emergency Management.** Develops emergency action plans and conducts ministry's response to emergencies related to internet issues.
- **Bureau of Planning and Finance.** Manages budget and expenses; organises internal audits and performance examinations; offers finance, taxation, and pricing recommendations and manages ministry finances and assets.
- **Bureau of Internet Social Work.** Promotes social networks for internet issues and takes part in the management of online communities.
- **Bureau of Network Comments.** Overseas public opinions on the internet. It has the authority to collect, check, issue warnings and delete certain internet posts and videos.
- **Bureau of Secretary.** Manages internal dissemination of information, communications, security safeguards.
- **Bureau of Cadre.** Manages human resources, including issues pertaining to retired cadres.

Cyberspace Administration of China also has the following affiliated institutional responsibilities:

- **Illegal Information Reporting Centre.** Standardises the reporting of bad and illegal information on the

Internet; helps in handling reports of illegal information on the Internet; encourages the construction of a public supervision and governance system, carries out international exchanges and cooperation, enhances contacts with relevant international organisations, reporting agencies and Internet enterprises abroad.

- **China Internet Network Information Centre.** Administers essential Internet resources conducts research on Internet development undertakes R&D and security work of fundamental Internet resources and improves international cooperation and technological exchange.
- **National Computer Network Emergency Response Technical Team/Coordination Center of China.** Initiates the discovery, prevention, early warning and integrated management of Internet network security incidents ensures the safe operation of basic information networks and important information systems, defends national public Internet security and carries out related security monitoring work of Internet + industry "integration" represented by Internet finance.
- **National Research Center for Information Technology Security.** Analyses and researches the security of IT products/systems ensures the network security of national key information infrastructure systems and develops indigenous information security technologies.
- **Chinese Academy of Cyberspace.** As CAC's think tank, the Academy is responsible for providing strategic support, research support, talent support and technical support for national planning and scientific decision-making in the field of network security and IT and publishing both the World Internet Development

Report and China Internet Development Report every year.

- **Institution Services Centre.** Responsible for general logistics services.
- **Network Security Emergency Command Centre.** Responsible for general network security and guiding emergency actions.
- **China Internet Development Foundation.** Raises public funding to support CAC's internet development agendas and supports ongoing projects to ensure internet safety and increase digitisation, particularly in rural areas.

On April 27, 2020, the CAC, together with 11 other government departments, published the 'Cybersecurity Review Measures', which applies to CII operators. The Cybersecurity Review Measures were implemented on June 01, 2020, as the "2020 rules". These rules were developed to implement China's Cyber Security Law. The aim was to address the risks to national security and business continuity created by the procurement of network security products and services by CII operators. Enforcement actions under the 2020 rules have never been taken or disclosed until July 02, 2021 when it was announced that China's top ride-hailing platform Didi Chuxing would be probed for cybersecurity review two days after its IPO in the U.S. This was closely followed by two similar probes against other Internet companies that were also US-listed very recently.

National Critical Information Infrastructure. CII includes network operators in the areas of public communications, information services, energy, transportation, water utilities, finance, public services, e-government, telecommunications, radio and television, postal services, emergency management, health, social security and national defence technology industry. The recently promulgated two-step review process for CII requires:

- To predict the national security risks associated with using the network products or services, the CII operator should conduct a self-assessment before executing a procurement agreement.
- If the self-assessment indicates national security risks, the CII operator should submit the required documents, including procurement agreements and risk assessment reports, to the CAC for a cyber security review.

Criteria for Cyber Security Review. The conditions are:

- If the risk due to the use of the network products or services cause CII operators to be unlawfully manipulated, destroyed or interfered or lead to the leak, loss or damage of important data.
- If there is continuous damages to CII's business due to supply disruptions of the products or services.
- Security, openness, transparency and diversity of sources, reliability of supply channels and any risk of supply disruptions resulting from political, diplomatic and trade factors.
- If the product or service provider is in compliance with Chinese regulations.

In addition to these four factors, the procedures also provide a 'catch-all' provision encompassing all other situations that could endanger CII security and national security. Based on this catch-all provision, the CAC will have enough discretion to determine potential risks in a particular procurement.

Requirements for Designated Personnel. Each operator of CII must nominate a designated person to be in charge of cyber security management. He is responsible to:

- Formulate cyber security regulations internally, operation manuals and overseeing their implementation.
- Coordinate testing of the technical skills of key technical personnel.
- Conduct and implement cyber security education and training programmes.
- Conduct cyber security inspections and contingency drills and dealing with cyber security incidents.
- Report important cyber security issues and incidents to competent authorities.
- Protecting CII is a common responsibility of government, businesses and the society.
- According to the laws, regulations, rules, and standards, adopt the necessary measures to ensure CII security.
- Expand input in areas of management, technology, talent and finance, synthesise measures and policies according to the law
- Realise that evaluation happens earlier and application later.
- Improve risk assessment of CII.
- Enhance security protection in government bodies and Party as websites in focus areas, Party and Government bodies' websites should be built, operated and managed according to the intensification model.
- Focus on identification, monitoring, prevention, early warning, response, handling and other such segments.

- Establish orderly cyber security information sharing mechanisms for government, sectors and enterprises and give full responsibility to the critical role of enterprises in protecting CII.

The Cybersecurity Review Measures introduces the condition of a mandatory review of any business with personal information of more than one million users that seek to list its securities abroad. It shows unambiguously Chinese regulators' concerns about data security and cross-border data transfer related to overseas listings. Inside China, it indicates that cyber security review will become a focus of future enforcement in data protection laws. The immediate effect of China's proposed changes is that many tech companies are announcing withdrawals of overseas IPOs.[4]

Recently, the CAC has been in the limelight for China's efforts to wrest control over one of its most valuable resources: data. On July 2, 2021, the CAC started a probe into Didi Global Inc., which can upend capital markets and overhaul the country's most successful businesses. The Didi inquiry came days after the ride-hailing giant's $4.4 billion U.S. listing, triggered a $130 billion stock sell-off and forced high-flying startups including Alibaba Group Holding Ltd. backed LinkDoc Technology Ltd. and Tencent Holdings Ltd. backed Meicai to stop their plans to go public. About 70 private firms based in Hong Kong and China that are about to go public in New York may in due course be affected.[5]

Research and Development. Chinese Institute of Contemporary International Relations works directly under the MSS. Tsinghua University and Peking University are closely related to the government's IT-related research work. The PLA runs profound strategic development through institutions such as the Academy of Military Science and the PLA Information Engineering University (IEU). Cyber Security Association of

China, consisting of academic institutes, individuals and internet companies such as Tencent was launched in March 2016 to develop industry standards and better coordinate research on cyber security.

Industry. Some of China's leading companies like Telecom, Huawei, Lenovo and China Unicom in telecommunications, technology and IT operate on a global scale. The management levels are directly linked to the CPC and the PLA. They are subject to various restrictions in the Western world, as it is assumed that their products and services may be the sources of PRC-based cyber espionage operations.

Many scientists, engineers, experts and network technology capable citizens working in the telecommunication, information and technology areas are natural members of a militia structure of the PRC. These individuals may not be directly associated with the CPC but have occasional exercises within the scope of contingency planning. They got training for lines of action against cyber-attacks against the PRC during these exercises. Chinese hacker groups operate independently or in the name of PRC in cyberspace.

Deficiencies in China's Cyber Security Mechanisms

No matter how large an internet company is, no matter how high its market value is, if it is heavily dependent on foreign countries for its core components, and if the "major artery" of the supply chain is in the hands of others, it is like building a house on someone else's foundation. No matter how big and beautiful it is, it may not stand up to wind and rain, and it may be so vulnerable that it collapses at the first blow.

- Xi Jinping, The Full Text of Xi Jinping's Speech at the Forum on Cybersecurity and Informatization Work

China is acutely aware of its weakness in cyber security. President Xi Jinping complained when he said, "The control of core technology by others is our biggest hidden danger."[6]

Chinese experts assess that the U.S. holds the advantage in cyber capabilities in overall IT industry dominance, control of Internet infrastructure, malware design and training of cyber forces. Big U.S. companies Apple, Cisco, Google, IBM, Intel, Microsoft, Oracle and Qualcomm, which the Chinese media call 'eight guardian warriors', dominate the IT industry. Chip, network switch, processor and other core technologies of U.S. are superior to other countries. China feels the dominance of these companies would give U.S. access to the CII that U.S. can exploit during conflicts. Cyber attacks could cause the breakdown of important information and industrial control systems, adversely affecting China's economic development and industrial security. Chinese computer networks are vulnerable to potential subversion by western actors especially U.S. According to China's statistics, 80 percent of Chinese chips, high-end components, universal protocols, and standards depend on imports. 65 percent of information security products like firewall, encryption machines, and others are also imported.

China's leaders consider its cyber defences weak. In 2017, China had to withdraw from its indigenisation plan for an operating system in favour of existing reliance on a special edition of Microsoft Windows developed for the Chinese government in a joint venture between Microsoft and a state-owned Chinese partner.[7] Windows 10 is in everyday use in China, providing security packages. In 2019, China's leading international bank, the Bank of China, and IBM announced a partnership in developing new cyber architectures for the bank, which has worldwide offices. China understands its reliance on foreign technology companies is likely to be long term. Some companies like Microsoft, IBM, Cisco and Intel were invited to join China's leading consultative group for writing national standards related to cyber security. In spite of several attempts to move away from Microsoft Windows, China is yet to develop its own operating system to replace those of Microsoft or Apple.[8]

International Evaluation of China's Cyber Security. The evaluation of China's cyber security mechanisms by international bodies does not augur well for China:

- According to the International Telecommunications Union's cyber-security index, China's overall cyber capability ranks 27th in the world, behind countries such as Croatia, Denmark, Egypt, Germany, Italy, Russia and Turkey. China and Turkey have among the highest rates of malware infections.[9]
- The Global Innovation Index (GII) for 2019, compiled by a consortium of reputable international organisations and not confined to cyber, ranks China 14th. China has not been in the top ten in any year since the GII was established, that range being dominated by the US and its allies.
- Comparitech, an industry website, has ranked China 23rd out of 76 countries based on 2019 data.
- The World Economic Forum's Global Information Technology Report ranked China 59th in network readiness in the several years up to 2016.

China's Assessment. China's assessments about its cyber security have been moderate:

- National Computer Network Emergency Response Technical Team in its 2017 report, stated that advanced persistent threat attacks from foreign states were frequent and becoming normal. These were directly threatening national security. The report noted serious damage to data, and the number of attacks against industrial control systems was increasing.[10]

- However, the country's overall cyber-security situation has worsened. In its six-monthly report released in September 2020, the China Internet Network Information Centre noted that personal cyber security in the area of online fraud had improved. It found a substantial increase in the number of websites affected, some of which were infected with 'backdoors'. The number of vulnerabilities found in high-risk systems more than doubled from the previous year. Though the proportion of backdoors installed in Chinese websites decreased significantly, the volume of webpage-tampering incidents increased by 20 percent across all sectors and 30 percent for government websites.
- China's National Internet Emergency Response Center, in its report released in 2018, stated that phishing cases in China decreased by 72.5 percent from 2016 to 2017. The number of active control terminals launching distributed denial-of-service (DDoS) attacks reduced by 46 percent, and the number of controlled sources launching DDoS attacks decreased by 37 percent. DDoS attacks against China became more powerful, with the number of high-volume attacks exceeding one terabyte per second, reaching 68 in 2018. The number of malicious sniffing and cyber attacks on industrial facilities, systems and platforms increased significantly. The report found that the top three foreign sources for malicious software in China in 2018 were Canada, Russia and the United States. The three top sources for hosting control servers distributing this software were Germany, Japan and the US.

- Tencent, one of the world's largest internet firms, in a report from Tencent Security Response Centre, gave out reasons for the weakness of China's cyber security sector:
  - High cost.
  - Focus on profit instead of security.
  - A general lack of talent.
  - Poor cyber security threat technology.
  - Concentration of the sector in Tier 1 and Tier 2 cities such as Beijing, Guangdong and Shanghai.
  - Reliance on foreign imports for basic information infrastructure.
  - Weak capability to track hostile activity especially advanced persistent threats.
  - Reliance on out-of-date methods of protecting data.
  - Limited legal foundations for countering and tracking illegal access of data.
  - Lack of national control in core technologies.
  - Under developed identity-authentication systems.
  - Chinese firms' cyber-security investment as a share of total investment (1.78 percent) was far lower than that in the U.S. (4.78 percent) and the rest of the world (3.75 percent).

Edward Snowden's Revelation. Edward Snowden, in June 2013, revealed widespread successful penetration of Chinese systems by the National Security Agency (NSA) and FBI of U.S. This dramatic disclosure put U.S in an embarrassing situation. It damaged the U.S. efforts to take the moral high ground against Chinese espionage. The impression created by big American IT companies that they are independent of U.S. government also took a big hit. President Barack Obama, in his State of the Union address in February 2013, suggested that the US had substantial knowledge of China's cyber-intelligence operations, stating that 'our enemies are also seeking the ability to sabotage our power grid, our financial institutions, our air traffic control systems'. Edward Snowden exposed the following: [11]

- The NSA had been hacking the majority of Chinese government and private systems since 2007. They relied on routers of the U.S. Company Cisco Systems.
- NSA penetrated Huawei's headquarters in Shenzhen to exploit the routers and switches made by Huawei and used by a third of the world's Internet population.
- NSA had hacked Chinese universities, telecommunications firms and submarine cables.
- 14 American secret cyber agencies had been closely tracking secret cyber operations by China for several years.
- NSA broke into a Chinese telecommunications company to obtain mobile phone messages and repeatedly attacked the backbone network of Tsinghua University and computers of the telecommunications company Pacnet in their Hong Kong headquarters.

China's Response to Snowden Revelation. China named the U.S. the reason for its cyber insecurity as cyber attacks originated from the U.S. China is worried about U.S. dominance in global network infrastructure and its influence on cyber technology. The entire Internet depends on thirteen root servers. Ten of those are in the U.S., while one each is in the Netherlands, Sweden and Japan. China is seriously concerned about the influence of companies like Microsoft and Oracle and is considering curtailing their use for government applications.

China is aware that some of the most sophisticated malware like Stuxnet and Flame have been developed in American labs. According to a scholar at the China Institute of Contemporary International Relations, "The United States holds the power of determining anyone's life or death in cyberspace and has the capability of dominating cyber information. The broadband information infrastructure development gap with developed countries has widened; the level of government information sharing and business collaboration is not high; the core technology is controlled by others, insufficient strategy coordination; weak critical infrastructure protection capability; mobile Internet and other technologies pose serious challenges." China had to deal with the humiliating exposure of a PLA cyber-espionage. Mandiant, a U.S. cyber-security firm, gave a detailed report of China's cyber-espionage activities and its main organisation, Unit 61398. This report also showed critical gaps in the PLA's cyber security system.[12]

Indigenous Digital Industrial Base

China wants to decrease its reliance on foreign cyber technology. It desires indigenous replacements for foreign software to protect its military and critical infrastructure from foreign interference. Indigenisation will also allow China to become more aggressive. Every country, including the U.S. has its own weaknesses in their cyber defences. China's problems are greater than those of its strategic rivals. It has a much weaker cyber-industrial base than the U.S., lower levels of nationwide informatisation and a less advanced and fertile educational system. In these conditions, new technologies such as 5G aggravate threats. Most notably, China has no cyber military allies, where the U.S. leads an impressive cyber military alliance network. U.S.–China Security and Economic

Review Committee, 2019 Report to Congress states: To achieve security in the long run, China must domestically produce chip technology, operating systems, and cryptographic techniques with independent intellectual property. Only with these steps can China guarantee the real safety of national networks.[13]

China has some advantages, like a vast internal market that provides solid foundations for winning a sizeable portion of the developing world's digital market. However, China has a modest domestic cyber-security industry, a fraction of the size of its American counterpart. According to the Cyber-security Association of China, its total revenue in 2019 was RMB 52.09 bn (US$8.09 bn), which represented less than 7 percent of the global cyber-security industry, estimated at US$120 bn in 2019.[14] The leading cybersecurity firms in China have much lower revenues than those in the U.S. and much smaller global footprints. For example, in the first quarter of 2020, Cisco Systems, Palo Alto Networks and Fortinet respectively accounted for 9.1 percent, 7.8 percent and 5.9 percent of the global market and the total U.S. share was estimated at around 40 percent.[15]

In recent years, there has been a rapid growth in this sector, a projected annual growth rate of 20 percent to the end of 2021. In comparison, in 2018, the security-related income of IBM, the leading U.S. cyber-security company, alone grew by 55 percent, and revenues reached $4 bn. In China the proportion of investment allocated to cyber security within informatisation projects is still low, demonstrating an evident gap with the more developed countries in Europe and the United States.[16] While the global footprint of China's cyber-security companies is improving, it remains underdeveloped. As a result, they do not benefit from internationalisation in the same way as firms such as Norton LifeLock, IBM and even Kaspersky have done.

More broadly, the Chinese government has not elevated its educational system to meet the cyber-power.[17]

President Xi Jinping has been pragmatic on this issue. He seems to be accepting the time and effort it will take to overcome the challenge posed by the U.S. In 2019 he summarised it succinctly, "No matter how large an internet company is, no matter how high its market value is, if it is heavily dependent on foreign countries for its core components, and if the major artery of the supply chain is in the hands of others, it is like building a house on someone else's foundation. No matter how big and beautiful it is, it may not stand up to wind and rain, and it may be so vulnerable that it collapses at the first blow.[18] The free market would not be sufficient. Market exchange cannot bring us core technologies, and money cannot buy core technologies. We must rely on own research and development. In a globalised environment such research and development could not be expected to take place behind closed doors. Only when we fight against masters can we know the gap in ability. China would not reject any new technology. It would strategically determine which ones can be introduced (from abroad), digested, absorbed, and then re-innovated versus which must be indigenously innovated on their own."[19]

In an article written in 2019, a noted Chinese scholar, Chen Zhaoxiong pointed out, the deficiencies of market forces when it comes to developing core technology and on the need for industrial policy. Chen wrote, money and the market neither brought the core technology of an operating system nor allowed that technology to be digested, absorbed and re-innovated. China, therefore, had no choice but to support indigenous innovation to build a safe and controllable IT system.

The Ministry of Industry and Information Technology and the State Electricity Regulatory Commission, in September 2012, alleged that Canada's RuggedCom grid equipment contained preset backdoors and required the Chinese electrical power sector to develop contingency plans and risk management to deal with potential problems posed by this technology. In the long run, to achieve security, China must domestically produce chip technology, operating systems and cryptographic techniques with independent intellectual property. Only with these steps can China guarantee the real safety of national networks.

Military Cyber Security

To a considerable degree cyber defence weaknesses in the civil domain carry over to the military sector. Armed forces of all countries' depend partly on non-military organisations to provide cyber defences for armed forces and national security. For example, the U.S. Department of Defense has a large civilian cyber-security workforce drawn largely from educational and training institutes. Same is in China. While China has made impressive breakthroughs in niche areas like quantum communications, these do not depend on distributed capabilities and mass interventions as cyber defence does. The cyber defence task for the PLA is huge, involving millions of uniformed personnel and a large number of civilian employees and external contractors supporting PLA systems.[20]

PLA planners must have compiled a list of cyber assets that are critical to national military operations in various contingencies and vulnerable to cyber attacks. The list is likely to be a long one given the weaknesses in China's civil and military-sector cyber defences. The top targets would most likely include the ten listed below. Many of these targets would be susceptible to some form of classic electronic warfare attacks. This list is not dependent on any particular scenario.[21]

Probable Chinese list of assets subject to US cyber attacks on China in a military crisis, in order of priority are:

- Strategic nuclear missile command and control.
- Medium range missile command and control.
- Strategic Support Force command and control.
- Naval headquarters.
- Eastern Theatre Command headquarters, opposite Taiwan, with primary responsibility for Taiwan contingencies.
- Electric grids around key naval and air bases.
- Satellite navigation systems used by Chinese forces.
- Naval weapons systems and platforms.
- On-board combat systems of military aircraft.
- Chinese intelligence, surveillance and reconnaissance capabilities.

Human Resource Development (HRD) Issues

One of the major obstacles of China becoming a cyber powerhouse is a shortage of cyber operators. The workforce deficit is immense. One Chinese corporation noted that the current supply of cyber security talent is approximately 100,000 while demand is expected to reach 1.4 million in 2020. Less developed areas of China have a deficiency of educational resources. It causes poor cybersecurity practices. PRC is well aware of the poor quality of cyber-security education. It has initiated several measures to alleviate this problem. As of now, this cannot overcome the shortfall in numbers or quality. By 2019, there was a 16 percent increase in enrolments in its five undergraduate cyber-security degrees compared with the previous year. The total numbers, fewer than 10,000, were much less than the requirement. Enrolment growth in master's degrees from 2017 to 2018 was more impressive.

The brain drain, either as entrepreneurs or as employees, from China to western country mainly U.S., is hurting China. A joint China–World Bank report of 2007 found that out of 600,000 students sent abroad in the previous 30 years to study, only 26 percent returned. According to U.S. immigration statistics, around 700,000 Chinese were given green card (permanent resident) status from 2002 to 2011. In 2007, the stay rate in the United States of students from China who had received their PhD degree from a U.S. university was around 90 percent. As the World Bank said, if China wants to retain these people, it will have to 'adjust' the settings. China has employed special incentives to bring skilled émigrés back to the country. Salaries and social conditions in China have improved. Until now, the problem remains.[22]

China has laid down a long-term policy till 2030 to realise the country's innovation objectives. But success would depend on the availability of a vast range of technical skills for research, design, fabrication, production, information and communication technology (ICT) support. China envisages that it would be producing more college graduates than the entire workforce of the United States. The quality of university education was improving rapidly. It is conscious of the quality of tertiary education.

Feng Huamin, the lead official for cyber security education in China, presented a very bleak assessment of cyber security training in 2019:

- The cyberspace security speciality and information security speciality are ambiguous in content and lack homogeneity within the specialities.
- There is a lack of high-level professional teachers who have in-depth engagement with cyber security research.
- The quality of teaching materials is uneven.

- There is a lack of good offensive and defensive training platforms, experimental opportunities, and students' exposure to actual network security problems.

China has proposed several measures to redress the problems:

- Further accelerate governance reform in universities, giving them greater autonomy.
- Diversify funding sources.
- Tighten ethical standards in research.
- Appoint faculty that ensures high-quality, cross-disciplinary graduate and post-doctoral programmes.
- Set up well-staffed, specialized research institutes.
- Develop innovative approaches to teaching and mentoring, especially in analytical skills.
- Encourage more leading foreign universities to set up campuses in China jointly with domestic universities to impart modern governance standards, teaching methods and research management.
- Increase investment by the private sector and the government to improve the quality of human resources.

The General Office of the Ministry of Education, in March 2019, issued the policy guidance under the heading of 'Key points of work about education informatisation and cyber-security in 2019'. Its main instructions on improving 'support capacity of cybersecurity talents' are listed below:[23]

- Improve the capacity to cultivate talents and enhance their quality.
- Enhance the guidance as to "double first-class" universities.
- Compile the Guide to Core Courses for postgraduate students.

- Strengthen the construction of disciplines related to cyberspace security and artificial intelligence.
- Explore new ideas, systems, and mechanisms for training cyber security talents to build.
- Implement the "Excellent Engineer" Training Plan 2.0.
- World-class cyber security colleges.
- Accelerate the construction of new engineering disciplines in the field of cyber security.
- Promote the collaboration between universities and the industry to cultivate cyber security talents.
- Encourage qualified vocational schools to set up cybers security-related majors.
- Expand the scale of training for cybers security talents.
- Continue to improve the national teaching standard system for vocational education.
- Carry out the second batch of work to revise teaching standards in high vocational schools.

The Ministry of Industry and Information Technology (MIIT), in September 2019, offered its perceptions into the education policy measures needed. For improving the talent training system, it called for the following proposals:

- More universities to establish cyber security colleges or cybersecurity-related majors.
- To intensify the establishment of first-class cyber security colleges and the development of teaching and research staff.
- To strengthen vocational education to produce more graduates.
- To promote the collaboration between universities and the industry by setting up joint laboratories for cyber security.

- To support high-level cyber security contests.
- To improve the talent discovery and selection mechanism.

Establishing the National Cybersecurity Center (NCC) is a huge step to get more cyber security professionals. CCP policymakers hope to see 2,500 graduates passing out from NCC each year. The first class of 1,300 students will graduate in 2022. The Talent Cultivation and Testing Center, the second talent-focused component, offers courses and certifications for early and mid-career cybersecurity professionals. The Talent Cultivation and Testing Center can teach six thousand trainees each month, more than seventy thousand in a year at full capacity. Combined, both components of the NCC could train more than five hundred thousand professionals in a single decade.

The Cybersecurity 'Ten Thousand Talents' Training Grant Program

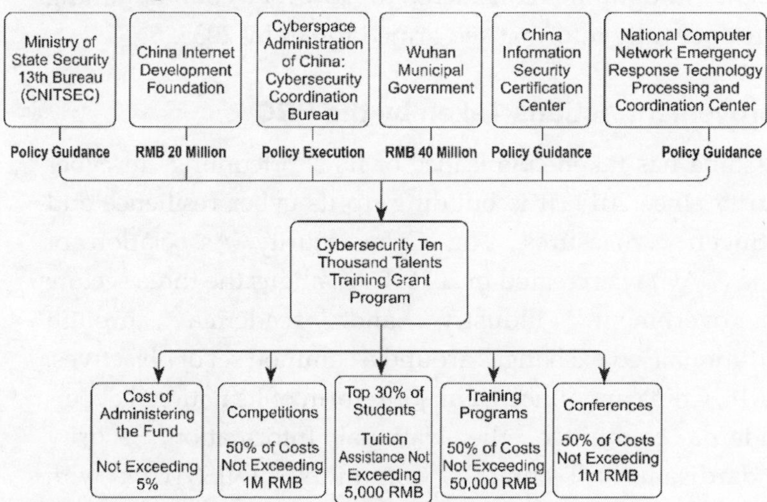

Source: Dakota Cary, China's National Cybersecurity Center, Center for Security and Emerging Technology, July 2021.

Cyber Training in Military Domain

The PLA has many key professional institutions at the university level that produce graduates in cyber security subjects. The PLA IEU in Zhengzhou comes under the Strategic Support Force. This university is now the only officially designated national cyber security personnel training institution for the PLA and is the most important. It has more than 2,000 teaching and research staff, including 153 doctoral supervisors and 447 master's supervisors. It takes a multi-disciplinary approach that integrates science, engineering, military affairs, culture and management. Four new majors have been created in 2019: artificial intelligence (AI), information security (information management), confidentiality management and electronic information engineering. In 2019, the total number of student places for all listed cyber disciplines was 737. This accounts for 64 percent of the positions available at the IEU. However, even this higher student throughput is considered too low for a country aiming to produce fully informatised armed forces by 2035.

Improvement Actions Taken by the PRC

China has taken cognisance of its shortcomings in cyber security since 2014. It is building up its cyber resilience and contingency measures. The Cybersecurity Association of China (CAC) was created in 2016. CAC aligns the three sectors of government, industry and academia through institutionalised exchanges around a common set of objectives. In 2016, China announced a major reform of its national cyber-standards committee, the National Information Security Standardisation Technical Committee (NISSTC), with representatives from across government, from Chinese companies, and a much smaller number of foreign companies.

By 2018 the NISSTC had published more than 300 new cyber-security standards, covering CII protection, product review and other areas. In December 2019, the Multi-level Protection Scheme 2.0 (MLPS 2.0) was implemented, broadening the scope for regulation of network operators and imposing heightened regulatory requirements.

In 2020, China published 'Cybersecurity Review Measures' to toughen up the security of its CII. This document outlined a set of rules to govern the review of supply-chain reliability and security underlying the products and services used by the infrastructure operators. The government also released a draft Data Security Law in July 2020 and a draft Personal Information Protection Law in October 2020, representing the first all-inclusive legislation relating to the security of personal data.[24]

China understands very well the value and power of technology, innovation and the internet. It is cautious in operating the double-edged sword of the internet. China is aware that once free information is released, it is impossible to stop. This has great potential to shake the foundation of the communist party and the political order of China. China has set up a doctrine of Seven Baselines for using the internet. It demands whatever is expressed online must respect seven elements: the country's national interest, laws and regulations, the socialist system, public order, citizens' lawful rights and interests, morality and accuracy. Apple was the first global company that faced the compelling provisions of this law. PRC warned Apple to remove the VPN40 applications in the AppStore in China in July 2017. Another world-leading company, Amazon, informed their customers about cancelling its services if the use of unapproved VPN's is detected, in accordance with this law.

China has taken steps to control social media. Some of these steps include banning some social media applications originating from the Western world, encouraging the use of national social media applications, and banning some websites altogether. For instance, in 2009 China banned the operations of Facebook. The ban on Facebook was followed by the ban on other social media applications having foreign origins, such as Twitter and Snapchat. After 2009, the Chinese government has tried to popularise national and local social media applications. A lot of progress through investment and incentive plans and significant progress has been made by 2018. The use of national and local social media applications in China is under serious auditing and control. CPC has regulated the use of the internet in public spaces and taken precautions against opening web pages or blog.

The PRC has implemented 'the Great Firewall of China' to control cyberspace, which is officially known as the 'Golden Shield Project'. This project was initiated by the Ministry of Public Security in 1998 and has been updated periodically. It is the Chinese government's project for internet censorship and surveillance. MPS operates this system in three stages:

- Stage 1: Blocking the Domain Names and IP Addresses.
- Stage 2: Censorship on Keywords; in other words, if any content is a pre-detected "critical" by the government, blocking of this message.
- Stage 3: The detection of VPN's; in other words, if they are used, taking criminal action against them.

National Cybersecurity Center

China has taken a significant initiative to establish the National Cybersecurity Center. NCC aims to bring together government, academia and the private sector with its focus on cybersecurity. Commercialisation of research and development activities and facilitating the quick deployment of new technologies are key to the NCC's impact on state capabilities. The NCC is an asset in national power that will prove critical to China's future success in the cyber domain. Despite a shortfall of 1.4 million cybersecurity professionals, China is considered a near-peer cyber power to the U.S. The current deficit leaves China's businesses and infrastructure vulnerable to attack while spreading thin its offensive talent. The NCC will bolster China's capabilities, making competition in the cyber domain fiercer.

When the Cyberspace Administration of China announced the NCC in 2016, CAC also enumerated 'five innovations' that should guide its development and ensure it achieved the CCP's original intentions. The CAC's five innovations are: Innovate New Methods for Administering Cybersecurity Schools, Innovate New Ways of Assembling Cybersecurity Talent, Innovate New Methods of Cultivating Cybersecurity Talent, Establish a System for Evaluating and Certifying Cybersecurity Talent and Construct a Top-Class Cybersecurity Industrial Park. Within a year of the NCC's announcement and its accompanying 'five innovations', the Wuhan Municipal CAC expanded on these broad concepts. The 'Wuhan Model' of Cybersecurity Talent Cultivation described how major components of the base are to be operated with varying levels of specificity.[25]

As of September 2020, 114 companies had decided to establish themselves in the NCC, promising more than $71.5 billion in investment. Representatives from across society, including powerful government ministries, top-tier cybersecurity firms and academic institutions, sit on the NCC's government committee. The NCC is being built in Wuhan. The 15 square mile campus, which China began constructing in

2017 is still being developed at speed. A report by Georgetown University's Center for Security and Emerging Technology (CSET) along with an interactive map of satellite photos, examines the NCC. The NCC includes seven centres for research, talent cultivation and entrepreneurship, National Cybersecurity School and two government-focused laboratories.[26] The NCC has support from the highest levels of the CCP. The Party's Cyberspace Affairs Commission established a committee to oversee the NCC's operations and policies, directly linking to Beijing.

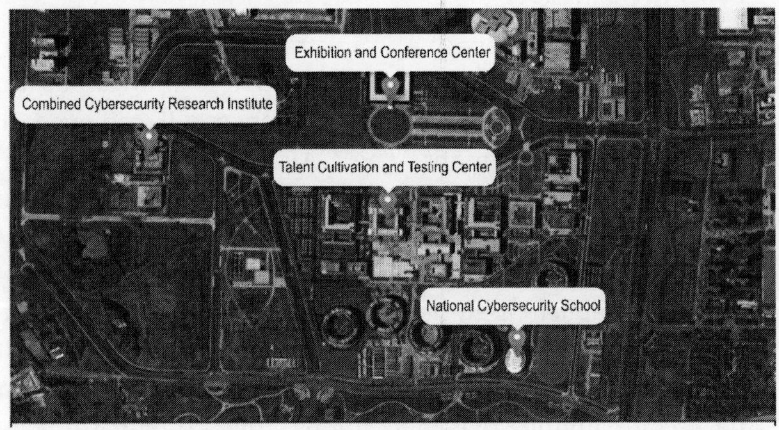

Layout of NCC

Source: https://ncc-map.cset.tech/

By 2030, the NCC aims to train over five hundred thousand cybersecurity practitioners, alleviating the shortage of trained professionals. The NCC will strengthen China's cyber capabilities. The NCC will improve China's offensive and defensive cyber capabilities. Unlike the tools for cyber defence, where there is a well-developed market in which companies innovate and compete for profits, offensive cyber capabilities have only one customer in China: the government. The NCC's goal is to advance China's cybersecurity capabilities in two ways: strengthening the talent pipeline and supporting innovation and entrepreneurship.

Concept Map for Components of the NCC

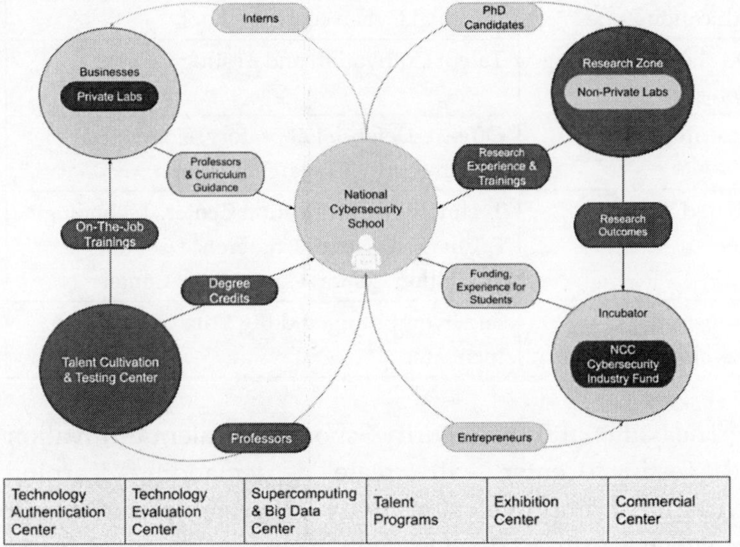

Source: Dakota Cary, China's National Cybersecurity Center, Center for Security and Emerging Technology, July 2021.

https://cset.georgetown.edu/wp-content/uploads/CSET-Chinas-National-Cybersecurity-Center.pdf

The NCC's focus on practical, hands-on learning and the substitution of school course credits with certifications from the Talent Cultivation and Testing Center makes its graduates particularly attractive for government and private sector employers seeking to bolster their cyber capabilities.

Students at the NCC can build relationships with companies they will ultimately work for, ask for support from the Incubator for their new startup, or attain certifications that give them preferential treatment when applying to jobs. Online programs may expand the talent pool.

The Five Zones of the NCC

Zone	Components
Education Zone	National Cybersecurity School
On-the-Job Training Zone	Talent Cultivation and Testing Center
Research Zone	Offense-Defense Laboratory, Combined Cybersecurity Research Institute
Shared Services Zone	Technology Certification Center, Technology Evaluation Center, Conference Center, Exhibition Center, Commercial Center
Industrial Development Zone	Supercomputing and Big Data Center, Incubator

The National Cybersecurity School and Talent Cultivation and Testing Center will create a demanding learning environment, improve connectivity between stakeholders in the cybersecurity ecosystem and represent a broad-based attempt to expand the talent pool. In due course, the NCC will become the foundation for technological progress and talent cultivation that meaningfully influences the dynamics of nation-state cyber competition. The NCC will help the PLA to progress on the three obstacles constraining its capabilities: talent, innovation and indigenisation. PLA's cyber operators, private sector mercenaries and state security services' hackers will slowly be filled by successive classes of NCC graduates. NCC graduates may well design the cyber tools they use.

National Cybersecurity School

The National Cybersecurity School is the 'leading mission' of the NCC. It presently shares the campus of Wuhan University and Huazhong University of Science and Technology (HUST). Originally it was planned to combine

Wuhan University and HUST educational resources. However, problems with integration led to the present "partially independent, partially shared" model. Members from national and local government, the private sector and sponsoring units conduct oversight, ensuring the divided institution meets its obligations to the central government.

Source: Apollo Mapping.

National Cybersecurity School

Rather than teaching primary content, the school plans to ensure that the best and brightest of academia and the private sector are training promising students under government direction, focusing on innovation, entrepreneurship and practical skills. The school for degree credits counts training programs, competitions, published papers, inventions and patents obtained and professional certificates. The school gives special attention to its doctoral program, providing a "strategic scientific" mentor and an "innovative entrepreneurship" mentor to help postgraduate candidates conduct and monetise applied research. To date more than RMB 2.6 billion has been invested in the National Cybersecurity School. Though its first graduating class includes only 1,300 students, CCP policymakers hope to increase that number to 2,500.

Talent Cultivation and Testing Centers

The Talent Cultivation and Testing Center offers a wide range of cybersecurity training programs and certifications for cybersecurity professionals, students and the general public. The centre's programs are anchored by two leading cyber-security firms: IntegrityTech and Qi'anxin Technology. Graduates would receive advance notice of job openings and preferential treatment in the hiring process at nearly 30 companies. The centre is capable of training 6,000 people per month.

The Centre hosts training programs for several different certifications, including:

- Certified Information Security Professional, a standard developed by Ministry of State Security 13th Bureau, China Information Technology Security Evaluation Center.
- Certified Information Security Manager.
- Information Security Management Auditor (ISO/IEC 27001 and ISO/IEC20000-1).
- Network Security Authentication Certification Engineer (NSACE), a standard developed by the Ministry of Industry and Information.

- Information Security Protection Evaluator, a standard developed by the Ministry of Public Security.
- Certified Information Security Assurance Worker (CISAW), a standard developed by the China Cybersecurity Review Technology and Certification Center.

Combined Cybersecurity Research Institute. The Combined Cybersecurity Research Institute is a pathway for government-directed research on innovative cyber capabilities. Designed as a joint effort between Qihoo360 and Wuhan University, it expanded to work in partnership with 12 companies, including Beijing TopSec, which has trained PLA hackers.

Exhibition and Conference Center. The Exhibition and Conference Center hosts large scale events and promotes investment in the NCC. The Exhibition Center is 100 sq m with three exhibition halls. The Exhibition and Conference Center has hosted several events since opening in July 2019, these include signing ceremonies for new participants in the NCC, a cybersecurity competition and a conference for the Shanghai Cooperation Organisation's Information Security Working Group and the opening of the 'Yellow Crane Cup'.

Supercomputing and Big Data Center. The NCC relies on two facilities to provide cloud computing and data storage solutions. The Supercomputing and Big Data Center host 2,000 servers, a 60,000-core vCPU, 8 petabytes (PB) of RAM and 80PB of data storage.

Data Valley (Supercomputing and Big Data Center). Data Valley, constructed by Centrin Data Systems, is an expansive complex of three large and four medium-sized data storage buildings, an operation and maintenance centre, a control centre and dedicated backup power supplies. Once construction is completed, Data Valley's total storage capacity will become 10 exabytes and computing power will reach one petaflop at a total investment of RMB 10.5 billion by Centrin Data Systems.

Technology Incubator. The facility has attracted investment of more than RMB 3 billion. Led by Tsinghua University's TUS Holdings, the Incubator will help commercialise research and fund startups. The Incubator will help scale up existing enterprises by providing accelerator programs for small businesses. More than 200 companies are involved with the Incubator.

Technology Evaluation Center. The Technology Evaluation Center would provide security and defensive services for the Supercomputing and Big Data Center, the National Cybersecurity School and laboratories. Although no public documents state who runs the facility, it is run by its namesake organisation, CNITSEC, also known as the 13th bureau of the Ministry of State Security.

Offense-Defense Laboratory. Wuhan University runs a similarly-named Cyber Offense-Defense Center in collaboration with the PLA. The Offense-Defense Lab is a facility for developing and testing new cyber tools for government use. Provincial propaganda departments describe the Offense-Defense Lab as a network simulation center with three purposes: to host personnel training, offer practical combat drills and support research and innovation. It invested RMB 20 million in outfitting the facility.

Technology Certification Center. The centre is run by the China Information Security Certification Center (ISCCC). It is responsible for the certification of essential cybersecurity for products, licensed personnel, management systems and information security services.

Commercial Center. The centre is made up of two office buildings with 42 companies in residence.

Hongxin Semi-conductors Defunct Factory. Hongxin Semiconductors began constructing this factory to produce semi-conductors in 2018. In early 2021, during the construction of their fabricator, the company was exposed as fraudulent and collapsed into bankruptcy.

Endnotes

1. Greg Austin, The Strategic Implications of China's Weak Cyber Defences, Survival, vol. 62 no. 5, October–November 2020, pp. 119–138 DOI 10.1080/00396338.2020.1819648
2. State Council Information Office of the People's Republic of China, 'China's Military Strategy', China Military Online, May 2015, http://english.chinamil.com.cn/news-channels/2015-05/26/content_6507716.htm.
3. The Cyber Index: International Security Trends and Realities. Report by the United Nations Institute for Disarmament Research, 2013, p. 15, available at: http://www.unidir.org/files/publications/pdfs/cyber-index-2013-en-463.pdf
4. China is outspoken about data security concerns in overseas IPOs by revising its cybersecurity review rules, July 14, 2021 available at: https://www.jdsupra.com/legalnews/china-is-outspoken-about-data-security-8251633/
5. Jamie Tarabay and Coco Liu, Obscure Cyber Agency Becomes Nemesis of China's Tech Giants, Bloomberg, July 13, 2021 available at: https://www.bloomberg.com/news/articles/2021-07 - 13 / xi-elevates-an-obscure-china-regulator-to-take-on-didi-big-tech
6. President Xi Says China Faces Major Science, Technology "Bottleneck"', Xinhua, 1 June 2016 available at: http://en.people.cn/n3/2016/0601/c90000-9066154.html.
7. Iain Johnson, 'Redmond Puts Wall Around Windows 10 for Chinese Government Edition', 23 May 2017, available at: https://www.theregister.co.uk / 2017/05/23/redmond_puts_wall_around_windows_10_for_chinese_government_addition/
8. Cyber Capabilities and National Power: A Net Assessment, International Institute for Strategic Studies (IISS), 28th June 2021 available at: https://www.iiss.org/blogs/research-paper/2021/06/cyber-capabilities-national-power

9. ITU Publications, 'Global Cybersecurity Index (GCI) 2018', p. 62, available at: https://www.itu.int/dms_pub/itu-d/opb/str/D-STR-GCI.01-2018-PDF-E.pdf.
10. China National Computer Network Emergency Response Team, 2016, National Computer Network Emergency Technology Processing Coordination Center, April 2017, pp. 14–20, available at: http://www.cac.gov.cn / wxb_pdf / CNCERT2017 / 2016 situation.pdf
11. Kurt Eichenwald, "How Edward Snowden Escalated Cyber War with China," Newsweek, November 1, 2013.
12. APT1, Exposing One of China's Cyber Espionage Units available at: https://www.fireeye.com/content/dam/fireeye-www/services/ pdfs/mandiant-apt1-report.pdf
13. U.S.–China Security and Economic Review Committee, 2019 Report to Congress of the US– China Economic and Security Review Commission, 116th Congress, 1st Session, November 2019, p. 135, available at: https://www.uscc.gov/sites/default/files/2019-11/2019 percent20Annual percent20Report percent20to percent20Congress.pdf.
14. Gartner, 'Gartner Forecasts Worldwide Security and Risk Management Spending Growth to Slow but Remain Positive in 2020', 17 June 2020 available at https://www.gartner.com/en/newsroom / press-releases / 2020-06-17-gartner-forecasts-world widesecurity-and-risk-managem.
15. Statista, 'Leading cybersecurity vendors by market share worldwide from 2017 to 2020', 2 July 2020, https://www.statista.com/statistics/991308/worldwide-cybersecurity-top-companies-bymarket-share.
16. China Cybersecurity Industry Alliance, 'China's Cyber Security Industry Analysis Report 2019', December 2019, p. 2, available at http://www.china-cia.org.cn/AQLMWebManage/Resources/kindeditor/attached/file//20191219/20191219092355_6832.pdf.
17. China Cybersecurity Industry Alliance, 'China's Cyber Security Industry Analysis Report 2019', December 2019, p. 2, available at http://www.china-cia.org.cn/AQLMWebManage/Resources/kindeditor/attached/file//20191219/20191219092355_6832.pdf.
18. 'China's Xi Jinping warns of new "long march" as trade war with US intensifies', Straits Times, 22 May 2019, available at

https://www. straitstimes.com / asia / east-asia / chinese-president – xi – jinpingwarns - of - new-long-march-as-trade-war-intensifies

19. The Full Text of Xi Jinping's Speech at the Forum on Cybersecurity and Informatization Work
20. Recruitment Announcement of the Academy of Electronic Warfare of the National University of Defence Technology in 2020', 19 October 2019, available at http://www.offcn.com/jzg/2019/1019/33384.html.
21. Greg Austin, The Strategic Implications of China's Weak Cyber Defences, Survival, vol. 62 no. 5, October–November 2020, pp. 119–138
22. Greg Austin and Wenze Lu, 'Five Years of Cyber Security Education Reform in China', in Greg Austin (ed.), Cyber Security Education: Principles and Policies (Abingdon: Routledge, 2020), pp. 173–93.
23. Greg Austin, Cyber Security Education: Principles and Policies, Routledge, 2021
24. Bryan Cave, 'China's Draft Personal Information Protection Law: What Businesses Should Know', Lexology, 2 December 2020, https://www.lexology.com/library/detail. aspx?g=f7f7b85c-545a-4fbe-a114-833044603750
25. Translation by Ben Murphy, Wuhan City Cyberspace Administration, "The 'Wuhan Model' of Cybersecurity Talent Cultivation"; Office of the Central Cyberspace Affairs Commission, Cyberspace Administration of China, September 19, 2016 available at: https://perma.cc/N98W-5VWU
26. Dakota Cary, China's National Cybersecurity Center, Center for Security and Emerging Technology, July 2021 available at: https://cset.georgetown.edu / wp-content / uploads / CSET-Chinas-National-Cybersecurity-Center.pdf

* * *

CHAPTER 7

China's Cyber Espionage Activities

"There are two kinds of big companies in the United States; there are those who've been hacked by the Chinese and those who don't know they've been hacked by the Chinese." – Former FBI Director James Comey

Introduction

For years, China has engaged in cyber espionage against the U.S. and other nations, mostly in Europe, to collect sensitive public and private information in support of national objectives laid out in its 12th Five Year Plan. These cyber espionage operations are part of a sophisticated, long-term campaign to get inside targeted networks so that once intruders are inside the network, they can exfiltrate information, manipulate data and implant stay-behind devices or software for future action.

China acquires technology through illegal means, like cyber theft, industrial espionage, human intelligence as well as through legal means like strategic investments, recruiting talent, open source information and acquiring knowledge through education in the U.S. and business deals with U.S. firms. The Pentagon, in 2017, informed that Beijing had conducted "an intensive campaign to obtain foreign technology through imports, foreign direct investment, industrial and cyber espionage, and establishment of foreign R&D centers."[1]

Chinese espionage activities are targeted at defence capabilities, diplomatic, economic and defence industrial base sectors that support U.S. national defence programs and other national security secrets and economic espionage activities. China is particularly interested in space, infrastructure, energy, nuclear power, technology firms, clean energy, biotechnology and healthcare.[2] Not only Chinese hackers were carrying out traditional state espionage, they were also busy stealing intellectual property from every major company in the Fortune-500, American research laboratories and think tanks. Chinese hackers were pilfering trade secrets from innovators, mostly from the U.S. By some estimates, they were passing trillions of dollars' worth of American research and development to China's state-owned enterprises. Chinese hackers had taken everything from the designs for the next F-35 fighter jet to the Google code, the U.S. smart grid and the formulas for Coca-Cola and Benjamin Moore paint.

China's Targets

Economic and Technical Domain. One of the aims of Chinese espionage activities is to strengthen China's economic effectiveness and strategic position. China is assessed to be responsible for 50 to 80 percent of cross-border intellectual property theft worldwide and over 90 percent of cyber-enabled economic espionage in the United States. The U.S.-China Economic and Security Review Commission has concluded that Chinese espionage "comprises the single greatest threat to U.S. technology." Chinese espionage helped China save on research and development expenses while catching up in several critical industries. China does this to "erode the United States' long-term position as a world leader in science and technology innovation and competitiveness." China is reverse engineering many of the U.S. military's technical and industrial advantages.[3]

China has concentrated cyber industrial espionage at high-technology and advanced manufacturing companies in the United States, Europe, Japan and Southeast Asia. Hackers have targeted firms' negotiation strategies and financial information in the energy, banking, law and pharmaceutical sectors. In the Five Year Plan for 2011-15, China identified seven priority industries to develop. Not surprisingly, the U.S. has been an innovator and leader in these very industries. Most of China's industrial espionage involves such industries as:

- New Energy (nuclear, wind, solar sower).
- Energy Conservation and Environmental Protection (energy reduction targets).
- Biotechnology (drugs and medical devices).
- New Materials (rare earths and high-end semi-conductors).
- New IT (broadband networks, Internet security infrastructure, network convergence).
- High-end Equipment Manufacturing (aerospace and telecom equipment).
- Clean Energy Vehicles.

At the end of the day foreign technology is converted into products and weapons in China at 'Pioneering Parks for Overseas Chinese Scholars', 'Innovation Service Centers', 'National Technology Model Transfer Organisations' and an unknown number of 'technology business incubators'. These large, sophisticated facilities are located strategically to ensure wide distribution of the foreign technologies obtained informally.[4]

Military Domain. PLA cyber forces want to build an operational picture of U.S. defence networks, military disposition, logistics and associated military capabilities that could be used before or during a conflict to deter, delay, disrupt and degrade U.S. operations. The skill sets and accesses required for these intrusions are similar to those necessary to conduct cyber operations. Chinese hackers have pilfered information from more than two dozen U.S. Defense Department programs, including the MIM-104 Patriot surface-to-air missile system and the F-35. They have targeted more than 24 universities in the United States, Canada and Southeast Asia to pinch research about maritime technologies being developed for military use.[5]

For PLA Command-and-control targets are principally attractive. A RAND Corporation report concludes, "Perhaps no U.S. military vulnerability is as important, in Chinese eyes, as its heavy reliance on its information network. ... Successfully attacking that system will affect U.S. combat capabilities much more profoundly than would directly targeting combat platforms. Chinese strategists also believe that the U.S. military information network is not just vulnerable but also fragile. Thus, the foundation of the U.S. military's success can also be its undoing."[6]

Chinese hackers want to know not only about the technology of the U.S. armed forces but also about its operational plans. Hacking efforts were concentrated against Pacific Command, which would be directly involved in any war with China. As per their military doctrine China wants to prevent the U.S.' ability to mobilise for war. Chinese hackers broke through a large number of the civilian organisations and contractors who work for the U.S. military's Transportation Command, responsible for movements of men and material in position for battle.

The Washington Post reported that Chinese hackers pilfered critical information relating to missile defence including "the advanced Patriot missile system, ... an Army system for shooting down ballistic missiles, ... and the Navy's

Aegis ballistic-missile defense system." The hackers also gathered information on planes, helicopters and ships, including "the F/A-18 fighter jet, the V-22 Osprey, the Black Hawk helicopter and the Navy's new Littoral Combat Ship, which is designed to patrol waters close to shore." These were the very weapons on which the U.S would depend in a conflict with China. China can now study the vulnerabilities of these equipments.[7]

Activities of Su Bin, a businessman from Canada can be an interesting case study of Chinese espionage activities. Su Bin's task was to track American military aerospace developments. He used his knowledge of the industry, aviation and English to channel the Chinese hackers toward the most important targets. One of his targets was the Boeing's giant cargo plane C-17, that the U.S. Air Force uses extensively in different missions. John Carlin, the senior Justice Department official wrote that "thanks to Su Bin, the Chinese were able to develop, build, and deploy their own copy, in barely a third of the time it had taken the U.S. to design, test, and build the original C-17." At an air show in November 2014, the PLA Air Force kept its C-17 clone, the Xi'an Y-20, right next to the original U.S. It was a spectacular visual symbol of what hacking can do. Su Bin and his hacker colleagues also targeted other advanced aircrafts in the U.S arsenal like the F-22, a fighter jet optimized for air-to-air dogfighting and the F-35, the Joint Strike Fighter that was the most expensive airplane project in history. China was closing the technological gap. The total cost of the team's effort was only one million dollars compared to multibillion-dollar price tags of these systems.

Examples of Miscellaneous Cyber Espionage

China has targeted foreign ministries, embassies and important government offices in India, Taiwan, Germany,

Indonesia, Romania, South Korea and other countries. Journalists and Tibetan and Uighur activists are tracked. Chinese hackers broke into telecommunications operators in Turkey, Kazakhstan, India, Thailand, and Malaysia to track Uighurs travelling in Central and Southeast Asia.[8]

GhostNet. China has been conducting cyber espionage operations against India for a long time. One of the earlier examples was the GhostNet episode. Between June 2008 and March 2009 the Information Warfare Monitor conducted an investigation focused on allegations of Chinese cyber espionage against the Tibetan community. GhostNet penetrated computer systems containing sensitive and secret information at the private offices of the Dalai Lama and other Tibetan targets. GhostNet, infected 1,295 computers in 103 countries. Almost a third of the targets infected by GhostNet included the ministries of foreign affairs of Iran, Bangladesh, Latvia, Indonesia, Philippines, Brunei, Barbados and Bhutan; embassies of India, South Korea, Indonesia, Romania, Cyprus, Malta, Thailand, Taiwan, Portugal, Germany and Pakistan; the ASEAN (Association of Southeast Asian Nations) Secretariat, SAARC (South Asian Association for Regional Cooperation) and the Asian Development Bank; news organisations and an unclassified computer located at NATO headquarters.

Operation Aurora. A spear-phishing and drive-by download effort, Operation Aurora, became public in 2010. Operation Aurora targeted thirty-four major companies, including Google, Microsoft, Juniper and other firms. The hackers had the following objectives for Operation Aurora:

- Spy on Chinese dissidents. Google wrote that "we have evidence to suggest that a primary goal of the attackers was accessing the Gmail accounts of Chinese human rights activists."
- Undermine the home-field advantage that hugely benefited the U.S. They wanted to find out which targets in China the U.S. was observing through Google's systems. With access to the legal-discovery system, the Chinese could see a list that former top Justice Department official John Carlin described as a 'who's who' of the spies, hackers and criminals known to the United States. China could see if the U.S. was using American technology companies to watch the activities of alleged Chinese intelligence officers.
- Access to those companies' secrets, beginning with their source code, a valuable form of intellectual property. It is easier to find software vulnerabilities and write software exploits to take advantage of them. Discovering and exploiting software vulnerabilities is critical for cyber operations.

- Obtain signing certificates which are cryptographically complex markers that authenticate that a particular piece of code came from a known source like Google and can be trusted.

In 2013, Mandiant, a U.S. cybersecurity company, publicshed a detailed report pinpointing a Chinese military unit's cyber espionage involvement.[9] In 2014, as part of the Office of Personnel Management (OPM) breach, Chinese hackers pilfered almost 22 million records of government employees. Stolen data included details of names, places of birth, dates, security background checks, data on intelligence and military personnel and 5.6 million employees' fingerprint data. The hackers accessed Standard Form 86, which includes records of drug use, alcohol addiction and financial problems. This data could be combined with medical data stolen from Anthem Insurance, travels documents from United Airlines and hotel reservation data from Marriott International to create a complete picture of U.S. personnel and their movement.[10] In 2017, people from the PLA's 54th Research Institute hacked into the protected computers of Equifax and took names, birth dates and social security numbers for approximately 145 million American citizens. The hackers obtained credit card numbers and other personally identifiable information belonging to approximately 200,000 American consumers. In a single breach, the PLA obtained sensitive identifying information for nearly half of all American citizens.[11]

A report written by a team of intelligence analysts and consultants from the Swedish intelligence and research agency, Defence Research Agency (FOI) titled 'Kina's Industriella Cyberspionage' ("China's industrial cyber espionage") was published in March 2019. It found that the Chinese cyber warfare division is largely operated directly by China's PLA with the assistance of its Ministry of State

Security (MSS). This organisation mostly focuses on corporate and industrial espionage.

The Hacking Game

There is a feeling in China that U.S. concerns about China's cyber espionage activities is an attempt to divert attention from America's own activities. China's criticism is triggered by hurdles posed against its following practices: [12]

- Militarisation of cyberspace.
- Pursuit of a double standard in claiming cyber freedom for itself while attacking or limiting such freedom for others.
- Engaging in completely groundless, destructive, and self-serving accusations against others.
- Dominating the current global cyber system through unfair means.

China's official report states that 63 percent of attempts to hack PLA military websites originate in the U.S. [13] Qihoo-360, one of China's premiere cybersecurity firms, reported that some of the tools used by U.S to hack Chinese government, military, science and industry targets since 2008 are the same ones that have been developed by the CIA as confirmed by Wiki Leaks in 2017.[14] After Edward Snowden's revelations about U.S. global surveillance efforts, China takes more assertive stance and points its finger at the U.S. government. American officials warn that Chinese manufacturer Huawei's equipment are riddled with Chinese backdoors. China can exploit that access to intercept communications, gather intelligence, carry out cyber war or shut down critical infrastructures in times of its choosing. But the reverse is also true. China is quick to point out that a study conducted on behalf of the U.S. Congressman and Chairman of the House Permanent Select Committee on Intelligence, found no clear evidence that Huawei spied on behalf of the Chinese government.[15,16]

Years ago, the U.S. National Security Agency (NSA) had snooped its way into Huawei's headquarters in Shenzhen, stolen its source code and planted its own malware/backdoor in Huawei's routers, switches and smartphones. NSA also penetrated Huawei's customers, particularly countries like Iran, North Korea, Cuba, Syria and Sudan who seriously avoided American technology. It further hacked into two of China's largest cellular networks. NSA's voice recognition and selection tools had been extensively deployed across Chinese mobile networks. NSA can sniff out voices of interest on Chinese cell networks, capture their conversations and get them back to Fort Meade, where NSA translators, decoders and analysts brake them down for critical intelligence. There has been several reports about the NSA spying on non-national security entities like Brazil's biggest oil company, the European Union Commissioner investigating Google, Microsoft and Intel and the International Monetary Fund and World Bank. [17,18] Even in the U.S. public and special interest groups pursuing to preserve civil liberties have condemned the NSA activities.[19]

United States does this to many other countries, friend or foe. Hundreds of thousands of NSA implants are deeply embedded in other foreign networks, routers, switches, firewalls, computers and phones worldwide. Many are actively siphoning texts, emails and conversations back to the agency's server farms every day. Many others are sleeper cells, dormant until called upon for some future shutdown or all-out cyberwar.

China's Cyber Espionage Resources

The PLA is in collaboration with various institutions within China's civilian sector and has raised a number of 'cyber militias' that are called upon to perform cyber espionage activities. These organisations are made from academic institutions, tele-communications companies, municipal governments and volunteers within China. China's telecommunications firms play a major role in strengthening China's activities in this domain. These are not technically part of the Chinese governmental apparatus or State-Owned Enterprises. Nevertheless, major Chinese telecommunications firms like Huawei act as *de facto* proxies for China. As per the FBI estimation, China has more than 30,000 military cyber spies, plus an additional 150,000 private sector cyber experts, "whose mission is to steal American military and technological secrets", according to former head of U.S. counter-intelligence, Michelle Van Cleave.[20]

The Shadow Brokers hacking group has released tools and files belonging to Equation Group in 2017. The Equation Group is linked to the U.S. intelligence agency's Tailored Access Operations (TAO) unit of NSA. Cybersecurity firm Check Point on February 22, 2021 reported that a Chinese group APT31, known as Judgment Panda, had gained access to a Windows-hacking tool known as EpMe created by the Equation Group and modified it as a tool called Jian. It was actively exploited between 2014 and 2017 before the vulnerability was patched. This is not the lone example of Chinese tools stealing and modifying Equation Group tools. In 2019, Symantec documented that APT3 Buckeye was linked to attacks using Equation Group tools in 2016 before the Shadow Brokers leak.[21]

Data War

The battle over data is defining the global conflict between U.S. and China. This war over data is of critical importance for spy agencies of both. In the intelligence world, information is king, and the more information, the better. During the Cold War, intelligence mainly came in piecemeal and partial form. Today, the data-driven nature of every activity creates huge volume of information that can be potentially used by intelligence agencies using techniques like big data analytics.

William Evanina, the U.S.' top counter-intelligence official, told the Foreign Policy that "China is one of the leading collectors of bulk personal data around the globe, using both illegal and legal means. Just through its cyber attacks alone, the PRC has vacuumed up the personal data of much of the American population, including data on our health, finances, travel and other sensitive information."

China also conducts influence operations by targeting media organisations, cultural institutions, academic, business and policy communities in the U.S. and other countries and international institutions. The Chinese Communist Party wants to condition foreign and multilateral political establishments and public opinion to accept China's narrative of its strategic priorities. In the next chapter China's Cyber Influence Operations will be examined.

Endnotes

1. U.S. Department of Defense, "Annual Report to Congress: Military and Security Developments Involving the People's Republic of China," May 15, 2017, page 72 available at: https:// www.defense.gov / Portals /1/Documents/pubs/2017_China_ Military_Power_Report.PDF
2. http://intelligence.house.gov / sites / intelligence.house.gov / files/documents/HuaweiZTE%20Investigative%20Report%20% 28FINAL%29.pdf
3. Michael Brown and Pavneet Singh, "China's Technology Transfer Strategy: How Chinese Investments in Emerging Technology Enable a Strategic Competitor to Access the Crown Jewels of U.S. Innovation," Defense Innovation Unit Experimental, January 2018, pages 3, 17-21.

4. https://www.judiciary.senate.gov / imo / media / doc / 12-12-18%20Mulvenon%20 Testimony.pdf

5. The Future of Cybersecurity across the Asia-Pacific available at: https://www.nbr.org / wp-content / uploads / pdfs / publications/ap15-2_cyberrt_apr2020. pdf

6. Roger Cliff, Evan Medeiros, and Keith Crane, "Keeping the Pacific: An American Response to China's Growing Military Might," RAND Corporation, Spring 2007 available at: https://www.rand.org/pubs/periodicals/rand-review/issues/spring2007/ pacific.html

7. Ben Buchanan, The Hacker and the State: Cyber Attacks and the New Normal of Geopolitics, Harvard University Press, Feb 2020

8. Jack Stubbs, "China Hacked Asian Telcos to Spy on Uighur Travelers," Reuters, September 5, 2019 available at: https://www.reuters.com / article / us – china – cyber-uighurs-idUSKCN1VQ1A5

9. "APT 1: Exposing one of China's Espionage Units," Mandiant, available at: http://intelreport.mandiant.com/Mandiant_APT1 _Report.pdf.

10. Richard J. Harknett & Max Smeets (2020) Cyber campaigns and strategic outcomes, *Journal of Strategic Studies,* DOI: 10.1080/01402390.2020.1732354

11. "Wanted by the FBI," linked from the FBI Home Page, https://www.fbi.gov / wanted / cyber / chinese-pla-members-54thresearch-institute, "Chinese Malicious Cyber Activity," linked from Department of Homeland Security Home Page, 15 Mar 2018, available at: https://www.us-cert.gov/china

12. Michael Swaine, "Chinese Views on Cybersecurity in Foreign Relations," China Leadership Monitor, July 30, 2013, page 14 available at : http:// carnegieendowment.org / email / South_Asia/img/CLM42MSnew.pdf

13. Bill French, "China and the Cyber Great Game," The National Interest, March 20, 2013 available at: http://nationalinterest.org/ commentary/china-the-cyber-great-game-8241.

14. Richard J. Harknett & Max Smeets (2020), Cyber campaigns and strategic outcomes, *Journal of Strategic Studies,* DOI: 10.1080/01402390.2020.1732354

15. Mike Rogers and Dutch Ruppersberger, "Investigative Report on the U.S. National Security Issues Posed by Chinese Telecommunications Companies Huawei Technologies and ZTE," U.S. House of Representatives, October 8, 2012, available at: https://intelligence.house.gov/sites/intelligence.house.gov / files / documents/Huawei-ZTE%20Investigative%20Report% 20%28FINAL%29.pdf.
16. "Huawei: Leaked Report Shows No Evidence of Spying," BBC News, October 18, 2012, available at: http://www.bbc.com/ news/technology-19988919.
17. Edward Moyer, "NSA Spied on EU Antitrust Official Who Sparred With U.S. Tech Giants," Cnet, December 20, 2013, available at: http://www.cnet.com/news/nsa-spiedon-eu-antitrust-official-who-sparred-with-us-tech-giants/.
18. Mark Hosenball, "Obama Halted NSA Spying on IMF and World Bank Headquarters," Reuters, October 31, 2013, available at: http://www.reuters.com/article/us-usasecurity-imf-idUSBRE99U1EQ20131031
19. Charlie Savage, "Watchdog Report Says NSA Is Illegal and Should End," The New York Times, January 23, 2014, available at: http://www.nytimes.com / 2014 / 01 / 23 / us / politics / watchdog – report - says-nsaprogram-is-illegal-and-should-end. html?partner=rss&emc=rss&smid=twnytimes&_r=1
20. Michelle Van Cleave, "Chinese Intelligence Operations and Implications for U.S. National Security," Testimony before the U.S.-China Economic and Security Review Commission, June 9, 2016, page 5. Available at: https://www.uscc.gov/ sites/default/files/Michelle%20Van%20Cleave_ Written%20 Testimony060916.pdf
21. Charlie Osborne, Chinese hackers cloned attack tool belonging to NSA's Equation Group, February 22, 2021, available at: https://www.zdnet.com / article / chinese – hackers – cloned - attack-tools-belonging-to-nsas-equation-group/

* * *

CHAPTER 8

China's Cyber-Influence Operations

"Wherever the readers are, wherever the viewers are, that is where propaganda reports must extend their tentacles."

–Xi Jinping, February 2016

Introduction

The digital era has transformed the way we communicate. Using social media like Facebook and Instagram and social applications such as WhatsApp and Telegram, one can be in contact with friends and family, share pictures, videos, messages, posts and share our experiences. Social media has become an effective way of influencing human society and behaviour and shaping public opinion. By sharing a post, tweeting an idea, contributing a discussion in a forum and sharing a sentimental picture, we can influence others and sometimes convince to agree with our opinion.

Use of cyber tools and methods to manipulate public opinion is called 'Cyber Influence Operation'. In the present day, many countries use cyberspace, especially the social media, to accomplish Cyber Influence Operations as a part of Information Warfare. Most of these operations are done covertly. It is difficult to differentiate between legitimate or malicious influence operations.[1]

Influence operations are meant to shape the perceptions of individuals, groups, and/or the public at large. In September 2020, General Paul Nakasone, Commander of the United States (U.S.) Cyber Command, called foreign influence operations as the "the next great disruptor." Russia is the most active player in this domain and uses many methods, including the social media. The U.S. is now much concerned with the spread of pro-Chinese propaganda in the country and has taken measures to reduce the "news employees" of the Chinese media organisations Xinhua, China Daily, the China Global Television Network (CGTN), China Radio and People's Daily from 160 to 100.[2]

China seeks a critical role in impacting the current international system. It conducts influence operations as a national strategic objective by targeting media organisations, cultural institutions, academic, business and policy communities in the U.S. as well as other countries and international institutions. The Chinese Communist Party (CCP) wants to condition public opinion and foreign and multilateral political establishments to accept China's narrative of its strategic priorities.[3]

Definition

There is no official definition of the term 'Influence Operations'. Influence operations include a broad range of non-kinetic, communications-related and informational activities that aim to affect the cognitive, psychological, motivational, ideational, ideological and moral characteristics of a target audience.[4] China sees the cyberspace domain as a platform providing opportunities for influence operations.

In 2009, the RAND Corporation defined influence operations as a coordinated, integrated and synchronized application of national diplomatic, informational, military, economic and other capabilities in peacetime, crisis, conflict and post-conflict situations to foster such attitudes, behaviours or decisions among foreign target audiences that further U.S. interests and objectives.[5]

Cyber-Influence Operations

Cyber-Influence Operations (CIO) use new digital tools like the 'bots' or social media. It focuses on utilising cyberspace to shape public opinion and decision-making processes through social bots, dark ads, memes and spread of misinformation.

Matteo E. Bonfanti defines CIO as "activities that are run in cyberspace, leverage this space's distributed vulnerabilities and rely on cyber-related tools and techniques to affect an audience's choices, ideas, opinions, emotions or motivations, and interfere with its decision making processes."[6] Influence operations thus encompass not only the activities referred to as information operations but also the non-military and coercive activities. These operations are designed to influence a target audience by changing, compromising, destroying or stealing information by accessing information systems and networks.[7]

If the purpose is to control the responses of the group members, it is called perception management. Russia follows the concept of reflexive control, a theory similar to perception management. Reflexive control is a means of expressing to a partner or an opponent specially prepared information to incline him/her to voluntarily decide the predetermined decision desired by the action initiator.

Herbert Lin and Jackie Kerr have coined the term 'Information/Influence Warfare and Manipulation' (IIWAM). They define this as "the deliberate use of information by one party on an adversary to confuse, mislead, and ultimately to influence the choices and decisions that the adversary makes." It is thus a hostile non-kinetic activity whose targets are the adversary's perceptions. IIWAM realm focuses on "damaging knowledge, truth, and confidence, rather than physical or digital artefacts. IIWAM seeks to inject fear, anxiety, uncertainty, and doubt into the adversary's decision making processes."[8]

Cyber-Influence Operations refers to actions designed to influence people through the combined use of sophisticated computational and social manipulation techniques. China's idea of CIO is stated as "cyber media warfare is a kind of combat operations with the Internet as the platform... Targeted information infiltration is made through the Internet media for influencing the convictions, opinions, sentiments, and attitudes of the general public to effectively control the public opinion condition, shape strong public opinion pressure and deterrence over the adversary and win an overwhelming public opinion posture for one's own side."[9]

The People's Republic of China (PRC) conducts influence operations for achieving outcomes favourable to its strategic objectives by targeting policy communities, cultural institutions, media organisations, business and academics in the U.S. as well as other countries and international institutions. The CCP wants to condition domestic, foreign, and multilateral political establishments and public opinion to accept Beijing's narratives. People's Liberation Army (PLA) organisations responsible for information operations include the Central Military Commission (CMC), particularly the Joint Staff Branch and its Intelligence Bureau, the Political Work Division's Liaison Branch and the Office for International Military Cooperation, the Strategic Support Force and PLA-controlled media enterprises. Free exchange of information also permits criticism of the ruling party. Therefore Chinese authorities go to great lengths to prevent access to Internet sites deemed subversive. The Great Firewall of China blocks the following:[10]

- Any content considered unfavourable to China. There are over 18,000 websites.
- Gmail, Google, YouTube, Facebook, Instagram.
- Many VPN providers.
- Intermittently, also the Twitter, Hotmail, and Flickr.

China has been trying to influence foreign thoughts and opinions for long. China's influence activities have moved from their focus on diaspora communities to target a far broader range of Western societies' sectors. These are stretching from universities, think tanks and media to national government, state and local institutions. The Hoover Institution, in a paper published in November 2018, claimed that over 30 of the West's foremost China scholars collaborated in disseminating findings of a working group on China's influence operations abroad. [11] China wants to:

- Promote views kind to the Chinese culture, society and government policies.
- Suppress alternate views and co-opt key American players to support China's foreign policy goals and economic interests.

These Chinese inference and influence operations come in various forms:[12]

- Manipulation of leading former European politicians working to promote Chinese interests.
- Penetration of regional organisations (Interpol, the Council of Europe) to orient their activities to align with Chinese interests.
- Manipulation of diasporas and Chinese communities living abroad, which the United Front Work Department (UFWD) agents can mobilise during diplomatic visits.
- Pressure on researchers and the academic research apparatus using the issuance of visas and financial programs.
- Distribution, in exchange for remuneration, of a news supplement 'China Watch' in major European daily papers, to create economic dependence and stimulate self-censorship in the treatment of news about China.

- To be in charge of the majority of Chinese-language European media.
- Retaliatory measures against governments that are critical or judged to be "unfriendly."

The PLA's influence operations are summarised in the 'Three Warfares' concept of media or public opinion warfare, psychological warfare and legal warfare. Media warfare is the control and exploitation of communications channels for disseminating propaganda. It sets the circumstances for dominating communications channels for the conduct of psychological and legal warfare. Psychological warfare uses propaganda, deception, threats and coercion to affect the adversary's decision-making. It conducts military operations through perception management and deception while countering opponent psychological operations. Legal warfare uses international and domestic laws to claim legal high ground, to sway target audiences, gain international support, manage political repercussions and to assert Chinese interests. The PLA uses online influence activities to support its overall Three Warfares concept and undermine an adversary's resolve in a contingency or conflict.

China has employed cyber operations to exert influence over opponents and potential partners. China's repetitive penetration of Taiwanese networks is part of a more extensive effort to wield economic and military pressure on Taiwan to lessen its autonomy. China has undertaken many network operations to harass sub-state actors, many of which are associated with its "Five Poisons": Tibetan separatism, Uighur separatism, Falungong activity, Taiwanese independence and pro-democracy activism. Many sophisticated operations against dissident groups indicate that China considers their suppression to be a high priority and worth the risk of an international backlash as they pose threats to China's internal stability.

China sees disinformation operations as an effective strategy for its government to achieve foreign policy objectives. In propagating disinformation, China is deliberately undertaking large-scale operations of producing and reproducing false or misleading information to deceive. The PLA, the State Council and the CCP's Central Committee participate in organised Information Operations, whether on domestic or international platforms. China utilises advancements in technology and uses 'deep fakes', 'deep voice' and artificial intelligence (AI) on Chinese social media. It is important to distinguish the political intent and national strategies underlying these campaigns from another perspective on the news.

French researchers, in an influential 2018 joint research report on Chinese influence operations, used the term 'information manipulation'.[13] They define information manipulation as "the intentional and massive dissemination of false or biased news for hostile political purposes." According to the French researchers, nation-state information manipulation comprises three conditions:

- A coordinated campaign.
- The political intention is to cause harm.
- Diffusion of information or false information that is consciously distorted.

Organisation

The CCP uses a wide range of party, state and non-state actors for its influence operations. In recent years it has considerably increased its investment and intensity of these efforts. In China, there is no single institution that is entirely responsible for China's influence activities. However, the CCP reigns supreme. Actors, who are nominally independent in other countries like academia, civil society, corporations and religious institutions, are obliged to the Chinese Government and are frequently made to press forward the state interests. The organisation and structure for carrying out influence operations are given below:

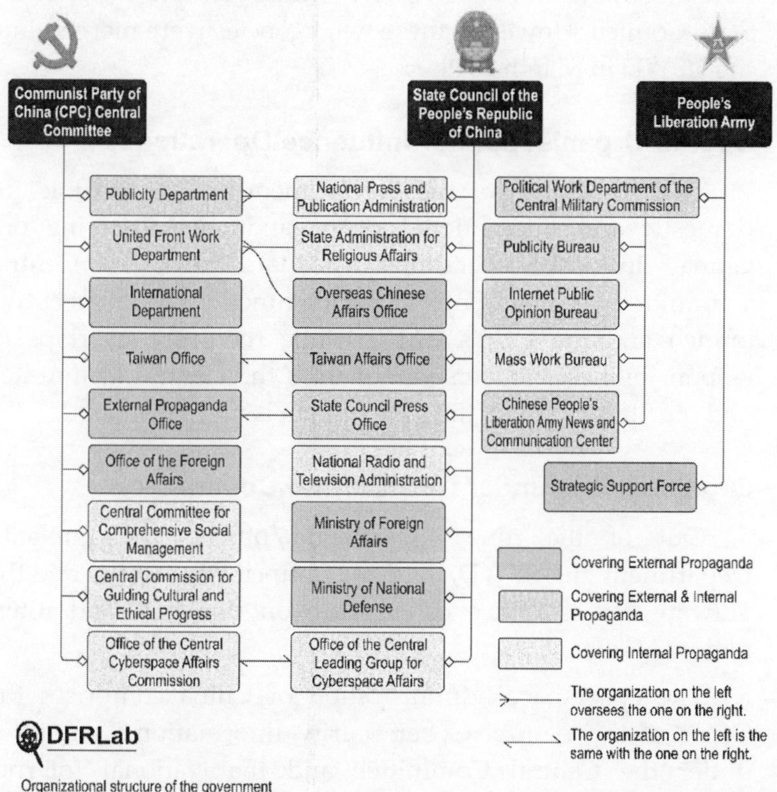

Organizational structure of the government offices responsible for discourse power.

Source: Alicia Fawcett, Chinese Discourse Power China's Use of Information Manipulation in Regional and Global Competition, Atlantic Council, December 2020 available at: https://www.atlanticcouncil.org/wp-content/uploads/2020/12/China-Discouse-Power-FINAL.pdf

The central organisation responsible for influence operations include the CCP's UFWD, the Central Propaganda

Department, the State Council Information Office, the International Liaison Department, the Chinese People's Association for Friendship with Foreign Countries and the All-China Federation of Overseas Chinese. These organisations are augmented by various state agencies like the Ministry of Foreign Affairs and the Overseas Chinese Affairs Office of the State Council. However, these two agencies were merged into the UFWD in March 2018.

Overall Organisation for Influence Operations

Three branches of the Government are responsible for domestic and international propaganda and carrying out China's influence operations. They are the CCP's Central Committee, the State Council, which functions as its executive branch and the CCP's CMC. While there are overlaps of responsibilities and personnel across the Central Committee and the State Council, the PLA branch is more insulated.

Organisations under CPC Central Committee

Out of the nine departments/offices, the Publicity Department, the UFWD, the State Council Press Office and the Taiwan Affairs Office concentrate on domestic and international issues.

The cyberspace administration of China comprises the Office of the Central Cybersecurity Information Committee under the Central Committee and the National Internet Information Office under the State Council. Under the Cyberspace Administration, there is the Internet News Dissemination Bureau, the Internet Comments Bureau and the Internet Social Work Bureau. The organisation's duties are: supervising the domestic information flow, making rules for online content and regulating internet companies to make sure compliance with laws and regulations.

The Internet News Dissemination Bureau controls online news production and dissemination by organising political training sessions to use the internet for more compelling storytelling and news professionals. It encourages information exchange between domestic and international online media outlets. The Internet Comments Bureau is responsible for investigating online comments trends and providing future projection on the online comment ecosystem. In a report on the 2019 Bluebook of Internet Comments, the China Internet Comments Development Report released by the Internet Comments Bureau, revealed its interest in "exploring the effective ways of expression in the new era of online commenting to promote government credibility, communication power and influence." Likely tactics of the agency include engaging experts, agenda-setting, government officials, and influencers to 'interfere at the right time' and targeting the younger generation with a 'positive' online commenting environment. The Internet Social Work Bureau is a more direct channel to engage with the domestic population.

The United Front Work Department (UFWD)

The United Front has been vital to China's soft power offensive. The UFWD is a department under the CCP Central Committee, one of four Central Committee departments. The department was created in 1938 by the CCP to garner support from civilians in the country. After the emergence of the PRC in the 1950s, the department was given the responsibilities to unite the country in both territorial and nation-state terms. Major worries of the department were: ethnic minorities issues, citizens not associated with the CCP, overseas Chinese diaspora, Taiwan, Hong Kong, Macau, Xinjiang and Tibet.

Methods adopted to engage these populations include inviting politicians, businessmen, journalists and civil society organisations from target countries to visit China for events like political summits, academic conferences and civil society organisations seminars. The purpose of these trips is to produce and promote propaganda that directly portrays China's positive image by influencing the respective population groups in these target countries. The UFWD has relations with prominent private corporations, business people, academics, intellectuals, minority groups, Chinese diaspora groups and Chinese students overseas.

The United Front cultivates pro-Beijing perspectives in the Chinese diaspora and the wider world by rewarding those it deems friendly with accolades and lucrative opportunities, while orchestrating social and economic pressure against critics. This pressure is intense but indirect. Clear attribution is difficult. But it has had an overwhelming effect on Chinese-language media in the diasporas.[14]

The Chinese President and General Secretary of the CCP, Xi Jinping, has energized the UFWD's operations. He has added 40,000 officials to its roster and raised it to the top tier of party organs. Under Xi Jinping's leadership, UFWD organisations play a crucial role in China's foreign policy. The UFWD performs targeted, low-intensity influence operations to shape influential individuals' perceptions of the CCP's goals and objectives. The UFWD is taking particular actions to co-opt and subvert ethnic Chinese individuals who are citizens of other nations. In the U.S., the 'Thousand Talents Program (TTP)' initiatives result in powerful business implications, including the loss of critical intellectual property, from some of the country's leading corporate giants.

The UFWD's primary target audience is Chinese diaspora. The mission of engaging and influencing non–ethnic Chinese audiences, individuals and foreign institutions is allocated to other specialized Chinese entities like the Ministry of State Security (MSS) e.g., China Institutes of Contemporary International Relations (CICIR), the Chinese Academy of Social Sciences (CASS), the Ministry of Culture, the Ministry of Education and other institutions that have well-trained professionals with long-standing ties with their counterparts overseas.

Organisations under the State Council of the PRC

The Ministry of National Defense and the Ministry of Foreign Affairs generally focus on international issues. However, they target both domestic and international audiences. The National Radio and Television Administration focuses primarily on internal issues for domestic audiences. It uses propaganda and content surveillance.

Organisations under the PLA

Political Work Department of the CMC seeks to influence foreigners by sponsoring visits to China by foreign groups with military affiliations. It maintains a liaison department, subordinate to which is an intelligence bureau and the China Association for International Friendly Contact (CAIFC). The group that is very active in such activities is the CAIFC. The Political Work Department controls CAIFC, but it works closely with the CCP's International Liaison Department and the PLA's Military Intelligence Department for selecting its foreign targets.

The International Liaison Department

The CCP's International Liaison Department is in charge of 'party-to-party relations'. Its primary mission is cultivating foreign political parties and politicians around the world. It maintains ties with over 400 political parties in 140 countries, receives about 200 delegations, and dispatches about 100 delegations abroad every year. Through its dealings with political parties worldwide, the International Liaison Department identifies promising foreign politicians before achieving national prominence and office. After identifying such people, the department usually brings them to China on all-expenses-paid visits and makes the best possible impression on them.

The International Liaison Department performs the following functions:

- Administering private sector liaison organisations to facilitate contact with think tanks, NGOs and individuals around the world.
- Collecting up-to-date intelligence and information on the foreign policies, domestic political scene and political parties and societies in various nations.
- Sending special study teams overseas to research important topics related to China's reforms.
- Contributing to the work of Chinese embassies around the world.
- Working with other CCP Central Committee departments and State Council ministries to assist their work overseas.
- Arranging overseas visits of central/provincial/municipal/sub-provincial level CCP officials.
- Introducing foreign political leaders, officials, ex-officials and foreign policy specialists on tours of China.
- Hosting biannual World Political Parties High-Level Meeting and the annual 'CCP in Dialogue with the World' meeting.

The International Liaison Department carries out very important roles overseas and is a crucial instrument in China's international influence activities.

Role of Intelligence Agencies

The People's Daily, China's largest newspaper group, is used by both the MSS and China's military intelligence department as cover for sending intelligence agents abroad and presents itself as offering a humane, Chinese viewpoint on global news. It also operates an English-language news site and regularly performs several U.S.-based social media platforms.

The intelligence agencies and the MSS have a significant task in shaping and influencing Western perceptions on China, similar to the UFWD's role, and the state-run media and propaganda systems. The strategic objectives are determined, prioritised and disseminated from Xi Jinping downwards. Each ministry and system uses its own methods and resources to achieve those goals. Each system has the same objectives but similar and dissimilar tools. Sometimes, there is an overlap of these resources, tools and competition against each other, degrading their efforts' effectiveness.

Traditionally, the intelligence services do not have a prominent role in influence operations. However, as Peter Mattis noted, they are one of multiple professional systems operating in parallel within China to achieve national-level goals and objectives. [15]

Gathering Intelligence from Non-Intelligence Sources

The CCP, to gain information relies on, in addition to the MSS, other non-intelligence sources. Chinese state-affiliated think tanks, for example, China Institute of International Studies (CIIS), CASS and China Center for Contemporary World Studies (CCCWS), not only seek to influence perceptions of China among scholars and policy makers but also function as sources of information for the Chinese

Party-State. The China Institutes of CICIR is a direct extension of the MSS.

Foreign contacts are an important part of China's intelligence efforts. Chinese intelligence agents rarely approach targets directly. As Peter Mattis notes, "for the Chinese, intelligence services seem to facilitate meetings and contacts rather than handling the dirty work of influencing foreign targets themselves."[16]

The PLA's influence operation capabilities are shared across its political, academic and militia groups. The Political Work Department of the CMC is the most crucial organ in the PLA, responsible for designing and promoting Chinese influence operations abroad ideologies. The Publicity Bureau or Propaganda Bureau, subordinate to the Political Work Department, supervises content production and dissemination, especially regarding the PLA's reputation both at home and abroad. Colonel Pan Qinghua, who is in charge of the Propaganda Bureau, released upcoming plans for establishing a more professional group of spokespersons, prioritising the impact of positive narratives around the CCP's rule and taking the initiative in 'storytelling' to shape the image of the PLA. PLA News and Communications Center implements content production and promotion and operates its media outlets and social media accounts, including official accounts on Weibo and WeChat. The Mass Work Bureau concentrates on the domestic audience and attempts to promote "positive energy" content. The Internet Public Opinion Bureau, which was established under the 2015 Deep Reform and the military reform, is responsible for online information operations. The Chinese influence operations bureaucracy is given at Appendix.

There is cross-organisational cooperation between the Internet Public Opinion Bureau with other organisations outside of the army branch. The Bureau's main aim is to shape PLA soldiers' positive reputation for both domestic and international audiences. The Public Opinion Bureau, with the Cyberspace Administration of China, organized an event in 2019 for internet media professionals to cover heartening stories about border patrols in celebration of the 70th Anniversary of the establishment of the PRC. In 2018, the bureau organized a seminar titled 'Innovation and Development of Army Internet Public Opinion in the New Era', with academic professionals from the School of Political Science of the National Defense University, officers from the army's political administration and officers in charge of active-duty troops participating. The topics included "operation and maintenance of novel online media platforms of the army" and "ideological and political work of the army in the era of the internet."

THE MEDIA

The Traditional Media

China Central Television (CCTV) has a number of stations operating overseas, broadcasting in the native language of the host country and in Chinese. It transmits the targeted messages of the CCP. State-owned Chinese media companies have created a substantial footing in the English-language market in print, radio, television and online. Simultaneously, the Chinese Government has restricted the U.S. and other Western media outlets' ability to conduct normal news-gathering activities and provide news feeds directly to Chinese listeners, viewers, and readers within China.

Since 2012, China has increased foreign direct investment in U.S. entertainment, media and education from nearly zero to some $9 billion. In 2015, the Reuters reported that China state-run media employed a series of shell companies to hide its ownership of 33 radio stations in the U.S. and 13 other countries.

In the digital television sector, Chinese firms like Star Times in Africa have become dominant players. They indirectly benefit Chinese state media. The most affordable and popular packages feature a combination of local stations and Chinese state-run outlets. The global news sources like the British Broadcasting Corporation (BBC) or Cable News Network (CNN) are considerably more expensive. Chinese companies are also expanding its roles in countries like Pakistan, Cambodia and East Timor.

Digital Media

The Chinese Government has used social media for its influence operations extensively. The proliferation of social media platforms, the progressively broad range of services offered and the ability to engage with the intended audience provide a lucrative platform for influence operations. In the U.S., "Americans spend more than 11 hours per day on average in social media reading, listening, watching or interacting with media."[17] They get their news equally from social media[18] and news sites and trust the reliability of the information on social media.[19]

Xinhua and the People's Daily are the two widely distributed and heavily digitised Chinese news services to promote the Party's will and protecting its authority. Xinhua News Agency is the authorised news agency of China. The 'Reporters Without Borders' has termed it as "the world's biggest propaganda agency." Since joining Twitter and Facebook in 2011 and 2013, People's Daily has accumulated 4.4 and 41 million followers respectively. Mobile applications of its media organisations, including the CGTN, brings out another aspect of China's propaganda outreach. It has delivered over 1 million downloads on the Android platform.

The PLA's Nanjing Political Institute is the home of its research and training for political warfare. Majority of the PLA's social media experts come from this institute. The PLA's premier academic journal on propaganda, the Military Correspondent, provides a fair idea of how the CCP wants to go about its influence activities. The journal contains ongoing research on tactics, current tracking methods and future information campaign goals. As per the Military Correspondent, the PLA's objectives with foreign social media include: improve and defend the PLA's image, correct misperceptions, address adverse reporting, communicate deterrence signals, communicate resolve and undermine enemy resolve. It calls upon the PLA to improve employment tactics in social media, advance its psychological warfare strategies and develop home-grown AI and data solutions.

Some of the recommendations from various publications in Articles in Military Correspondent are as under:

- The necessity for engaging in Western social media platforms. "...if a blog has more than 10 million followers, then one's influence may match that of a TV station". Make use of the viewpoints and opinions of third-party media and experts, amplifying voices advantageous to our side."
- China's global discourse power was weak because more than 80 per cent of the essential international news in the world is provided by a few major news outlets of developed nations in the Western world. So create Western social media accounts, employ them to maximum effect.

- Target audiences with tailored content to draw them to the official English language resource, China Military Online, with hyperlinks.
- Cultivate a group of opinion leaders or 'influencers' from within the PLA and using realistically plain language on the Western social media sites, facilitate subconscious acceptance without betraying its foreign origin.
- The Chinese Military Online could be used for foreign interference. It can seek to understand what the Western target audience wants and project different perspectives over domestic propaganda.

Chinese Investments in the Media

The U.S.-China Economic and Security Review Commission's report to the Congress in 2011 noted that China Daily, a Communist Party-affiliated state-owned newspaper, paid for inserts in newspapers such as The Washington Post and The New York Times.

A U.S. scholar has estimated that the Chinese Government is spending on propaganda in foreign countries $10 billion per year. The Government has paid to place news like propaganda supplements in prominent international newspapers.[20] China has been playing propaganda videos on billboards in New York City's Times Square since 2011, likely to cost millions of dollars.[21]

Since 2012, China has increased foreign direct investment in the U.S'. entertainment, media, and education from nearly zero to some $9 billion. A 2015 Reuters investigation reported that China state-run media employed a series of shell companies to obscure its ownership of 33 radio stations in the U.S. and 13 other countries. These radio stations actively sought to influence U.S. listeners' perceptions of key topics, from the South China Sea to democratic elections in Hong Kong.

A New York Times report confirms that the Chinese Government does pay to deliver its propaganda to foreign audiences. China "spends hundreds of thousands of dollars" on Facebook advertising alone to promote its content on the network. It was observed that Xinhua's Twitter followers were growing at an unnatural rate. It was felt that other Chinese propaganda organisations might also be buying influence and followers on the Western social media. The New York Times investigated in January 2018 and found that Xinhua had bought social media followers and reposts from a "social marketing" company called 'Devumi'. The Chinese Government is ready to exploit U.S. social media companies for its propaganda purposes.

It was reported that China Daily, mouthpiece of the CCP, paid $19 million to American newspapers in advertisement and printing charges alone between 2016-2020. In its report to the U.S. Department of Justice, China Daily stated that it had spent $11 million in advertising in prominent U.S. newspapers like Chicago Tribune, The Los Angeles Times, The Houston Chronicle, etc. It disclosed that it spent $2,65,822 on Twitter advertisements. The U.S. President Trump found propaganda ads in various newspapers by China, including The Wall Street Journal and Washington Post, disturbing.

The People's Daily, China's largest newspaper group, is part of a collection of papers and websites. The Daily is used by both China's military intelligence department and the MSS as cover for sending intelligence agents abroad.[22] It Daily operates an English-language news site and is active on several U.S. based social media platforms.

Chinese-Language Media

By 2018, all of the significant official Chinese media outlets had developed deep roots in the communications and broadcasting infrastructure of the U.S. CGTN or CCTV, the semi-official Hong Kong-based Phoenix TV and some Chinese local TV channels are available as add-on packages of two major satellite TV providers in the U.S. - DirecTV and DISH Network. CCTV channels (English and Chinese) are included in the cable systems of all the major metropolitan areas of the U.S.

The CCTV, major Chinese provincial TV networks and the quasi-official Phoenix TV, are all available in the Chinese TV streaming services that are popular among Chinese communities in the U.S. There are four primary Chinese streaming services in the U.S.: Charming China, iTalkBB Chinese TV, KyLin TV and Great Wall. All these services are accessible nationwide and carry the major official Chinese TV channels, including major provincial channels.

Chinese media social media presence

(E) = English version; (C) = Chinese version

Platform	Official organizations and subscribers/followers				Quasi-official
	CCTV (CGTN)	Xinhua	People's Daily	China Daily	Phoenix TV (fully Controlled by Chinese government)
Twitter	CCTV: 532K (E+C) CGTN: 7.19M (E)	11.8M (E) 11.6M (C)	4.54M (E) 221K (C)	1.8M (E)	7K (C)
Facebook	CCTV: 48.04M (E); 3.44M (C) CGTN: 58.28M (E) CGTN America: 1.2M (E)	46.92M (E)	43.15M (E) 171K (C)	35.17M (E)	14K (C)
YouTube	289K (C)	173K (E)	25K (E)	3K (E)	75K (C)
Instagram	550K (E)	111K (E)	696K (E)	23.5K (E)	N/A

The principal official Chinese media organisations - the People's Daily, and China Daily (the only major official newspaper in English), Xinhua, CCTV (CGTN), have a substantial presence on all major social media platforms of the U.S. and have many followers. Even though Facebook and Twitter platforms are blocked in China, these outlets use the same platforms in U.S. Quasi-official Phoenix TV, a global TV network with links to the PRC's MSS and headquartered in Hong Kong with branches worldwide, has a significant presence on all the major social media platforms in the U.S.

Social Media

In the social media domain, Chinese companies' growing role in content delivery systems creates opportunities for the CCP to influence foreigners' views about China and the news they receive about their own countries and political leaders. On social media platforms, Xinhua, CGTN and the Global Times were the most active content generators. Posts by the People's Daily, Xinhua, and CGTN were liked at the highest rates.

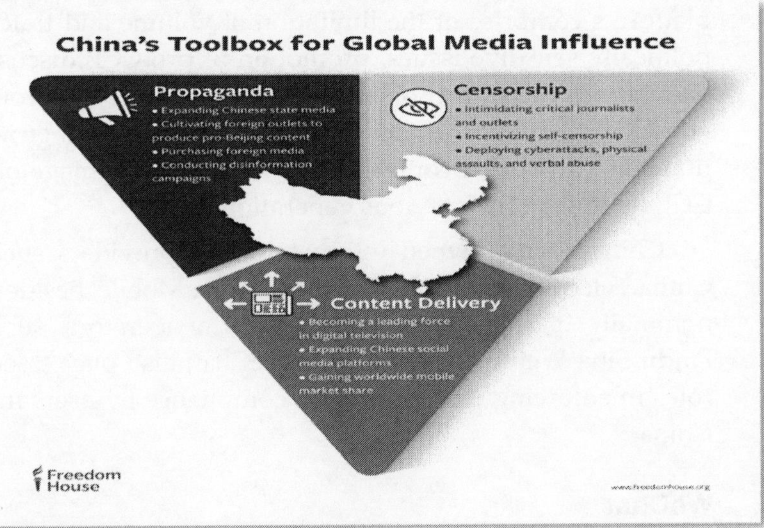

Source: www.freedomhouse.org

The role of WeChat in the 2016 U.S. election is interesting.[23] Reuters reported in August 2020 that the Chinese tech firm ByteDance had censored articles critical of the Chinese Government on its Baca Berita (BaBe) news aggregator app based on instructions from a company's team's Beijing headquarters. Millions use this app in Indonesia. The regulated content included references to 'Tiananmen' and Mao Zedong', as well as to China-Indonesia tensions over the South China Sea and a local ban on the video-sharing app TikTok, which ByteDance owns.

Influence Operations on China's Domestic Platforms

China's influence operations targeting mainly the internal audiences on domestic social media apps Weibo, Wechat and TikTok China are both overt and effective. Social media companies are under close scrutiny by the Government regarding trending topics and user management response-bilities. The methods of information operations on these platforms comprise of the limitation of volume and traffic of politically sensitive issues, promotion of pro-CCP discussion and narratives and censorship of users considered to promote anti-CCP discourse. Under the name 'Little Pink', growing numbers of young people embrace the positive image of the CCP more than the previous generations.

Chinese state-owned internet service providers such as China Telecom, China UniCom and China Mobile, besides the nominally 'private' technology platform operators, such as Baidu Sina Weibo and Tencent's WeChat, also play essential roles in enforcing censorship and compliance by users inside China.

WeChat

WeChat is the most popular social media platform and instant messaging (IM) app in China. It is owned by Tencent, a Chinese internet company with close ties to the Chinese Government. As of the first quarter of 2020, the monthly active users of WeChat exceeded 1.2 billion.[24] In addition to Chinese citizens, many people of the global Chinese diaspora use WeChat to connect with their friends and business partners in China. Numerous reports indicate that Chinese-Americans had initiated political groups on WeChat to mobilise voters for their preferred candidate, mostly Trump.[25] Besides the IM capabilities, WeChat also provides a miscellaneous set of supplemental services and payment services. It limits politically sensitive narratives.

WeChat was found to censor Chinese activists' posts and the independent media while allowing pro-Beijing media and narratives to spread widely among Chinese diaspora communities. Its server identifies politically sensitive information and prevents the message from showing up on the recipients' end without informing the user who sent the message. The growing use of WeChat among non-Chinese speakers in locations ranging from Malaysia and Mongolia to Australia and Canada creates a solid base for future CCP disinformation campaigns or election meddling.[26] Its Influence Operations deal with limiting information transmission, jeopardising domestic and international users' ability to communicate and to organize with other users. It provides the Government with desired stability and protects the majority of the public from taboo topics.

Sina Weibo

Sina Weibo is a Chinese micro-blogging website similar to Twitter. With 516 million monthly active users in 2019, it is the second-largest social media platform in China, after WeChat.[27] It is a robust environment for discussion on a variety of topics, like Twitter. This platform has a highly educated user population; about 80 per cent of the population holds a bachelor's or other technical degrees. The 2011 Wenzhou High-speed Rail Incident, in which two high-speed rail trains collided in Zhejiang Province, put the platform in the limelight. At that time, the platform's users directed passionate anger and demanded justification from the Ministry of Railways officials in dealing with the rescue work. Facing the criticism, the Government carried out a series of "reforms" to exert greater control over content and users. At least 2,500 words are banned on the platform, including words and phrases like 'one-party dictatorship' and 'today we are all Hong Kong citizens'. Banning specific words or phrases on Weibo prevents communities from mobilizing personnel and garnering support online, which proved to be helpful in organizing the Arab Spring protests.

Western Social Media Platforms

Western social media platforms have been restricted or banned in China for the last decade. Facebook and Twitter were banned in July 2009 after the Urumqi riots. YouTube was blocked permanently in 2009. Since then, there have been no official CCP accounts on Western social media. While Facebook, Twitter and YouTube are blocked in China, Chinese Party-State media have put together lively presences on these platforms. Chinese ambassadors worldwide have been opening Twitter accounts to feed their government's positions into global debates on China.[28] The CCP aims to change international discussions about China and bring them closer in line with its own position. It intends to gradually shift the conversation and increase, what they call, the Party's "discourse power."[29]

Initially, the focus was on English and Chinese language content. It remains the principal languages used even today. However, since 2015 CCP media has been following a media localisation strategy, offering content in other languages and targeting specific countries. Xinhua started, in 2015, a German language Twitter account, @XHdeutsch, and its country-specific Romanian and Italian Twitter channels (@XinhuaItalia and @XHRomania). In the same year, Xinhua and the China Daily newspaper started using automatic geo-location to redirect users to a specific language version of their page on Facebook. China's influence operations for engaging foreign actors depend mainly on outsourcing the operation to third parties and utilising 'astroturfing' and 'sockpuppets'.

Astroturfing is the exercise of obscuring the source of an idea or message that would look less reliable if the audience knew its true source. Government or political organisation could conceal an influence operation by making it appear as if it were originating from local politicians, civil society organisations or civilians. Sockpuppet accounts are manually administered social media accounts created and used to manipulate public opinion. In this method, the account stresses news on sports and fashion to capture the audience's attention then combines with more pro-China content, while bots are automated programs that replicate user activity to undertake a specific action for promoting particular messages.

Puma Shen, assistant professor at National Taipei University, states that the CCP has 'Content Farms' in Malaysia and Taiwan to spread pro-party messaging. A Content Farm is a website that creates a high volume of highly trafficked articles. Content Farms crowdsource articles without any editorial control. It leads to many articles having false and with excessive information. After creating the articles, the Content Farm operators recruit and pay individual social media users to spread them. As many of the fake Facebook pages used during the 2020 Taiwanese election were shut down or deleted, the PLA depends on outsourced freelancers in Malaysia or overseas Chinese nationals to disseminate Content Farm originated dis-information across the Facebook. It circumvents detection and direct association between these entities and the Chinese Government.

For example, a popular Content Farm, KanWatch, was considered to be remunerating for sharing its content. To sign up for an account, a user has to fill up basic information and an associated PayPal account. User can then share articles on their social media accounts or write articles. A single user can make about $7 for every thousand views a shared article receives. Users can also rewrite articles by using a clone button. They can track their cash flow to see how much money they have made. Given the ease with which its participants can make money and the ease by which content can spread on platforms, it is likely that Content Farm websites similar to the KanWatch will continue to increase.

While the PLA does not maintain an official Twitter account, there has been a spike in creating Twitter accounts since January 2020 by the Chinese Ministry of Foreign Affairs spokespeople, embassies, diplomats and the state media. The Wall Street Journal reported that the CCP bought a large number of Twitter accounts from foreign entities and used them for political content. These lacked the sophistications needed for a successful influence campaign. Chinese Influence Operations on Twitter have shown their operators to be sloppy, speedy, disorganized and overt. The Twitter account handles repeatedly consist of a random string of numbers and letters, and either have an absurdly high number or a nearly complete lack of followers, both being signs of inauthenticity. These accounts present clear indicators that these are repurposed. These indicators also pointed to a number of these accounts and pages formerly belonging to operators in Bangladesh.[30]

Most of the content comprises regular news stories. The emphasis is on more positive news and success stories about

China, such as development achievements in minority areas like Tibet and Xinjiang. The #Tibet and #Xinjiang hashtags are filled with images of animals and landscapes by Party-State media on Twitter. Most CCP media use attractive visuals and human-interest stories featuring cuddly pandas, other baby animals, impressive landscapes and China's technological achievements to draw in users. Some editors of state media are quite active on platforms such as Twitter. Hu Xijin, editor-in-chief of the English-language newspaper Global Times has over 100,000 followers, so has the China Daily's Europe bureau chief Chen Weihua.

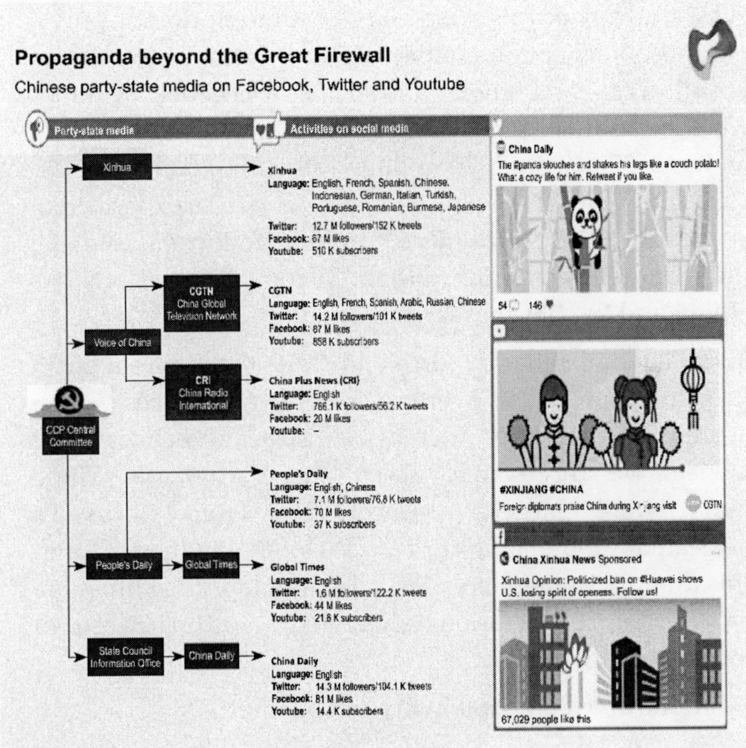

Source: Mareike Ohlberg, Propaganda beyond the Great Firewall, Dec 05, 2019 available at: https://merics.org/en/short-analysis/ propaganda-beyond-great-firewall

In June 2020, Twitter suspended thousands of accounts linked to China that were a part of a manipulated and coordinated campaign to spread disinformation about COVID-19 and Hong Kong. Chinese Influence Operations try to cultivate relationships with key foreign decision-makers, opinion leaders and the business community; inject Chinese narratives into foreign educational establishments, media and public opinion and tarnish the reputation of foreign politicians. China is largely interested in achieving longer-term policy objectives.

It is difficult to guess how successful these operations are. The vast number of followers suggest, though do not prove, that Chinese Party-State media may have artificially inflated their followers and their 'likes'. On Facebook, China's international news channel CGTN, Xinhua and the People's Daily have 87, 67 and 70 million 'likes' respectively. On Twitter, the English language version of Xinhua's principal news account @XHNews has 12 million followers, and the People's Daily has over 5.5 million. In comparison, CNN has 31 million and the BBC has 49 million 'likes'.

The Economist has reported in 2019 that the state-run media's follower counts were artificially high. These state-sponsored 'bot' activities attempt to distract audiences away from negative discussions about the Party-State. These attempts were largely unsuccessful. Unlike Russia's sophisticated understanding of Western audiences and organisation for content creation and targeted dissemination, China's influence operations show less coordinated social engineering skills.

From the above, the following can be inferred:

- China's English-language social media Influence Operations are seeded by state-run media, which present a positive, kindly and helpful image of China.

- China used paid advertisements to target the American users with political or nationally important messages.
- State propaganda authorities issue weekly guidance to propagate positive messages regarding special events.
- China did not attempt a large-scale campaign to influence American voters in the run-up to the November 6, 2018 midterm elections.
- China's state-run social media operations are mainly positive and coordinated because those techniques support Chinese strategic goals.

Domestic Issues

Chinese state-owned internet service providers like China Telecom, China UniCom and China Mobile, and private technology platform operators such as Baidu, Sina Weibo and Tencent's WeChat play essential roles in enforcing censorship and compliance by users inside China. CCP appointments to managerial positions control such firms. They are subject to being fined or shut down if they host banned content.[31]

Other than the restrictions imposed by the Great Firewall and content censorship, the Chinese state also uses several active disinformation and distortion measures to influence domestic social media users. One of the most widely studied organisation is the 50 Cent Party. It is a group of people hired by the Chinese Government to covertly post large numbers of fabricated social media comments to show them the genuine opinions of ordinary Chinese people.

The Great Firewall

The Great Firewall, introduced in the mid-90s, is a strict government-controlled filter of internet content that prevents the Chinese people from accessing news on major Western media sites, including news outlets such as the New York Times and social media platforms such as Twitter and Facebook. It was designed to keep Chinese cyberspace free of the outside world's influence by mandating internet service providers to block access to problematic sites abroad. Ever since, the techniques of information control have expanded exponentially. China's Ministry of Industry and Information Technology undertook a drive against illegal internet connections, including Virtual Private Network (VPN) services that enable internet users to bypass the Great Firewall.

The Great Firewall of China is constantly updated to restrict transnational internet connections and to block potentially subversive sites. A research project from Counter-Power Lab at the School of Information, UC Berkeley, has measured the blocking technology deployed by the Chinese Great Firewall in recent years. The HikingGFW.org website has displayed domain names of 1382 blocked websites, compiled from Alexa's top 10,000 globally ranked websites. These websites include YouTube, Google, Facebook, Flickr, Twitter and WordPress. The Great Firewall of China is constantly updated. Some of the techniques used are:

- Blocking traffic via IP address and domain.
- Mobile application bans.
- Protocol blocking, specifically Virtual Private Network protocols and applications.
- Filtering and blocking keywords in domains (URL filtering).
- Resetting TCP connections.
- Packet filtering.
- Distributed denial-of-service (DDoS) attacks (the so-called Great Cannon).
- Man-in-the-middle (MiTM) attacks.

- Search engine keyword filtering.
- Government-paid social media commenters and astroturfers.
- Social media account blocking, topic filtering, content censorship.
- State-run media monopoly and censorship.
- Social Credit System.
- Mandatory real-name account registration.

The above toolset, along with the mass physical surveillance systems, put China at the vanguard of integrating influence operations, information technology, surveillance and censorship.

Methods of Influence Operations

China's influence operations have become far more sophisticated. It has moved from its focus on diaspora communities to target almost all sectors of Western societies, including media, universities, think tanks and state/local/national government institutions. China wants to promote views sympathetic to Chinese government policies, Chinese society and culture; suppress different perspectives, and get critical Western players on board to support China's foreign policy goals and economic interests. These Chinese inference and influence operations come in the following forms:[32]

- Manipulation of leading former European politicians working to promote Chinese interests.
- Penetration of regional organisations (Interpol, the Council of Europe) to orient their activities so that they align with Chinese interests.
- Manipulation of diasporas and Chinese communities living abroad, which UFWD agents can mobilize during diplomatic visits.

- Pressure on researchers and the academic research apparatus using the issuance of visas and financial programs.
- Distribution, in exchange for remuneration, of a news supplement (China Watch) in major European daily papers, to create financial dependence and to stimulate self-censorship in the treatment of news about China.
- Taking control of the majority of Chinese-language European media.
- Retaliatory measures against governments that are critical or judged to be "unfriendly."

The PRC's Influence Operations are coordinated at the highest level and executed by a range of actors such as the Propaganda Ministry, UFWD, the State Council Information Office, the MSS and the PLA. The CCP has been using Influence Operations for domestic purposes, including its 'United Front Work', even before the formation of the PRC and thereafter. The CCP strives to condition domestic, foreign and multilateral political establishments and public opinion to accept Beijing's narratives. It considers open democracies as more susceptible to Influence Operations than other types of governments.

China depends heavily on its citizens living overseas and members of Chinese diaspora populations, regardless of their citizenship, to advance the Party's objectives. The PRC is not averse to using pressure or threat to its citizens overseas to conduct Influence Operations on behalf of the PRC. One example is of threatening ethnic Uyghurs living in the U.S. with their family members' imprisonment in China.

China has been increasingly assertive in the online media space. China's presence on the internet belongs to its 'sharp power'. It reveals a more coercive and aggressive presentation of the Party-State. Russell Hsiao from the Global Taiwan Institute described China's use of sharp power as a process that employs propaganda, disinformation and other information operations to weaken democratic institutions and abuse cultural institutions to affect political activities for preservation of absolute authority of the Chinese Party-State. Notable Chinese scholars recommend using a combination of official and unofficial propaganda to deter opponents, boost influence and increase power projection.

'Wolf Warriors' on Social Media

Many new and very active official social media accounts of Chinese embassies and leading diplomats have been observed in recent times. This has become termed as "wolf warrior" diplomacy. The most visible account belongs to Zhao Lijian of the Chinese foreign ministry. He tweeted articles suggesting that corona virus originated in the U.S., which caused massive controversy in March, 2020. As per research from the Digital Forensic Research Lab, these Tweets have been shared more than 40,000 times and referenced in 54 different languages.[33] In China, popular hashtags referencing posts have become viral. These have been viewed more than 300 million times by users of the Chinese social network Weibo.[34]

In December 2020, Zhao Lijian was widely condemned for sharing an Australian soldier's fake image killing an Afghan child. China did not apologise for this. China also disseminates propaganda through Chinese 'institutes' on American campuses.

The 'Thousand Talent Program'

China's Thousand Talents Program, a massive and sustained talent recruitment campaign, aims to encourage and recruit the best talent available worldwide to support China's modernisation drive. The stress is on science, technology, engineering, and manufacturing (STEM). Initially, the program aimed to recruit one thousand overseas talents over a period of 5 to 10 years. Official Chinese TTP websites show more than three hundred U.S. government researchers and six hundred U.S. corporate personnel have accepted TTP money. These individuals, in many cases, do not disclose receiving the TTP money to their employer, which is illegal for U.S. government employees. Financial rewards and peer pressure are used to obtain advanced technologies, including often evolving trade secrets, from laboratories and university research centres.

The Chinese Government has established and funded over 500 institutes or research bodies in many universities worldwide. There are 86 in the U.S. While the professed purpose is to develop friendship, the institute staff have been involved in spying on Chinese students abroad and other such espionage activities.

The 'Fifty Cent Party'

To control online public opinion, China utilises many internet commentators, known as the *Fifty Cent Party*. Fifty Cent Party refers to internet commentators who are organized and paid by the government to write online in favour of government policies, boost Xi Jinping's image and monitor netizens' activities, often using fake identities. The Fifty Cent consists of civilian government employees who are required to post pro-CCP narratives on the internet as a part of their political position. This is a significant example of strategic state-directed cheer-leading activity. China uses astroturfing which means the creation of fake persona accounts to organise online trolling.

Scholars at the University of Michigan found that the government fabricated at least one in every six posts on

Chinese domestic social media. Less than 40 per cent of astroturfed comments could be classified as 'cheerleading'. The rest were a combination of racism, vitriol, insults and rage against events or individuals. In August 2019, the Facebook and Twitter deleted accounts associated with the PRC which were promoting disinformation regarding the protests in Hong Kong. There is much disagreement among scholars of the Chinese domestic social media environment regarding government-paid astroturfers' goals or objectives. They believe that censors and state-sponsored influence campaigns focus most on opinion leaders and users with many followers.[35]

In recent years, China has mobilised over 10 million college students through its *Communist Youth League* organisation to take on "online public opinion struggle" tasks. A website, *fiftycentsleaks.info*, has been set up by *China Digital Times* to publicise the leaked emails, making them searchable and accessible by the general public outside of China.

Role of The PLA

Chinese military thinkers have propagated a theory of "cognitive domain operations" to defeat the enemy by employing the method of "mind superiority." According to the PLA, the next evolution of warfare will be cognitive warfare. Dai Xu, a professor at the National Defense University in China, relates "information-driven mental warfare" to a modern day Trojan horse, arguing that the internet is a newly "deformed domain shaped by the interweaving of people's minds and the main form of power competition between nations." The CCP realises that subsets of Information Warfare, such as cyber, electronic and psychological, are a new way to win without kinetic war.

The PLA has a basic understanding of social media analytical tools and how to use them for influence. It used social media analytic tools, *Tweet Binder* and *BuzzSumo* to gather basic statistics on the number of re-tweets and people reached. The PLA uses intangible spaces like social media as a place to deploy psychological warfare. Here the generation, transmission, and influence of information can be manipulated for shaping its targets' perceptions. According to Zeng Huafeng of the PLA, "the ultimate goal is to manipulate a country's values and achieve strategic goals without an actual overt military battle." Zeng identified disinformation as a perfect tool for achieving an unnoticeable victory.

The PLA conceives and executes influence operations through the use of social media.[36] Chinese military theorists have written extensively on information dominance. To achieve information dominance, the PLA employs social media to engage in the three warfare strategy: public opinion warfare, legal warfare and psychological warfare.[37] An example of the PLA's use of social media for strategic messaging is releasing a photo of a PLAAF H6-K strategic bomber flying over the disputed Scarborough Shoal in July 2016 through the PLA Air Force's (PLAAF's) official Weibo microblog account. The PLAAF has also taunted Taiwan on Weibo after increasing flights around the Island in 2017.

A vast majority of the PLA's social media experts come from the home of its research and training for political warfare, the PLA's Nanjing Political Institute. The PLA's premier academic journal on propaganda, the Military Correspondent, contains ongoing research on tactics, current tracking methods and future information campaign goals. It provides a close look into the heated discussion within the CCP about improving its discourse power. According to Military Correspondent, the PLA's plans for foreign social media are to enhance and defend its image, address adverse reporting, correct misperceptions, communicate deterrence signals, communicate resolve and undermine enemy resolve. The Journal calls on the PLA to develop its tactics on social media, advance its psychological warfare strategies and improve home-grown AI and data solutions.

The PLA authors have argued that by leveraging propaganda spread through email, short messages, cell phone communications and other interpersonal communications, including social media, China can do all of the following:[38]

- Seize the initiative.
- Bolster debilitating psychological and morale-killing effects of kinetic attacks.
- Deceive enemy intelligence operations and degrade adversary understanding of the battlespace, making it "hard for people to distinguish the true from the false and thus more easily drive the enemy into a trap."
- Target enemy leadership more precisely and at lower costs.
- Defend one's morale and decision making autonomy.
- "Sow discord in the enemy camp... to perplex, shake, divide and soften the troops and civilians on the opposing side."

Under General Secretary Xi Jinping, the CCP has put enormous resources, estimated at $10 billion a year, into influence operations abroad. As stated, the CCP aims to suppress dissenting and negative voices at home and overseas, and influence civil societies and governments abroad. Its targets range from prominent politicians and business people to academics, students, the media, Chinese diaspora communities and the general public. With deep pockets and Western enablers' help, the CCP uses money, rather than Communist ideology, as a potent source of influence. CCP funding has meddled into the realm of ideas, influencing think tanks, academia, newspapers and other media outlets. Cash-starved Western media is increasingly willing to accept doubtful sources of revenue. Prominent news outlets publish Chinese propaganda knowingly, labelled as an advertisement. Retired Western politicians readily push pro-CCP agendas for monetary benefits.

Tactics to Influence Foreign Information Environments

'Beijing's Global Megaphone', a Freedom House report of January 2020, found that the PRC's media techniques' constant evolution and expansion have accelerated since 2017. The pace of change has intensified as the CCP attempts to restore its international reputation after its initial cover-up of the COVID-19 outbreak and take advantage of the economic weakness and political divisions within and among democracies during the crisis.

Different tactics employed by China to manipulate foreign information environments can be divided into four categories: propaganda, disinformation, censorship and gaining influence over crucial nodes in the information flow. Over the past decade, these tactics have developed to such a level that millions of news consumers worldwide are routinely reading, viewing or listening to information created or influenced by the CCP without knowing its origins.

Propaganda

Soon after becoming the general secretary of the CCP, Xi Jinping stated at the August 2013 National Meeting on Propaganda and Ideology that China needed to "strengthen media coverage ... use innovative outreach methods ... tell a good Chinese story, and promote China's views internationally." Propaganda has been an essential part of the CCP's United Front strategy since the 1940s to convince people to join the Communist cause and justify Mao's draconian policies. Leading agencies for carrying out external propaganda are the Central Propaganda Department (CPD), the State Council Information Office, the State Administration of Radio, Film, and Television (SARFT) and state-owned media groups. These agencies make every effort to promote the CCP-sanctioned version of domestic and international events. China is also funding and indirectly owning cash strapped Western media through intermediaries.

Propaganda has been the foundation for Chinese state-run foreign influence operations. A RAND Corporation Report found that the overt propaganda efforts of China are highly effective due to the following reasons:[39]

- People are poor judges of actual versus wrong information. They do not necessarily remember that certain information was false.
- Familiar messages or themes can be appealing, even if they are wrong.
- Information overload makes people take shortcuts in determining the trustworthiness of messages.
- Statements are more likely to be believed if backed by evidence, even if that evidence is false.
- Peripheral cues, such as the appearance of objectivity, can increase the credibility of propaganda.

China is spending huge money to spread its messages around the world. Some of these activities can be within the ambit of public diplomacy or soft power strategies. But there are sufficient clues to suggest that Beijing uses dishonest and corrupt methods to send its messages.

The Chinese state media have been diversifying their foreign-language output. Major state media like the CGTN expanded from providing English and Chinese to Spanish,

French, Russian and Arabic programmes. Today, their footprint is in a much broader range of languages and markets. Thai vernacular media is full of content produced by Chinese state media. Content-sharing agreements signed by Xinhua and other such partnerships established over many years are now resulting in vast amounts of Chinese state media content dominating portions of the news in places like Italy and Thailand. Most of the China-related news coverage of one of Italy's major news agencies is from Xinhua. In Portugal, Kevin Ho, a Macau-based businessman, purchased a 30 percent ownership stake in the Global Media Group in 2017. He has got a seat as a delegate in China's parliament, the National People's Congress. This media group is looking for new partnerships in other Portuguese-language markets like Brazil and Mozambique.

There is a trend of hostile and belligerent narratives targeting CCP adversaries. As protests against a proposed Extradition Bill flared in Hong Kong during the summer of 2019, videos appeared comparing Hong Kong activists to the Islamic State militant groups and the rise of student protesters to use of child soldiers in Twitter and Facebook feeds of Chinese state media. With U.S.-China relations going south following the coronavirus outbreak, anti-American narratives have been aggressively promoted.

Disinformation

China thinks of disinformation operations as an effective strategy to achieve its foreign policy objectives. In propagating disinformation, China is deliberately undertaking large-scale operations of producing and reproducing false or misleading information to deceive. The created content depends on the psychological bias to promote paranoia, one-dimensional critical thinking and cognitive blind spots. The PLA, the State

Council and the CCP's Central Committee participate in organized Information Operations on domestic and international platforms.

Russians, in 2016, used disinformation tactics to influence the U.S. elections. There was no evidence of China getting involved in any such activities. This has since changed, though the Chinese methods and goals are different from that of the Russians.[40] Both the Chinese and Russian state-run media proclaim themselves as simply countering the conventional English-language media's narrative and bias against their nations and peoples. The state-run English-language media in both the countries hire confident western-educated journalists and hosts. The difference between Russian and Chinese approaches are their tactics, strategic goals and efficacy.

The Oxford Internet Institute reported in 2019 that the Chinese government displayed "new-found interest in aggressively using Facebook, Twitter, and YouTube."[41] These social media platforms have taken down many inauthentic China-linked accounts in the last two years. There has been repeated and persistent campaigns to spread false and demonising information about Hong Kong pro-democracy protesters, Taiwanese politicians, electoral candidates from the Democratic Progressive Party (DPP), CCP critics, Chinese civil society activists inside and outside China, and COVID-19.[42]

Tools employed by the Chinese are varied. These are: content farms that push out information simultaneously across multiple platforms; purchased or hijacked Facebook groups, pages and accounts; coordinated trolling activities meant to manipulate search results; text-messaging campaigns; automated 'bot' networks to affect Twitter hashtags etc.[43] Though direct attribution to Chinese Party-State actors is difficult, enough evidence of such ties has been found in several instances.[44] In all such cases, the campaigns and networks seemed to support well-documented political and content preferences of the CCP.[45]

Propagating Influence Tools

China's drive to finance and build infrastructure empowering online surveillance and censorship through its *Digital Silk Road* has helped widespread adoption of systems that mirror China's own. This has affected information environments worldwide, particularly in the Indo-Pacific regions. Outside the Southeast Asia, Tanzania and Uganda have passed strict laws on online media based on China's models of censorship that sacrifice individual freedoms to support broader social stability.

GONGO

China has created a 'Government Organized Non-Government Organisations' (GONGO). These organisations promote China's party line in the international arena.

Use of Economic Ties as Political Leverage

China has formed a global network of strategic partners through its Ministry of Commerce, the National Development and Reform Commission, the State-Owned Assets Supervision and Administration Commission of the State Council (SASAC), Chinese state-owned enterprises and private companies. This allows the CCP to gain political leverage. The attraction of market access to China or Chinese investments is an encouraging factor. For example, Greece and Hungary, both major beneficiaries of Chinese financing and investments, have refused to sign European Union (EU) statements criticising China's human rights record and actions in the South China Sea.

THE RISE OF CHINESE "GONGOS"

One tactic employed by China to marginalize its critics within international organizations and promote favorable voices is the creation of Government-Organized Non-Governmental Organizations, or GONGOs. This is a type of international astroturfing. A nonexhaustive list of China's GONGOs includes the following:

Internet and Media	Labor and Migrants	Law and Governance
• China Writer's Association • All-China Journalists Association • Internet Society of China	• Beijing Yilian Labor Law Aid and Research Center • Suzhou Migrant Workers Home • Shenzhen Chunfeng Labor Disputes Services Center	• Justice for All • Equity & Justice initiative • Dongjen Center for Human Rights Education and Action
Environment	**Ethnic Minorities**	**Education**
• Huai River Eco-Environment Research Center • Center for Legal Assistance to Pollution Victims • Center for Environment Development and Poverty Alleviation	• Preservation and Development of Tibetan Culture • Yothok Yonden Gonpo Mecical Association • Lanzhouj Chongde Women Children Education Center	• Guangzhou Grassroots Education Support Association • China Zigen Rural Education & Development Association • Beijing Hongdandan Education and Culture Exchange Center

Source: Organizations retrieved from China Development Brief's NGO Directory. http:/www.chinadevelopmentbrief.cn/directory/

The CCP frequently exploits economic leverage and market access for Western companies in China as powerful leverage. In January 2018, under CCP pressure, the Marriott International was forced to apologise for listing Tibet, Taiwan, Hong Kong and Macau as separate countries. BMW apologised after posting an innocent self-help quote from the Dalai Lama on its Instagram account.[46] Of late, different Chinese government agencies have forced companies like American Airlines, Marriott, and Zara to remove references to Taiwan as a country on their websites. The Apple Inc. bowed under pressure from the Chinese government and took out the app *HKmap.live* from its online store. The app helped Hong Kong protesters in 2019 in tracking police movements. Apple also deleted the Taiwanese flag emoji from iPhones in Hong Kong and Macau during the same period.

Simultaneously, China's crackdown on VPNs makes American social media platforms very difficult to access within China's borders. China's technology remains responsive to Beijing's domestic system of digital censorship and control. China funds Western enablers through Chinese institutions and companies. After retirement, Top Western politicians look for well-paid jobs, which Chinese companies can offer. Former British Prime Minister Cameron is now working for a British-Chinese fund, promoting the Chinese state-driven project with geopolitical ambitions - the One Belt One Road (OBOR) initiative.

There are also accusations of corruption by proxy, where Western enablers and family members get paid through less-traceable funding. Another method is politicians selling their houses to connections or mysterious third parties for above the market prices.

Weaknesses in China's Influence Operations

There are apparent weaknesses in China's strategy. Chinese state actors have amassed large numbers of followers on social media sites, including Facebook and Twitter. But they find it difficult to build up much follower engagement, whether measured by likes or retweets. China was not able to create real influence to sway the result of elections. In the 2020 Taiwanese presidential elections, the DPP's Tsai Ingwen won convincingly.

China's disinformation campaigns need refining. Twitter, in August 2019, took down 936 troll accounts that it linked to

Chinese state actors. The accounts pushed conspiracy theories about pro-democracy protesters in Hong Kong. As per the Atlantic Council's Digital Forensic Research Lab analysis, little effort was put into making the accounts look like plausible human personas. Many of the accounts had been used earlier to push spam-like promotional links. They would tweet in a wide range of languages, including Chinese, Indonesian, Arabic, English and Spanish. China's efforts to win 'hearts and minds' in Hong Kong and Taiwan, have rebounded. Heavy-handed Chinese messages attacking student protesters and promoting reunification made young people in both places increasingly unwilling to identify as Chinese. They felt alienated and scared by the prospect of being under the thumb of the CCP.

Researchers at the *Graphika* recognised a pro-Chinese network called *Spamouflage Dragon*. It posted ineptly made English language videos attacking U.S. policy and the Trump administration on Twitter, YouTube and Facebook. The videos with robotic voice-overs in English criticised the U.S. over issues like how police treated anti-racism protesters.[47]

Censorship

Earlier, the CCP's efforts to censor external media focused on international outlets operating within China and Chinese-language outlets abroad, including those in Hong Kong and Taiwan. This has changed now. PRC officials use economic leverage to hush up adverse reporting in local-language media with more frequency.

The CCP's censorship methods can be grouped into four main categories: direct action by Chinese government representatives, indirect pressure through proxies like advertisers and local governments, positive and negative incentives for self-censorship among media owners and physical, cyber or verbal attacks.

Controlling Content Delivery Systems Outside China

Over the past decade, Chinese companies have become ever more active in building information infrastructure and content delivery systems abroad. Technology giants like Huawei and Tencent, although privately owned, maintain close ties with the PRC Government and its security services. They usually make available censorship and surveillance assistance to the Party-State within China.[48] The international expansion of these companies has got the explicit blessing of the CCP.[49]

CASE STUDIES

The Stanford Internet Observatory, on July 20, 2020, published a joint White Paper[50] with the Hoover Institution examining China's covert and overt capabilities in Influence Operations. The CCP depends on extensive influence machinery covering a range of print and broadcast media to consolidate its domestic monopoly on power and its claims to global leadership. The White Paper looks at the impact of technological innovations on these strategies and tactics. The questions asked are: what is the scope and nature of China's covert and overt capabilities and how do they complement each other?

	Official Presence On Platform			
Outlet	**Twitter**	**Facebook***	**Instagram**	**YouTube**
Xinhua News	12.6M	79.9M	1.2M	894K**
CCTV	1M	49M	779K	857K**
CGTN	13.9M	105M	2.1M	1.66M**
People's Daily	7.1M	84M	1M	64.3K
Global Times	1.7M	54M	174K**	34.5K**
China Daily	4.3M	93M	603K	27.9K**
China.org.cn	1.1M	32M	N/A	11K**

Number of followers of official Chinese state media accounts on social media as of 5/29/20.

*Facebook number represents how many people have Liked the Page (**indicates the account has not been verified).

Key takeaways of the study are:

- China's overt propaganda apparatus is vigorous. It manages both inward and outward-facing messaging, which is a top priority for the CCP.
- This apparatus's two pillars are the CPD and the United Front, which organizes state organs and manages influence groups outside the Party.
- Xi Jinping has improved the UFWD's operations, enhancing 40,000 officials to its roll and elevating it to the Party organs' top level.
- China's overt messaging efforts cover both broadcast and social media.

U.S. Elections

A study on U.S. elections gave out the following:

- China's English-language social media influence operations are started by the state-run media, presenting China's positive, benign and cooperative image.
- China uses paid advertisements to target American users with political or nationally important messages and distorted news about China.
- State propaganda authorities' weekly guidance drives accounts to publicise positive messages regarding special events once or twice a month.
- China did not attempt a large-scale campaign to influence American voters in the run-up to the midterm elections of November 6, 2018. However, on a small scale, state-run influence accounts propagated breaking news and biased content concerning President Trump and China-related issues.

- Russian social media influence operations are disrupttive and destabilising. Conversely, China's state-run social media operations are mainly positive and coordinated.
- The Government fabricates one in every 178 social media posts. The comments and campaigns are focused and directed against specific issues.[51] Domestic social media influence operations focus mainly on 'cheerleading' or presenting or furthering a positive narrative about the Chinese state.

A report on Foreign Threats to the 2020 U.S. Federal Elections by the National Intelligence Council states that:[52]

"Key Judgment 4: We access that China did not deploy interference efforts and considered but did not deploy influence efforts intended to change the outcome of the U.S. Presidential elections. We have high confidence in this judgment. China sought stability in its relationship with the U.S., did not view either election outcome as being advantageous enough for China to risk getting caught meddling, and assessed its traditional influence tools – primarily targeted economics measures and lobbying – would be sufficient to meet its goal of shaping U.S. China policy regardless of the winner... however, that China did take some steps to try to undermine former President Trump's reelection."

Taiwan

The focus of the CCP's international Influence Operations is Taiwan. This may well be the assessment of how China will operate elsewhere. Taiwan's local elections in 2018 were subjected to numerous online disinformation campaigns. China tried to weaken democratic integrity and methodically attacked democratically elected politicians who did not align with China's strategic interests.[53] The 'Base 311', the PLA unit formally known as the 'Public Opinion, Psychological Operations and Legal Warfare Base' was the lead agency for this operation. The Taiwanese government and social media platforms were caught off guard by the amount of disinformation, the extent of actors and issues it targeted, and its impact on political discourse. Targets included government's policies, political parties and political figures.

Tactics. China aims to subvert democracy and weaken governance in any target country by planting doubts and chaos in its society, weakening its self-confidence and increasing polarisation and disunity. Its tactics are:

- Worsen existing political, social, economic and generational divides.
- Exploit weaknesses in the informational system.
- Financially control traditional media.
- Employ its cyber army.
- Obscure the attack source through technological, commercial, and legal means.
- Make the attacks partisan so that one side will not condemn it at worst and magnify the effects of its attacks at best.

Agencies. The Chinese Cyberspace Administration, United Front Department, CPD, State Council's Taiwan Affairs Office, People's Liberation Army Strategic Support Force, 50-Cent Party or the Cyber Army, its Content Farms and agents employed by the Chinese government from the target country are the leading players. The CCP used its Cyber Army to exercise sharp power in three ways: spreading disinformation online and *PTT* (Taiwanese equivalent of Reddit), creating and circulating depressing propaganda about Taiwan and spreading fake news in *LINE* (similar to WhatsApp). These were enlarged online, on television and in newspapers by compromised Taiwanese media. These fake news stories changed perceptions and dictated the narrative and topic of the day. Sixty per cent of controversial information and fake news on the LINE came from China.

Obfuscation of Attack Sources. China conceals and hides its attack sources by technological, commercial and legal means. IP addresses of its Cyber Army accounts and locations bounce to Australia, Singapore and other places. It was very difficult for Taiwan's national security apparatus to obtain technical proof of where the cyber information attacks were initiated. For 'advertisements or propaganda in traditional media, China formed companies such as 'Jiuzhou Culture Communication Center' and 'Publishing Exchange Center' to purchase stories. Reporters are not told that what they were writing are advertisements. When a Financial Times journalist blew the whistle on China's influence on the *Want Group*, the Group sued her, sent people to harass her and attempted to make an example out of her to warn anyone who wished to speak out.

The Private Sector. Facebook and LINE were vital in combating Chinese sharp power. Facebook does not have a policy that everything on its platform has to be true, but it does remove content and accounts that violate its community standards, hide contents that break local laws and downgrade fake news. Facebook did all these during the election. As part of the effort to protect Taiwan's election integrity, Facebook removed 118 fan pages, 99 groups, and 51 duplicate accounts for artificially inflating their posts' reach. In December 2019, Facebook cooperated closely with Taiwan's Central Election Commission during the election period to remove false election information that could suppress votes and to hide posts that broke Taiwanese electoral laws. Facebook worked with a third-party fact-checking organisation to downgrade incorrect information.

One of Facebook's most significant contributions to countering Chinese sharp power during the elections was establishing an 'Election Operation Center' or the 'war room'. Its goal was to ensure the elections' integrity by rooting out disinformation, monitoring false news and deleting fake accounts as quickly as possible. The *war room* brought together Facebook's policy, legal and security representatives, content moderators and local experts on politics, elections, and law, so they could meet face to face and expedite the decision-making process on what accounts to delete and what fake news to downrank/remove. The war room operated 24/7. The war room was able to block a significant amount of foreign-produced fake news. It was one of the main reasons as to why Chinese propaganda and disinformation did not affect Taiwan's elections this time.[54] The Taiwanese government's success against these operations was due to increased public communication, enhanced credibility with Taiwanese society, and swift and uniform reaction.

Instagram

Instagram post from the People's Daily

An example of *Instagram* was taken to see how the Chinese state exploits Western social media. Both Xinhua and The People's Daily are regular users and have verified accounts on Instagram. On average, both accounts posted around 26 times per day. Both have a huge number of followers and follow a few other accounts. The posts are mainly photographs and videos. These are significantly positive and present many variations of a few core themes. Some of the themes are:

- China's immense natural beauty.
- Appealing heritage and cultural traditions.
- Visits by Chinese leaders Overseas or visits of overseas leaders to China.
- Positive impact of China in the world of science, technology, sports etc.
- Breaking global news.

Paid Advertisements

It was observed that People's Daily, Xinhua, CGTN and China Daily run paid advertisements. Many of these paid advertisements were recognised and retained by Facebook as part of their collection of 'ads related to politics or issues of national importance'. For Facebook, advertisements of this kind are required to be authorised and reviewed. Besides the notation indicating that the post is a paid advertisement, it carries a specific "paid for by" disclaimer.

Chinese Model of English-Language Social Media Influence Operations

In late 2018 and early 2019, a study was carried out about the English-language social media posts from accounts run by the People's Daily, Xinhua and four other Chinese state-run media organisations concentrating on the foreign audience in Western social media platforms. It was found that China has

China Xinhua News
Sponsored

What has China achieved over 40 years of #ReformAndOpeningUp? President Xi Jinping sums up:

Xi summarizes achievements of China's 40-year reform, opening-up
XINHUANET.COM

taken a completely different approach to influence foreign audiences from its policy in the domestic social media space.

Chinese state-run accounts, on average, posted 60 to 100 times per day across several Western platforms. CGTN, Xinhua and the Global Times were the most active content generators on these social media platforms. Posts by Xinhua, People's Daily and CGTN were favourited or liked at the highest rates.

Confucius Institutes (CI) and Targeted Organisations

Confucius Institutes are education organisations sponsored by the CCP to teach Chinese culture, language and history at the primary, secondary and university level worldwide. China likes to compare the CIs with branches of France's *L'Alliance Francaise*, U.K.'s *British Council*, Germany's *Goethe Institute* and Spain's *Cervantes Institute*. As per Xinhua, there were more than 500 CIs in 142 countries as of late 2017.

There were at least 110 CIs and 501 Confucius Classrooms in (secondary schools) across the U.S alone.[55]

According to Li Changchun, a former CCP Politburo Standing Committee member responsible for propaganda, CIs' Chinese-language instruction serves as an essential platform for a more extensive program to increase China's soft power and advance Beijing's version of history. In the sphere of perception management and image shaping, this idea of CIs from the Chinese Communist Party's UFWD and PRC's Ministry of Education is a sophisticated example of the Chinese Government's and the Communist Party's Influence Operations.

As per Richard Fadden, former director of the Canadian Security Intelligence Service, CIs are funded by the CCP Propaganda Department, formally affiliated with the UFWD. Confucius Institutes are supervised by personnel based in Chinese embassies and consulates. Liu Yandong, a former Chinese vice-premier and Politburo member, was the head of the UFWD when she launched the program in 2004. Ms Liu now serves as chair of the Office of Chinese Language Council International, the CIs' parent organisation, known as the 'Hanban'. Confucius Institutes provide the Chinese government with access to U.S. student bodies.

In late 1970s, when the Chinese government first allowed its citizens to attend western universities, the CCP created a 'Chinese Students and Scholars Association' (CSSA) to monitor Chinese students and mobilize them against views different from the CCP's stance. This has not changed. Directly supported by the Chinese embassy and consulates, CSSAs now report on and compromise other Chinese students' academic freedom as well as the American faculty. Events that are considered politically offensive by the CCP have been subject to increasing pressure and retaliation by diplomats in the Chinese Embassies, consulates, and CSSA branches. Some essential aspects of CSSA are:

- The CCP's UFWD oversees the CSSAs, whose purpose is to influence local elites and community leaders.
- Many of the 150 CSSA chapters on U.S. campuses limit membership to Chinese citizens, violating the principle that student organisations should not differentiate based on nationality.
- The PRC diplomatic missions regularly provide guidance and funding to separate CSSA chapters, such as directing members to disturb lectures or events that question CCP ideology or views.
- Academic brilliance requires the free flow of ideas. Chinese students are valued contributors. However, CSSA chapters actively inhibit debate and interactions with non-Chinese peers.
- In 2018, the congressional U.S.-China Commission stated that CSSAs "frequently attempt to conceal" their ties to the CCP and "are active in carrying out overseas Chinese work consistent with Beijing's United Front strategy."

Funding

The Associate Editor of the *Weekly Standard*, Ethan Epstein, argued that the key reason for the spread of CIs in U.S. universities is "an alarming willingness to accept money at the expense of principles that universities are ostensibly devoted to upholding." According to expert John Fitzgerald, "Universities that accept CIs on Beijing's terms with all the compromises they entail, they signal their willingness to set aside academic principles to build good relations with China and indicate that normal due diligence does not apply to relations with Chinese universities and firms."

Confucius Institutes are co-founded by several host universities and secondary schools. The *Hanban* arranges a Chinese university to supply teachers, textbooks and other materials. The Chinese university pays the teachers. They do not have to hold green cards or pay U.S. taxes. On average, depending on the institution, the Hanban provides a $150,000 start-up grant with $100,000–$200,000 per year follow-on funding directly to the American university. Secondary schools usually receive $50,000 in initial funding and $15,000 subsequently per annum. There are two worrying provisions in the Hanban contracts with U.S. host institutions: forbidding the CIs from piloting any activities that contravene Chinese law and the enabling contract remain confidential, making oversight by the academic community difficult.

In addition to sending many teachers to provide Chinese language instruction, China sponsors trips for U.S. students to study in China. Through its 'Chinese Bridge Program for Secondary School Students', the Hanban has paid for more than 6,000 U.S. high school students to visit China since 2007. These exchanges' main goal is to build a friendly environment for China's interests by giving participants favourable views of China, which they then propagate.

Many universities worldwide see China as a fund provider and think that partnering with it and establishing CIs is a practical way of getting more funding. With schools in Latin America and the Caribbean in need of funding and the generous amounts of funding provided by the Hanban, it would be interesting to see how much influence the CIs will have in the region.

Adverse Opinions

Allegations against the CIs are mainly about the exclusive use of PRC materials that support Chinese viewpoints, terminology, and simplified characters; the avoidance of discussion in American classrooms and programs on controversial topics such as Tibet, Tiananmen, Xinjiang, the Falun Gong and human rights; and potential infringement on theoretically independent studies curricula on American campuses.

The U.S. policymakers, in recent years, have increased their scrutiny of the activities of CIs and their relationship to the Chinese government. Their concerns are propaganda, censorship and interference in U.S. universities' decision-making processes, for which some universities had to withdraw from the program. A U.S. organisation advocating for intellectual freedom, the National Association of Scholars, in its 2017 report on Confucius Institutes, made several observations:

- Institute faculty "face pressure to self-censor."
- Contracts between Confucius Institutes and host universities are "rarely publicly available."
- Universities with financial incentives not to upset China "find it more difficult to criticise Chinese policies."
- Confucius Institutes present students with "selective knowledge" of Chinese history, including "avoiding Chinese political history and human rights abuses."

Headwind

Some of the steps taken by the U.S. policymakers are:

- Senator Marco Rubio (R-FL), Chairman of the Congressional-Executive Commission on China, in

February 2018, wrote to five universities in Florida asking them to end their affiliations with the CIs, citing the risk posed by Beijing's "increasingly aggressive attempts to use CIs to influence foreign academic institutions and critical analysis of China's history and present policies."

- Representative Seth Moulton (D-MA), in March 2018, urged Tufts University and the University of Massachusetts, Boston, to close their CIs.
- Two Texas representatives, Michael McCaul (R) and Henry Cuellar (D), in April 2018, urged several Texas universities to severe ties with the Confucius Institute.

Some legislative measures undertaken are:

- Representative Joe Wilson (R-SC) and Senators Rubio and Tom Cotton (R-AK) presented legislation in March 2018, titled the Foreign Influence Transparency Act. It would require organisations that promote foreign governments' political agendas to register as foreign agents and would require universities to disclose gifts and donations from foreign sources.
- Senator Ted Cruz (R-TX) announced the Stop Higher Education Espionage and Theft Act in May 2018, which tries to strengthen the U.S. government's ability to counter foreign intelligence organisations working inside the U.S. educational system.
- Senator Rubio and his Congressional-Executive Commission on China co-chair Representative Chris Smith (R-NJ), along with co-sponsors, introduced bills in the Senate and House in June 2018 for the creation of an inter-agency task force to prepare an unclassified report on CCP influence operations targeting the U.S. and certain allies.

- The National Defense Authorization Act for 2019 covers important provisions to coordinate the U.S. government's response to harmful foreign influence operations and campaigns, including specifically by China.

The PRC has been carrying out its influence operations through CIs aggressively. A July 20, 2015 report by the 'Council on Hemispheric Affairs on Big Dragon on Campus', on China's soft power-play in the academia states, "The administrations of many universities hosting CIs worldwide have self-censored their activities to keep from offending China". North Carolina State University, in 2009, cancelled a visit by the Dalai Lama. This was due to the director of the school's Confucius Institute's warning stating that hosting the Tibetan leader would disrupt "strong relationships we were developing with China." In Australia, Sydney University cancelled a lecture by the Dalai Lama in 2013.

The U.S. policymakers believe that more rigorous standards of academic freedom, transparency and university oversight be exercised over the CIs. Though the U.S. is open to Chinese scholars studying American politics or history, China restricts access to American scholars and researchers seeking to explore politically sensitive areas of China's political system, society and history.

A non-profit advocacy group, The National Association of Scholars, informed that the number of CIs in the U.S. fell from 103 in 2017 to 55 in 2021. Universities quoted several reasons for terminating the Institutes, including the potential for Chinese government influence and risks to U.S. national security; concerns about academic freedom; differences between U.S. educational institutions and the Institutes over missions and objectives; declining interest or enrollment; changing curricular needs; difficulties of the operation due to the COVID-19 pandemic; the desire to keep DoD Chinese Language Flagship funding and encouragement by Members of Congress.

Some Confucius Institutes and Classrooms have recently been shut down in countries including Australia, Canada, Belgium, Denmark, France, Germany, and Sweden. The Vrije University of Brussels shut its Confucius Institute in 2019 after 13 years. Other universities that have or are doing the same include the University of Chicago, Penn State, Tulane, Texas A&M, NC State, Michigan (a total of 33 in the U.S. and abroad), the Université of Lyon in France, Stockholm University and the University of Leiden in the Netherlands.

Targeting Societies

Today, as stated, China's Cyber influence operations target a broad segment of Western societies, including universities, think tanks, media and state, local and national government institutions. It has moved far beyond the traditional focus on diaspora communities. China wants to promote views sympathetic to the Chinese Government's policies, stifle different ideas and co-opt important players to support China's foreign policy goals and economic interests. China also exploits usual public field diplomacy like paid media inserts, visitor programs, educational and cultural exchanges, and government lobbying, which many countries use to project soft power. But, besides, China makes use of assertive and opaque 'sharp power' activities.

In the U.S., China tries to identify and cultivate promising politicians. It employs top lobbying and public relations firms and obliges influential civil society groups. China arranges visits to the middle kingdom by members of Congress and their staffs. In some rare cases, It has used private citizens or companies to take advantage of loopholes in U.S. regulations prohibiting direct foreign contributions to elections for funding. China uses its business, companies to press forward their strategic objectives abroad and gain political influence. China has supported the dozens of local Chinese chambers of commerce in the U.S. to have ties to the Chinese Government.[56]

OTHER CHINESE PROGRAMS

Thousand Talents Programs

China's Foreign Thousand Talents Program wants to attract "high-end foreign scientists, engineers, and managers from foreign countries." Chinese research institutions that manage individual programs send invitations and advertisements to participate. These institutions report to and are supervised by the government and the party, which provides financial compensation for participation.

Film Industry

There is growing apprehension over PRC-directed control and censorship of the film industry. It is implemented through purchases of theatre and production companies by Chinese companies, editorial changes demanded by the CCP and visa denials to directors, actors and others critical of Chinese policies. *PEN America,* a free-speech watchdog, in a report titled 'Made in Hollywood, Censored by Beijing', describes how Hollywood has almost wholly submitted to China's censorship demands through production modifications or anticipatory self-censorship.[57]

Think Tanks

The CCP has also turned to think tanks to expand its influence in the U.S. and Europe. Chinese diplomats and other intermediaries' regularly attempt at think tanks, researchers, scholars and other staffers to influence their activities. The Chinese-U.S. Exchange Foundation, linked to the Chinese Government, provides grants to prominent American think tanks like the *Carnegie Endowment for International Peace, Brookings* and *the Asia Society*. The PRC has made networking arrangements in Europe, such as the *16+1* think tank network and *eSilks*, a think tank network aligned with the OBOR.[58] The *Chinese Academy of Social Sciences*, a government think tank, in 2017, opened a branch in Budapest as a reward for Hungary's political cooperation and to influence future European debate on cooperation with China.[59] As a result of their connections to the Chinese Government, think tanks may significantly undermine their credibility as centres of independent expertise on China.

While China is establishing its network of think tanks in the U.S., it has been restricting American think tanks operations in China. It curbs the access of American think-tank researchers and delegations to China and Chinese officials. The U.S. Department of Education has investigated to determine whether U.S. academic institutions had correctly reported foreign contracts and gifts. Its report disclosed that many American universities accepted billions of dollars in unreported foreign funds. Though receiving foreign funds is not illegal, the law requires disclosure. Georgetown University did not report more than $2 million from an arrangement with the CCP Central Committee to host academic exchanges with CCP officials through the Central Committee's Party School. Cornell University did not disclose more than $1 million in contracts with Chinese telecommunications company Huawei Technologies.

Georgetown and Cornell Universities were not alone. Nearly every U.S. institution investigated had received some finance from Huawei. Moreover, most of Huawei's sponsored arrangements involved sensitive industries like robotics, cloud computing services and semi-conductors. The University of Maryland was cooperating with Chinese e-commerce giant Alibaba Group Holding Ltd. to develop algorithms for crowd-surveillance technology. The U.S. Justice Department declared criminal indictments involving a Harvard Department Chair who lied to federal authorities about his ties to Chinese government entities and his acceptance of Chinese funding.

The U.S. Secretary of State Michael Pompeo issued an ultimatum in November 2020 to think tanks and academic institutions worldwide: either publicly disclose funding received from foreign governments or risk losing access to State Department officials. This move was initiated due to growing concerns about foreign governments' role in shaping academic and policy debates, especially the risk posed by the CCP's robust influence apparatus.[60]

In contrast to China's investments in U.S. academic institutions, Chinese government funding for U.S. think tanks is negligible when compared to that of other foreign countries. This was revealed by a review of information compiled by the Center for International Policy (CIP), an independent nonprofit center for research, public education, and advocacy on U.S. foreign policy. According to CIP's research, only three U.S. think tanks received Chinese government funding. However, the report acknowledges that think tanks have no legal obligation to reveal their funders, foreign or domestic, publicly.

Cyber Penetrations

China has no hesitation in using cyber penetration for influencing its adversaries and potential partners. China penetrated the Taiwanese networks to exert economic and military pressure to reduce its autonomy. Even when China does not have a hostile relationship with the target entity, it uses cyber operations to support diplomatic and trade efforts.[61] Significantly, many of the cyber penetrations undertaken by China target sub-state actors, which the Chinese call a "Five Poisons": Uighur separatism, Tibetan separatism, Falungong activity, Taiwanese independence and pro-democracy activism. There have been many instances of Chinese cyber penetrations harassing activist groups abroad who fight for the rights of minority ethnicities within China. Extremely sophisticated cyber-attacks targeting Tibetan advocacy groups were made by the *Red Alpha* and *Ghostnet* campaigns. These featured *phishing* and *watering hole* attacks with malware, software exploits designed to work across multiple platforms.

THE COVID-19 CAMPAIGN

Wolf Warrior Diplomacy

China has an old stratagem known as 'Borrowing a Boat Out to Sea' to exploit foreign media to deliver Chinese propaganda. During the COVID-19 pandemic, PRC government officials aggressively used social media through 'wolf warrior' diplomacy and global disinformation campaigns to sow confusion and promote conspiracy theories. Named after two action movies in which the Chinese military conquers American forces and coined by Chinese state media, *wolf warrior diplomacy* pronounces the new ethos of Chinese diplomat - a more aggressive push of CCP messaging through various mediums. As the coronavirus outbreak originated from Wuhan city, China's main effort was to suppress information about it. When China could control the pandemic within its borders, it launched an influence campaign to sidetrack blame from Beijing's failings and highlight other governments' failures to portray China as the model and first-resort partner for other countries.

China uses both overt and covert tactics for its Influence Operations on COVID-19. It used domestic censorship, state media messaging in English-language, and fake accounts to influence Western social media platforms' conversations. Chinese diplomats and embassies took active part in overt messaging to augment the CCP's narratives on COVID-19. Covert state-sponsored activity leveraged fake Twitter accounts to acclaim the CCP's pandemic response and criticised the U.S., Hong Kong and Taiwan's responses.[62]

In 2019, the CCP created many official accounts of its government offices and embassies on Twitter and Facebook through which the Chinese state media started posting actively. Between the end of December and mid-March, the Chinese media published seven thousand articles on coronavirus in English on Facebook alone. The Chinese profiles on social networks regularly share *Russian Television (RT), Sputnik* and *Iranian Press TV*. However, direct cooperation between the Chinese and pro-Russian media could not be confirmed. Chinese diplomats used Twitter extensively during the COVID-19 crisis to strengthen its 'mask diplomacy' charm offensive, deluge the internet with the propaganda about the virus' origin and rebut any criticism about the CCP's handling of the outbreak.

The wolf warrior tactics have largely backfired. The French Foreign Ministry summoned the Chinese Ambassador after Chinese diplomats claimed France negligently allowed its elderly to die of COVID-19. European public attitudes toward China are hardening and the EU approach toward China is stiffening. According to recent *Pew* polling, negative views of China reached historic highs in Australia, Canada, Germany, the Netherlands, South Korea, Spain, Sweden, the United

Kingdom, and the U.S. COVID-19 is not the only cause of this shift, but it certainly is an accelerant.

China started sending medical aid to European countries facing COVID-19. There was an increase in forceful messaging to publicise this assistance focusing on China's donations of masks to other countries. It was supplemented by negative messages on the failings of the U. S. and its slow response to the virus. Some of the examples are:

- Zhao Lijian, the Foreign Ministry spokesperson, tweeted, "Countries like Singapore, ROK took necessary measures & put the epidemics under control because they made full use of this precious time China bought for the world. As for whether the U.S. availed itself of this window, I believe the fact is witnessed by U.S. & the world." He tweeted again, "Be transparent! Make public your data! U.S. owe us an explanation!"
- Hu Xijin, the editor in chief of *Global Times* tweeted, "What really messed up the world is failure of the U.S. in containing the pandemic."
- In Paris, the Chinese embassy issued a press release hailing the success of China's "dictatorship" over the United States' "flagship of democracy," pushing the message that Beijing's model was superior.

China made clandestine efforts to manipulate information and propagate chaos using false messages that went viral in the U.S. It cautioned that President Trump was about to order a two-week national quarantine. The messages triggered such panic that the National Security Council had to tweet that this was false.[63] When China was facing criticism over its management of the early stages of the pandemic and some U.S. officials stated that the virus could have escaped from a Wuhan lab, CGTN started its own conspiracy theory. The station advocated, without any evidence, that the virus originated at a military base in Maryland in the U.S. and was brought to China by American soldiers during an athletics competition.

Mask Diplomacy

While the world was stuck in the chaos of the COVID-19 outbreak, China grabbed the opportunity to improve its image as a "responsible global leader" under the claim of "peaceful rising." The discourse on mask diplomacy concerning different countries and the volume varied across nations. It showed the custom-tailoring of messaging for the respective country. There was a radical increase in CCP-affiliated Twitter accounts, connected with the COVID-19 time period, from January 2020 to July 2020.[64]

One example of this is the media coverage of the donations of Jack Ma, the founder of Alibaba and a Party member. On 16 March, 2020, Jack Ma announced that his foundation would send 500,000 testing kits and one million masks to the U.S. as well as 20,000 testing kits, 100,000 masks, and 1,000 sets of personal protective equipment to all 54 African countries.[65] Depending on China's exact relationship with the respective country, China's donation are portrayed as an iron-clad friendship/all-weather friendship. Examples are Cambodia, Serbia, Pakistan, Saudi Arabia and Zimbabwe. It also tries to depicts a jointly built community of shared future with U.S., Japan or South Korea.[66] An example is when Aleksandar Vučić, the Serbian president, on 15 March, stated that "European solidarity does not exist. That was a fairy tale, the only country that can help us is China."[67]

Anti-U.S. messaging is spread through unofficial channels, which provide a level of plausible deniability. An appropriate example of this is the PRC Ministry of Foreign Affairs' spokesman Zhao Lijian's Twitter post on 12 March, blaming the U.S. Army for deliberately spreading COVID in Wuhan. This was shared by over a dozen Chinese diplomats on Twitter.[68]

Lijian Zhao 赵立坚
@zlj517

2/2 CDC was caught on the spot. When did patient zero begin in US? How many people are infected? What are the names of the hospitals? It might be US army who brought the epidemic to Wuhan. Be transparent! Make public your data! US owe us an explanation!

From **Global Times**

10:37 AM · Mar 12, 2020 · Twitter for iPhone

7.7K Retweets **15.4K** Likes

Analysis

China's influence strategy on COVID-19 involved a full spectrum of overt and covert tactics to manage Beijing's image both domestically and abroad. Some of the critical aspects are:

- Censorship of individuals and information channels offered China control over the virus's domestic perception and limited international reporting on China's emerging outbreak.
- English-language state media Facebook Pages, with over 50 million followers, bolstered their reach even further via targeted ads on the platform, allowing China's desired narratives to reach many worldwide audiences.

- Chinese diplomats and embassies engaged in increasingly hostile messaging toward other countries on Twitter to criticise other governments and amplify the CCP's preferred narratives to demonstrate China's strength and to combat its negative images internationally.
- Covert state-sponsored activity on Western social media platforms paralled overt narratives by praising the CCP's pandemic response and criticizing other actors' responses, such as the U.S., Hong Kong, and Taiwan.

Comparison with Russia

The Chinese and the Russian approaches for Cyber Influence Operations are different. Comparison between the Chinese and Russian Influence Operation is given below:[69]

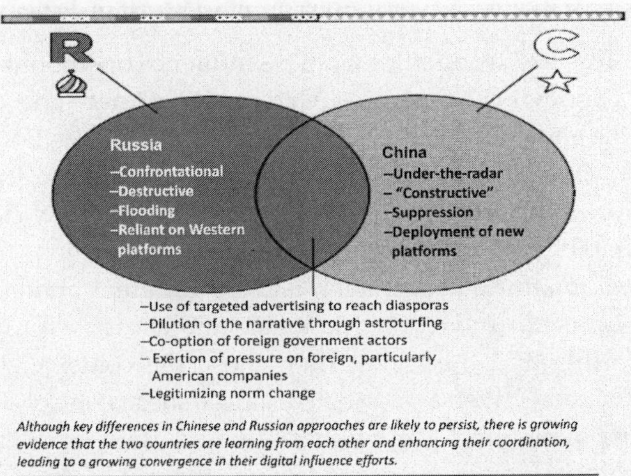

Although key differences in Chinese and Russian approaches are likely to persist, there is growing evidence that the two countries are learning from each other and enhancing their coordination, leading to a growing convergence in their digital influence efforts.

Russia overwhelms readers with disinformation. China rewrites the reality with positive news. The Stanford Cyber Policy Center analysis of the COVID-19 social media landscape shows that China's state media in times of pandemic emphasised the positive international responses to Chinese aid, the pace of China's crisis response and on the numbers and stories of people cured. China is more confident about its brand than Russia. While RT only mentions Russia in 4 percent of its reports and prefers to focus on other countries' mistakes, Chinese CGTN and CCTV talk about China in 50 percent of its articles.[70]

While crucial differences in Chinese and Russian approaches are likely to continue, there is growing evidence that the two countries are learning from each other and enhancing their coordination, leading to an increasing convergence in their digital influence efforts.[71]

Artificial Intelligence and Big Data

"China to explore the application of AI for news collection, production and dissemination to comprehensively increase our ability to lead public opinion"

- Xi Jinping, National Academy of Governance, January 25, 2019.

The next frontier for Chinese influence operations is in big data and AI. The PLA uses AI to run its bot networks on social media and manage its clandestine accounts' attributions better. The Military Correspondent pressed for AI's use in foreign influence operations. It called for the PLA to "fully exploit AI technology to recommend military information to broad media platforms accurately, and for different audiences and make even more international audiences see our PLA reporting and think that they chose the content." China is using data-driven analytics to exercise social control over their own population. Over 1 billion Chinese users conduct over 60 percent of their transactions through the app WeChat. WeChat "is state-recognized, electronic social-security identification and ID card that is the dream of the surveillance state." China uses WeChat to crack down on anything that threatens the state's harmony and stability.

China's data collection from abroad and domestic environments are not separate issues. These are linked to national security. Examples are:

- The China-owned company Tencent is one of the largest gaming companies in the world. It owns significant stakes in popular games like console-based computer games Fortnight Riot Games and mobile Supercell. Lately, the U.S. Congress has raised questions about as to what data is being gathered and collected by the company and sent back to China's servers.
- Due to lack of clarity over what is gathered from individuals' devices and sent back to China, TikTok and Zoom have also come under enquiry.
- WeChat has 75 behavioural indicators such as growing a beard or calling a relative overseas that allegedly indicate potential religious radicalisation.
- Chinese companies TikTok, Baidu and Douyin have explored the possibility of making deep fakes available to the consumer on their apps. These tools can be deployed as a part of influence operations later.

The CCP's latest Influence Operations project is propaganda powered by AI. It is meant for domestic and international application. The system will identify early warning pointers of social turbulence, assist state journalists in producing effective content and propagating approved narratives to target audiences. It is expected that AI will strengthen the Party's voice and increase its influence over public opinion. The CCP's CPD, with several government ministries, in August 2019, issued a document titled "Guiding Opinions on the Promotion of Deeper Integration of Culture and Technology." The paper recommends exploring "the use of AI for newsgathering, production, distribution, reception, and feedback; for comprehensively improving the state's ability to guide public opinion; and for making personal customization… and intelligent push notification services to serve positive publicity".

In 2017, the Institute for Cyberspace Studies stated that the PLA could use AI and big data to improve public opinion detection, determination and handling especially sensitive topics.

Thought Management

The CCP is emphasising propaganda and ideological indoctrination throughout Chinese society.[72] The recent Chinese government statements, publications in government publications, state media and academia points to China's propaganda and 'thought management' apparatus and the intent of the CCP to dominate the electronic media. China's current propaganda foundation will integrate domestic and international thought management. The Communist Party thinks of the internet as "the frontline in the struggle over people's opinions."[73]

The CCP perceives a weakness in its control over the issues that people focus on, and its failure to respond to those issues in a timely and compelling manner. This weakens its influence over public opinion on the internet. The heart of these challenges is the plurality of voices and the speed at which public opinion changes online.[74] The CCP's communications specialists especially stress the necessity to reform the type (text, video, etc.), the superiority of Party content, and improvement in its dissemination speed.

China's method to next-generation thought management is built on three main pillars: early warning, practical content and targeted distribution.

Early Warning

To create effective propaganda content, the CCP thinks authorities and state media must record the issues around which ideologically improper thinking exists and detect future crises. AI is therefore a mean to "continuously monitor websites, forums, blogs, Weibo, print media, WeChat and other information to reach a timely, comprehensive and accurate understanding of trends in public opinion and public attitudes and sentiment."[75] Artificial Intelligence can:[76]

- Build and correctly interpret audiences' "comprehensive profiles of ideological behaviour" from big data.
- Identify "ideological confusion".
- Support the development of "personalised counter-measures."

Chinese experts hope that natural language processing and machine learning will permit authorities to identify potentially contentious domestic and international stories before unapproved narratives go viral.[77]

Effective Content

China's AI systems help to generate compelling and ideologically correct content. This improves the quality and production speed of content for managing public opinion. AI assists with content planning, lead identification, data collection, data visualisation, writing and video production.[78] For international audiences, AI would help identify the keywords so that the journalists can use the correct terms to maximise viewership and resonance.[79] Machine translation will thus increase the reach of China's messaging around the world.[80]

Targeted Distribution

Big data on the audience's online behaviour helps the state media officials to tailor content distribution to meet personalised needs. AI selectively sends propaganda based on 'interest tags' derived from the individual's profile.[81] AI helps tailor content based on variable factors such as how long individuals spend consuming news, what time of day they are online, the type of content they engage with etc.[82]

Artificial Intelligence is envisioned to support real-time distribution to improve the timeliness of propaganda. Interest-based distribution is possible because CCP propaganda is frequently not overtly political. Narratives are economic, cultural and social in nature. For international audiences, the contents highlight the positive aspects of the country's culture, history, economy, and global affairs participation.[83]

Future Trajectories in AI and Big Data

For foreign interference, especially around elections, China is likely to employ AI and aggregated social media management software, especially on *WeChat* and on Southeast Asian messaging app LINE. Using AI to generate fake content would give the PLA chance to use 'deep fakes'. Deep fakes are digital representations created with AI to produce realistic but wholly fictitious images and sounds. Chinese companies TikTok and Zao could develop deep fake capabilities, which the PLA could easily use to propagate biased or false deep fake content.

Facial scanning raises fears of possible adoption for facial recognition purposes by law enforcement agencies. The parent company of Chinese apps TikTok and Douyin, the ByteDance, as of January 2020, was reportedly developing deep fake technology that the app refers to as 'face swap'. This capability would enable a biometric scan of a user's face to be applied to various videos. However, as of August 2020, TikTok was banning deep fakes altogether from its platform.

China's news services are vigorously working to enlarge their reach and messaging across the media matrix, including websites, newspapers, online interactive and mobile apps, personal social media, official social media, and third-party representations.[84] AI requires vast amounts of data to generate perceptions. This data is mined from the media matrix, pulled from sources like WeChat, Weibo or the mobile apps developed by state media outlets.[85] Internationally, the data will be harvested from news websites, Facebook, Twitter and other platforms.

The PLA plans to use sentiment analysis to detect high-profile or very high trafficked events and provide earlier warning of items to censor. This would create another comprehensive and intelligent information dissemination model.

Challenges

Changing over to AI and big data would face a lot of challenges. Collecting, organising and integrating information would necessitate advanced computer applications. China is already building an industrial base to harness big data. Dependence on AI to disseminate content may reduce editors' discretion to determine what content is consumed. Not surprisingly, Xinhua's vice president told the 2018 China Internet Media Forum attendees that "humans lead, machines assist."[86] CCP experts on propaganda and communications see AI as a means for a sustained and responsive online presence. AI will anticipate, identify and take action on emerging crises in public opinion, send government messaging before unapproved narratives go viral, and circulate personalised content to individual readers and viewers. As in every communications revolution, processors and algorithms will form the foundation of next-generation 'thought work'.[87]

At its present state, PLA is far from perfecting its influence operations. It has not been successful in connecting with non-Chinese audiences. However, PLA is trying hard.

Conclusion

China is now the world's second-largest economy. It has become the world's largest trading nation and produces many of the top multinationals' prized products. It plays a leading role in global financial institutions like the Asian Infrastructure Investment Bank, in global bodies like the World Health Organisation, and is one of only five countries with a veto-power seat on the United Nations Security Council, a power it increasingly uses. It has one of the most powerful militaries globally and is testing the once-untouchable U.S. forces in places like the South China Sea and the Taiwan Strait. China unquestionably has become more dominant in hard power, but its ability to push a "China story" and its soft power capability is suspect.

China is promoting its image as a stable, strong and leading country to the rest of the world. It is using civil unrest in the U.S. following police violence against African Americans to counter criticism of police abuse against protesters in Hong Kong. China is using propaganda and the manipulation of social media at home to reinforce popular support for the CCP. This is important now as its economy faces significant obstacles as demography, debt and unfinished reforms are slowing down growth.

With its growing assertiveness in the international arena, China uses new technologies to achieve its foreign policy goals and project an image of "responsible global power." These efforts closely correspond to China's geopolitical interests - territorial demands around the South China Sea, institutional power projection in the Asia-Pacific region and beyond and increasing aggression toward Taiwan, Hong Kong, Xinjiang and Tibet.

China is spending billions on influence operations across the world. This fits in with China's larger aim of expanding its soft power alongside its growing economic and military power. The reach of Beijing's overseas media is impressive and should not be underestimated.[88] But the results are mixed.

China has been successful at home to effectively censor unwanted content on the Web and shaping online conversations. The Chinese online propaganda campaigns targeting Taiwan and protesters in Hong Kong are not as effective as China struggled to weaponise social media. Here, China has to contend with competing narratives that cannot be suppressed easily.

China's influence operations are different from the Russian interference in the 2016 U.S. presidential election. Chinese influence operations are long term. Its actions are highly targeted, long-winded and aim to influence critical American people who can shape U.S. policy. China strives to shape influential businesspeople and companies' perceptions and enlist them as advocates for China by irregular means, like bribery, coercion, and information distortion.[89]

China is learning its lessons. China's Internet regulator advertised for a contract to help it "operate and grow" overseas social media accounts on platforms such as Facebook. The project sought a team of experts who could "tell China's stories with multiple angles, express China's voice and get overseas audience recognition and support for Jinping Thought." The *China News Services* announced that it had started a new project to build its social media presence overseas. It specifically seeks to increase Twitter followers on its two accounts by 580,000 within six months. It wants at least 8 percent of the accounts to come from North America, Australia, and New Zealand. Overall, China is spending more than $1 million on both accounts.

On the domestic front, China has successfully established convincing narratives and propagated those to its citizens with the help of censorship and government-affiliated content production. China has shown its intent to propagate its ideology by entering Western social media platforms and developing its platforms. Simultaneously, the CCP uses censorship and content regulation heavily. But China has not won the acceptance and recognition of the international community.[90]

China has a long way to go internationally. China does not have an official PLA presence on Western social media platforms. Its efforts to conceal *sockpuppet* accounts are sloppy. Western social media platforms can easily identify content farms. Foreign audiences are not impressed by the Chinese influence operations on Taiwan, Tibet, Hong Kong and the country's treatment of its Uyghur population.

The PLA still has a long way to go in perfecting its influence operations. However, The PLA has displayed a remarkable aptitude to learn, adjust and merge their strategies. This trend is likely to continue.

Appendix

Chinese Influence Operations Bureaucracy

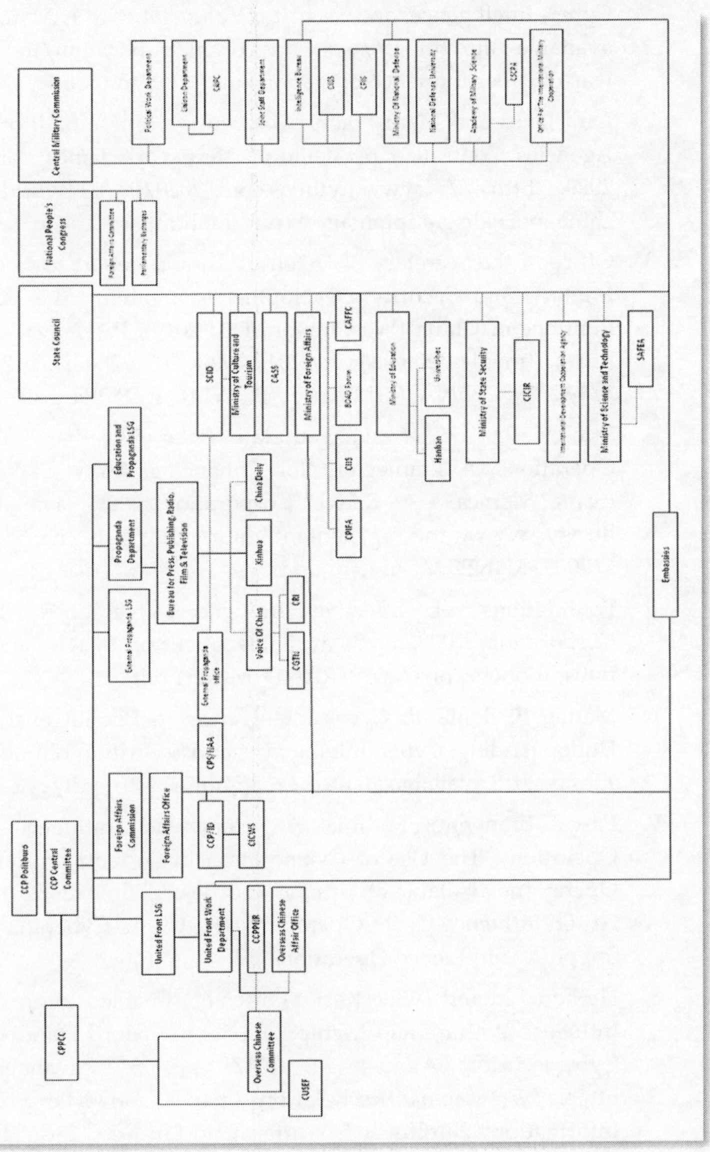

Endnotes

1. David Tayouri, The Secret War of Cyber Influence Operations, Cyber, Intelligence, and Security, Volume 4, No. 1, March 2020 available at: https://www.inss.org.il/publication/the-secret-war-of-cyber-influence-operations-and-how-to-identify-them/
2. Lara Jakes and Marc Tracy, "US Limits Chinese Staff at News Agencies Controlled by Beijing," New York Times, March 2, 2020. https:// www.nytimes.com/2020/03/02/world/asia/china-journalists-diplomats -expulsion.html
3. Office of the Secretary of Defense, Annual Report to Congress: Military and Security Developments Involving the People's Republic of China (Washington, DC: 2019), P.112 available at: https://media.defense.gov / 2019/May / 02 / 2002127082 / -1 /-1/1/2019_CHINA_MILITARY_ POWER_ REPORT.pdf
4. Eric V. Larson et al., Foundations of Effective Influence Operations: A Framework for Enhancing Army Capabilities (Santa Monica, CA: RAND Corporation, 2009), available at: https://www.rand.org/content/dam/rand/pubs/monographs/2009/RAND_MG654.sum.pdf,
5. Foundations of Effective Influence Operations, RAND Corporation, 2009, p. 2. available at: http://www.rand.org/pubs/monographs/2009/RAND_MG654.pdf,
6. Matteo E. Bonfanti, Cyber Intelligence: In Pursuit of a Better Understanding, Cyber, Intelligence, and Security, Volume 2, No. 1, May 2018 available at: http://din-online.info/pdf/cy2-1e.pdf
7. Pascal Brangetto, Matthijs A. Veenendaal, Influence Cyber Operations: The Use of Cyberattacks in Support of Influence Operations available at: https://ccdcoe.org/uploads/2018/10/Art-08-Influence-Cyber-Operations-The-Use-of-Cyberattacks-in-Support-of-Influence-Operations.pdf
8. Herbert Lin and Jackie Kerr, "On Cyber-Enabled Information/Influence Warfare and Manipulation," in Oxford Handbook of Cybersecurity, August 14, 2017, pp. 5–7 available at: https://www.semanticscholar.org / paper / On-Cyber-Enabled-Information%2FInfluence - Warfare-and-Lin-Kerr/1adbcd318efc84eb53dbb0c23d6433aa93aa58c4

9. Chen Zhengzhong, "Preliminary Thoughts About Strengthening Cyber News Media in Wartime," Military Correspondent, July 2014 available at: https://encyclopedia.1914-1918-online.net/article/propaganda_media_in_war_politics
10. See "List of Blocked Websites and Apps in China 2020," Travel ChiThevicna Cheaper website, https://www.travelchinacheaper.com / index-blocked – websites – in - china. Retrieved April 7, 2020. Updated periodically. available at: https://cyber.harvard.edu/filtering/china/China-highlights.html
11. China's Influence & American Interests, Report of the Working Group on Chinese Influence Activities in the United States, Hoover Institution Press, Stanford University, available at: https://www.hoover.org/sites/default/files/research/docs/chineseinfluence_americaninterests_fullreport_web.pd
12. Jeangène Vilmer, A. Escorcia, M. Guillaume, J. Herrera, Information Manipulation: A Challenge for Our Democracies, report by the Policy Planning Staff (CAPS) of the Ministry for Europe and Foreign Affairs and the Institute for Strategic Research (IRSEM) of the Ministry for the Armed Forces, Paris, August 2018 available at: https://bg.ambafrance.org/IMG/pdf/report_information_manipulation.pdf?10364/0ced9e06f6ba84738088accbf0928cbc809ef42f
13. Jean-Baptiste Jeangène Vilmer, Alexandre Escorcia, Marine Guillaume, Janaina Herrera, Information Manipulation A Challenge for Our Democracies, August 2018 available at: https://www.diplomatie.gouv.fr/IMG/pdf/information_manipulation_rvb_cle838736.pdf
14. Kelsey Munro and Philip Wen, "Chinese Language Newspapers in Australia: Beijing Controls Messaging, Propaganda in Press, Sydney Morning Herald, July 8, 2016 available at: https://www.smh.com.au / national / chineselanguage-newspapers-in-australia-beijing-controls-messaging-propaganda-in-press-20160610-gpg0s3.html
15. Peter Mattis, A Guide to Chinese Intelligence Operations, War on the Rocks, August 18, 2015 available at: https://warontherocks.com / 2015 / 08 / a-guide-to-chinese-intelligence-operations/

16. Profile of MSS-Affiliated PRC Foreign Policy Think Tank CICIR, Open Source Center, August 25, 2011 available at: https://fas.org/irp/dni/osc/cicir.pdf

17. The Nielsen Total Audience Report: Q1 2018, Media, July 31, 2018 available at: https://www.nielsen.com/us/en/insights/reports/2018/q1-2018-total-audience-report.html

18. Elisa Shearer, Social media outpaces print newspapers in the U.S. as a news source, December 10, 2018 available at: http://www.pewresearch.org / fact-tank / 2018 / 12 / 10 / social-media-outpaces-print-newspapers-in-the-u-s-as-a-news-source/

19. People don't trust social media -- that's a growing problem for businesses, June 18, 2018 available at: https://www.cbsnews.com /news/edelman-survey-shows-low-trust-in-social-media /

20. Chris Buckley and Jane Perlez, "By Buying Hong Kong Paper, Alibaba Seeks to Polish China's Image," New York Times, December 13, 2015 available at: https://www.nytimes.com/2015 / 12 / 14 / world / asia / alibaba-south-china-morning-post-hong-kong.html

21. Kristina Cooke, "China News Agency Leases Plum Times Square Ad Space," Reuters, July 26, 2011; Angela Doland, "Watch the Chinese Propaganda Ad Playing 120 Times a Day in Times Square," AdAge, July 27, 2016 available at: https://www.reuters.com / article / industry-us-media-xinhua-timessquare / china – news – agency – leases – plum – times – square - ad-space-idUSTRE76P71T20110726

22. Brian Fung, Are China's Journalists Spying on Us?, The Atlantic, January 12, 2013 available at: https://www.theatlantic.com/international / archive / 2013 / 01/are-chinas-journalists-spying-on-us/267098/

23. For an overview of Chinese-Americans in the 2016 election, see "Chinese-Americans Are Becoming Politically Active," Economist, January 19, 2017 available at: https://www.economist.com / united-states / 2017 / 01 / 19 / chinese-americans-are-becoming-politically-active

24. Louise Lucas, "Questions over Pace of Growth As Wechat Nears 1bn Users," Financial Times, August 30, 2017; Mengzi Gao, "Chinese Trump Supporters Thank WeChat," Voices of New

York, November 11, 2016 available at: https://www.ft.com/content/b557d6c8-8891-11e7-8bb1-5ba57d47eff7

25. Eileen Guo, "How We chat Spreads Rumors, Reaffirms Bias, and Helped Elect Trump," Wired, April 20, 2017 available at: https://www.wired.com / 2017 / 04 / how-wechat-spreads-rumors-reaffirms-bias-and-helped-elect-trump/

26. Sarah Cook, China's Global Media Footprint Democratic Responses to Expanding Authoritarian Influence, National Endowment for Democracy, February 2021 available at: https://www.ned.org / wp-content/uploads/2021/02/Chinas-Global - Media -Footprint-Democratic-Responses-to-Expanding-Authoritarian-Influence-Cook-Feb-2021.pdf

27. Shulin Hu, "Weibo–How Is China's Second Largest Social Media Platform Being Used for Social Research?" Impact of Social Sciences, March 29, 2020 available at: https://blogs.lse.ac.uk/impactofsocialsciences / 2020 / 03 / 26 / weibo-how-is-chinas-second – largest – social – media - platform-being-used-for-social-research/

28. Mareike Ohlberg, Propaganda beyond the Great Firewall, December 05, 2019 available at: https://merics.org/en/short-analysis/propaganda-beyond-great-firewall

29. Mareike Ohlberg, Propaganda beyond the Great Firewall, December 05, 2019 available at: https://merics.org/en/short-analysis/propaganda-beyond-great-firewall

30. Tom Uren, Elise Thomas, and Jacob Wallis, "Tweeting through the Great Firewall," International Cyber Policy Center (blog), October 2019 available at: https://s3-ap-southeast-2.amazonaws.com/ad-aspi/2019-12/Tweeting%20through%20the%20great%20fire%20wall.pdf?TRGkGXh8FPY5KXLSc_4SfDUy7sMfNkw0

31. Meng Jing and Celia Chen, "China Fines Tencent, Baidu, Weibo over Banned Contents in On-Going Crackdown," South China Morning Post, September 26, 2017 available at: https://www.scmp.com / tech / china-tech / article / 2112921 / china-fines-tencent-baidu-and-weibo-over-banned-contents-ongoing

32. Jeangène Vilmer, A. Escorcia, M. Guillaume, J. Herrera, Information Manipulation: A Challenge for Our Democracies,

report by the Policy Planning Staff (CAPS) of the Ministry for Europe and Foreign Affairs and the Institute for Strategic Research (IRSEM) of the Ministry for the Armed Forces, Paris, August 2018.

33. Weaponized: How Rumors about Covid-19's Origins Led To a Narrative Arms Race, DFR Lab, February 2021 available at: https://www.atlanticcouncil.org/wp-content/uploads/2021/02/Weaponized-How-rumors-about-COVID-19s-origins-led-to-a-narrative-arms-race.pdf

34. Krassi Twigg and Kerry Allen, The disinformation tactics used by China, BBC News, March 12, 2021, available at: https://www.bbc.com/news/56364952

35. Mary Gallagher Blake Miller†, Who Not What: The Logic of China's Information Control Strategy, January 13, 2019 available at: https://drive.google.com/file/d/1xjHWI0Ih3abONxL0WoXj2swlcBuiRCXO/view

36. For an overview of the PLA's approach to political warfare, see Mark Stokes and Russell Hsiao, "The People's Liberation Army General Political Department: Political Warfare with Chinese Characteristics," Project 2049 Institute, October 14, 2013 available at: https://www.yumpu.com/en/document/view/22551366/pla-general-political-department-liaison-stokes-hsiao

37. Chinese Academy of Military Science Military Strategy Department, ed., Science of Military Strategy, 3rd edition, Beijing: Academy of Military Science Press, 2013, p. 129 available at: https://deterrence.ucsd.edu/_files/Chinas%20Science%20of%20Military%20Strategy%20Cross - Domain%20Concepts%20in%20the%202013%20Edition%20Qiu2015.pdf

38. For an overview of the PLA's approach to political warfare, see Mark Stokes and Russell Hsiao, "The People's Liberation Army General Political Department: Political Warfare with Chinese Characteristics," Project 2049 Institute, October 14, 2013 available at: https://project2049.net/wp-content/uploads/2018/04/P2049_Stokes_Hsiao_PLA_General_Political_Department_Liaison_101413.pdf

39. Christopher Paul and Miriam Matthews, The Russian "Firehose of Falsehood" Propaganda Model Why It Might Work and Options to Counter It, Rand Corporation available at:

https://www.rand.org/content/dam/rand/pubs/perspectives/PE100/PE198/RAND_PE198.pdf

40. Peter Mattis, "Contrasting China's and Russia's Influence Operations," War on the Rocks, January16, 2018 available at: https://warontherocks.com / 2018 / 01 / contrasting – chinas - russias-influence-operations.

41. Samantha Bradshaw and Philip N. Howard, The Global Disinformation Order, Oxford Internet Institute, University of Oxford, 2019 available at: https://comprop.oii.ox.ac.uk/wp-content/uploads/sites/93/2019/09/CyberTroop-Report19.pdf

42. Tom Uren, Elise Thomas, and Jacob Wallis, Tweeting through the Great Firewall: Preliminary analysis of PRC-linked information operations against the Hong Kong protests, Australian Strategic Policy Institute, 3 September 2019, www.aspi.org.au/report/tweeting-through-great-firewall; Edward Wong, Matthew Rosenberg, and Julian E. Barnes, "Chinese Agents Helped Spread Messages that Sowed Virus Panic in U.S., Officials Say," New York Times, April 22, 2020 available at: www.nytimes.com / 2020 / 04 / 22 / us / politics / coronavirus – china - disinformation.html

43. Tom Uren, Elise Thomas, and Jacob Wallis, Tweeting through the Great Firewall: Preliminary analysis of PRC-linked information operations against the Hong Kong protests, Australian Strategic Policy Institute, 3 September 2019, www.aspi.org.au/report/tweeting-through-great-firewall; Edward Wong, Matthew Rosenberg, and Julian E. Barnes, "Chinese Agents Helped Spread Messages that Sowed Virus Panic in U.S., Officials Say," New York Times, April 22, 2020 available at: www.nytimes.com/2020/04/22/us/politics/coronavirus-china-disinformation.html

44. "Information operations directed at Hong Kong," Twitter (blog), 19 August 2019, https://blog.twitter.com/en_us/topics/company/2019/information_operations_directed_at_Hong_Kong.html; "China Media Bulletin: Student indoctrination, surveillance innovation, GitHub mobilization," Freedom House, April 2019 available at: https://freedomhouse.org/china-media/china-media-bulletin-student-indoctrination-surveillance-innovation-github-mobilization-no-135.

45. Sarah Cook, "Welcome to the New Era of Chinese Government Disinformation," Diplomat, 11 May 2020, https://thediplomat.com/2020/05/welcome-to-the-new-era-of-chinese-government-disinformation; Uren, Thomas, and Wallis, "Tweeting through the Great Firewall"; Raymond Zhong, Steven Lee Myers and Jin Wu, "How China Unleashed Twitter Trolls to Discredit Hong Kong's Protesters," New York Times, September 18, 2019 available at: www.nytimes.com / interactive / 2019 / 09 / 18 / world/asia/hk-twitter.html
46. Peter Harrell, Elizabeth Rosenberg, Edoardo Saravalle, "China's Use of Coercive Economic Measures" (Center for a New American Security, June 11, 2018) available at: https://s3.amazonaws.com/files.cnas.org/documents / China_Use_FINAL-1.pdf?mtime=20180604161240
47. By Ben Nimmo, C. Shawn Eib, L. Tamora, Cross-Platform Spam Network Targeted Hong Kong Protests, Graphika, September 2019 available at: https://public-assets.graphika.com/reports/graphika_report_spamouflage.pdf
48. Sarah Cook, "Worried About Huawei? Take a Closer Look at Tencent," Diplomat, 26 March 2019, https://thediplomat.com / 2019 / 03 / worried-about-huawei-take-a-closer-look-at-tencent; Nathan Vanderklippe, "Huawei providing surveillance tech to China's Xinjiang authorities, report finds," Globe and Mail, November 29, 2019 available at: www.theglobeandmail.com / world / article – huawei – providing-surveillance-tech-to-chinas-xinjiang-authorities.
49. Elsa Kania, Samm Sacks, Paul Triolo, and Graham Webster, "China's Strategic Thinking on Building Power in Cyberspace," New America, September 25, 2017 available at: www.newamerica.org / cybersecurity-initiative / blog / chinas-strategic-thinking-building-power-cyberspace.
50. Renée Diresta, Carly Miller, Vanessa Molter, John Pomfret, And Glenn Tiffert, Telling China's Story: The Chinese Communist Party's Campaign to Shape Global Narratives, Hoover institution available at: https://fsi-live.s3.us-west-1.amazonaws.com/s3fs-public/sio-china_story_white_paper-final.pdf
51. Gary King Jennifer Pan Margaret E. Roberts, How the Chinese Government Fabricates Social Media Posts for Strategic

Distraction, not Engaged Argument, April 9, 2017 available at: http://gking.harvard.edu/files/gking/files/50c.pdf?m=1463587807

52. Foreign Threats to the 2020 U.S. Federal Elections, National Intelligence Council, March 10, 2021 available at: https://www.dni.gov/files/ODNI/documents/assessments/ICA-declass-16MAR21.pdf

53. Rush Doshi, "China Steps Up Its Information War in Taiwan," Foreign Affairs, January 9, 2020 available at: https://www.foreignaffairs.com/articles/china/2020-01-09/china-steps-its-information-war-taiwan

54. Aaron Huang, Combatting and Defeating Chinese Propaganda and Disinformation: A Case Study Of Taiwan's 2020 Elections, Harvard Kennedy School of Government, July 2020 available at: https://www.belfercenter.org/sites/default/files/files/publication/Combatting%20Chinese%20Propaganda%20and%20Disinformation%20-%20Huang.pdf

55. Confucius Institutes in the United States: Selected Issues, Congressional Research Service (CRS). March 18, 2021 available at: https://crsreports.congress.gov/product/pdf/IF/IF11180

56. Larry Diamond, Orville Schell, China's Influence & American Interests Promoting Constructive Vigilance Report of the Working Group on Chinese Influence Activities in the United States, Hoover Institution Press Stanford University Stanford, California, 2019 available at: https://www.hoover.org/research/chinas-influence-american-interests-promoting-constructive-vigilance

57. Tager, James. Made in Hollywood, Censored by Beijing. PEN America available at: https://pen.org/report/made-in-hollywood-censored-by-beijing

58. Benner, Thorsten, et al. Authoritarian Advance: Responding to China's Growing Political Influence in Europe. Global Public Policy Institute/Mercator Institute for China Studies, Feb. 2018, https://merics.org/sites/default/files/2020-04/GPPi_MERICS_Authoritarian_Advance_2018_1.pdf. And "Follow the New Silk Road: China's growing trail of think tanks and lobbyists in Europe." Corporate Europe Observatory, April 08. 2019

available at: https://corporateeurope.org/en/2019/ 04/follow-new - silk -road-chinas-growing-trail-think-tanks-and-lobbyists-europe

59. “China launches "China-CEE Institute" think tank in Hungary.” Xinhua, April 25, 2017 available at: http://www.china-ceec.org/eng/zdogjhz_1/t1456482.htm
60. Craig Singleton, Follow the Money: Exposing China’s Influence Operations at Academic Institutions and Think Tanks, March 16, 2021 available at: https://www.fdd.org/analysis/2020/11/24/china-influence-institutions-think-tanks
61. Robert Morgus, Brian Fonseca, Kieran Green, & Alexander Crowther, Are China and Russia on the Cyber Offensive in Latin America and the Caribbean? July 2019 available at: http://newamerica.org/cybersecurity-initiative/reports/russia-china-cyber-offensive-latam-caribbean
62. 1st Lt Peter Loftus, Eric Chan, Chinese Communist Party Information Warfare US–China Competition during the COVID-19 Pandemic, Journal of Indo-Pacific Affairs, Summer 2020 available at: https://media.defense.gov/2020/Jun/08/2002311968/-1/-1/1/DO_CHAN.PDF
63. Laura Rosenberger, China’s Corona virus Information Offensive, Foreign Affairs, April 22, 2020 available at: https://www.foreignaffairs.com / articles / china / 2020-04-22 / chinas-coronavirus-information-offensive
64. Samantha Cole, “‘Deep Voice’ Software Can Clone Anyone’s Voice With Just 3.7 Seconds of Audio,” VICE, March 7, 2018 available at: https://www.vice.com/en_us/article/3k7mgn/baidu – deep-voice-software-can-clone-anyones-voice-with-just-37-seconds-of-audio.
65. Jack Ma, Twitter, March 16, 2020 available at: https://twitter.com/
66. China Ready to Boost Cooperation with Japan to Fight COVID-19: Chinese Ambassador, Xinhua News, February 23, 2020 available at: http://www.xinhuanet.com/
67. Nemanja Cabric and Shi Zhongyu, “Iron-clad China-Serbia Friendship Stronger in COVID-19 Fight,” Xinhua News, April 2, 2020 available at: http://www.xinhuanet.com

68. Zhaoyin Feng, "China and Twitter: The Year China Got Louder on Social Media," BBC, December 29, 2019 available at: https://www.bbc.com/
69. Daniel Kliman, Andrea Kendall-Taylor, Kristine Lee, Joshua Fitt, and Carisa Nietsche, Dangerous Synergies: Countering Chinese and Russian Digital Influence Operations, May 2020 available at: https://www.cnas.org/publications/reports/dangerous-synergies
70. Carolyn Kenney, Max Bergmann, and James Lamond, Understanding and Combating Russian and Chinese Influence Operations, February 28, 2019 available at: https://www.americanprogress.org/issues/security/reports/2019/02/28/466669/understanding-combating-russian-chinese-influence-operations
71. Alžběta Bajerová, China Is Learning the 'Russian Way' of Disinformation on COVID-19, April 3, 2020 available at: https://chinaobservers.eu / china-is-learning-the-russian-way-of-disinformation-on-covid-19/
72. China Brief, April 24, 2019; China Brief, December 10, 2019; China Brief, December 31, 2019; China Brief, April 13
73. Cyberspace Administration of China, December 17, 2019
74. Cyberspace Administration of China, December 29, 2016
75. Ibid
76. University of Electronic Science and Technology, April 27, 2018.
77. China Social Sciences Net, January 4, 2017.
78. People's Daily Online, April 18, 2019; Cyberspace Administration of China, August 2, 2018).
79. China Social Sciences Net,January 4, 2017.
80. People's Daily Online, April 18, 2019.
81. People's Daily Online, April 18, 2019; Reference News, June 18, 2019.
82. People's Daily Online, May 24, 2019; University of Electronic Science and Technology, April 27, 2018.
83. People's Daily Online, February 22, 2019.
84. Xinhua, April 7, 2017; People's Daily Online, September 3, 2018,

85. People's Daily Online, August 15, 2019; Cyberspace Administration of China, December 29, 2016.

86. CCTV, September 6, 2018.

87. China Brief, Volume 20, Issue 9, May 15, 2020 available at: https://jamestown.org/wp-content/uploads/2020/05/Read-the-05-15-2020-CB-Issue-in-PDF-2.pdf?x50971

88. Alicia Fawcett, China's Use of Information Manipulation in Regional and Global Competition Chinese Discourse Power, Atlantic Council, December 2020 available at: https://www.atlanticcouncil.org/wp-content/uploads/2020/12/China-Discouse-Power-FINAL.pdf

89. America's Weaknesses – Foreign Policy available at: https://foreignpolicy.com / 2018 / 10 / 04 / chinas-influence-operations-are-pinpointing-americas-weaknesses/

90. Elsa Kania, The Right to Speak: Discourse and Chinese Power, November 27, 2018 available at: https://www.ccpwatch.org/single-post / 2018 / 11 / 27 / The-Right-to-Speak-Discourse-and-Chinese-Power

* * *

CHAPTER 9

Military Civil Fusion

"We must accelerate the formation of a full-element, multi-domain, and high-return military-civil fusion deep development pattern, and gradually build up China's unified military-civil system of strategies and strategic capability."

–Xi Jinping, speaking to the Central Commission for Military-Civil Fusion Development, June 20, 2017.

Introduction

Military-Civil Fusion (MCF) is an aggressive, national strategy of the Chinese Communist Party (CCP). The Party's leaders see MCF as a vital element of their strategy for China to become a "great modern socialist country," which includes developing a "world-class" most technologically advanced military and becoming a world leader in science and technology (S&T). To achieve this, MCF will allow the seamless flow of knowledge, technology, resources, materials and talent back and forth between the military, defence industrial sectors and academia. The CCP is executing this strategy through its own research and development (R&D) efforts and acquiring the world's cutting-edge technologies, including theft.

The Science of Military Strategy states: "In light of the ambiguous boundaries between peacetime and wartime in cyber countermeasures, and the characteristic that military and civilian attacks are hard to distinguish, persist in the integration of peace and war in military–civil integration; in peacetime, use civilians to hide the military; in wartime, the military and the people, hands joined, attack together." China's concept and national strategy of military civil fusion stress leveraging synergies between defence and commercial developments. It also wants to utilise the skills of civilian personnel for cyber defence and force development. PRC President and CCP General Secretary Xi Jinping personally supervises the strategy's implementation. He chairs the CCP's Central Military Commission and the Central Commission for Military-Civil Fusion Development.

The United States Influence

China is a keen observer of western especially American theories and practices. It has analysed U.S. concepts of Civil-Military Integration (CMI), third offset strategy, Public Private Partnership (PPP) and Defense Advanced Research Projects Agency (DARPA). After careful scrutiny of all these concepts, China arrived at the strategy of MCF. Military-Civil Fusion caters to China's specific conditions, requirements and goals.

The term MCF looks like the opposite number to the American term CMI. However, it is far deeper and more complex. As per the U.S. Congressional Office of Technology Assessment, America's CMI is "cooperation between government and commercial facilities in R&D, manufacturing, and/or maintenance operations."[1] But China's MCF strategy is a state-led, state-directed program that leverages the state and commercial power to strengthen and support the People's Liberation Army (PLA), the Communist Party of China's armed wing. In the American ecosystem, the level of integration has emerged over the decades. In China, MCF is a state-driven strategy for rapid implementation. The full scope of MCF is much broader than the PPPs the Pentagon has been promoting.

Chinese scholars feel that MCF is not a new thing. They note that the developed nations promote MCF in the following ways:

- They adopt a whole-of-society approach to promote the informatisation of their military forces by using private firms and technological platforms for their Armed Forces.
- Big Defence industrial companies like Lockheed Martin, Boeing, General Dynamics, Northrop Grumman and others maintain a high proportion of outside contractors, many of which became major enterprises in military research fields.
- In recent conflicts, the concept of contractors of the private military companies in the battlefields has come into existence. More than 80 percent of the U.S. Military's logistical and technical support personnel nowadays are provided by contractors.
- The national education system normally trains military cadets. In developed countries, about 70-80 per cent of cadets come from universities. Comparatively, the PLA's proportion of cadets trained by its national education system is less than 30 per cent.
- Developed countries successfully use their civilian infrastructure for military use by constructing expressways, tunnels and service stations.

There are striking similarities between U.S. and Chinese organisations. The new Chinese Central Military Commission Science and Technology Commission resembles the DARPA. 'Rapid response small group', established by the Central Military Commission Science and Technology Commission is reported in Chinese media as 'China's DIUx (defence innovation unit)' for innovation to improve the PLA's capability to leverage commercial technologies.

Importance of MCF to the Chinese Communist Party

Military-Civil Fusion is critical for advancing China's regional and global ambitions. A U.S. China Economic and Security Review Commission report stated that the PLA "is heavily reliant upon China's commercial IT sector to aid R&D into dual-use and military-grade microelectronics and telecommunications and to improve the military's C4ISR capabilities."

At an address in the annual parliamentary session, Chinese President Xi Jinping called for deepening civil-military fusion while emphasising technical innovation's strategic importance for the PLA's military modernisation, including training, recruitment, weapons innovation and strategic planning. He said, "Military innovations should take a central role in producing indigenous military wares; and that the governments from the state to the local levels should promote integration between the civilian and the military sectors."

Key technologies that are targeted under MCF include quantum computing, big data, semi-conductors, 5G, advanced nuclear technology, aerospace technology and artificial intelligence (AI). China especially wants to exploit the inherent 'dual-use' nature of many of these technologies, which have both military and civilian applications. China is developing and acquiring niche technologies through licit and illicit means. These include investment in private industries, acquiring intellectual property, talent recruitment programs, academic and research collaboration programs for military advantage, intelligence gathering, forced technology transfer and outright theft. MCF permits selected civilian enterprises to undertake classified military R&D and weapons production. China exploits the open and transparent nature of the global research creativity to bolster its own military capabilities through bodies like the China Scholarship Council. It requires academic scholarship recipients to report on their overseas research to Chinese diplomats.

Military-Civil Fusion development can contribute to the following key positive results:

- It can support China's transformation into a powerful nation. There is an immediate need for significant improvements in China's national defence capabilities.
- It can help China gain advantages in global technological and military competitions. China needs to close the gap in the development of disruptive technologies by advanced countries.
- It provides a tremendous opportunity for the improvement of China's governance system. It will enable the creation of a governing system across sectors, government bodies and domains.
- It supports the creation of a world-class military. The MCF strategy is to work with China's other great power strategies in the manufacturing, maritime, space and cyberspace domains.

China's 13th Five-Year Plan (FYP) (2016–20) describes the 2020 goal for MCF as: "form a basic military-civilian S&T collaborative innovation system, and promote the formation of comprehensive, multi-domain, and high-efficiency military-civilian technology fusion." To ensure the completion of this objective, the plan charted following seven specific goals:[2]

- Strengthen macro-coordination of science, technology, military and civilian integration. Improve the scientific and technological MCF system and mechanism. Promote coordination and integration of plans.
- Strengthen the capacity of S&T collaborative innovation between the military and civilian sectors. Coordinate basic research and layout of cutting-edge technology

research. Implement key S&T MCF projects. Implement major national S&T projects.

- Promote planning and sharing of S&T innovation resources. Strengthen the joint construction and sharing of scientific research platforms. Promote the sharing of military and civilian S&T resources.
- Promote the two-way transformation of military and civilian S&T achievements. Promote the transformation of the system overseeing the conversion of military and civilian S&T achievements. Promote the implementation of an intellectual property rights protection strategy.
- Carry out pilot demonstrations. Focus on building a military-civilian S&T collaborative innovation platform. Encourage the construction of a new type of MCF scientific research institution. Explore an MCF financial service model.
- Strengthen the cultivation of innovative personnel. Improve the training and utilisation mechanism of military and civilian creative talents and build a new type of think tank for S&T MCF.
- Improve the policy system. Strengthen the construction of an MCF system.

Management and Implementation

The importance the CCP gives to MCF can be seen from the overall management and implementation of the MCF Development Strategy. It includes the most powerful organs in the party-state: the Politburo, the State Council and the CMC. The CCP Central Committee's rise of the MCF Development Strategy to a national-level strategy is aimed to overcome hindrances to implementation across the party-state. The Central Commission for Military Civilian Fusion Development

(CCMCFD) was established in 2017, chaired by General Secretary Xi Jinping, Premier Li Keqiang, several other Politburo Standing Committee members, two State Councilors, both CMC Vice Chairmen, 12 Ministry-level leaders, and others. The specified objective of the CCMCFD is to build China's "national strategic system and capabilities" and overcome impediments to implementation.

The graphic below illustrates the core components of the MCF deep development pattern:

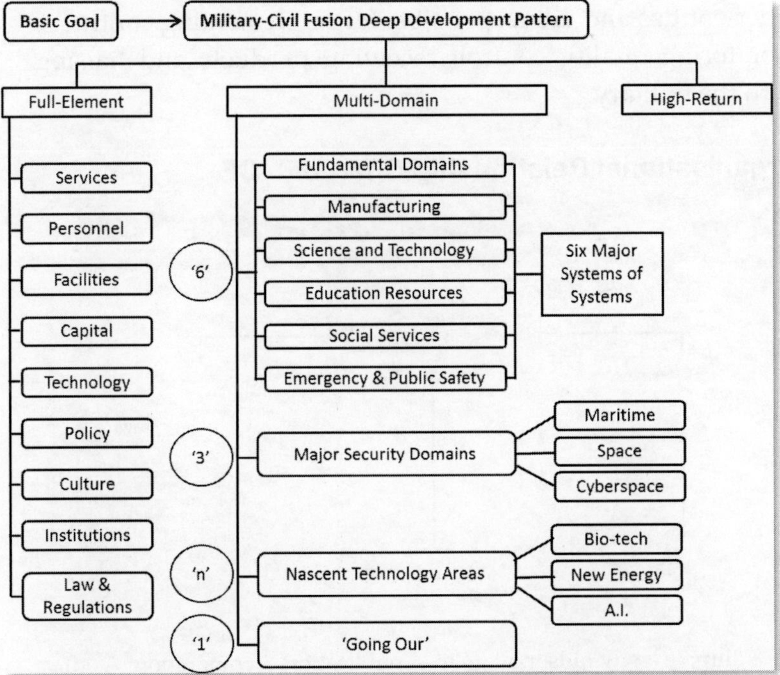

Source: Alex Stone and Peter Wood (2020), China's Military-Civil Fusion Strategy: A View from Chinese Strategists, Montgomery, AL: China Aerospace Studies Institute, Air University available at https://www.airuniversity.af.edu/Portals/10/CASI/documents/Research/Other%20topics/CASI%20China's%20Military%20Civil%20Fusion%20Strategy-%20Full%20final.pdf?ver=2020-06-15-152810-733

In the military, the Military-Civil Fusion Bureau was established in the Office for Strategic Planning of the CMC in 2016. This bureau is the driving force behind civilian participation in the defence industries. The State Administration for Science, Technology and Industry for National Defense (SASTIND), is the force behind "eliminating barriers to defence conversion." The SASTIND is responsible for the management of national defence company policy. Also, military representative offices have been established at each level as representatives of the PLA in defence contractors and other entities and are responsible for implementing contracts, monitoring quality control, receiving products and liaising with the military.

Organisational Relationship Chart of MCF

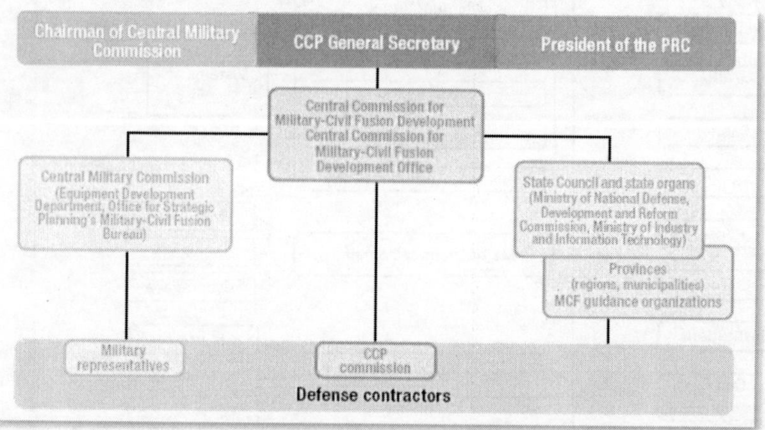

Source: http://www.nids.mod.go.jp / publication / chinareport / pdf / china_report_EN_web_2021_A01.pdf

China pursues MCF through six interrelated efforts. Each effort overlaps with the others and has both domestic and international components. The Party seeks to implement the MCF Development Strategy across every level of China's party-state from the highest national-level organs down to provinces and township. The six systems in the MCF Development Strategy are:

- **The Advanced Defense Science, Technology and Industrial Systems.** This system focuses on fusing China's defence industrial base, civil industrial base and technology. This would transfer mature technologies across military and civilian sectors. This system intends to improve the competitiveness within China's defence industrial base and self-reliance in manufacturing key industrial technologies such as aerospace, communications and transportation, equipment and materials to reduce its dependence on imports.
- **The Military-Civil Coordinated Technology Innovation System.** This system would maximise the full potential and benefits of the country's S&T development. It concentrates on fusing innovations and advances in basic and applied research, specifically strengthening and promoting civilian and military R&D in advanced dual-use technologies and cross-pollinating military and civilian basic research.
- **The Fundamental Domain Resource Sharing System.** This system deals with building military requirements into the erection of civilian infrastructure from the inception and leveraging China's civilian construction and logistics capacities and capabilities for military purposes. This includes infrastructure projects in dual-use domains such as space and undersea as well as mobile communications networks and topographical and meteorological systems. This is evident in China's major land reclamations and military construction activities in the South China Sea, which brought together the PLA, law enforcement, several government

entities, construction companies and commercial entities.

- **The Military Personnel (Talent) Cultivation System.** This system would blend and cultivate military and civilian S&T expertise through education programs, personnel exchanges and knowledge sharing. It would improve China's human capital, build a highly skilled workforce and recruit foreign experts to access know-how, expertise and niche technology.
- **The Socialised Support and Sustainment System for the PLA.** This system wants to streamline PLA's logistics and support services. It would harness civil and private sector resources to improve the PLA's essential services and support functions like food, housing and healthcare services. This would provide the PLA with modern transportation and distribution, warehousing, information sharing, and other types of support in peacetime and wartime. This fusion will give the PLA with a logistics system that is more efficient, higher capacity and quality and global in reach.
- **National Defence Mobilisation System.** This would expand and deepen China's national defence mobilisation system to include all relevant aspects of its society and economy for use in competition and war.

Military-Civil Fusion Linkages

Each MCF system has linkages between a number of organisations and government entities including:

- Ministry-level organisations from the State Council.
- Lead military organs subordinate to the Central Military Commission.
- State-sponsored educational institutions, research centres, and critical laboratories.

- Defence industry.
- Other (SOEs) and quasi-private companies.
- Provincial governments.

Funding

The Chinese government is promotion MCF by leveraging guidance funds as an important mechanism to drive capital and activities. For example, the MCF industrial development fund launched in September 2016 involved 30.2 billion RMB or $4.4 billion in its initial funding round. According to some estimates, the total funding for a wide variety of guidance funds is in the range of several hundred billion dollars. As of mid-2019, several billion dollars of funding has been allotted to MCF through funds launched in cities and provinces that include Shanghai, Sichuan, Guizhou, Hebei, Henan, Hunan, Guangdong, Zhejiang, Liaoning, Shaanxi and Heilongjiang.

Quietly, China has invested vast sums of money in Silicon Valley firms with technology relevant to national security. Crucial defence related targets include sensitive or military-grade equipment such as computer circuits, radiation-hardened programmable semi-conductors, accelerometers and military sensors, high-grade carbon fibre, restricted micro-wave amplifiers, proprietary and export restricted technical data and thermal imaging systems. Chinese investors are mainly involved in AI, robotics, augmented reality/ virtual reality, and financial technology. It is estimated that China participated in 10-16 per cent of all venture capital deals, including 271 early-state technology investment deals worth $11.5 billion in 2015 alone. Examples are: [3]

- Neurala, an AI company, struggled to get funding from the U.S. military. It got funding from a Chinese group associated with a state-owned company.[4]

- Quanergy, which develops sensors for military applications, accepted venture funding from the Chinese fund GP Capital.
- China's State Council financed an initial investment in Canyon Bridge Capital Partners in its attempted $1.3 billion takeovers of Lattice Semi-conductor. Later this was blocked by the Trump administration on national security grounds.[5]

However, China maintains strict control over inbound investment.[6] Not all China's technology companies are keen to pursue close collaboration with the PLA. Commercial considerations drive them in a fiercely competitive ecosystem. Those with international aspirations, like Alibaba, may tend to be less transparent about collaborations with the Chinese military and defence industry, with some important exceptions. Baidu, a global leader and member of China's national team in AI, and the China Electronics Technology Group Corporation started a joint laboratory to apply AI, big data and cloud computing to command and control.

Espionage

As explained earlier in the Chapter on Cyber Espionage, to bring the western, innovations into its industrial ecosystem, China has increased its cyber and technology espionage activities. Such illegal transfers can occur through exports, foreign direct investment and acquisitions, cyberespionage, traditional industrial espionage, research collaboration, talent acquisition, and influence operations. FBI Director Christopher Wray stated, "Over the past decade, the FBI has seen economic espionage cases with a link to China increase by approximately 1,300 per cent." There are many examples. PLA Navy submarines and frigates are now having German-produced engines exported to China for commercial use.

As per the Australian Strategic Policy Institute estimates, the PLA has sponsored over 2,500 military scientists and engineers to study abroad, especially in Five Eyes countries (U.S., UK, Canada, Australia and New Zealand) since 2007. China's application of the MCF abroad threatens the democratisation of science and the philosophy of academic openness and collaboration.

China has intensified its regulatory actions deep into private Chinese enterprises to ensure that they will function as arms of the state. It has renewed emphasis on technology independence. China provides massive subsidies for the development of domestic technologies and support for "national champion" firms designed to meet China's domestic technology needs and erode Western multinationals' global market share.

Technology

China considers that the key to 21st century geopolitical and military competition lies with emerging technologies like AI and machine learning, cyber, electromagnetic spectrum, quantum cryptography, swarm robotics and biotechnology. Currently, the U.S. dominates in these areas of international R&D. Remarkably, Chinese assessments about these technologies' criticality were significantly influenced by strategic thinking from within the U.S. government, especially the Department of Defence's Obama-era Third Offset Strategy.

The high impact area of Bio-technology is identified as MCF focus technology. Elsa Kania and Wilson Vorndick contended that the PLA is using MCF to "weaponize biotech" such as the advanced biomimetic systems, CRISPR gene-editing technology, biological and biomimetic materials and human performance enhancement. China is trying to leverage their Artificial Intelligence/Machine Language expertise to achieve their objectives, including through collaboration with foreign partners.

Chinese supremacy in 5G technology has alarmed the United States and others. Huawei, the world leader in 5G IT infrastructure, has substantial personnel overlap with the PLA. The U.S. is alarmed that the Chinese dominance in U.S. IT infrastructure would give the Chinse government access to colossal data about American companies and citizens. For a number of legal violations, including theft of trade secrets, wire fraud, in January 2019, the U.S. State Department put Huawei on the Entity List.

Artificial Intelligence

China may have lost out on the "Revolutions in Military Affairs" (RMAs) of the early 90s. Now it is determined to lead the era of the Fourth Industrial Revolution. As explained in the Chapter on Concepts and Doctrines of Cyber Warfare, Chinese strategic thinkers believe that AI will drive the next revolution in military affairs, which the Chinese termed, "intelligentized warfare". This concept is driven by applying AI and AI-enabled technology into military systems and doctrine. Intelligentized warfare is defined as the operationalisation of AI and its enabling technologies, such as autonomous systems, big data analytics, cloud computing and quantum computing, for military applications.

As China moves toward intelligentized warfare, MCF will be a crucial element of the PLA's overall strategy to achieve "complete military modernisation" by 2035 and become a "world-class" military by 2049. In July 2017, the State Council issued the Artificial Intelligence Development Plan for a

New Era, which stated that China will "promote the two-way transfer and application of military and civilian scientific and technological achievements, and jointly build and share the innovative resources of the military and civilian, to form a full-element, multi-domain, and high return MCF deep development pattern." This plan specifically attempts to "direct the results of AI technology toward defense applications and encourage civilian S&T researchers to participate in major national defense-related AI research."

Role of PLA

Historically, the Chinese defence sector has been part of the Chinese military domain and about a dozen SOE. The MCF strategy intends to break down the obstacles between the PLA, academia, technology and private sectors. This would facilitate the PLA to employ dual-use industries and technologies for military advancements and capabilities development.

The Central Military–Civil Fusion Development Commission, led by Xi Jinping himself, has made the Cyberspace Security Military–Civil Fusion Innovation Centre, Qihoo-360, a leading Chinese cybersecurity company. He is guiding the centre with an aim to improve national cyber defences. China wants to leverage 'cyber militias' for its cyber defence. Xi Jinping has continuously emphasised the dynamism and potential of MCF in cybersecurity and informatisation, calling China to 'grasp the historical opportunity of the current information technology transformation and new transformation of military affairs'. In April 2018, in a speech delivered at the National Cybersecurity and Informatization Work Conference, Xi Jinping highlighted the inherent relationships between the market and the battlefield while 'promoting the creation of a full-factor, multi-domain and highly efficient development structure for MCF'.[7]

The PLA's Strategic Security Force (PLASSF) will have to keep pace with the rapid, disruptive technological changes, often driven by R&D in the private sector. These technological changes make SSF pursue civil military fusion as an integral aspect of its mission. This involves taking advantage of dual-use technological advances and leveraging civilian talent. The PLASSF recruits a large number of civilian personnel as specialist professionals in cyber defence, aerospace and AI. Individual PLASSF units are conducting research projects with universities. The quality of education at the SSF's Information Engineering University and Aerospace Engineering University will be crucial to its cultivation of personnel for command and technical career tracks.

Strategic Security Force has been active in pursuing its goals of MCF. Some of the initiatives undertaken are:

- Partnerships with over nine different universities and companies, such as the University of Science and Technology of China and the CETC, to focus on "fostering high-end talent" through education, training, cooperation, talent selection and exchanges.
- Signed an MCF strategic agreement with China Mobile in December 2016, that enables cooperation in areas of joint construction of information infrastructure, information system and resource development and utilization, emergency communications support, command and dispatch, "smart" military camps, information security and informatization talent training.
- Establishment of the Military-Civil Fusion Intelligent Equipment Research Institute in November 2016, as a

collaboration between the North China University of Technology and a private technology company. The institute received support from the Rocket Force's Equipment Research Academy, the Army Equipment Department, the Naval Equipment Research Institute and other military organisations. It was tasked to pursue AI research in intelligent robotics, unmanned systems and military brain science.

- 13th Five-Year S&T Military-Civil Fusion Special Projects Plan released in September 2017, focused on intelligent unmanned and cross-disciplinary technologies. It called for integrated space, cyber, biology, new energy and maritime technologies that have both commercial and military applications.

Education System

The complete Chinese university system is known to be the front line of MCF. The Chinese government certifies universities to carry out classified R&D on military matters and certifying them for weapons production. This policy is known in China as the 'three certifications'. More than 80 Chinese universities have already been permitted to undertake Top Secret or Secret level military R&D under this program. There are many joint laboratories and research partnerships that facilitate closer research cooperation between the military, defence industry, academia and commercial enterprises.

Tianjin's new Artificial Intelligence Military-Civil Fusion Innovation Center was raised in partnership with the Academy of Military Sciences. Today it leads military science research for the PLA and in defence innovation initiatives. Qingdao has expertise in undersea robotics systems and applications of AI in this domain. In Beijing, the high-tech zone of Zhongguancun has focused on emerging technologies, including establishing new industrial parks and starting several projects such as robotics and intelligent equipment. Beijing Military-Civil Fusion Expo 2019 was organised to market commercial technologies to military users. New armoured, multipurpose drone launching vehicles capable of launching a dozen drones to conduct reconnaissance or even suicide attacks were displayed.

Challenges to MCF

Though MCF could offer significant benefits to the PLA, some senior Chinese leaders, scholars and experts have underlined many internal challenges that will play a significant role in translating MCF from policy into reality. Although the CCP reigns supreme, there is the reluctance of many companies to embrace MCF. They think that MCF will affect their ability to access foreign markets and that may put civilian companies out of the defence sector.

There are observations on the lack of access to large-scale and high-tech facilities and experimental instruments for private sector companies. It is also unclear whether the private sector companies will get permission to work on very sensitive projects. On the other hand, some Chinese companies may try to take advantage of the resources available rather than provide real contributions to military modernisation. The heavy increase in funding, including the guidance funds dedicated to MCF can aggravate corruption in the Chinese military and defence industry.

Though there has been noticeable progress in MCF, some experts are worried that, in their current state, the defence industrial base and the innovation base are not in a position to meet both defence and commercial needs. Another cause of worry is the defence industrial base's low self-sufficiency on the core, critical technologies and the innovation base's inability to produce original innovations and breakthrough technologies. Bi Jingjing, Deputy Commandant of NDU between 2012 and 2017, noted the following problems:

- "I'm willing to 'fuse' others but not willing to 'be fused' by others."
- "It is okay for others to share resources with me, but I will not share my own resources."
- "My game, my turf, my rules."

A report on the Development of MCF in China (2016) by PLA's NDU observed that an evaluation of economic and defence construction at the end of the 12th FYP concluded that progress had been unsatisfactory. The CCP had tried to pursue similar policies earlier without any success. Finding the balance between the role of the government and the market is and will be one of the toughest challenges in implementing the MCF strategy.

Xi Jinping, since he took office, has been pressing hard on CMF. He argued that there is a pressing need to transition from "early-state fusion" to "deep fusion," a process that had been held up by problematic mindsets, systemic barriers and vested interests. To effect change and drive results, Xi Jinping, at the first meeting of the Central Commission for Military-Civil Fusion Development on June 20, 2017, highlighted the task's urgency. He urged officials to "break down ramparts, break through solid ice, remove barriers…wade through dangerous shoals, move people's cheese, resolve difficult problems, overcome obstacles, try out new ideas and open new paths."[8]

As China has become increasingly dependent on information networks in all aspects, including defence, its networks both civil and military have been vulnerable to cyber attacks. Chinese policymakers are acutely aware of this problem. In the next chapter China's Limitations and Vulnerabilities in Cyberspace will be evaluated.

Endnotes

1. China's Military-Civil Fusion Strategy available at: https://www.airuniversity.af.edu / Portals / 10 / CASI / documents / Research / Other-Topics / CASI_China_Military_Civil_Fusion_Strategy.pdf
2. The Thirteenth Five Year Plan's Special Plan for Military-Civil Fusion, Xinhua, August 23, 2017 available at: http://www.xinhuanet.com / mil / 2017-08 / 23 / c_1121531750.html
3. Paul Mozur and Jane Perlez, "China Bets on Sensitive U.S. Start-Ups, Worrying the Pentagon," The New York Times, March 22, 2017 available at: https://www.nytimes.com/2017/03/22/technology/china-defense-start-ups.html
4. China's Approval Process for Inbound Foreign Direct Investment: Impact on Market Access, National Treatment and Transparency available at: https://www.uschamber.com/sites/default/files / legacy / reports / 020021_China_Investment Paper_hires.pdf
5. Liana B. Baker, Koh Gui Qing, and Julie Zhu, "Exclusive: Chinese government money backs buyout firm's deal for U.S. chip maker," Reuters, November 28, 2016 available at: https://www.reuters.com / article / us-lattice-m-a-canyonbridge / exclusive-chinese-government-money-backs-buyout-firms-deal-for-u-s-chip-maker-idUSKBN13N1D5
6. China's Approval Process for Inbound Foreign Direct Investment: Impact on Market Access, National Treatment and Transparency, 2012 available at: https://www.uschamber.com/china%E2%80%99s-approval-process-inbound-foreign-direct-investment-impact-market-access-national-treatment
7. Rogier Creemers, Paul Triolo and Graham Webster, 'Translation: Xi Jinping's April 20 Speech at the National Cybersecurity and Informatization Work Conference', New America, 30 April

2018, available at: https://www.newamerica.org /cyber security initiative / digichina / blog / translation – xi – jinpings – april -20- speech – nationalcybersecurity – and – informatization – work - conference

8. Alex Stone and Peter Wood (2020), China's Military-Civil Fusion Strategy: A View from Chinese Strategists, Montgomery, AL: China Aerospace Studies Institute, Air University available at https://www.airuniversity.af.edu/Portals/10/CASI/documents/Research/Other%20topics/CASI%20China's%20Military%20Civil%20Fusion%20Strategy-%20Full%20final.pdf?ver=2020-06-15-152810-733

* * *

CHAPTER 10

China's Limitations and Vulnerabilities in Cyberspace

Introduction

China has become increasingly dependent on information networks in all aspects, including defence. China's digital economy is now the largest in the world, reaching approximately $4.6 trillion and accounting for 35 per cent of GDP in 2018. The total value of online transactions in China exceeded $1.5 trillion in 2019, compared to $600 billion in the United States (U.S.). While China has a fairly developed technology industry and can compete with the U.S. in some fields, most core network technologies and key software and hardware are dependent on U.S. companies. As the PLA gets further networked, it will be progressively reliant on foreign technology, a potential weakness that an opponent could exploit.

Earlier, the PLA relied on the landline, sea-based fibre optics and land based servers, routers and network switches, to be reasonably insulated from cyberattacks. As the PLA modernises it has become more reliant on information technology in its military operations.[1] A 2015 RAND study noted that China's integrated air-defense systems; maritime intelligence, surveillance, and reconnaissance systems and dual-use networks would be "obvious targets" for cyber operations in the event of a conflict.[2] Chinese policymakers are acutely aware of the problem of the increasing dependence of the economy on information technology and substantial technological and regulatory vulnerabilities. The July 2019 defence white paper states, "Cybersecurity remains a global challenge and poses a severe threat to China." Chinese military experts are openly worried about China being attacked in cyber domain.

Despite the increasing importance of information and communications technologies to the economy, adequate priority is not given to cybersecurity investment and expertise. A 2019 report estimates that Chinese companies spend around $7.3 billion on cybersecurity annually. This is nine times less than the U.S. private sector. It is true that the domestic cybersecurity industry is growing faster than the global average. Chinese specialists believe that the country's firms lack core technologies and innovation capacity.[3] As per the ICT Development Index (IDI), which is based on 11 indicators to monitor and compare developments in information and communication technology across countries, China is ranked 80th, 81st, and 82nd among 176 states in 2017, 2016, and 2015 respectively.[4] Apart from China's disadvantages in critical technological self-sufficiency, as mentioned above, it is not as advanced in other aspects as well. In the last five years, China has rapidly developed new cybersecurity institutions, laws, guidelines and standards. It has taken steps to replace foreign suppliers with domestic counterparts. In 2019 the CCP ordered every government office and public institution to remove all foreign software and hardware within three years.[5]

China's Limitations

Hardware and Software. At the current state of development China still needs to depend on foreign corporations in most sub-fields of cyber core technologies.

These companies all have core technology in some sub-fields. Eight U.S. companies which China terms 'eight King Kongs': Cisco, IBM, Google, Qualcomm, Intel, Apple, Oracle, and Microsoft, are identified by China's state-run media as U.S. government proxies that posed a "terrible security threat." Products from Huawei and Lenovo are examples of immense Chinese progress in hardware. China has nationalised its portion of the web. But, U.S. firms still rule international software and decide the software-related standardisation process. No Chinese firm can come near to challenge this corporate influence. At least in the next 5 years, no Chinese firm will be able to do so. Of the top 100 companies ranked by software revenue in 2014, U.S. companies occupied 67 spots. Chinese companies held only two, and the largest of those, Neusoft, was ranked 71st and had software revenue 0.8 percent as large as Microsoft's.

Many Chinese experts believe that U.S. companies report to the U.S. government. They also feel that the United States can disrupt or corrupt the functioning of any device with U.S.-made software. Most of China's personal computers use pirated versions of Microsoft Windows operating systems. The extensive use of illegal software regularly comes from unreliable sources. These pirated systems are harder to keep patched than their legal counterparts. According to a Spanish security vendor Panda Labs report of 2015, 49 percent of Chinese computers are infected with malware, the highest proportion of infected computers in the world. A 2012 spot check by the Microsoft Corporation found that pirated versions of its software are preloaded into new computers sold in China. Malware were also implanted in the software.

Network Management. Keeping systems functional in the face of malware attacks, accidents, user errors and poor administration are the indicators of a country's ability to alleviate the effects of a concerted attack. Compared to U.S., China's network management can be termed as between underdevelopment and modernity. According to the book Pirates of the ISPs,[6] nearly all internal networks used by Chinese firms have been attacked at least once during the past year, and hackers managed to take control of at least 85 percent of them. According to a China Internet Network Information Center study, in 2010, more than 45 percent of Chinese Internet users complained of viruses or Trojans on their computers. About 22 per cent reported that their accounts or password had been stolen.

China's internet is one of the most commonly attacked. As per the Beijing Knownsec Information Technology report published in February 2019, China suffered the highest rate of distributed denial of service attacks (DDOS) globally in 2018, averaging over 800 million attacks per day. An increasing percentage came mostly from the U.S., South Korea and Japan. The attacks that targeted government and financial websites mostly outnumbered those on other targets. China's efforts to keep its 'Great Firewall' provide indicators of its cyber competence level. The result is mixed. Internet users in China use diverse methods, including virtual private networks (VPNs), proxy servers and mirror sites of blocked pages hosted on U.S. cloud computing services to circumvent censorship.[7] However, now China has become more aggressive in stopping such methods. It has made the blocking of VPNs more automated and dynamic. China has developed a new offensive tool, named the 'Great Cannon', designed to divert traffic to denial-of-service attacks against sites hosting mirror sites of blocked web pages.[8]

Centralised Structure of Internet Governance. It is difficult to disable internet in countries where different internet providers operate networks. It is much easier to paralyse the Chinese internet through sophisticated attacks.

Industrial Control Systems. China's Industrial Control Systems (ICS) are exposed to damaging attacks. Over 80 percent of China's economy and critical infrastructure involve some type of industrial control system. These systems are vulnerable to attack due to:

- Operators have low security awareness and ICS are connected to the internet.
- Chinese industry is heavily reliant on foreign suppliers for ICS and these suppliers have access to service or update software.

Space. China's space systems face a variety of potential threats. China's greater reliance on space brings increased vulnerability. The countries that are developing counter-space capabilities could threaten Chinese satellites.

Cyber Range. China lacks a testing range for a simulation environment to prepare for and defend against cyber attacks.

Thinking on Offensive Aspects. China tends to inflate the effectiveness of cyber weapons. Chinese military experts over-emphasise the positive benefits of offensive Information Warfare while downplaying the limitations. This selective analysis can adulterate the decision-making process. China's writings on information warfare show a lack of thorough research and analysis on its use and consequences. Chinese operational research on cyber warfare has also not reached a sufficient level of sophistication.

Military Domain. CCP leaders are aware that China is vulnerable to cyber attacks. Adversaries will try to penetrate Chinese connected and air-gapped networks to gather intelligence, corrupt operations or disrupt operations. The PLA emphasis on "informationized" warfare will try to provide its warfighters with broad access to information. As Chinese forces depend more on information systems, they would become more vulnerable to interference, manipulation and jamming.

Foes like the U.S. would like to target the Chinese Interactive Analysis and Display Software (IADS) and maritime ISR systems. Attacks on IADS could disconnect those systems from one another or create false radar images. Russian-made IADS systems in Syria and Iraq have supposedly been successfully attacked in cyberspace. IADS systems of China have similar origins and will be vulnerable. China's maritime ISR capabilities may be attacked to prevent the PLA from targeting U.S. ships or incoming aircrafts. These cyber attacks against Chinese IADS and ISR targets have more chances of success, especially early in a conflict.

Integration Challenges. The PLA views technological improvements to C4I systems is essential to improve the speed and effectiveness of decision-making while providing secure and reliable communications to fixed and mobile command posts. The PLA needs to integrate all the disparate ISR capabilities and integrate them into the targeting process. It could adversely affect the speed, reduce the reliability or diminish the PLA's effectiveness over the horizon targeting capabilities. This has technical challenges associated with integrating such a variety of new technologies and complex systems and procedural weakness such as insufficient coordination among numerous intelligent organisations, operators and higher-level decision makers. Chen Weizhan, Head of the Military Training and Service Arms Department of the Guangzhou Military Region, said, "Many generations of weapons and equipment exist at the same time... incompatible software systems, unmatched hardware interfaces, and non-unified data formats. There are considerable gaps in the fundamental conditions of the units, and the level of informationization is not high."

Hacking the Hackers. Snowden had revealed that the NSA hacked Chinese targets including mobile phone operators, China's education and research network and Tsinghua University Beijing, home to one of six network backbones that route all of mainland China's Internet traffic as well as the Hong Kong headquarters of Pacnet, which operates one of the Asia-Pacific region's largest fiber optic networks. The case of hacking the hackers of China by the NSA is an interesting example of the state of cybersecurity in China. The Chinese hackers group named BYZANTINE CANDOR focused mainly on breaking into the U.S. Department of Defense, while also spying on economic transactions of geopolitical interest, like oil deals. Tailored Access Operations (TAO) cell of NSA was tasked to hack the hackers. The TAO unit is the centre piece of the NSA's SIGINT operations consisting of over 1,000 military and civilian employees. TAO's specialty is hacking foreign targets, especially the ones that are hardest to breach.

The Chinese had hacked computers from which they hacked American targets. The TAO found and hacked those same computers to spy on the Chinese effort. TAO gained insight into the PLA's activities against the U.S. government, defence contractors, foreign governments and more. TAO could clearly conclude: the hackers behind BYZANTINE CANDOR were from the Third Department of the Chinese PLA. The NSA found that one of the Chinese targets was the United Nations' computer network. The Chinese hackers frequently found documents and other files of interest on United Nations computers and copied them back to China. It enabled the NSA to get its own copies of many documents stolen by the Chinese. The NSA used this knowledge to defend American networks into a program named TUTELAGE that attempted to learn and block adversaries' hacking efforts before they made entry into their target networks.

Human Resources. There is a huge shortfall in China in the number of people trained or educated in information security to match the ever growing demand. As per Feng Huaming, Vice president of the Beijing Institute of Electronic Science and Technology Institute this deficit is expected to be around 1.4 million people by 2020, up from 700,000 in 2019. In the field of cybersecurity, the workforce is extremely diverse. There are many levels of capability, ranging from basic through intermediate, advanced and super expert. Since cybersecurity is a socio-technical phenomenon, Knowledge sets for cybersecurity can be a single discipline (such as electrical engineering, management or law and policing) or be multi-disciplinary. It is not likely that the Chinese education system, training networks and labour market will fill this gap soon.

The PLA faces challenges in enlisting and training highly skillful personnel as there is competition from China's private technology sector. Though online training and simulation tools have been introduced, problems persist in improving military training. Efforts to get fresh graduates with high-tech expertise into the PLA has not yielded desired results. As one official states, "it is not easy for these professional technicians to adapt to the troops, and it is equally difficult for the force commanders to adapt to the new."

In July 2016, the Central Leading Group on Cybersecurity and Informatization approved "Suggestions on Strengthening the Construction of Cybersecurity Discipline and Personnel Training" [Cyberspace Administration of China (CAC, 2016)] that were subsequently attributed to Xi Jinping. Recognising that the talent gap is huge and that the talent structure is not rational, the document outlined following measures:

- Speed up investment in research and building of laboratories.

- Transform delivery mechanisms by having universities deliver professional training courses and bringing in specialists from think tanks to help the transformation.
- Create reasonable cybersecurity text books that meet the national requirements.
- Build strong teams of educators by relying more on experts, internationalising the teaching staff, especially by employing high-end foreign talents.
- Encourage enterprises to participate in the policy setting and training of cybersecurity talents in universities.
- Strengthen on-the-job training for cybersecurity employees and establish classifications and competency standards for cybersecurity jobs.
- Strengthen cybersecurity awareness and skills training for the public through full use of the internet, radio, film and television, newspapers and magazines and other platforms, especially educational curricula.
- Improve the economic incentives for cybersecurity talent cultivation to promote internationally competitive and influential talents.

Measures Taken

China's political leaders feel that its citizens are involved in high risk online behaviour for political or personal reasons. PLA is struggling to come to terms with cyber war concepts and technologies beyond cyber espionage. Chinese leaders recognise that they are vulnerable to cyber attacks. Though the Chinese internal security agencies are among the world leaders in domestic cyber surveillance and catching its own cyber criminals, its capability to protect national critical infrastructure in cyberspace is suspect.

China is serious about the threats and vulnerabilities that were seen from Stuxnet, the Arab Spring and the Snowden revelations. This has resulted in the development of a more robust framework to enhance national security and resilience. Led by the CAC, founded in 2014, China has carried out a complete overhaul of legal and regulatory regime overseeing information security. National Cybersecurity Law (NCL) was implemented in June 2017. The law has acted as an enforcement mechanism under which agencies have implemented new regulatory regimes over content management, device management, encryption, cybersecurity information sharing and supply-chain security.

In February 2014, President Xi Jinping declared that there is "no national security without cybersecurity," and since then, cybersecurity has been a national priority for China. Cybersecurity has been made a priority for top leadership. China considers cybersecurity as a key part of its sovereignty. By 2016, China changed to the current concept of cybersecurity that conformed to the whole-of-system approach. President Xi Jinping gave it out in the National Meeting on Cybersecurity and Informatization. The key points of this concept are given below:

- Cybersecurity is holistic rather than fragmented. In the information age, cybersecurity has a close relationship with many other aspects of national security.
- Cybersecurity is dynamic rather than static. Information technology changes faster and faster, and the networks, which used to be scattered and independent, become highly connected and interdependent. The threat sources of cybersecurity and the means of attack are constantly developing. The idea of relying on a few pieces of security equipment and security software to keep safety is outdated. It needs to establish a dynamic, integrated protection concept.

- Cybersecurity is open rather than closed. The cybersecurity level can continue to improve only if we strengthen international exchange, cooperation and interaction to absorb advanced technology.
- Cybersecurity is relative rather than absolute. There is no absolute security, we should consider basic national conditions and avoid the pursuit of absolute security regardless of cost.
- Cybersecurity is common rather than isolated. Cybersecurity is for people and relies on people. Cybersecurity is the responsibility of the whole society, and it needs the joint participation of the government, enterprises, social organisations and most Internet users to build a line of defence.

In its 13th Five Year Plan released in 2016 China took the courageous step of elevating national cyberspace security to be one of only six high priority development areas in science and engineering, along with quantum computing and communications. The Computer Emergency Response Team (CERT) of China, CNCERT/CC, offered the following positive trends through 2016:

- Cybersecurity situation is generally stable.
- No significant impact on normal operations.
- Cyberspace Law and governance are clearer.
- Domain name system security is in good condition and anti-attack ability increased significantly.
- New security technology based on artificial intelligence is in full swing.

On the threat side, the list was longer:

- Volume of mobile malware continued to rise rapidly and to have a significant impact on profits.

- Attacks from foreign sources were frequent.
- Large-scale distributed denial of service attacks, particularly through networked Intelligent devices.
- Serious damage to data.
- Personal information disclosure, and 'derivative disaster' arising from that rampant fraud.
- Government-launched advanced persistent threats (APT) directly threatening national security and stability are becoming normal and are a grave threat.
- The number of network security attacks against ICS is increasing, with many essential safety incidents.
- The dark web business model has matured.
- Ransomware and extortion software are proliferating.
- The use of Internet of Things intelligent device network attacks will continue to increase.
- The security threat posed by the integration of the internet and traditional industries is more complex.
- The national origin of attacks continues to become more important.

President Xi Jinping launched a new agency, the CAC. It was given the responsibility of bolstering cybersecurity, controlling online content and developing the digital economy. The President himself now chairs the recently established Central Commission for Cybersecurity and Informatization to drive policy from the top. The Chinese government has now developed an interlocking framework of laws, regulations, and standards designed to increase cybersecurity and data integrity. The National Security Law, Counter-terrorism Law, Cybersecurity Law and Multi-Level Protection System, include provisions for online content management, the protection of critical information infrastructure, security reviews for network products and services, and measures that require data localisation.

There is a new regulation for foreign companies operating in China. Foreign companies now have to use Chinese security technologies and encryption. Encrypted connections are switched off and the source code produced or used in China has to be disclosed to the Chinese government. These measures can become a model for other countries striving to achieve cyber sovereignty.

Intelligence Agencies

China has excelled in its internal surveillance and intelligence collection system in the cyber domain. The Chinese term for this activity is "public security intelligence" (PSI). China's internal security agencies are prime targets for cyberattack by adversary intelligence agencies. From the open domain information, the following aspects are not clear:

- The quality of cyber defences of these internal agencies.
- The ability to protect their own cyber secrets.
- Where and in what manner electronic data is collected and stored by these agencies.
- There is considerable evidence that the security ecosystem for this information is in a rather poorly developed state.

It seems that the security ecosystem for this information is in a below par developed state. Suppose the intelligence agencies can't deliver high standards of cybersecurity for themselves. In that case, it is questionable just how effective they can be in supporting information security of other government agencies across the breadth of the country. The agencies involved in China's comprehensive PSI ecosystem have been identified as comprising two types: intelligence units found in public security comprehensive command centres (CCC) and intelligence units established in the offices of the Ministry of Public Security (MPS). Inside the CCC, there are two main types: the China Crime Information Centre (CCIC) and the Super Intelligence System (SIS). Little else is known in the public domain about these centres.

The workhorses of the CCP's cybersecurity defence system domestically are 'cybersecurity bureaus' under the MPS that are spread around the country. The mission sets of these bureaus are:

- Supervision, inspection, guidance of information system security work.
- Organisation and implementation of security assessments of information systems.
- Investigating and dealing with cyber crime.
- Collations of data on major security incidents.
- Prevention and management of intrusion by viruses and other malware.
- Provision of information system security services and products for management.
- Managing information system security training.
- Other duties prescribed by laws, regulations and regulations.

The lead organisation for content security is the Central Propaganda Department (CPD) which organises centralised monitoring and take-down of material deemed inappropriate. The CPD works with parts of the CAC, the Cyber Emergency Bureau and the Coordination Bureau for Cybersecurity. The Ministry of Industry and Information Technology (MIIT) also has a Cybersecurity Administration Bureau, which is responsible for industry supervision in the interests of both content and technical security. It is not clear what role the Ministry of State Security (MSS) has for domestic information security (either technical or content related). It can be assumed that it has a direct interest in monitoring state secrets' possible leaking in cyberspace. Several ministries and agencies apart from the MPS, CPD and MIIT play important roles in day-to-day cybersecurity operations. All national ministries and peer agencies have a cybersecurity unit that reports directly to a very senior official. Still, there is little public domain information on how capable these teams are.

Assessment by a Chinese specialist finds that the country's PSI system is far from perfect appears credible. The six challenges were identified:

- The informatization of the intelligence system is inadequate. There is no unified standard for intelligence reporting. Updating of intelligence data is slow.
- Inadequate data integration.
- Security risks in the preservation of intelligence data.
- Some investigation personnel are not capable of collecting useful information.
- In certain places, intelligence collection has not yet attracted enough attention.
- Conflicts between the work of PSI and the privacy of citizens.

Another scholar reports three major short comings in their PSI work in general, "clogged intelligence sharing, limited analytical and quality control capabilities, and old ways of policing based on obsolete ideas". In a 2017 study attributed to officials of the MPS the following shortcomings were observed:

- Security vulnerabilities in software.
- Lack of standardisation of hardware between MPS offices, resulting potential for data leakage.
- Unsecured nodes and terminals linking to secured systems.
- Lack of cybersecurity awareness among colleagues.
- Access by non-authorized police to MPS systems.
- Improper use of USBs and mobile hard disks.
- Storage of confidential documents in unsecured computers.

China is well aware of this western dominance in the cyber field. China is coordinating with others to define technology standards and other important global issues to put forward its interests in pursuit of economic and political interests. In the next chapter China's Expanding Role in International Cyber Order will be scrutinised.

Endnotes

1. Adam Segal, "U.S. Offensive Cyber Operations in a China-U.S. Military Confrontation," in Bytes, Bombs, and Spies: The Strategic Dimensions of Offensive Cyber Operations, ed. Herb Lin and Amy Zegart (Washington, D.C.: Brookings Press, 2019).
2. Fiona Cunningham, "Maximizing Leverage: Explaining China's Force Postures in Limited Wars" (PhD diss., Massachusetts Institute of Technology, September 2018); and Eric Heginbotham, U.S.- China Military Scorecard: Forces, Geography, and the Evolving Balance of Power 1996–2017 (Santa Monica: RAND Corporation, 2015), 259–83.
3. China's Cybersecurity Market to Expand 20% in 2019, China Daily, December 10, 2019 available at: https://www.chinadaily.com.cn/a/201912/10/WS5def5812a310cf3e3557d39e.html

4. Lyu Jinghua, What Are China's Cyber Capabilities and Intentions?, Carnegie Endowment for International Peace, April 01, 2019 available at: https://carnegieendowment.org/2019/04/01/what-are-china-s-cyber-capabilities-and-intentions-pub-78734
5. 22 Yuan Yang and Nian Liu, "Beijing Orders State Offices to Replace Foreign PCs and Software," Financial Times, December 8, 2019 available at: https://www.ft.com/content/b55fc6ee-1787-11ea-8d73- 6303645ac406.
6. Noah Schactman, Pirates of the ISPs: Tactics for Turning Online Crooks into International Pariahs, Washington, D.C.: Brookings Institution Press, July 2011.
7. Activists Are Finding New Ways Around China's Great Firewall," Time, November 21, 2013.
8. "China's Great Firewall Gets Taller, Wall Street Journal, January 30, 2015.

* * *

CHAPTER 11

China's Expanding Role in International Cyber Order

"Cyberspace is the common space of activities for mankind. The future of cyberspace should be in the hands of all countries. Countries should step up communications, broaden consensus and deepen cooperation to build a community of shared future in cyberspace jointly."

– Xi Jinping, December 16, 2015.

Introduction

President Xi Jinping, in his opening speech at the 19th Party Congress in October 2017, called for the "deep integration of the Internet, big data, and artificial intelligence (AI) with the real economy for building a science and technology superpower, quality superpower, aerospace superpower, cyber superpower..." To achieve these goals, China has developed a template of interlocking cybersecurity strategies, laws, regulations, measures and standards at home. Abroad, it uses diplomatic efforts to preserve and expand the concept of cyber sovereignty in international organisations and forums.

Chinese Foreign minister Wang Yi, in an address following the 19th Chinese Communist Party (CCP) National Congress, laid down the course of China's diplomacy and international relations in the 'new era' in this way: "General Secretary Xi Jinping made it clear in his report to the Congress that China will endeavour to foster a new form of international relations and build a community with a shared future for mankind...

These twin objectives are inspired by the fine traditions of the 5000-year Chinese culture emphasizing the pursuit of the common good, by the core values championed by China's peaceful foreign policy for over six decades, and by the CPC's global vision of delivering benefits to the people of China as well as those of all other countries."[1]

Michael Hayden, a former NSA director, justified NSA's intelligence-gathering activities by saying, "This is a home game for us. Are we not going to take advantage that so much of data goes through Redmond, Washington? Why would we not turn the most powerful telecommunications and computing management structure on the planet to our use?"[2] Influence of global information and communication technology markets by U.S. technologies and standards surely enhanced U.S. intelligence and cyber offensive capabilities. China is well aware of this western dominance in the cyber field. China is coordinating with others to define technology standards in pursuit of economic and political interests. President Xi, at the 2015 World Internet Conference in Wuzhen, called for "respecting each country's right to choose its own internet development path, its own internet management model, and its own public policies on the internet."

The U.S. and its allies believe that Chinese efforts will be a less open and less free internet. China will strengthen other states' capacities looking to block the flow of information and tighten their control over their populations. Chinese intelligence and military agencies will undoubtedly look to exploit familiarity with Chinese technology and standards searching for home-field advantage.

Cyber Sovereignty

Xi Jinping, in his keynote address to the World Internet Conference in 2015 said, "In order to promote reforms in global cyberspace governance, we should insist on the following principles: first, respect Internet sovereignty. The principle of sovereign equality enshrined in the Charter of the United Nations is one of the basic norms in contemporary international relations. It covers all aspects of state-to-state relations, which also includes cyberspace... We should respect the right of individual countries to independently choose their own path of cyber development and model of cyber regulation and participate in international cyberspace governance on an equal footing."

Over the past 25 years, China has methodically promoted the introduction and deployment of digital technologies in social, economic and political life. The foundation of China's digital policy is the concept of cyber sovereignty, which shapes its domestic policy and its digital and cyber diplomacy on the international level. Globally, China is pushing for a state-centred, Westphalian understanding of sovereignty, where the state holds ultimate authority in the digital space. It means every state shall have the right to establish national online spaces and fully control content and data flows within its borders. Though this principle may seem agreeable, it must be understood within the context of China's resolve to defend its own model of internet management: sophisticated, systematic censorship through a well-developed 'Great Firewall' and rigid requirements for local data storage imposed upon all firms operating within its borders.

While the term "cyber sovereignty" has been used repeatedly, there is no precise, agreed-upon definition for it. The most comprehensive description of cyber sovereignty by China is given in the 2017 International Strategy on Cooperation in Cyberspace: "As a basic norm in contemporary international relations, the principle of sovereignty enshrined in the UN Charter covers all aspects of state-to-state relations, which also includes cyberspace. Countries should respect each other's right to choose their own cyber development path, model of cyber regulation and Internet public policies and participate in international cyberspace governance on an equal footing. No country should pursue cyber hegemony, interfere in other countries internal affairs, or engage in, condone or support cyber activities that undermine other countries' national security."

Further, it is explained that "Upholding sovereignty in cyberspace reflects governments' responsibility and right to administer cyberspace by law and enables countries to build platforms for sound interactions among governments, businesses, and social groups. This will foster a healthy environment for the advancement of information technology (IT) and international exchange and cooperation. National governments are entitled to administer cyberspace by law. They exercise jurisdiction over ICT infrastructure, resources and activities within their territories and are entitled to protect their ICT systems and resources from threat, disruption, attack and destruction to safeguard citizens' legitimate rights and interests in cyberspace. National governments are entitled to enact public policies, laws and regulations with no foreign interference. Countries should exercise their rights based on the principle of sovereign equality and also perform their due duties. No country should use ICT to interfere in other countries' internal affairs or leverage its advantage to undermine the security of other countries' ICT product and service supply chain."[3]

Four important dimensions of the Chinese concept of Cyber Sovereignty are:

- **Target of Sovereignty.** China rejects the applicability of universal rights and foreign attempts to intervene in its internal affairs. It targets businesses, non-governmental actors, civil society and the technology community. This challenges the multi-stakeholder model for cyber governance. China believes that international cyber diplomacy and governance processes should be brought into the United Nations' fold.

- **Nature of Sovereignty Claim.** China wants that it should be recognised that governments hold supreme authority within their national cyberspace in international law.
- **Objectives of the Pursuit of Sovereignty.** It primarily includes territorialisation and indigenisation. With territorialisation, Beijing wants to make sure that online processes affecting vital Chinese interests take place within its boundaries and unwanted activities can be excluded from entering. Indigenisation tries to substitute foreign actors and technologies with homegrown equivalents.
- **Means to Realise Sovereignty.** These are legal-regulatory tools that support the development of China's digital capabilities through greater education, government procurement, research and development funding to infrastructure construction and the establishment of specific investment channels and vehicles.

Cyber sovereignty has become the foundation of China's global cyber diplomacy stance and the guiding principle for its domestic digital policies. It outlines China's participation in international processes under the United Nations umbrella and organisations such as the Internet Corporation for Assigned Names and Numbers' (ICANN) and the formulation of regulations for data protection, content control, product certification and critical infrastructure protection. On the domestic front, it has become the basis of stringent laws, regulations and policies that aim to enhance the Chinese government's ability to control online processes, indigenise software and hardware value chains and improve strategic autonomy. As China is the emerging leader in the digital world, its interpretation of cyber sovereignty will undoubtedly impact the global cyber order.

Internet Governance

China wants to prevent the U.S. from interfering with its domestic cyber policies. It also intends to set the tone for how the rest of the world governs the internet. China wishes to transform international norms and institutions to accommodate the Chinese internet governance model, diametrically opposed to U.S. and allied interests. The problem with China's model is that it clashes with the foundational principles of the internet in market-based democracies, online freedom, privacy, free international markets and broad international cooperation.[4]

Internet governance is still a contested space. China has tried to assume active roles in global internet governance, signaling its potential to lead and challenge existing institutions and international norms. It is trying to impose its approach to internet governance on the global system. The concept of control conflicts with universally recognised principles including freedom of speech and freedom of information. The Chinese model has several inadequacies. The government imposed content-control measures were not effective in fighting online extremism.[5]

According to the Cyberspace Administration of China (CAC), "Cyberspace has become a new field of competition for global governance, and China must comprehensively strengthen international exchanges and cooperation in cyberspace to push China's proposition of Internet governance toward becoming an international consensus." The U.N. is a key focus for that effort.

International Strategy of Cooperation on Cyberspace

China's Ministry of Foreign Affairs and the Cyberspace Administration identified four basic principles: Principle of Peace, Principle of Sovereignty, Principle of Shared Governance and Principle of Shared Benefits. It outlines six strategic objectives:

- Safeguard Sovereignty and Security.
- Develop a System of International Rules.
- Promote Fair Internet Governance.
- Protect Legitimate Rights and Interests of Citizens.
- Promote Cooperation on Digital Economy.
- Build Platform for Cyber Cultural Exchange.

China's cyber governance system is designed to achieve the following goals:[6]

- Maintain rigid control over the flow of information to ensure domestic stability, regime legitimacy and the CCP's continued rule.
- Reduce security vulnerabilities in critical networks and protect the country against a range of cyber operations, including disruptive and destructive attacks and cyber espionage.
- Ensure technological autonomy, reduce reliance on foreign suppliers and support Chinese companies to dominate markets in emerging technologies.
- Expand its importance over cyberspace and limit the room for manoeuvre for the U.S. and its partners. It should be able to shape the global internet.

Internet Corporation for Assigned Names and Numbers. China has strongly contested the existing multi-stakeholder model of Internet governance promoted by the U.S. The multi-stakeholder model involves traditional states and international organisations and a range of new institutions, non-governmental organisations (NGOs), non-state actors, civil society, technical advisory bodies and private entities operating in distributed and networked fashion.

In 1998, a few individuals, private standards bodies, several corporations, and the U.S. Department of Commerce established the ICANN. As a California-based, non-profit entity, ICANN pioneered multi-stakeholder Internet governance beyond national jurisdictions' traditional purview. The ICANN collectively determine the rules of Internet operations, which in turn shape the fundamentals of cyberspace. To fulfil its global mandate as the facilitator of a free and open Internet, ICANN endorsed a charter with by-laws that encourage inclusivity and openness. Since then, the Internet has relied on U.S.-centric architecture in both technical and organisational sense.

In 2013, Edward Snowden revealed the National Security Agency (NSA) surveillance activities. Countries like Germany and Brazil enacted privacy protections that could undermine the Internet's global inter-connectivity. Chinese academic scholars examined the use of social media to organise street protests in Iran and China's Xinjiang. They concluded that U.S. will leverage such technologies to spur regime change in other countries. Russia and China exploited the global controversy surrounding NSA surveillance to push their Internet governance model, which cedes control of crucial Internet operations to national governments.

The multi-stakeholder nature of ICANN governance and its close relationship with the U.S. government annoyed China, leading it to advocate bringing ICANN into the fold of the United Nations' International Telecommunications Union (ITU). Recognising China's growing importance in global cyber affairs, ICANN and its officials went to considerable lengths to build confidence. In 2013, ICANN opened its first Global Engagement Centre in Beijing. China welcomed ICANN's transition away from U.S. government oversight. China remains worried that the U.S. government might still use residual control over ICANN to target Chinese networks' functioning. Since the early 2000s, China has worked consistently to achieve its aim. In 2012 and 2013 China hosted ICANN meetings. The Ministry of Industry and Information Technology (MIIT), the Internet Society of China and Chinese Internet giants such as Alibaba and Tencent have participated actively in ICANN's affairs.

September 2016 has been a landmark for Internet governance issue. China and its allies had been working tirelessly to counter U.S. influence over ICANN by forcing the U.S. Department of Commerce to abandon a contract with ICANN. For over a decade, the U.S. Department of Commerce's National Telecommunications & Information Administration (NTIA) handled a component of Internet operations under contract with ICANN's Internet Assigned Numbers Authority (IANA). In September 2016, NTIA's contract with IANA expired. The NTIA transferred IANA stewardship to ICANN. This decision was regarded as a victory for China and Russia. The Deputy Director of the National Internet Information Office described the handover a progressive step in global cyber governance and a valuable attempt to bridge the digital divide between developing and developed countries. The transition raised concerns about the staying power of multi-stakeholder governance. A few experts fear an impotent ICANN untethered from U.S. underwriters could gradually allow national governments to compartmentalise cyberspace.

China and its allies persisted with the ICANN issue to reimpose multilateralism on multi-stakeholderism. At the same time, Russia and China have worked tirelessly in regional fora like the Shanghai Cooperation Organisation (SCO) and international organisations like the ITU to undermine the American position.

Multilateral versus Multitasking. Lawrence Strickling, Assistant Commerce Secretary of U.S., testifying before Congress in 2015, defended America's support for multi-stakeholder Internet governance. As head of the NTIA, Strickling criticised China and Russia for pursuing greater control over the Internet. China along with Russia rejected the idea of an open Internet. However, China's cyber sovereignty approach holds national governments accountable for the behaviour of their citizens. Such accountability could incentivise straggler countries to tackle cybercrime originating from within their borders more enthusiastically. Despite these advantages, the U.S. believes multi-stakeholder governance guarantees Internet freedom and protects the innovative ecosystem that drives prosperity. The U.S. rejects China's push for a new multilateral approach.

Domain Names and Traffic. Chinese authorities view the architecture of the DNS as run by ICANN with suspicion. It has taken several measures to mitigate the risk this architecture posed. In 1997, the China Internet Network Information Centre (CNNIC), under the Chinese Academy of Sciences, became responsible for administering the Chinese aspects of the DNS, including administration of the '.cn' domain. China unilaterally took the initiative to create an alternative system to handle Chinese-language domain names, which is globally compatible.

New DNS regulations from 2017 onwards show the growing trend pointing to localisation. These regulations depend upon entities running DNS root servers registered in China to locate their servers inside Chinese territory. Domain name registrars must be Chinese entities handling their systems within Chinese territory. The registries and registrars must establish domestically-based emergency response systems and create localised back-ups of their databases. Suspicions against foreign intelligence services' surveillance capabilities led to the inclusion of an article in draft regulations on data protection published in May 2019. It necessitates domestic Chinese Internet traffic be exclusively routed through Chinese territory. With only a few international gateways, the topography of China's Internet may facilitate the implementation of this requirement.

Role of United Nations

China uses international organisations like the UN to give its efforts legitimacy. This serves two crucial strategic objectives:

- It reduces China's negative image as a hacking state by showing that it is trying to work collectively and within the defined rules of established international organisations.
- It helps China implement non-kinetic asymmetric means to pursue its political and economic objectives, avoiding the need to use military force or influence.

Group of Government Experts. China and Russia gained international support so that all states have equal rights to the Internet's governance. The agreement updated an old U.N. telecommunications rule. While non-binding, 89 countries signed it with 55 reserving the right to sign it later, showing widespread support. This initiative required the ITU to play an active role in the Internet's multi stakeholder model.

In June 2013, China joined a landmark consensus of the UN Group of Government Experts (GGE) that addressed the fundamental issues:[7]

- Confirmed that existing international law, including the UN Charter, applies to cyberspace and that the law of state responsibility should guide state behaviour concerning the use of cyberspace.
- Expressed the need to promote international stability, transparency and confidence in cyberspace.
- Explored how the international community can help build the cybersecurity capacity of less-developed states.

China, along with Russia, Tajikistan and Uzbekistan, in 2011, submitted a draft resolution on an international code of conduct for information security to the UN General Assembly. The resolution, enhanced and resubmitted in 2015 by a larger group of SCO member countries, emphasised individual states' sovereignty and stability within the digital space. The code invites states to agree that they will not "use information and communications technologies, including networks, to carry out hostile activities or acts of aggression, pose threats to international peace and security." The code also reaffirmed "that policy authority for Internet-related public issues is the sovereign right of States, which have rights and responsibilities for international Internet-related public policy issues."

Likewise, the 2017 BRICS (Brazil, Russia, India, China and South Africa) Leaders Declaration stressed "the paramount importance of the principles of international law enshrined in the Charter of the United Nations, particularly the state sovereignty, the political independence, territorial integrity and sovereign equality of states, non-interference in internal affairs of other states and respect for human rights and fundamental freedoms." The resolution states it aims to "push forward the international debate on international norms on information security, and help forge an early consensus on this issue."[8]

Though China endorsed the norms of responsible state behaviour included in the 2013 and 2015 reports from the UN GGE, it has resisted U.S. efforts to administer international law, including the laws of armed conflict and the right of self-defence to cyberspace. In 2017, the countries engaged in the GGE failed to issue a follow-on report in part due to China and Russia opposed language endorsing the right of self-defence. China's 2017 International Strategy of Cooperation in Cyber-space articulates that "the United Nations, as an important channel, should play a leading role in coordinating various parties' positions and building international consensus" on internet governance."

China took part in all five rounds of a U.N. GGE process established to study cyberspace. In the fourth round, China added to the GGE list of governance principles the term state sovereignty which effectively thwarted the group's ability to institute how international law should apply in the cyber domain. The last round failed to produce a report because China, Russia and Cuba objected to principles put forward by other nations, along with the right to respond to inter-nationally wrongful acts. After this deadlock, the process split into two groups. One is led by the U.S. and other democracies that will continue to focus on international law. The other is organised by regimes like China, Russia, North Korea and Venezuela, that depicts itself as an alternative "open-ended working group (OEWG) acting on a consensus basis."[9]

Open-Ended Working Group. China has been proactive in establishing an international set of responsible behaviour norms for nation-states in cyberspace. The proposal tendered at the UN revealed China's desire to gain consensus among the international community. These efforts can be construed as China's mitigation of the negative press by presenting itself as responsible and collaborative. The GGE had 25 handpicked member states. The OEWG is open to all involved UN member states. During the 2018 UN General Assembly, rather than voting to endorse one process over the other, UN member states permitted both a new GGE and an OEWG in two separate UN General Assembly resolutions. China voted against a US-sponsored resolution for the next GGE round and supported the Russian initiative to establish the OEWG on cyber affairs. Potentially open to all UN members, the OEWG provides a space where Beijing and Moscow believe they hold greater advantages. The OEWG first met in June 2019.

At the September 2019 meeting of the OEWG, the partition between those supporting state sovereignty in cyberspace and those emphasising an open, free and secure internet was obvious.[10] At the first session of this OEWG, China submitted a detailed paper outlining a broad plan with demands going far beyond the classical cybersecurity debate. It included claims concerning supply chain security and the limitation of export bans. China insisted that the participation of NGOs should be limited. China's insistence on sovereignty may become a problem for China itself. While China has banned foreign content, Western countries are now showing concern about data transfers to Beijing, leading to banning Chinese-developed apps like TikTok. As China wants to reduce reliance on imported technology, Huawei is facing increasing headwinds in global markets.

Budapest Convention. The Council of Europe's Budapest Convention is the international agreement concerning human rights safeguards that criminalises computer crimes such as fraud and child pornography. It prohibits illegal access and interception, data and system interference and intellectual property theft. Sixty-four countries have already signed the treaty, including the U.S., Japan, Turkey, Australia and Argentina. Russia has argued that the convention is only a regional agreement that violates principles of state sovereignty and non-interference and wants to replace it. China will work with Russia to promote a new UN cybercrime treaty.

In December 2019, member states approved a resolution backed by Russia that established a committee of experts to consider a new treaty. U.S. officials, before voting, warned that the proposal was an opportunity for China, Russia and others to create UN approved standards for regulating the flow of information. However, some of the large democracies have found Russia and China's arguments on the need to fight cybercrime and terrorism convincing.[11]

International Telecommunications Union. The ITU is the specialised U.N. agency that sets international standards and protocols for ICT. The ITU formulates technology standards, for example, 5G wireless communication standards based on merit. When new communication technologies like wireless phones and networks emerged, the companies driving those innovations send domain experts to the ITU to present their technical contributions for a potential new standard. Members of ITU assess these contributions, select the solutions that best meet global demand needs and announce those solutions as the new global standard.

China is leveraging the ITU to support its techno-nationalist industrial policies. China thinks that the ITU is a platform that it can leverage to reduce its dependence on overseas intellectual property and increase the royalties other nations pay to China. It is particularly interested in wireless communication technology. China is leveraging state resources to promote Huawei technology within 3rd Generation Partnership Project (3GPP), which is the ITU sub-group developing global 5G standards. The 3GPP is a private sector partnership composed of seven telecommunications standards development organisations. The 3GPP examines the range of technologies that make up mobile telecommunications, including radio access, core networks, cellular technologies and services. The number of Chinese representatives serving in the chair or vice-chair leadership positions in the 3GPP is rising. Due to this prominence in the organisation's leadership, China is now able to influence the 3GPP to its advantage.

Since 2014, Houlin Zhao, a former delegate at the Designing Institute of the Ministry of Posts and Telecommunications of China, is the ITU Secretary-General. Houlin Zhao was reelected as secretary-general of the ITU in 2018 to serve for another term until 2023. In cooperation with Chinese companies, the Chinese government has intensified its activism and leadership at the working levels of the global standards-setting bodies. China provides financial support to Huawei and other Chinese firms for sending personnel to attend 3GPP meetings and deluge the process with Chinese technical contributions. Private companies from other nations find it difficult because of the cost factor. Huawei had submitted over 19,000 technical contributions and dispatched over 3,000 engineers to participate in the 5G standard-setting process. Among U.S. companies, Qualcomm and Intel have the most significant 3GPP presence. Qualcomm has made 5,994 technical contributions and sent 1,701 engineers to attend 3GPP meetings. Intel has created 3,656 technical contributions and dispatched 1,259 engineers to attend the same. Huawei is leading in approved technical contributions. Member of 3GPP have approved 5,855 Huawei contributions, making them part of the official 5G standard. In comparison, Qualcomm and Intel had 1,994 and 962 contributions, respectively. So far, Chinese firms own an estimated 36 percent of the patents essential for the global 5G standard. U.S. firms hold about 14 percent of those.

China's growing IP portfolio in the worldwide 5G standard will give Chinese companies, especially Huawei, a price advantage in international market competition. When manufacturing and selling 5G equipment, the companies who own the crucial patents in the international 5G standard will not require to pay royalties to other firms. Whereas other firms will pay royalties to them. This will give Chinese manufactures a cost advantage that they can use to further expand China's 5G market dominance.[12]

China's strategy of using multilateral institutions to its advantage is paying off at the ITU. In 2019 Zhao supported Huawei, when he defended against the U.S. security concerns of 5G by calling them driven by politics rather than evidence. He has backed China's proposal of the "New Internet Protocol". Some western nations like the U.S. U.K. and Sweden have raised concerns that China's New IP plan, if enacted, would fracture the global Internet and give state-run Internet Service Providers too much control.

Cyber Norms. Worldwide cybersecurity has become a serious problem. Nation states and other stakeholders want to enhance stability for cyberspace. New ecosystem of 'cyber norm' processes has emerged. Norms are explicit, agreed-upon rules of behaviour, procedures or codes of conduct. These may be established and agreed to by experts, NGOs or nation-states. Some of the agencies working to identify or operationalise various normative standards of behaviour for states and/or other stakeholders in cyberspace are: the GGE and the OEWG of United Nations, expert commissions like the Global Commission on the Stability of Cyberspace, industry coalitions like the Tech Accord, the Charter of Trust and multi-stakeholder collectives like the Paris Call for Trust and Security in Cyberspace.

Since 2004, the United Nations has regularly convened meetings to develop cyber norms. From 2012 to 2015, the meetings yielded some important but measured steps forward. The working group arrived at a consensus that international law does apply to cyberspace, a conclusion that China and Russia publicly signed on to. The Global Commission on the Stability of Cyberspace brought together a diverse set of experts on global cybersecurity. Its final report, issued in November 2019, lends validity to the broader cyber norm project. It has seeded the content of other norm processes like the Paris Call, still its legacy may be limited as focus shifts to declaring already established norms.

Uniformity of Standards. Industries and technologies around the world have standards that define how they work and their interoperability with others. Interoperability means the ability for two or more systems to work together. Standards affect 96 percent of global trade. Nations that set and deliver these standards will own the IP and formation, development and control of relevant supply chains. Control of key supply chains creates capabilities to access and control broad systems.

Industry bodies, experts and companies collaborate between them to create technical standards. This ensures that standards are uniform, improve efficiency and ensure they work worldwide. Major western technology companies, such as Qualcomm and Ericsson, have been part of the standards-setting process. China is playing an active role in standards-setting. Huawei, one of the leading Chinese players in 5G networking equipment, has been a significant player in this activity. In 5G related field it has the highest number of patents and is ahead of its closest European rivals Nokia and Ericsson.

Emerging Technologies. While U.S., European and Japanese companies have traditionally dominated global standards, China is making a concerted effort on the standards of emerging technologies such as 5G, AI and the Internet of Things (IoT). This may increase the intelligence and cyber offensive capabilities of Chinese intelligence agencies and the PLA. Chinese officials would know about NSA's efforts to weaken the random number generator in the encryption standard Dual_EC_DRBG and alleged payments to RSA Security to include it in its BSAFE software library.[13] Chinese intelligence agencies will try to do the same thing to Chinese standards. China has formed a new committee focused on creating standards for blockchain technology. Some of China's major IT companies, including Huawei and Tencent, are part of that committee. In international standards-setting forums, Chinese technology companies have become more active and effective participants.

The New Generation Artificial Intelligence Development Plan has a big focus on standards-setting for technological interoperability, safety procedures and ethical norms for deployment of AI-enabled systems.[14] China has taken a major initiative in asserting leadership in AI governance by hosting international AI standards meeting in Beijing and put out an AI standards white paper that emphasised the need for rules of the road for AI ethics, privacy and safety. China uses these methods to take a leading role in international governance as it feels that Chinese representatives were not at the high table to help set the rules of the game for the global Internet. Since China has become a technology power with a sizeable market and leading technology companies, it wants to make sure that this does not crop up with the next generation of transformative technology.

China's Cyber Standards

China views standards as its basic goals to reshape global governance and expand geostrategic power. China aims to promote its own technical standards as China Standards through a multipronged, all-of-party-government-and-nation, domestic and international campaign. China Standards give vital technical connectivity for the Belt and Road Initiative and the Digital Silk Road, expanding Chinese control of global ICT.

A 2015 article in the Zhejiang Daily by then-deputy director of the Policy Research Office of the Zhejiang Provincial Party to Committee provides a succinct example of the competitive, strategic value China assigns to standards: "Under the conditions of economic globalization and modern market economy ... Standards are the commanding heights, discourse power, and the power to control. Therefore, the one who obtains the standards gains the world and the first-rate enterprises sell standards. Second-rate companies sell-brands, and third-rate companies sell products"

In 2016, Xi Jinping declared that China would "actively implement a standardization strategy to strengthen and export Chinese technical standards. We must accelerate the promotion of China's international discourse power and rule-making power in cyberspace and make unremitting efforts towards the goal of building a cyber great power."[15] In recent times, China has issued numerous domestic standards by excluding foreign companies from taking part in the process. This state-led process is different from the European model of private actors coordinating under the national non-governmental organisation's auspices and the American model. There are more than 600 standards organisations, most of them industry associations.

China is expanding its influence over international standard boards such as the ITU, the International

Organisation of Standardization (ISO), and the International Electrotechnical Commission (IEC). After France and Germany, China has the third highest participation in IEC technical committees and holds ten secretariats. While China holds no formal chairmanships of study groups at the ITU, representatives of Alibaba, Huawei, ZTE, China Telecom, China Mobile and CAICT hold vice chairmanships at ITU. These firms get solid financial backing from the Chinese state. They play a supporting role in advancing China's strategic interests across the world. For instance, Chinese telecom companies have taken an extremely proactive stance to influence international standards, such as those governing 5G networks. This drive to sway standards directly impacts China's efforts to improve its position within the network domain. The dual nature of standards writing is appropriately summarised by one observer who noted that telecom standards authorship is a "commercial advantage which parlays itself into a security advantage...Whoever controls the technology knows, intimately, how it was built and where all the doors and buttons are." Critically, Chinese telecom firms that operate abroad are still subject to PRC law. Hence, these firms would be required to divulge information that passes through their networks to PRC military and intelligence authorities.[16]

China's Cyber Interest

China's interest in setting the standards extends much beyond ICT sector. In its 'standards harmonisation action plans', China showed its interest in ICT and ICT infrastructure, industrial communication, railway construction, satellite navigation, civil aviation links, roads, waterways, electric grids, energy (oil, gas, and nuclear) power stations, aerospace, infrastructure and construction machinery, urban IT infrastructure projects like smart cities, movie theatres, digital television services, home electronics, building materials, textiles, steel, non-ferrous metals and new materials, explosives, engineering equipment, agriculture, shipbuilding, marine transport and logistics, online shopping networks, green products, media, publishing, radio, movies, television, the arts, medical equipment, pharmaceuticals and international banking and financial services.

China's Standards Development System

In 2018, as part of a larger government reorganisation, China reorganised several government agencies and offices to align standards-related work with quality control and other market supervision offices. It placed the Standardization Administration of China (SAC) under the new State Administration of Market Regulation (SAMR).

The majority of standards in China are developed in technical committees and subcommittees that are under MIIT, SAMR and SAC. The key technical committees for the high-tech sector are:

- SAMR/SAC
  - National Technical Committee on Information Technology (TC260).
  - National Technical Committee on Communications (TC485).
  - China National Institute of Standardization (CNIS).
  - China Association for Standardisation (CAS).
- MIIT
  - China Communications Standards Association (CCSA).
  - China Electronic Standards Institute (CESI). Both CCSA and CESI participate in the TC260and TC485.

These groups often perform dual roles as expert standards developers and playing a part in the governance of standards and regulation. CESI looks after technical research and standards development while also providing product and organisational certifications based on those standards. MIIT is the primary regulator for ICT. It drafts technology regulations that prescribe the creation of standards. SAC coordinates "China Standards" setting and revision on a dedicated website. SAC is China's lead agency to coordinate the PRC's industrial and commercial technical standards, the SAMR's China National Institute of Standards (CNIS) and the SAC's National Center of Standards Evaluation (NCSE). The CPC Committee Chairman of the top SASAC energy State-Owned Enterprise (SOE) 'China Huaneng Group' is the president of the IEC since 2019.

The CAC, MIIT, MPS, China Academy of Information and Communications Technology and National Information Security Standardization Committee (TC260) and CESI: all have some say over standards, regulations and implementation. It is estimated that TC260 has issued close to 300 standards related to cybersecurity since 2015.[17] It has about 700 more in the pipeline. Its membership was increased from 48 members to 81 members, basically from representatives of Chinese technology companies and Chinese officials. Sometimes foreign companies have been allowed to take part in working groups. Seven working groups of the committee are focusing on encryption, big data and other cybersecurity issues.

TC260 is not an enforcement body. But it is very influential. In October 2020, it released the latest personal information security standard with recommended practices for data governance and security. About three weeks later, China's National Computer Virus Emergency Response Center published a list of over 20 mobile applications that violates existing personal information protection laws and recommended users to be cautious of downloading them. The list largely includes Chinese apps, but also named Amazon. To maintain their China operations, multinational companies have to ensure that their technologies align with Chinese standards to pass regulatory checks. This is why several foreign companies sit on TC260's working groups.

China's big tech companies take maximum interest in the IoT. Of the 16 regulations related to IoT that have been released, almost 50 percent of them have one or more of Baidu, Alibaba, Tencent and Huawei (BATH) companies involved in drafting the regulation. Huawei's dominance in TC260 would give the company a more significant say in its future technology infrastructure. It has been involved with TC260 regulations and standards related to data security, telecommunications and cloud computing. Huawei's 5G technology in all probability will form part of China's smart cities' key infrastructure. Alibaba and its subsidiaries, like Taobao and Ant Financial, have helped draft many policies involving safety standards and regulations for cloud computing, big data and cloud security.

With the 2017 revision to the standards law, social organisations have been authorised to develop standards. Social organisations are loosely modelled on U.S. standards consortia, resulting in growth in Chinese standards activity. Whereas there are a few hundred technical committees, there are thousands of social organisations. These standards will make it difficult for foreign firms to operate in China due to the following reasons:

- China uses vague language in standards to avoid issues. It allows the government maximum flexibility and discretion to apply difficult provisions when it deems fit. Internationally China must disclose required standards to the WTO.

- Chinese standards give a competitive advantage for Chinese companies. Chinese companies do not have the same concerns about providing the sensitive information to the government as the foreign companies have. Chinese regulators may also judge Chinese companies as more secure.
- Foreign firms will require to redesign products for the China market where they are not compatible with international standards to comply with certain standards.

China's Cyber Laws

Internal Laws. President Xi Jinping has put lot of importance to reduce reliance on foreign suppliers in core technologies.[18] These activities coincide with China's comprehensive cybersecurity laws (CSLs) and regulations. An interconnected system of laws, regulations and standards create a labyrinth of rules covering data, online content and critical infrastructure.[19]

Cybersecurity Law. In June 2017, The CSL was officially promulgated. It focused on critical information infrastructure (CII). Initially the definition of CII was not clear. Earlier sectors like "public communication and information services, power, traffic, water resources, finance, public service, and e-government," were identified as CII. Following draft regulations media, healthcare, cloud computing and big data providers were added.

Data Security. To protect personal data many countries have taken legal or regulatory steps. As on date about 140 countries have some form of law or regulation on data protection. Europe is dependent on the U.S for data. 80 percent of European data are stored or flow through American servers. There is a clear point of divergence on rules for data privacy between Europe and U.S. France wants to establish more robust rules based on the ground that data privacy is a right and not a privilege. General Data Protection Regulation (GDPR) of the EU is one of the better known and strictest frameworks, which is being used as a gold standard for other countries to follow. GDPR has forced American technical giants like Twitter and Facebook to change their cybersecurity practices and pushed them to look beyond America's borders to identify important compliance hurdles.

Though the CSL is the most authoritative law protecting personal information, China is building a framework for user consent and the collection, storage, processing and use of personal data.[20] The 'Personal Information Security Specification' became effective from May 2018. It requires identification of data before sharing, limitation on secondary uses of data beyond the original purpose and security assessments of third-party vendors handling data.[21] The MIIT has fined number of companies for apps and websites that excessively collected private data.

China's CSL is skewed towards national security rather than personal data protection. However, China has made efforts to safeguard personal information security and data security. A draft Data Security Law was sent for comments in July 2020. The first civil code in China, released in 2020, identifies data privacy as a personal right.

The CSL requires the storage of personal information and 'important data' inside China. It created a review procedures for transferring some information out of China if it is likely to impact national security, damage public interest or is not fully secured. What constitutes important data is not clear. The CSL established a regime to review critical network equipment and specialized cybersecurity products.[22] Certification was prescribed for 15 types of products, including servers and routers to access the domestic market. Overseas companies such as IBM, Cisco, Dell, Juniper and Siemens AG gave feedback to the MIIT, which drafted this set of rules.[23]

Chinese laws will impact foreign companies operating in China immediately. They will indirectly shape the regulatory standards in regions like Africa and South America where China has invested heavily.

Security Aspects. There are problems. The need for protection is offset by the economic harm from excessive limitations and the actual ability of government to administer and enforce data export rules. This is evident from the long winding development of China's regulatory framework for data protection. Draft data export regulations of 2017 covered critical infrastructure operators including network operator, the owner of a network, a manager and a network service provider. Draft regulation of 2019 required all network operations to conduct security assessments before exporting personal data and file such operations with provincial cybersecurity authorities. Foreign entities had to go through a local representative or organisation for data collection. The draft Data Security Law of 2020 is mostly silent on cross-border data flows and localisation. It has fuzzy provisions for the government to implement export limitation measures. It unambiguously established authority for China to reciprocate against "any country or region that adopts discriminatory prohibitions, limitations or other such measures toward the People's Republic of China with respect to investment or trade related to data, data development and use, or technology."

Cross-border Communications. Companies operating in China should have authorisation from the MIIT for using internal company virtual private network (VPN) services. The MIIT 2017 mandates that companies can only use internal VPN services from three state-owned telecommunications carriers. The Cloud service platforms have to route communications with their overseas facilities through channels permitted by MIIT.

Internet Technologies and Apps. New technologies and apps used in internet news/information services will require a new security review process. Service providers have to conduct security evaluations before the introduction of new technologies or applications on their platforms. But details are murky.

Data Localisation. Under national law, transferring data from one country to another could undercut protection granted to data subjects. This leads data protection regimes to impose rules on data transfer to other countries. Such rules have trade implications. Restrictions on cross border data flows is the bone of contention for U.S. companies in China. Article 37 of China's Cybersecurity Law states: "critical information infrastructure operators that gather or produce personal information or important data during operations within the mainland territory of the People's Republic of China, shall store it within mainland China." This provision requires certain kinds of data to be stored within mainland China and require security approvals for cross border data transfer. There are also views in China promoting more alignment with international practices. Important players in China's private sector seeking global markets argue that cutting off cross-border data flows will hurt China' global economic goals.

Collection and use of the data, AI, the IoT, present new challenges for technology norms and governance. The rules are not yet finalised on difficult questions connected to ethics, safety, privacy and discrimination. Chinese government, scholars and practitioners are struggling with these challenges. Immediate impact of these overlapping spheres and authorities will be:

- Uncertainty for Chinese and foreign firms.
- Impose cost by means of security audits and IP and source code submissions.
- Bring companies under greater supervision and control.

Goal of Cyber Super Power

Under President Xi Jinping, China has sets itself the goal to become a 'cyber superpower'. Governance has moved from being predominantly focused inward to actively projecting outward. Chinese leaders determined that controlling the domestic internet was needed but not sufficient. They would have to shape the global internet. To achieve these goals, China has developed a matrix of interlocking cybersecurity strategies, laws, measures, regulations and standards at home. Globally it has used diplomatic efforts to preserve and expand the concept of cyber sovereignty in international organisations and forum.

China's cyber governance system is vast. It not only covers cybersecurity, but also establishes a top-down plan for advancing China's domestic ICT industry. The strategy and planning focus to the need for China to be a global leader in advanced ICT, with Chinese companies leading. The plan is to reduce reliance on foreign technology, boost self-sufficiency in key fields and increase the global influence of China's national technical giants.

Latest Developments

Paris Call for Trust and Security in Cyberspace. In November 2018, France's President Emmanuel Macron called for all cyberspace actors to come together to face digital threats endangering citizens and infrastructure. Around 79 states, 33 public authorities, 374 civil society actors and 688 companies had signed the Paris Call.

The 9 Principles of the Paris Call. It is based on nine principles to secure cyberspace and encourages states to cooperate with private-sector partners and civil society. These are:

- **Principle 1.** Protect individuals and infrastructure.
- **Principle 2.** Protect the Internet.
- **Principle 3.** Defend electoral processes.
- **Principle 4.** Defend intellectual property.
- **Principle 5.** Non-proliferation of malicious software and practices.
- **Principle 6.** Strengthen digital lifecycle security.
- **Principle 7.** Support cyber hygiene.
- **Principle 8.** No private hack back.
- **Principle 9.** Promote international cyber norms.

The problem is how to ensure that Paris Call will build trust and security in cyberspace. The United Nations is the most important platform to define rules of behaviour in cyberspace globally. But unstable relations between major powers on cybersecurity have made compromise and consensus difficult. The limits of the intergovernmental process to shape or implement norms are exposed.

Diversity of the Paris Call Community. The Paris Call aims for global reach. The signatories of the Paris Call come from diverse geographies and sectors. All EU member states are signatories. However, Asia and Africa are under-represented. The United States, China, India and Russia have not signed. On the other hand, several corporate and civil actors in those countries signed; for example, Huawei did so in 2019.

Uncertainty in UN Diplomacy. The future of the UN cyber negotiations is not clear. The current UN negotiations are gridlocked and no universal agreement is in sight. Individual governments may take actions that violate norms to protect their sovereignty against state and non-state actors that conduct malicious cyber operations. This type of unilateral actions threatens the Paris Call's core mission of trust-building.

China Standards 2035

China Standards 2035 is blueprint for China's government bodies and leading technology companies to resolve global standards for emerging technologies areas where global standards are being set and China has the opportunity to leapfrog present occupants. Chinese companies can make Chinese standards in emerging areas where it has market, technology and application advantages. Focus areas of China Standards 2035 are niche technologies like AI, the IoT, big data, 5G, blockchain, cloud computing, smart cities and geographic information. It calls for China-developed standards for biological products, advanced medical equipment and bio-based materials. This new plan builds on that foundation of Made in China 2025 plan. With China Standards 2035, China is increasing its efforts to define the standards for the 4th Industrial Revolution with a 15 years strategic economic development program.

China Standards 2035 is a deliberate national-level strategy to set global rules especially in emerging technologies. China's

Standardization Administration describes it succinctly: "Qualcomm once monopolized the world's mobile phone standards through communication chip standards. It became the ruler of 3G and 4G. The strategic game among big powers is no longer limited to market scale competition and technological superiority competition. It is more about system design competition and rule-making competition. Huawei has broken Qualcomm's monopoly in the 5G situation. Huawei not only makes products, but also technology; not only technology but also standards. The Huawei mobile phone is a product. The mobile phone and AI chips are technology. And the Polar Code proposed by Huawei is the 5G standard. Currently, Huawei is planning and operating an AI standard. Huawei did it. It also proved a truth: Chinese companies can establish Chinese standards in emerging areas where we have market, technology, and application advantages."[24]

China's Challenges

China may be ambitious, but displacing the dominance of the U.S. and Europe would not be easy. Naomi Wilson, senior director for policy in Asia at the Information Technology Industry (ITI) Council, in a written testimony to the U.S.-China Economic and Security Review Commission stated that "While increased Chinese participation and government involvement has created some procedural challenges, it has not created undue influence or tipped the competitive scales in favour of the Chinese.[25] In fact, U.S. and multinational companies are still largely regarded as the most influential participants in ICT-related standards bodies based on their technical leadership and expertise, deep understanding of standards processes and rules, quality of contributions, and consistent participation over time."

China will have to improve the quality of the companies contributing to global standards. The country will need to develop companies like Huawei with advanced technology. China will not be able to proceed further with dominating standards regimes in various areas with subpar technology.[26] The Cybersecurity Law of the PRC has been effective since June 1, 2017. The CSL does not provide much guidance on how the cybersecurity assessment should be done. Draft regulations and guidelines that set out the framework for formally assessments in greater detail have been issued. However, they have not been passed yet. Now, foreign companies face at least six different security reviews by various Chinese government agencies. This can be used to delay or block market access. The jurisdiction, specific criteria, metrics and individual reviews conducting the evaluations are not clear.

The U.S. industry representatives have petitioned the Chinese government to accept international security certifications like ISO as a basis for compliance. The stand of the Chinese government is not clear. The different cybersecurity reviews and their practical implications are given below.

The Multi-level Protection Scheme (MLPS). The MLPS is managed by the Ministry of Public Security (MPS). The MLPS involves ranking networks by the level of sensitivity and then assigning certain compliance obligations. The MLPS will go through revisions as part of the new ICT legal regime. How the changes will be coordinated with other similar security reviews remain to be seen.

Cybersecurity Review Regime. An important question is how MLPS will work concerning the Cybersecurity Review Regime (CRR) or Cybersecurity Review Measures of Network Products and Services. These measures need network products and services used in CII to go through a cybersecurity review administered by the CAC and other sector-specific regulators. The final definition of CII is still undecided. The complete criteria for assessments and a list of those conducting them are unidentified. Without these, the practical implications of this system remain muddy.

Reviews of Cross-Border Data Transfer. There is a separate security review of data that companies want to transfer outside mainland China. The government is refining the process and conditions through which data would go through a security assessment under two draft regulations: Personal Information and Important Data Cross Border Transfer Security Evaluation Measures and Guidelines for Data Cross-Border Transfer Security Assessment. The exact scope is unclear.[27]

China's Initiative Faces an Uphill Task. China's multilateral approach is going parallel to the U.S Clean Network Initiative. The U.S. initiative is essentially targeted at China. A U.S. State Department official announced, "The Clean Network program is the Trump Administration's comprehensive approach to guarding our citizens' privacy and our companies' most sensitive information from aggressive intrusions by malign actors, such as the CCP". The Internet Society, an industry group with members including Google, AT&T, COMCAST and Eriksson, have sharply criticised the Clean Network Initiative. The society in a statement on their website wrote: "Policies like these only increase the global momentum towards a "Splinternet" – a fractured network, rather than the Internet we have built over the last four decades and need now more than ever". However, there will be little support for China's initiative from the U.S. at this stage. Other countries have not yet expressed their views. China's initiative could induce other countries to develop their proposals and principles that a broad set of countries may support.

Another critical issue is the continued erosion of online anonymity. The CAC added four regulations in August and September of 2017 regarding the online activity that effectively reduce online anonymity. These four regulations are: the Internet Forum Service Management Regulation, the Internet Threat Comments Service Management Regulation, the Internet User Public Account Information Services Management Regulation and the Management Rules of Internet Group Information Services.[28]

China's Cyber Aspirations

At the World Internet Conference in 2015, Xi Jinping announced that China will forcefully implement the strategy to make China a cyber great power, by constructing a community of common destiny in cyberspace, appropriate internet governance norms and global internet infrastructure. Officials of the CAC describes expanding influence of China over global internet governance is a key goal in developing cyber great power status.

A new digital architecture worldwide is taking form. This architecture will outline communications and resource flows, information, global norms, security and prosperity. Industry, technology and innovation are developing rapidly. The new generation of ITI exemplified by AI, cloud computing, big data, 5G, Quantum computing etc., is emerging. Global technical standards are still being formed. China senses the opportunity to realise the superiority of China's industry and standards.

Control over IT standards is pronounced as the core of U.S. and Western global power. China thinks it has the chance to break U.S. and Western monopoly over international standards and challenge U.S. and Western influence. According to Yang Zhen, the chairman of the Council of Jiangsu Institute of Communications, "The standards and core technologies of the internet are set by the U. S. The internet is and the IoT is a huge system that connects all things in the world ... If the key technologies and main standards of the IoT are in the hands of Western developed countries, and China has no independent intellectual property rights, then China will have no chance of achieving its peaceful rise and national rejuvenation."

China's standardisation plan goes beyond China. The China Standards outline is unambiguous about its intentions to proliferate standards internationally. It will do so by integrating and coopting global standard-setting bodies. China uses the ITU for its radical proposal to reinvent the Internet. China will use its position in ISO and the IEC to make sure Chinese practices and Chinese solutions are adopted globally. The Chinese Academy of Sciences has explained China's new geopolitical strategy to build a "ubiquitous and universally used information network system." China is now following a two-pronged standardisation strategy:

- Engage in international standardisation bodies such as ITU and ISO and implement existing standards for friction-less trade at a global scale.
- Design and implement the next wave of standardisation in cyber-physical trade and military supply chains with its ambitious China 2035 Standards strategy.

China is doing a complex tight rope walking in external Chinese government and commercial messaging on IT and its totally opposite domestic counterpart. This has been brought out succinctly by a report in Brookings.[29] The external Chinese government and commercial messaging on IT emphasises free markets, openness, collaboration and interdependence. It advocates Huawei and other Chinese companies be treated like other global private sector actors and welcomed into foreign networks. At the same time, domestic Chinese government, commercial and academic discourse stresses the limitations of free markets and the pitfall of reliance on foreign technologies. They suggest industrial policy and government control to protect technologies, companies, and networks. It points out that commercial communication networks may be used to project power and influence offensively.

To become a great cyber power, China wants to leapfrog legacy industrial leaders and define the digital revolution's architecture. The report finds the following:

- Though China discusses its cyber great power ambitions internally, those are rarely acknowledged in its messaging outside.
- While the Chinese government encourages foreign audiences to purchase Huawei products, its leaders warn domestic audiences of the dangers of foreign technology reliance. Xi Jinping argued that "the control of core technology by others is our biggest hidden danger and that allowing foreigners to control core technology is like building a house on someone else's foundation. China must have its own technology, and it must have strong technology."
- The Chinese government encourages foreign audiences sceptical of Huawei to adhere to market principles. Simultaneously, the government cautions domestic audiences that IT network development requires industrial policy and cannot be entrusted to market forces.

- Xi Jinping has declared categorically that "market exchange cannot bring us core technologies, and money cannot buy core technologies."
- China calls foreign security concerns over Huawei lame excuses and pure politics. At the same time, China articulates similar worries over incorporating foreign technology into its domestic networks. The MIIT finds that foreign technology networks are not controllable. China should build its own networks that are both independent and controllable.

Chinese academic and commercial sources suggest that the international community's security concerns over Chinese telecommunications might not be misplaced. China may use telecommunications and other commercial networks to project offensive power globally. When deliberating standard-setting with overseas audiences, the Chinese government stresses win-win collaboration.

Endnotes

1. Speech by Foreign Minister Wang Yi at the Opening of the Symposium on International Developments and China's Diplomacy, December 10, 2017 available at: https://www.fmprc.gov.cn/mfa_eng/wjb_663304/wjbz_663308/2461_663310/t1518130.shtml
2. Michael Hirsch, "How America's Top Tech Companies Created the Surveillance State," National Journal, July 25, 2013 available at: http://www.nationaljournal.com/magazine/how-america-s-top-tech-companies-created-the-surveillance-state-20130725
3. International Strategy of Cooperation on Cyberspace, Ministry of Foreign Affairs, the People's Republic of China available at: https://www.fmprc.gov.cn/mfa_eng/wjb_663304/zzjg_663340/jks_665232/kjlc_665236/qtwt_665250/t1442390.shtml
4. Hon. Kevin Rudd, "Xi Jinping, China and the Global Order," June 2018, available at https://asiasociety.org/sites/default/files/2019-01/Xi%20Jinping_China%20and%20the%20Global%20Order.pdf.

5. Samm Sacksjune, Beijing Wants to Rewrite the Rules of the Internet - The Atlantic 18, 2018, available at https://www.theatlantic.com / international / archive / 2018 / 06 / zte-huawei-china-trump-trade-cyber/563033/

6. Adam Segal, China's Alternative Cyber Governance Regime, Prepared before the U.S. China Economic Security Review Commission March 13, 2020 Hearing on A 'China Model?' Beijing's Promotion of Alternative Global Norms and Standards

7. LYU JINGHUA, What Are China's Cyber Capabilities and Intentions?, APRIL 01, 2019 available at: https://carnegieendowment.org/2019/04/01/what-are-china-s-cyber-capabilities-and-intentions-pub-78734

8. Amy Thomson, "UN Telecom Treaty Approved Amid U.S. Web-Censorship Concerns,"Bloomberg, December 14, 2012, available at: http://www.bloomberg.com/news/articles/2012-12-13/u-s-and-u-k-refuse-to-sign-unagreement-on-telecommunications.

9. General Assembly, "International Code of Conduct for Information Security", UN document A/66/359, 14 September 2011; Letter from the Permanent Representatives of China, Kazakhstan, Kyrgyzstan, the Russian Federation,

10. China's Submissions to the Open-ended Working Group on Developments in the Field of Information and Telecommunications in the Context of International Security available at: https://unoda-web.s3.amazonaws.com / wp-content/uploads/2019/09/china-submissions-oewg-en.pdf.

11. Ellen Nakashima, "The U.S. is urging a no vote on a Russian-led U.N. resolution calling for a global cybercrime treaty," Washington Post, November 16, 2019 available at https://www.washingtonpost.com / national-security / the-us-is-urging-a-no-vote-on-arussian-led-un-resolution-calling - for-a-global-cybercrime-treaty / 2019 / 11/16/b4895e76-075e-11ea-818cfcc65139e8c2_story.html

12. Federal Register / Vol. 81, No. 17 / Wednesday, January 27, 2016 available at: https://www.govinfo.gov/content/pkg/FR-2016-01-27/pdf/FR-2016-01-27.pdf.

13. Joseph Menn, "Exclusive: Secret Contract Tied NSA and Security Industry Pioneer," Reuters, December 20, 2013 available at: http://www.reuters.com / article/2013/12/20/us-usa-security-rsa-idUSBRE9BJ1C220131220.

14. "Chinese Interests Take a Big Seat at the AI Governance Table, DigiChina, New America, June 28, 2018 available at: https://www . newamerica . org / cybersecurity – initiative / digichina/blog/chinese-interests-take-big-seat-ai-governance-table

15. Xi Jinping, The Political Bureau of the CPC Central Committee Conducts the 36th Collective Study on the Implementation of the Strategy of Network Power, Xinhua, October 9, 2016 available at http://www.gov.cn/xinwen/2016-10/09/content_5116444.htm.

16. Adam Segal, "When China Rules the Web," Foreign Affairs, September/October 2018 available at: https://www.foreignaffairs.com/articles/china/2018-08-13/when-china-rules-web

17. Samm Sacks and Manyi Li, "How Chinese Cybersecurity Standards Impact Doing Business In China," CSIS Briefs, August 2, 2018 available at: https://www.csis.org/analysis/how-chinese-cybersecurity-standards-impact-doing-business-china

18. Paul Triolo, Graham Webster, Lorand Laskai, and Katharin Tai, "Xi Jinping Puts 'Indigenous Innovation' and 'Core Technologies' at the Center of Development Priorities," DigiChina, New America, May 2, 2018, available at https://www . newamerica . org / cybersecurity – initiative / digichina / blog / xi - jinping – puts – indigenous - innovation-andcore-technologies-center-development-priorities/

19. Samm Sacks and Manyi Kathy Li, "How Chinese Cybersecurity Standards Impact Doing Business in China," CSIS Briefs, Center for Strategic & International Studies, August 2 2018, available at https://www.csis.org / analysis / how – chinesecybersecurity - standards-impact-doing-business-china.

20. Mingli Shi, Samm Sacks, Qiheng Chen, and Graham Webster, "Translation: China's Personal Information Security Specification," DigiChina, New America, February 8, 2019, available at https://www.newamerica.org/cybersecurity-initiative / digichina / blog / translation - chinas - personal - information-security-specification/

21. Samm Sacks, "China's Emerging Data Privacy System and GDPR," CSIS Commentary, March 9, 2020 available at https://www.csis.org/analysis/chinas-emerging-data-privacy-system-and-gdpr

22. Paul Triolo, Samm Sacks, Graham Webster, and Rogier Creemers, "China's Cybersecurity Law One Year On," DigiChina, New America, November 30, 2017 available at https://www . newamerica . org / cybersecurity – initiative / digichina/blog/chinas-cybersecurity-law-one-year
23. Yuko Kubota, "American Tech Shudders as China Cyber Rules Are Expected to Get Tougher," Wall Street Journal, July 29, 2019, available at https://www.wsj.com / articles / chinas-cybersecurity-regulations-rattle-u-s-businesses-11564409177
24. Emily de La Bruyère & Nathan Picarsic, Beijing's Platform Geopolitics and "Standardization Work in 2020", China Standards 2035, Horizon Advisory, April 2020 available at: https://issuu.com / horizonadvisory / docs / horizon_advisory_china_standards_series_-_standard
25. https://www.uscc.gov/fileas/001269
26. Arjun Kharpal, Power is 'up for grabs': Behind China's plan to shape the future of next-generation tech, April 26, 2020 available at https://www.cnbc.com/2020/04/27/china-standards-2035-explained.html
27. Bert Hofman, China's New Data Security Initiative, EAI Commentary No. 18, September 16, 2020 available at: https://research.nus.edu.sg/eai/wp-content/uploads/sites/2/2020/09/EAIC-18-20200916.pdf
28. Samm Sacks & Paul Triolo, "Shrinking Anonymity in Chinese Cyberspace," Lawfare, Sept. 25, 2017, available at: https://www.lawfareblog.com / shrinking – anonymity - chinese-cyberspace
29. Rush Doshi, Emily De La Bruyère, Nathan Picarsic and John Ferguson, China as a "Cyber Great Power" Beijing's Two Voices In Telecommunications, Foreign Policy at Brookings, April 2021 available at: https://www.brookings.edu/research/china-as-a-cyber-great-power-beijings-two-voices-in-telecommunications/

* * *

Conclusion

China's Cyber War

Cyberspace is a crucial area for national security, economic growth and social development. China is fast building its cyberspace capabilities consistent with its international standing and status as a significant cyber power country. China's 2019 Defense White Paper gave a clarion call to the armed forces to "accelerate the building of their cyberspace capabilities." This capacity is all-encompassing. A 2016 NATO Cooperative Cyber Defence Centre of Excellence study concluded that the "Chinese government, together with the Chinese military, private corporations, and unaffiliated citizens, conduct intrusions against major Western powers as well as in the neighbouring region every day, targeting academia, industry and government facilities for the purpose of amassing technological secrets."

Cyber warfare is reckoned to be part of information operations. Information operations, in the PLA's glossary of military terms, is defined as: "integrating modes such as EW, cyber warfare, and psychological warfare to strike or counter an enemy to interfere with and damage the enemy's information and information systems in cyberspace and electro-magnetic space; to influence and weaken the enemy's information acquisition, transmission, processing, utilisation, and decision-making capabilities; and to ensure the stable operation of one's own information systems, information security, and correct decision making." Information warfare has a broader definition than information operations. It refers to a fight for initiative between two adversaries involving the use of IT in the political, economic, science and technology, diplomatic, cultural, military and other domains.

Informatisation

Information warfare is essentially shaping the PLA, including its organisation. Establishing information dominance involves waging information warfare. Information Technology is incorporated into different weapon systems making them more lethal and precise. The networking of weapons with each other and with sensors provide higher operational tempos. Erstwhile constrains of night and weather conditions no longer exists for military forces. The PLA uses the term "informatized or informationized warfare" to describe the process of acquiring, transmitting, processing and using the information to conduct joint military operations across the domains of land, sea, air, space, cyberspace and the electromagnetic spectrum during a conflict. Informationized warfare obscures the lines between peacetime and wartime. Informationized warfare is superset of cyber warfare; cyber warfare is just one piece of the larger whole.

Informationized warfare goes beyond the addition of IT into individual weapons or broader systems. It is creating systems-of-systems, including the inclusion of IT into every facet of military activities, e.g., logistics, intelligence collection and exploitation, transportation, etc. One of the characteristics of informationized warfare is that conflicts are not platform-versus-platform or system-versus-system. Battles are now between rival arrays of systems-of-systems. By 2019, various PLA publications and experts were writing about the possibility that the acceleration of changes in military strategy along with new technological opportunities may lead to an arms race in 'intelligentisation'. It alluded to the use of AI in military operations, intelligence collection and decision-making.

China does not want to only integrate AI into existing war-fighting functions. China wants to use it to shape a new cognitive domain and thus revolutionise their entire approach to war-fighting. Xi Jinping and China's leadership believes that China should pursue global leadership in AI technology and reduce its dependence on imports of international technology. China's aim is to overtake the West in AI R&D by 2025, and more importantly, to be the world leader in AI by 2030.[1]

Concept and Doctrine

The PLA leadership believes that information has become decisively crucial in the conduct of current and future wars. Focusing on fighting wars, China's armed forces have innovated military doctrines and strategy, joint operations and informationization. This has provided theoretical support to defence and military development. In both peace and war, China employs its cyber warfare abilities to enhance its overall strategic position. These network warfare capabilities are not used in a vacuum but work as part of cross-domain efforts.

In 2016, China's first national Cyberspace Security Strategy was published.[2] The strategy set nine core tasks, with a serious emphasis on sovereignty and improving cyber defence enablers of industry and education. The strategy was supported by China's first Cyber Security Law (CSL) published in 2017.[3]

The Chinese concept of Integrated Network and Electronic Warfare (INEW) is using electro-magnetic attack and defence and information attack as the main techniques for degrading adversary ability to gather and exploit information, treating networked information systems as the domain of operations.

The INEW is more than adding EW techniques to network warfare. It enhances information warfare beyond the virtual world of data to include the physical world. The INEW is envisaged as a critical example of the new kind of unified jointness necessary to successfully fight local wars under informationized conditions in the unified joint operations environment. It combines cyber and electro-magnetic attacks and conventional firepower. It integrates soft-kill and hard-kill measures. The PLA feels that cyber warfare can be more effective by simultaneously conducting kinetic strikes that cause physical damages. It believes that electronic and cyber warfare can be adapted to information operation missions in battlefields under an integrated command. The Network Systems Department (NSD) of Strategic Security Forces has been made responsible now for both cyber and EW.

China's investments in advanced EW systems, counter-space weapons, and computer network operations (CNO), combined with cyber influence operations, show the emphasis and priority China's leaders place on capacity building for information advantage

Reorganisation

China has undertaken a major transformation of the PLA in 2015. The PLA Strategic Support Force (PLASSF) is a significant component of the reorganisation. The PLASSF is an essential driver for the growth of new combat capabilities. It consists of supporting forces for battlefield environment, information, communications, information security and new technology testing. The PLASSF is trying to achieve big development strides in critical areas and accelerate the integrated development of a strong and modernised strategic support force.

The PLASSF is the first step in the development of a cyber force by combining cyber reconnaissance, cyber attack and cyber defence capabilities into one organisation to reduce bureaucratic hurdles and centralise command and control of PLA cyber units. Official pronouncements offer little details on the organisation's makeup or mission. On December 31, 2015, during the SSF founding ceremony, President Xi Jinping said that the SSF is a "new-type combat force to maintain national security and is an important growth point for the PLA's combat capabilities." In the SSF, space, cyber and the electro-magnetic spectrum have been consolidated as a unique warfighting domain. The unified force will be able to carry out the complex, multidimensional information operations that the PLA anticipates in future conflicts. Psychological, cyber and electronic warfare and kinetic actions can be integrated into a single information warfare strategy.

On the occasion of the 70th anniversary of the People's Republic's founding, a grand parade was organised on October 1, 2019. The parade reflected the organisational and doctrinal shifts in the PLA. The incorporation of personnel from all branches in the PLASSF and Joint Logistics Support Force sections of the parade highlighted China's progress towards joint operational capability across services. The presence of officers and scientists from the National Defense University, Academy of Military Sciences and University of Defense Technology emphasised China's focus on civil-military integration.

As China continues to modernise its armed forces, the continued advancement of its cyber capabilities through the Strategic Support Force will provide the PLA with new options to deter, coerce or even gain an advantage in a conflict scenario. The Ministry of State Security (MSS) and other agencies can conduct Chinese strategic and industrial espionage activities. However, the reorganisation is at an early stage. It would limit the SSF's ability to conduct multi-dimensional information warfare operations in the short and medium term.

Influence Operations

Along with the technical aspects of information operations, the PLA combines psychological warfare in manipulating public opinion, media warfare and the legal warfare that influences legal arguments to strengthen China's diplomatic and security position. China calls this Three Warfare. China effectively integrates this Three Warfare in a comprehensive information operations doctrine. China is targeted by two of the most powerful cyber actors in the world. One of these two perpetrators is evident in U.S. The other one is the government of China. It operates the most extensive cyber-enabled internal security surveillance system in the world.

In addition to government-owned media and party officials' involvement, the Chinese government has progressively included psychological warfare, technology companies, and internet influencers to increase domestic and foreign audiences' engagement with government propaganda. The propaganda starts with the Chinese domestic population, while at the same time, it exerts influence on the Chinese diaspora, seeking to disseminate pro-China narratives globally.

Law

The National Cybersecurity Law (NCL) was made law in November 2016 and implemented in June 2017. Under this law, various state agencies have implemented new regulatory regimes over content management, device management, cybersecurity information sharing, encryption and supply-chain security. Given China's interest in industrial espionage, these activities have been a cause of extreme concern abroad. These have wider strategic implications for the Chinese economy. It provides a model for other countries trying to achieve cyber sovereignty.

China, in 2020, published Cybersecurity Review Measures. It gave out a set of rules to govern the supply-chain reliability and security of the products and services used in the critical infrastructure.[4] The government also released a draft Data Security Law in July 20, 2061 and a draft Personal Information Protection Law in October 2020, representing the first comprehensive legislation relating to the security of personal data.

Vulnerabilities

China is emerging as a cyber super-power. This, along with economic and military capabilities, enhance its overall national power. Cyberspace is a double-edged sword for China presenting new risks and critical benefits. It confronts a range of challenges and potential vulnerabilities in the cyber domain, including the insecurity of its own IT ecosystem.

In the unfolding era of the fourth industrial revolution, China has invested heavily in today's emerging technologies like big data, robotics and AI. These technologies open up new economic opportunities and contribute to the diffusion of techniques and technologies that can be readily exploited for repression.

Future

As per Bell Labs, cybersecurity has these distinct problem sets: hardware, software, networks, electricity supply power, ecosystem, people and policy. Individually all these factors are very complex. As technologies like advanced AI, IoT, mobile computing, cloud computing and quantum computing come into play, things get compounded. The PLA will try to integrate the disruptive technologies of AI, quantum computing and communications, hypersonics, nano-materials and biotechnology with its military concepts over the next 15 to 20 years to attain joint informatised capabilities. The PLA identifies that military use of such state-of-the-art technologies holds the key to future warfare's fate.

The National Defense White Paper (NDWP, 2019) on China's National Defense in the New Era published in July 2019, stated precisely: "Driven by the new round of technological and industrial revolution, the application of cutting-edge technologies such as AI, quantum information, big data, cloud computing and the IoT is gathering pace in the military field."

The PLA has been progressively developing a doctrine for its reorganised conventional forces, combined with its expanding space and information warfare capabilities. It has devoted considerable intellectual capital to thinking about future warfare and how best to fight it. The PLA is not interested in only acquiring new equipment. It is trying to figure out how to best exploit all the technologies, whether new or old, by developing an appropriate set of doctrine and attendant tactics, techniques and procedures to implement that doctrine.

The PLA has been keenly following all the advancements that have taken place recently in warfare. It has studied the foreign military experiences, especially from the U.S., and learned what works, what should be ignored and what should be adopted to serve its goals. It has been innovative enough to develop solutions to its operational challenges, creating entirely new capabilities or operating in new and creative ways to challenge its adversaries operating in proximity to its shores.

China has been progressively expanding its ability to operate in information space, including the electromagnetic spectrum, cyberspace and outer space. No nation has so far fought a war through profound and intense dependence on integrated electronic and computer networks. In these domains therefore PLA has no disadvantage against other nations.

Endnotes

1. Maj Gen PK Mallick, VSM (Retd), Defining China's Intelligentized Warfare and Role of Artificial Intelligence, Vivekananda International Foundation, March 2021 available at: https://www.vifindia.org/sites/default/files/defining-china-s-intelligentized-warfare-and-role-of-artificial-intelligence.pdf
2. Cyberspace Administration of China, 'National Cyberspace Security Strategy', 2016, available at: https://chinacopyrightandmedia.wordpress.com/2016/12/27/national-cyberspace-security-strategy.
3. Rogier Creemers, Paul Triolo and Graham Webster, 'Translation: Cybersecurity Law of the People's Republic of China (Effective June 1, 2017)', New America, 2018, available at: https://www.newamerica.org / cybersecurity - initiative / digichina/blog/translation-cybersecurity-law-peoples-republic-china.
4. Lauren Dudley et al., 'China's Cybersecurity Reviews Eye "Supply Chain Security" in "Critical" ndustries [Translation]', New America, 27 April 2020available at: http://newamerica.org /cybersecurity-nitiative/digichina / blog / chinas-cybersecurity reviews – eye – supply – chain – security – critical – industries - translation.

* * *

Index

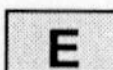

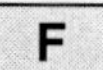

H

M

N